GREEN LINE

GREEN LINE
BY A. McCALL

The history of London's
Country Bus Services

London

ACKNOWLEDGEMENTS

It is obvious that a book of this calibre could not have been written without some assistance.

First of all, my thanks to the Publicity Officer of London Transport for making available various photographs and other items.

Many good friends have assisted, but special mention must be made of the following:

Laurie Akehurst, who not only supplied some of the tickets illustrated herein, but also provided me with timetables of the wartime operations, plus many useful statistics.

Mervyn Gibson, for supplying the majority of the tickets.

David Penrose, for preparing the route maps.

The late Leslie Nicholson, who loaned me his unique collection of the handbills and timetables issued by the independent operators, many of which later joined the Green Line organisation.

John G. Smith, Frank Mussett, Noel Jackson and Reg Westgate (as curator of the J. F. Higham negatives) for supplying photographs.

To Allen Levy of New Cavendish Books, who helped me achieve an ambition by accepting this book for publication.

Last but not least, I must tender my gratitude to my wife for her forbearance whilst this book was being written, and also for having lived with Green Line and other buses for over forty years.

A. W. McCall,

Godalming, Surrey.

**First edition published in Great Britain
by New Cavendish Books — 1980.**

Design — John B. Cooper
Text production and supervision — Carole Montague
Editorial direction — Allen Levy

Copyright © New Cavendish Books — 1980
All rights reserved, this book or parts thereof may not be reproduced in any form without permission in writing from the publisher.

Phototypeset, printed and bound
by Waterlow (Dunstable) Limited, England.
Illustration and colour reproduction
by Aragorn Colour Reproduction Limited, England.
New Cavendish Books Limited, 11 New Fetter Lane, London EC4P 4EE

ISBN 0 904568 26 1

CONTENTS

Introduction PAGE 6

Before it all began CHAPTER ONE 8
Early motorbuses to Brighton — Railway buses at Slough and Watford — Country bus routes from London 1912–1914 — Wartime decline — Postwar revival — Independent coach proprietors — The problems facing them.

The opening years CHAPTER TWO 11
The individual stories of the various operators who later joined the Green Line organisation, also the early operations of the L.G.O.C. and its associates.

Green Line builds up CHAPTER THREE 42
Formation of the Company — its rapid build up — proposals for cross-London routes — Poland Street Coach Station — more new routes in 1931 — the first double decker — acquisition of independents in 1932 and 1933.

Licensing systems CHAPTER FOUR 60
Licensing of staff and vehicles in London and country areas — Licensing under the Road Traffic Act — its affect on Green Line — the Amulree Committee and its results.

London Transport CHAPTER FIVE 68
The new Board takes over — acquisition of remaining independents — the network change in October 1933 — subsequent developments and route changes — the withdrawal due to war circumstances.

The war years CHAPTER SIX 86
Bus services replace some coach routes — partial resumption of coaches in 1939–1940 — restoration of the network to relieve the railways — withdrawal in September 1942.

Back again CHAPTER SEVEN 90
Coaches return from war service — the new routes — comparison with pre-war network — fares — subsequent developments — services to the New Towns.

Decline sets in CHAPTER EIGHT 98
Railway electrification — traffic congestion — fare increases — attempts to stimulate off-peak traffic — route withdrawals and changes — Express operations at Windsor and Amersham — Cheap Day returns once again — new orbital routes — Tunbridge Wells garage closes — G.L.C. to be responsible for London Transport — Green Line leaves London Transport.

London Country CHAPTER NINE 113
The new company takes over ageing fleet — first route changes — new coaches arrive — one-man operation increases — more fare revisions — season tickets introduced for commuters — more garage closures — the renaissance commences.

The vehicles CHAPTER TEN 130
The whole story of the vehicles used by Green Line from 1929 onwards, including the coaches inherited from the various independents acquired between 1932 and 1934.

Ticket systems CHAPTER ELEVEN 156
The story starts with the paper tickets used at first, followed by the Bell Punch system used by Green Line. It quotes extensively from instructions on ticket issue to the conductors, and ends with the modern ticket machines.

Insignia & publicity CHAPTER TWELVE 177
Part one deals with the story of the uniforms and equipment issued to the operating staff, and Part two discusses Green Line publicity throughout the years.

APPENDIX A 183
List of operators and services not included in the text.

APPENDIX B 185
List of local licences applied for by L.G.O.C. on Green Line before the Road Traffic Act.

APPENDIX C 187
Original proposals for through London workings — November 1930.

APPENDIX D 188
Original allocations of Green Line route letters — February 1931.

APPENDIX E 189
The second allocation of route letters — October 1933.

APPENDIX F 190
The third allocation of route letters — 1935 to 1937.

APPENDIX G 191
Wartime allocation of route numbers — December 1940.

APPENDIX H 192
Postwar allocation of route numbers.

Index 203

INTRODUCTION

The network of Green Line coach routes now operated by London Country Bus Services Limited, celebrate their fiftieth anniversary on Wednesday, 9 July 1980.

Although Green Line will have been operating for fifty years on that date, the provision of this type of service involving the operation of fast coaches between Central London and places within a 30-mile radius, commenced three years earlier in August 1927, when Glenton Coaches introduced the first route between London (Victoria) and Sevenoaks, with six daily journeys in each direction.

By the end of the year, two further services had been introduced, one from Tunbridge Wells to London, operated by Redcar Services (one of the town's local bus operators), and the other from London to Luton, operated by Imperial Motor Services. All three routes were operated on the pre-booking principle, whereby tickets were purchased at booking offices before boarding the coach. It was not until March 1928, when E. Gray and Sons started a London – Oxford service upon which the fares were collected by the drivers thus abolishing the need for pre-booking, that the rush to start new routes commenced.

Many services to various destinations were started in the next two years. Some flourished, but others failed. Many failures stemmed from Green Line Coaches appearing on the scene with their extensive fleet of A.E.C. Regal coaches providing services at regular and frequent intervals, staffed by courteous crews in smart green uniforms, and supervised by uniformed officials (a luxury which most other operators could not afford). Others survived the competition from Green Line and other operators, only to have their applications for licences to continue operation, refused by the Traffic Commissioners when the 1930 Road Traffic Act became law. Those who survived all this, either sold out to Green Line when it was rumoured that a Transport Board was to be formed to control and operate all of London's road services, whilst a hardy few, discounting the rumours, carried on until they were acquired by the new Board in 1933.

The London General Omnibus Company (a subsidiary of The Underground Group), together with its associate, The East Surrey Traction Company, noted the commencement of each new service in their respective areas with interest, at the same time watching the effect the new coach services were having on their long-established networks of bus routes in the countryside around London, and after two years of watching, decided they would join the growing ranks of operators in the short-distance express service world.

The East Surrey made a cautious start in August 1928 with two experimental services from Reigate and Redhill to London, both of which were withdrawn in the following March, as the new venture had not generated sufficient traffic to justify their continuance. The 'General' company started coaching in a small way late in 1929 with two routes from Watford, which ran to Golders Green and Charing Cross respectively, both being worked by Reliance all-weather coaches from the Private Hire fleet.

In the meantime, a new type of coach was being developed by the A.E.C. and L.G.O.C. jointly, and in April 1930, the L.G.O.C. entered the coaching business in earnest with a service from London to Windsor via Slough, which was soon followed by routes to other destinations. In June of the same year, they were joined by their associates (East Surrey and Autocar), who started services to London from Dorking, Reigate, Redhill and Tunbridge Wells.

At first, the coaches of all three companies were painted in the same red livery used on their buses, thereby causing much confusion in the public mind, as, particularly on the Windsor route, passengers thought the new red coaches were just a new type of single-deck bus, and were annoyed when they were told that there were no penny fares in operation. As a result of this, it was decided to form a new company entitled Green Line Coaches Limited, which was registered on 9 July 1930.

Upon the formation of the Company, it was officially announced that it had been formed for the purpose of convenience in operation, and in order to distinguish the coaches from the ordinary single-deck buses of the 'General' and its associate companies.

The first Green Line route as such commenced operating to Guildford just eight days after the Company was formed, and during the next few months many new routes were started, whilst the existing routes of the General, East Surrey and Autocar companies were also merged into the new undertaking, so that by the end of 1930, there were 24 routes in operation, requiring no fewer than 200 coaches to work them.

This book describes the operations of the smaller companies which later became part of the Green Line network; the start and build-up of the Green Line organisation; the effect of the Road Traffic Act; the acquisition of the smaller companies, and the merging of Green Line into London Transport in July 1933. Its subsequent successes and failures are also dealt with, right through to the transfer of responsibility from London Transport to London Country Bus Services on 1 January 1970. It also tells of the trials and tribulations experienced by the new company, and ends with the 'renaissance' of 1978, which still continues today as London Country attempts to find its proper share in the medium distance passenger market.

THE UNDERGROUND GROUP
THE UNDERGROUND ELECTRIC RAILWAYS OF
LONDON LTD, (formed 1902)

SUBSIDIARIES

The London Electric Rly Ltd
The Metropolitan District Rly Ltd
Central London Rly Ltd
City & South London Rly Ltd
London General Omnibus Co Ltd
Metropolitan Electric Tramways Ltd
London United Tramways Ltd
South Metropolitan Electric Tramways and Lighting Co Ltd
East Surrey Traction Co Ltd
Autocar Services – Tunbridge Wells Ltd
Green Line Coaches Ltd

BEFORE IT ALL BEGAN
CHAPTER ONE

Although the provision of fast coach services between London and towns within a 30-mile radius did not commence until the late twenties, it should not be thought that there were no connections by road to and from the capital.

Stage coaches, of course, had provided some sort of service for a large part of the 19th century. These consisted not only of the long distance services to the large provincial towns, but also a network of short-distance operations to the towns and villages within the areas served by the present-day Green Line services. Although the majority of them disappeared after the railway system developed around London, there were still some stage-coach services in operation as late as 1890.

In 1905 a service between London and Brighton, using double-deck motorbuses in the summer and single-deck vehicles in the winter, was started by the London Motor Omnibus Company Limited. Unfortunately, this route came to a sudden end when one of the Company's buses, carrying a private party, was involved in a fatal accident at Handcross in July 1906. The operation of this service is commemorated in Brighton by a public-house at the lower end of West Street which is called 'The Vanguard' (which was the fleet name of the bus company), and which depicts one of their double-deck buses on its sign.

After this unfortunate incident there were still local bus services operated by the railway companies at Slough, Watford and Hemel Hempstead, and a short route between Reigate and Redhill was started by The East Surrey Traction Company in 1911, although no further operations direct from London were to operate for quite some time.

Initially, services between London and the surrounding countryside were brought about to carry the Londoner out to the country on weekends and not by the need to bring the country folk into town. The motor-bus was a great novelty in those far-off days, and a ride on the open-top deck a great adventure, eagerly sought after by people keen to leave the sounds and smells of the big city for a few hours. Motorbuses of that time were somewhat mechanically unreliable and only ventured out as far as Richmond, Hampton Court and the southern outskirts of Epping Forest.

After much development the London General Omnibus Company at last produced a reliable bus in 1910, and two years later it appeared on the streets in increasing numbers. It was so reliable that it tempted the Company to try an experimental bus route on Sundays through the countryside from Hounslow to Windsor. Numbered 62, it commenced in July 1912, running at first every half-hour, but within a few weeks a 5-minute service was required to cope with the crowds wishing to enjoy the new facility. It was possible to purchase a through ticket from Charing Cross to travel on the District Railway to Hounslow and then on the bus to Windsor for 1/- (5p) single, whilst the London United trams from Shepherds Bush and Hammersmith issued through tickets by tram to Hounslow and then bus to Windsor. In these circumstances it is not surprising that by September it was running daily, and renumbered 81. It was also joined by a daily service to Staines, numbered 82, which was further extended on Sundays via Egham to Virginia Water. Over on the other side of London a new Saturday and Sunday service numbered 84 was commenced in the same month from Golders Green to St. Albans, which also became a daily service from December 1912.

By the summer of 1914, daily services were running to Sidcup, Farnborough and Westerham Hill in Kent; Esher, Egham, Caterham and Reigate in Surrey; Windsor and Maidenhead in Berks; St. Albans and Watford in Herts and Romford, Buckhurst Hill and Woodford Bridge in Essex. Although some of these destinations are today suburbs of London, in those days they were deep in the countryside surrounding the capital. On Sundays, the network was extended by extra services to several of the destinations mentioned above, as well as services to Lower Kingswood, Walton on-the-Hill, Godstone, Epsom, Leatherhead, Dorking and Virginia Water in Surrey; Burnham Beeches (Bucks); Hatfield and Wormley (Herts); whilst the Epping and Hainault Forest areas were well-served with routes to Epping Town, The Wake Arms, High Beech, Warren Wood, Chingford, Lambourne End and Chigwell Row.

All this activity was soon to come to an end as a large number of the London General Omnibus Company's buses were commandeered by the Government for troop movements when war was declared on Germany in August 1914, many of them being transported to France, whilst quite a number of the operating staff were Army or Navy reservists who had to report for war service. 2,500 men were lost to the Armed Forces in the first few months of the war, whilst over 1,300 out of a fleet of around 3,000 buses were commandeered.

In these circumstances it was inevitable that the needs of Central London and the inner suburbs had to come first when decisions were made on the question of route withdrawals. By the middle of 1915, the daily services to Maidenhead, Egham and Windsor had been withdrawn, the Woodford Bridge route had been curtailed at Wanstead on weekdays, but the Buckhurst Hill service was extended to Loughton. A fairly extensive programme of Summer Sunday services was worked, however, in order to provide recreational facilities for war-workers, but the following places were no longer served: Walton-on-the-Hill, Godstone and Virginia Water in Surrey; Maidenhead (Berks); Burnham Beeches (Bucks); Wormley (Herts) and High Beech (Essex).

The vehicle situation improved later in the year when the Company was permitted to buy back about 100 buses from the military authorities and later they were allowed to purchase some new buses, both single-deck and double-deck, but this only allowed for the introduction of a daily service to Dorking in May 1916, plus a slight increase on London routes which served the factory areas involved in war work. Petrol supplies became restricted, rationing was introduced in August 1916, and the amount available for operating bus services was progressively reduced.

In order to keep the public informed as to what bus routes were operating at any one time during this difficult period, printed folders were issued weekly showing a list of routes in operation for that particular week. The issue for the week from 22 to 28 July 1918, reveals the following facts: Ten daily services to the countryside were in operation, the destinations served being: Sidcup, Farnborough and Westerham Hill (Kent); Caterham, Merstham, Dorking and Esher (Surrey); Watford and St. Albans (Herts) and Loughton (Essex). The most frequent of these was the 47 route to Farnborough with a 7-minutes service; the Esher and Westerham Hill routes ran at irregular intervals, whilst the remainder operated at intervals varying from 12 to 20 minutes. The Summer Sunday extensions to the countryside were also restricted, consisting of extensions of some of the normal weekday services to Hampton Court, Kew Gardens, Belmont and Epsom (Surrey); Loughton, Woodford Bridge, Warren Wood, Chadwell Heath and Rippleside (Essex). Passengers wanting to visit other beauty spots in the countryside around London had to use the train, and then walk if the place they wished to visit was any distance from the railway station.

Hostilities ceased towards the end of 1918, but things could not return to normal immediately. Whilst some buses were being returned from France, they required extensive overhaul both to engine and bodywork before they could be placed in service, and new vehicles were still in short supply. However, the Company managed to improve both daily and Sunday operations to the countryside for the summer of 1919. The number of daily services was increased from 10 to 14, the four new destinations being Woodford Green, Kenley and Belmont, whilst the pre-war daily service on Route 10 to Woodford Bridge was reinstated. The Summer Sunday extension programme was greatly increased and services were resumed to Epping Town, Chingford and Lambourne End (Essex); Hadley Woods (Herts); Windsor (Berks); Leatherhead, Virginia Water and Lower Kingswood (Surrey). The frequency of some of both the daily and Sunday services had been reduced in some cases, half-hourly buses being provided to Watford, St. Albans, Belmont and Reigate instead of the 20-minute service of previous years. The weekday service to Dorking was hourly (half-hourly previously), whilst the remainder generally ran at 12–15 minute intervals, as did most of the Summer Sunday extensions.

Despite the fact that the new improved 46-seat K-type double-deck bus was beginning to appear on the streets in 1920, the position as far as bus services to the countryside was concerned, was bleak. A daily service had been reinstated to Windsor on Route 81 (half-hourly), also to Egham and Virginia Water (117) every 15 minutes. New destinations served were Boxmoor (Herts) from Golders Green every 12 minutes; Burnham Beeches from Hounslow every 15 minutes; Pinner from Somerset House every 15 minutes and Wormley (Herts) every 10 minutes from Finsbury Park. All these new destinations were served on Summer Sundays only.

1921 was a year of great development in the country bus scene, new buses entered service every week, and by the end of the year there were 26 daily services running out to the country towns. New places served daily were: Abridge, Epping, Brentwood, Upminster, Chigwell Row (Essex); Farningham, West Wickham, and Crayford (Kent); Godstone, Byfleet, Weybridge, Walton-on-the-Hill and Guildford (Surrey); Harpenden and Hertford (Herts); Uxbridge and Pinner (Middlesex) and West Wycombe (Bucks). New destinations served on the weekends were Rainham (Essex) and Ascot (Berks).

Open top NS-type bus en route to Windsor in 1926. (London Transport).

From then onwards, the network gradually grew and spread outwards until most towns and villages within twenty-five miles of London were able to boast of a service which would take their citizens either right into the centre of London or to a suburban terminal where they could continue their journey by another bus or else by Underground.

By the time that Green Line appeared on the scene, in late 1930, the London General Omnibus Company had over thirty daily services either running out from London directly, or starting their journeys in the outer suburbs and London buses could be seen as far afield as Farningham, Green Street Green, Keston and Dartford in Kent; Abridge, Rainham, Chigwell Row, Brentwood, Epping, Stapleford Abbots, Upminster, Aveley and Grays in Essex; Reigate, Chertsey, Dorking, Woking, Guildford and Lower Kingswood in Surrey; Staines, Uxbridge, Northwood and Potters Bar in Middlesex; Slough (Bucks); Windsor (Berks) and Watford, St. Albans, Arkley and Wormley in Hertfordshire.

Whilst all this was happening, a large number of independent bus operators had sprung up in Central London, most of whom were a thorn in the sides of the London General Omnibus Company and its associates, as these 'pirate' buses (as the public soon named them) tended to congregate on the more remunerative routes. Naturally, the 'General' organisation took preventative measures by putting extra buses on the routes concerned in order to counteract the opposition, with the result that the streets of London became very congested and whilst the public was enjoying a bus service never to be experienced again, the results were far from satisfactory as far as the police were concerned, as they had to deal with the ever-increasing congestion. Traffic lights did not exist in those days, and large numbers of policemen had to be employed for traffic control duties.

In 1924, the Government passed the London Traffic Act, which was designed to regulate the number of buses allowed to ply for hire on certain streets in the capital. In the main, the Act had the desired effect especially when the Ministry of Transport later declared several more thoroughfares as 'Restricted Streets' and the independent operators found that more routes were closed to them. From 1926 onwards, many of the smaller operators sold out to the 'General' or other larger independent concerns, which left them with money enough to invest in fresh spheres of operation.

Many of them observed that, although motor coaches were licensed as stage carriages in the Metropolitan Police District in the same way as buses, the restricting regulations of the 1924 Act only applied inside the Metropolitan Police District, and not throughout the London Traffic Area, which covered the territory approximately 20 to 25 miles from Charing Cross, so that in effect, there was no regulation of motor coach routes.

At this time, these motor coach routes consisted of services from London to the coastal towns and larger provincial cities and there were no services of the Green Line type in operation. It is not surprising, therefore, that some of the former independent bus operators decided to try their luck by providing this type of service.

They were facing a different problem, however, to the one they faced when starting their bus businesses in Central London. There they had watched the obvious successes of the L.G.O.C. and its associates on the various routes and it was simply a matter of deciding on which route they should place their new bus, but, in the case of the new venture on which they were proposing to embark, there was nothing to guide them.

Here then, are some of the problems which faced these early pioneers:

(a) Whilst they knew that a single-deck vehicle would be more suitable than a double-decker, the seating capacity remained a problem. Would a 20-seater be too small or a 30- or 32-seater too large?

(b) What frequency of service should be provided? Would an hourly service be sufficient, or should one start from there and build up, or should one commence with a half-hourly service, in the hope that there would be sufficient passenger traffic to justify it?

(c) Would the service attract enough passengers to ensure even a modest profit after all expenses had been met?

Looking at the existing ordinary bus services from London at that time, there was a reasonable weekend traffic from London particularly in the summer, as the private car was a luxury only enjoyed by the moneyed classes. The Monday to Friday traffic was mainly confined to trips to the nearest town on market days or for shopping and a visit to the cinema on Saturdays.

It will thus be seen that before deciding on the route to be served with a short-distance coach operation, careful planning was required if the operation was to be a success. An adequate financial reserve was necessary to cover the lean period while the business was developing and the public was becoming accustomed to the new service. For a route to become a successful venture, plentiful publicity was vital. Even if the operator proposed to use conductors and sell tickets on the coaches, it was advisable for him to appoint booking agents on the line of route and pay them a small commission on ticket sales. The agent would then, in his own interest, display posters advertising the service and distribute handbills and timetable leaflets.

Many of the routes started by small operators between 1927 and 1930 failed through lack of attention to the matters discussed in the previous paragraph. Others, who had achieved a reasonable success on the routes they had chosen, gave up when competition in the form of more frequent services over their routes, by larger organisations, stole most of the traffic they had painstakingly built up.

Some of them managed to survive all this, only to lose their right to operate, when, having submitted an application to continue operating, as required by the Road Traffic Act (1930), they were refused a Road Service Licence by the Traffic Commissioners.

Unfortunately, when they finally gave up and withdrew their services, though they undoubtedly posted withdrawal notices on their vehicles, none of them seemed to produce handbills advertising the fact and in consequence, the dates of their withdrawals have been lost in the mists of time.

These short-lived operations will be found listed in Appendix A, and we shall only discuss in detail the routes and companies which were acquired by Green Line Coaches Limited or London Transport, or which are still running at the present time, some of them as subsidiaries of the National Bus Company.

THE OPENING YEARS
CHAPTER TWO

Green Line Coaches Limited did not commence operations until July 1930, but many of the companies which ultimately joined them, started operating much earlier, and this chapter deals with their individual histories. Each organisation will be presented in the order in which operation commenced and, to maintain continuity, they will be dealt with as separate entities, ending with their acquisition by Green Line, London Transport or the National Bus Company.

NEW EMPRESS SALOONS
CITY COACH COMPANY LTD:

New Empress Saloons was the first company to start a short-stage carriage express service. Arthur Edward Young commenced running on 27 May 1927 with a service from Wood Green (Jolly Butchers Hill) to Southend-on-Sea, under the title of 'The Empress Bus', this being the fleet name he used whilst operating a bus on Route 29. Between Wood Green and Romford the service was worked on a pre-booking basis, but from there onwards the coaches plied for hire in the same way as a bus or Green Line coach does today.

There was severe competition beyond Romford, mainly from the bus services of the Westcliff Motor Services, but Young managed to survive this and was joined by two other former London bus operators with money to invest in the business. Together they formed New Empress Saloons Limited, which took over the operation of the route on 10 July 1928.

The City Omnibus Company Limited of Peckham, who were at that time running a very successful bus business in London, were also looking for fresh fields in which to invest capital. They purchased 1,000 of the 1,500 £1 shares, thus gaining control of New Empress, which passed to them on 19 December 1928.

Once City obtained control things began to happen very quickly. New vehicles were injected into the fleet, the older vehicles being repainted in the Spanish brown livery used by City for their buses. The City fleet name was adopted, but New Empress Saloons Limited were shown as the legal owners on the lower panels. The route was extended from Wood Green via Finsbury Park and Camden Town to Kentish Town Station, and after the opening of a new garage in Leighton Road, Kentish Town in December 1929, the service terminated there.

At this time an hourly service was being worked daily and timetable folders printed on art paper were produced which were available from agents and coach conductors, as well as being placed in small tin boxes on all the City's London buses.

About this time, Westcliff Motor Services commenced an hourly service to Wood Green over the same route as New Empress, using single deck buses and numbered Route 16, obviously competing with that service.

Leyland 'Lion' PLSC3 coach of New Empress Saloons Ltd. (a subsidiary of the City Omnibus Company) en route to Southend-on-Sea at Brentwood. (J. F. Higham).

11

City lost no time in eliminating this by consultation with the Westcliff company resulting in a joint timetable commencing on 1 January 1929, and which by 1930 gave a 15-minute joint service from Southend to Wood Green, with the New Empress coaches continuing to Kentish Town every half-hour.

The London bus business of the City Omnibus Company was taken over by London Transport in November 1934, and at the same time City was negotiating with Westcliff for the purchase of their timings on the Wood Green – Southend section of the route. They were successful in their negotiations and the whole route passed to New Empress Saloons, the new timetable becoming operative from 12 January 1935.

The renaming of the company to The City Coach Company Limited took place in March 1936, at the same time transferring its headquarters from Kentish Town to a new office building in Ongar Road, Brentwood, behind which a garage for the coaches was built. The Kentish Town and Southend depots were retained to allow for early morning buses and late night journeys to the respective terminals. The Southend route continued to prosper, and the company expanded its interests by the purchase of several small local bus operators in the Brentwood, Ongar and Laindon areas.

When the Second World War started it had no effect on the Southend route until the fuel and rubber situation worsened in 1942 necessitating modifications to the route by order of the Ministry of War Transport. As the route worked as a bus service from Southend to Brentwood and the section between there and Wood Green and Kentish Town was worked as a short-stage express operation, the Company were allowed to work two isolated sections as follows: Southend to Brentwood and Romford to Wood Green. The sections between Kentish Town and Wood Green and Romford and Brentwood were adequately covered by London Transport bus routes and were abandoned for the rest of the war. Through working from Southend to Wood Green was resumed in the spring of 1946, but the Kentish Town section was abandoned permanently and the route terminated in the garage and coach station in Lordship Lane, Wood Green, which is now an Eastern National garage. With the resumption of through running, double-deck vehicles were gradually introduced on the route, a practice which continues today.

When nationalisation appeared on the horizon, rather than wait to be acquired on the Government's terms, the company sold to the British Transport Commission on its own somewhat more advantageous valuation of its assets.

By a strange quirk of fate, the British Transport Commission placed the City company under the control of its old rival, Westcliff Motor Services, which was then a subsidiary of the Eastern National Omnibus Company and today that company still operates a frequent service on the former City route, which is now numbered 251.

REDCAR SERVICES LIMITED
MAIDSTONE & DISTRICT:

On 16 September 1927, Redcar Services commenced a service from Victoria (Buckingham Palace Road) to Tunbridge Wells (Monson Road), running four daily journeys, plus a special late journey on Wednesdays and Saturdays for theatre-goers. Conductors were not used at first, and passengers were required to purchase their tickets at the company's offices in Tunbridge Wells and Tonbridge and from booking agents in London. A notice on the reverse side of the handbill, advertising the new service, stated that on Sundays only, bookings at Tonbridge would be carried out by the Inspector on duty at the Omnibus Stand at Tonbridge Station and not at the local agents. On journeys to London, passengers were not picked up after Tonbridge Station, neither were they picked up south of Bromley on outward-bound coaches. I feel that this operation was started as an experiment to ascertain if there was a need for this type of service, as it was withdrawn on 1 January 1928. It was reinstated, minus the theatre coach, from 5 April presumably after the traffic returns of the original operation had been well scrutinised and satisfactorily proven. On reinstatement the service terminated in London at the temporary coach station in Lupus Street (Pimlico) owned by London Coastal Coaches Limited, who also became the London agents for the service.

The service was increased to eleven daily journeys by March 1930, and a picking up point had been established at Sevenoaks (Tubbs Hill Station), but tickets still had first to be purchased from a booking agent.

At this time the return fare from London to Sevenoaks was 4/- (20p), whilst that to Tonbridge was 5/- (25p) and Tunbridge Wells 5/6 (27½p), but once Green Line appeared on the scene, with lower fares, the Redcar fares were reduced to the Green Line scale, the only difference being that Green Line had fares from London to Bromley and Green Street Green, but Redcar did not introduce such fares until August 1932, when they also abolished the picking-up

restrictions which had applied since the service commenced.

Redcar adopted the full Green Line type of operation on 4 October 1933, when an hourly service was introduced and the London terminal was transferred from Victoria Coach Station to Eccleston Bridge. Many extra fare stages and picking up points were introduced at this time, but there were still no local fares between Sevenoaks and Tunbridge Wells.

The company was acquired by Maidstone and District Motor Services in February 1935, and they continued the London route until 31 July when it was passed to London Transport, together with five Leyland TS2 and four Leyland TD1 coaches. The Board continued the operation as a separate hourly service on Route C for a short while, but as Route AC only operated from Woking to Sevenoaks on Mondays–Fridays (extended to Tunbridge Wells on Saturdays and Sundays), this route was altered to a daily operation to Tunbridge Wells from 8 January, and the separate hourly service withdrawn.

Maidstone and District also acquired (on 10 March 1931) an old established hourly service from Charing Cross to Gillingham via Dartford and Gravesend. When London Transport was formed, this service was not acquired by the new Board, but was diverted at Crayford via Princes Road and the A2 road, Green Line Route A being extended from Dartford to Gravesend (Denton) in its place. This extension commenced on 1 July 1933.

Maidstone and District also had a frequent service from London to Maidstone via Farningham and Wrotham which, until 1 July 1933, carried passengers for Farningham, West Kingsdown and Wrotham. On the date mentioned in the last sentence, the responsibility for this section of road was passed to London Transport, and Green Line Route I was extended from Farningham to Wrotham to cover it.

IMPERIAL MOTOR SERVICES
SAFEWAY MOTOR SERVICES
BEAUMONT SALOON COACHES
BEAUMONT-SAFEWAY:

The story of the above four companies is somewhat involved and spans from November 1927 to April 1934, when Beaumont-Safeway was acquired by London Transport.

Imperial Motor Services commenced operations in November 1927 with a service from Kings Cross (York Road) to Luton (Manchester Square). At first, seven round trips were worked on weekdays and five on Sundays. All seats on the coaches were numbered and reserved and the timetable leaflet stated that 'tickets not showing seat numbers thereon would not be accepted'. Although booking agents were appointed at Harpenden and St. Albans, no fares are quoted from London or Luton to these points and it must be presumed that the through fares from Luton to London and vice-versa were also charged to Harpenden and St. Albans.

Evidently the initial operation was successful, and before long, nine weekday and seven Sunday journeys were being worked and the route was extended to Bedford via Clophill in February 1928. In September of that year, another Bedford service was started, this time via Welwyn, Hitchin, Henlow and Shefford, on which six daily journeys were worked, and the original service, via Clophill, was withdrawn between Bedford and Luton.

In October 1928, Harry Hill commenced operating his

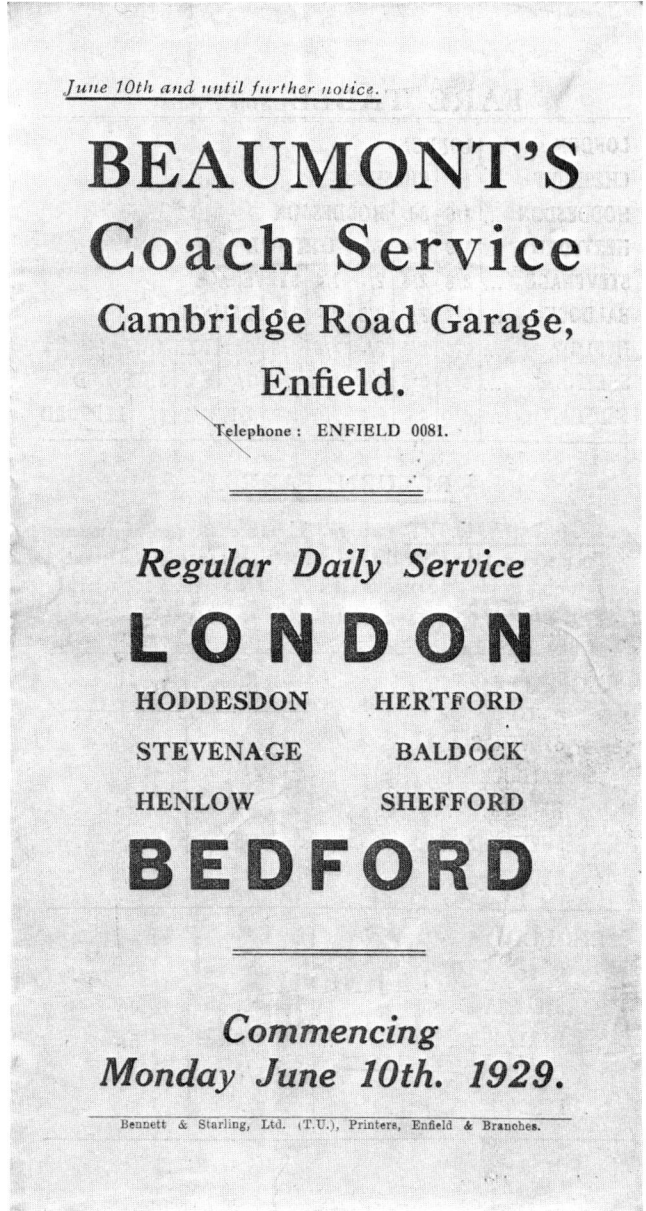

Strawhatter coaches from Park Street, Luton to Kings Cross, working four round trips daily, running in between the Imperial timings. In November this was followed by the introduction of the Birch Brothers operations on the Bedford rout with six daily round trips via Hitchin which started in London from Aldwych, and then ran via Kings Cross to compete with Imperial.

Faced with the competition from these two operators, who were covering the routes which he had pioneered, Ralph Priest (the Imperial proprietor) decided to sell out in March 1929 to Venture Transport Services Limited of Hendon.

Two months later, Ralph Priest formed a new company entitled Safeway Motor Services and commenced a London – Reading service via Staines, Ascot and Bracknell, the London terminal which was initially at Kings Cross, but was later transferred to Victoria (Vauxhall Bridge Road).

The initial service consisted of four daily round trips, one of which was described as a theatre-goer's coach, which left Reading at 5.30 pm, being extended to Charing Cross on weekdays. The return coach at 11.40 pm, from Charing Cross, was covered by the 8.30 pm departure from Reading. The normal London – Reading return fare was 4/- (20p), but

13

on the 5.30 pm, departure, a special return fare of 2/6 (12½p) was charged in order to stimulate traffic growth. By April 1930, six daily return trips were being worked, and to encourage weekend pleasure traffic, all single and return fares were reduced after midday on Saturdays and all day on Sundays.

In August 1929, Arthur Priest joined his brother Ralph, and they started a service from Kings Cross to Hertford via Hoddesdon and Ware, five daily return journeys being worked. It would seem that passengers were not picked up south of Hoddesdon as fares were not quoted in the handbill for places south of that point. A queer notice found in this handbill states that passengers must book at least one day in advance with one of the booking agents. This was an unusual request for a short distance service of this type. Evidently this operation was not very successful, as the goodwill of the service was disposed of to W. S. Ray of Harringay in October 1929, and henceforth it was worked by him as Regent Motor Services, whose story will be discussed later.

A few weeks later, in November, Safeway commenced three daily journeys to and from Leighton Buzzard via St. Albans and Dunstable, serving an area which was poorly provided with railway connections to London. This was the route which evidenced the merging of the Safeway organisation with that of Beaumont Saloon Coaches in 1931.

Meanwhile, in January 1930, Safeway commenced a new route from Victoria (Vauxhall Bridge Road) to Sevenoaks via New Cross, Lewisham, Bromley and Farnborough on which five daily return journeys were operated. Once again, a theatre facility to London was provided on weekdays with the normal return fare of 2/6 being reduced to 1/9, but, unlike the Reading service, cheap fares were not provided at weekends.

This service appeared on the scene at a somewhat unfortunate time, as Redcar was already well-established and, on 6 June, Autocar Services Limited of Tunbridge Wells started an hourly service from that town to London, which was stepped up to half-hourly from 24 June subjecting Safeway to some fairly heavy competition.

The Reading service also started to experience severe competition at the end of July 1930, when Thackray's Way introduced their hourly service from Oxford Circus to Reading which followed the same route. Safeway withdrew both the Reading and Sevenoaks operations on 26 August 1930.

Arthur Priest carried on with the remaining Safeway service to Leighton Buzzard, but Ralph left the company to become manager of Beaumont Saloon Coaches of Enfield.

William Douglas Beaumont, owner of the fleet of coaches bearing his name, had commenced a route from Kings Cross to Bedford on 10 June 1929. Two daily round trips were worked over a very roundabout route via Stoke Newington, Tottenham, Edmonton, Palmers Green, Enfield, Waltham Cross, Hoddesdon, Hertford, Stevenage, Baldock, Stotfold, Henlow and Shefford.

Single fares were issued throughout the route, and although the minimum fare out of London was 1/- (5p) to Cheshunt, there were lower fares after that destination examples being: Cheshunt – Hoddesdon, 8d (3½p); Hoddesdon – Hertford, 6d (2½p); Baldock – Henlow, 9d (3·75p). Return fares only applied from London to Stevenage, Baldock, Henlow, Shefford and Bedford, and in the reverse direction from Bedford to Stevenage, Hertford, Cheshunt and London.

In February 1930, Beaumont purchased the goodwill of the Venture Transport service to Bedford which operated over the more direct route via Welwyn, Codicote, Hitchin and Henlow and, as this was a more populated route, offering better traffic potential, he withdrew the service via Hertford in order to develop this route.

A timetable dated April 1931 shows four round trips on Mondays to Fridays and six on Saturdays and Sundays, whilst a later one shows six daily trips. This was the service in operation when Beaumont made his application to continue operations under the Road Traffic Act, a Road Service Licence being granted by the Traffic Commissioners.

In March 1931, Beaumont Saloon Coaches and Safeway Motor Services joined forces, the new company being entitled Beaumont-Safeway Saloon Coaches, and working two routes, as follows:

London – Welwyn – Codicote – Hitchin – Henlow – Bedford.

London – St. Albans – Markyate – Dunstable – Hockliffe – Leighton Buzzard.

As stated previously, the Bedford service consisted of six daily return journeys, whilst the Leighton Buzzard route consisted of four trips to and from Leighton Buzzard and two trips to and from Dunstable on Mondays to Fridays, with an extra journey to Leighton Buzzard on Saturdays. The Sunday service was four Leighton Buzzard journeys and one to Dunstable.

The Bedford route was disposed of to Messrs. Birch Brothers Ltd., on 30 November 1932 and henceforth Beaumont-Safeway concentrated on the Leighton Buzzard route until it was acquired by London Transport on 27 April 1934. Why London Transport found it necessary to acquire Beaumont-Safeway is a mystery. London Transport had been operating an hourly service to Dunstable from East Grinstead since 4 October 1933 and, as they were prohibited by one of the provisions in the Act which set up the Board from operating north of Dunstable, by acquiring Beaumont they deprived the towns between that point and Leighton Buzzard of a direct service to the metropolis. London Transport did not increase its service to Dunstable after the acquisition, but, of course, it is possible that the introduction of the Green Line service deprived Beaumont-Safeway of quite a fair amount of its traffic, making the route unprofitable, and so the company decided to sell out.

WEST LONDON COACHES:

The market town of Aylesbury was the destination chosen by West London Coaches when it commenced operation on 19 May 1928. At first, three round trips were worked daily, starting from the Lupus Street Coach Station of London Coastal Coaches and then calling to pick up at the company's office at 202 Sutherland Avenue, Maida Vale. The route followed was via Harlesden, Wembley, Harrow, Pinner, Northwood, Rickmansworth, Amersham, The Missendens and Wendover.

Despite the fact that the route ran parallel to the Metropolitan Railway from Harrow to Aylesbury, there was a good response to the new service, no doubt due to the fact that the railway stations in many cases were so far from the towns and villages after which they were named. As a result, a further two return trips were added to the timetable, introduced on 15 September 1928.

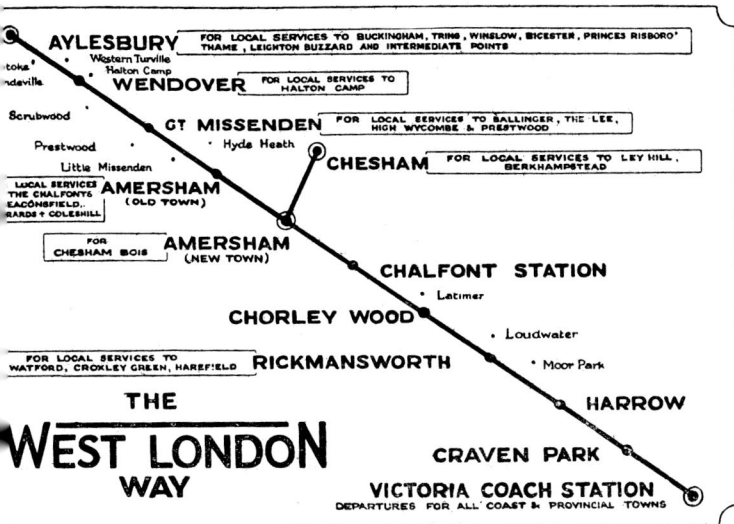

From a study of the timetable leaflets issued over the years, it would seem that the company closely studied the traffics which they carried at various periods of the year. The Summer timetable for 1929 showed a slight reduction in service, as it consisted of four round trips on Mondays to Fridays with three on Saturdays and Sundays. The winter timetable was put into operation on 28 October 1929, and one round trip daily was worked between London and Aylesbury, but a new facility was provided with a service to Chesham, consisting of two journeys to and from London on Mondays to Fridays, and one on Saturdays and Sundays.

The summer timetable for 1930, introduced in May was fixed at five round trips to Aylesbury on Mondays to Saturdays and four on Sundays, whilst Chesham received three daily round trips from London. Of course, in those far-off days, the area served by West London Coaches was not the dormitory area for the metropolis that it is today.

With the timetable introduced on 24 June 1931, the service reached its zenith with eight weekday and five Sunday trips in each direction on the Aylesbury route, all of which also served Chesham by means of a shuttle coach operating to and from Amersham (Sycamore Corner), where it met the coach on the main route on both the Aylesbury and London journeys.

A unique way of using the services of the shuttle coach driver in between making the necessary connections, was evolved. I met the driver many years later, and was told that, after he had transferred his passengers to the London coach, he boarded it himself and checked all the tickets in issue thereon. He would then travel with it until it met the outward-bound coach, when he would transfer, once again checking all the tickets in issue. On arrival at Sycamore Corner, he would supervise the transfer of passengers for Chesham to the shuttle coach, and then drive them to their destination.

This company was one of the few independents working under the wing of London Coastal Coaches and it transferred to Victoria Coach Station when that replaced the Lupus Street terminal.

The company was successful in obtaining a Road Service Licence to continue operation under the Road Traffic Act (1930), but Green Line Coaches Limited, who had

Daimler CH6 coach for West London Coaches Limited at the Hendon body works of Duple's before delivery to the company. (McCall collection).

Dennis 'Arrow' coach of Red Rover Saloon Coaches at Seymour Street terminus of the Aylesbury route. (J. F. Higham).

applied to extend their Rickmansworth service hourly to Chesham, were not so lucky, as their application was refused.

West London carried on quite successfully after this, still running at the times introduced in June 1931 until the company was acquired by London Transport on 17 January 1934.

I possess a copy of the first timetable folder for the service issued by London Transport. Although printed in the style then used by the Green Line section of the Board, it is headed 'WEST LONDON COACHES'. The times and number of journeys have not been altered, but the route has been lettered 'S' in the Green Line series.

Eight coaches passed to the new owners, comprising a mixed bag namely two Saurers, two T. S. Motors, three Gilford 1680T and a Daimler CH6. The Saurers and T.S. Motors were soon disposed of, whilst the Gilfords and Daimler were transferred to the Country bus fleet, who ran the Gilfords until 1936 and the Daimler until 1937.

Route S made its last journeys on 10 July 1934, being replaced the following day by the extension of Route B from Rickmansworth, which then ran hourly to Amersham (Oakfield Corner), where alternate coaches bifurcated to Chesham and Aylesbury respectively. With the extension of Route B to cover Route S, the operation at the northern end was transferred from Watford (Leavesden Road) to Amersham, and the coaches which formerly worked Route S were also transferred from their out-station in the County Garage at Aylesbury to Amersham London Transport Garage.

RED ROVER SALOON COACHES:

This company was started by Edward Maurice Cain, the proprietor of a double-deck bus on Route 14, who embarked on a coaching venture in August 1928. He also chose Aylesbury as the outer destination for his coach route, which ran six daily return journeys from Marble Arch (19 Edgware Road) via Cricklewood, Edgware, Brockley Hill, Watford-by-Pass, Kings Langley, Boxmoor, Berkhamsted and Tring.

The reason why the route chosen was not through the more populated route via Bushey and Watford was that Watford Council were responsible for licensing all vehicles to ply for hire through their area until 1930, and they were reluctant to license extra vehicles, particularly if the proprietors were not resident in the town. In any event, Watford was well-served by L.M.S. electric trains to Euston and Broad Street, as well as an all-day service on the Bakerloo Line at that time.

The situation north of Watford, however, was a different kettle of fish. Outside the peak hours on weekdays, trains were few and far between, and there were only fourteen trains on Sundays serving Boxmoor, Berkhamsted and Tring. The London Midland and Scottish Railway had a branch line to Aylesbury High Street Station in those days, but the trains operated on weekdays only, at widely spaced intervals, and all passengers had to change at Cheddington, with a long wait there for the London trains.

An undated Red Rover timetable which was probably issued around 1930 indicated eight Monday–Friday journeys; ten trips on Saturdays and eight on Sundays. The 9 am coach from London on weekdays, plus the 12 noon coach on Saturdays, only ran from London to Tring, returning at 10.30 am and 1.30 pm respectively. Initially, all seats had to be booked in advance, and it was not until Green Line introduced an hourly service to Tring, on which tickets could be purchased on the coach, that Red Rover adopted the same system.

The service was quite successful and by 1931 the company had established an office in Kingsbury Square (Aylesbury) and all journeys were now being operated right through to that town. The company was a booking agent for London Coastal Coaches and this fact also undoubtedly increased bookings for their own service. On the London service, through bookings were available to and from Whitchurch, Winslow and Buckingham on a bus service operated by P. J. Simmonds, and which was ultimately acquired by Red Rover in the Summer of 1932.

The London service was sold to Green Line Coaches Limited on 29 November 1932. Red Rover then concentrated on establishing itself as a bus operator in the Aylesbury area, changing its title to The Red Rover Omnibus Company Limited. Since 29 December 1955, when the Cain family retired from the business, it has been under the control of Keith Coaches Limited, but the fleet name 'Red

Rover' still lives on.

The coach service, consisting of ten weekday journeys and eight Sunday trips, carried on under Green Line control as Route AT. As Red Rover were continuing as a bus operator, the Road Service Licence for the coach route was transferred to Green Line Coaches Ltd, and the timetable leaflet issued by the new organisation was headed 'GREEN LINE (formerly operated by Red Rover)'. Through tickets were still issued to the Buckingham bus service, although these were withdrawn soon after London Transport took over in July 1933. When the Green Line network was reorganised, in October 1933, Route AT was relettered as AS, and carried on until it was merged into Route E (Chelsham–London–Tring–Aylesbury) on 11 July 1934.

BALDOCK MOTOR TRANSPORT LIMITED
QUEEN LINE COACHES LIMITED:

Known as Baldock Transport Limited this coach operating organisation started initially in the private hire field, operating excursions to coastal resorts in the summer seasons of 1927 and 1928. Operations were carried out from a garage in High Street, Baldock.

During the Summer of 1928 the company explored the possibility of operating a daily service to London via Letchworth, Hitchin and the Great North Road to Hatfield (Oldings Corner), where it would then follow the Barnet-by-Pass to South Mimms (Bignells Corner), carrying on through Barnet, North Finchley and Highgate to Kings Cross, where it was proposed that it should terminate in the Central London Road Transport Station, in Cartwright Gardens.

The route commenced on 30 October 1928 with four daily journeys to and from London from Baldock. Three started from Biggleswade, whilst all the coaches from London also ran through to that town. On Wednesdays, Thursdays, and Saturdays, a late journey was worked from Baldock at 9.30 pm which left London at 11.30 pm for Biggleswade. This journey was for the theatre-goers and reached Biggleswade at 1.45 am.

By the early part of 1929, the company had nine coaches in service and later in the year, became associated with Queen Line Coaches of Willesden Green in North-West London. This organisation operated long distance coach services from London to the coast in the summer seasons, as well as services to the North of England. The Baldock – Biggleswade section had been withdrawn by this time, and some competition was experienced from the Bedford – London service operated by Beaumont's Saloon Coaches between Baldock and Stevenage. This competition became more serious when the former Venture Bedford route was acquired by Beaumont who started running over the whole of Baldock Transport's route from Hitchin to London.

More serious competition was experienced from September 1930, when Green Line Coaches commenced a half-hourly service from Welwyn Garden City to London, especially when they extended the route to Hitchin soon after.

In the meantime, to meet this competition, Queen Line, whom had now taken charge of the Baldock Transport service, introduced an hourly service from Baldock to London from 14 November 1930 and also extended the route from Kings Cross to the London Terminal Coach Station in Clapham Road (just south of Oval Tube Station), which they reached via Oxford Circus and Victoria. They also set up an office here to control operations at the London end of the route. By the beginning of 1931 the fleet had grown to some thirteen vehicles. Not all of these were

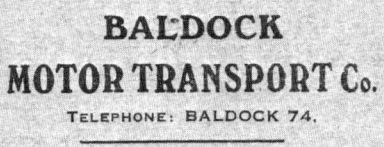

A.E.C. Regal coach of Queen Line Coaches Limited at Kings Cross en route to Baldock. (McCall collection).

employed on the London service, but were a useful standby when it was necessary to operate duplicates. At this time, Queen Line purchased the six A.E.C. Regal coaches with London Lorries bodywork, which operated the basic timetable.

On application to the Traffic Commissioners to continue the operation of their route under the Road Traffic Act (1930), Queen Line were granted a licence to continue the hourly service, but were required by the Commissioners to cut back the route to the new Kings Cross Coach Station (just opposite the railway station) in order to avoid causing extra congestion in Central London. Queen Line did not appeal against this decision and the service was curtailed at Kings Cross in February 1932.

The shadow of the coming Transport Board was hanging over the London bus and coach operators early in 1933, and the Company realised it would only be a matter of time before their undertaking would be acquired by the Board at a price which would be decided by the new organisation, and preferring to sell on their own terms, the London service passed to Green Line Coaches Limited on 26 April 1933, the new owners acquiring the six A.E.C. Regal coaches used on the route, plus the use of the Baldock garage.

Upon acquisition, the Queen Line times and fares were maintained by Green Line, and remained unchanged, except for a change in route letters from AR to AK on 3 October 1933. Under London Transport control it also remained undisturbed until 8 January 1936, when the Hitchin – Baldock section was added to Route K1, whilst the Queen Line route via South Mimms and the Barnet By Pass was diverted to Welwyn Garden City, operating from Dorking as Route K2 and passing its former terminus in Clapham Road on the way.

STRAWHATTER COACHES:

As the name implies, Strawhatter was a company based on the Bedfordshire town of Luton. Owned by Harry Hill, it operated coastal services during the summer, excursions and private hire until October 1928, when Hill decided to try his luck with a Luton-London service following the same route as Priest's Imperial Motor Services.

At this time, Priest was operating nine weekly round trips, with seven on Sundays, whilst Hill operated five on weekdays and four on Sundays, both operators charging a fare of 2/- (10p) single; 2/6 (12½p) return.

On 3 November 1928, Priest decided to meet the competition he was experiencing from Strawhatter by reducing the Monday-Friday fare to London to 1/6 (7½p) single; 1/9 (8½p) day return, at the same time revising his running time so that he made a faster trip to London. Hill's reply to this was to increase his service to eight daily trips, but only reduced the single fare to the same level as Priest, leaving his day return fare at 2/6. Hill had one advantage over Priest in that his coaches started from the Central London Road Transport Station in Cartwright Gardens (near Russell Square). He was also the booking agent in Luton for that organisation, and could book for services to all parts of England, a fact which no doubt led to the success of his own operation, as passengers from his coaches could change to long-distance services without having to spend extra money on transfer fares in London.

The competition proved too much for Priest, who disposed of his service to Venture Transport in March 1929. The writer possesses a handbill issued by Venture showing the timetable commencing on 14 January 1930. This shows eight weekday and six Sunday journeys from Bush House (Aldwych), all of which also called at Kings Cross. The weekday journeys were spaced out at two-hourly intervals timed to run between the Strawhatter timings, with fares at the same rates as charged by that company.

Co-ordination of timings between the two companies was introduced from 7 March 1932, with return tickets available for the return journey on the coaches of either company, but Venture sold out to Strawhatter later in the year, and from 1 January 1933, Strawhatter was operating a basic hourly service which was increased to half-hourly at certain times of the day.

Having killed off all the opposition, Strawhatter continued to prosper, building up a fleet of 24 Gilford coaches, all of which passed to London Transport when it acquired the company on 1 February 1934. The fleet of coaches and the London service were retained by the L.P.T.B., the route becoming BH in the Green Line series. The coastal services were passed to Eastern National (who were then the local bus operator in that area), whilst the garage in Park Street West became a London Transport depot (coded LS – Luton Strawhatter), passing to London Country Bus Services in 1970. They closed it in January 1977, when a reorganisation of their bus and coach services in the Luton area took place.

ACME PULLMAN SERVICES LIMITED:

Acme commenced operations on 5 October 1928 with twelve daily journeys at intervals varying from hourly to every 90 minutes from London (Liverpool Street Tram Terminus) to Bishops Stortford via Stratford, Wanstead, Woodford, Epping New Road, Epping, Old Harlow and Sawbridgeworth. A feature of the first timetable was the 5.30 pm departure from Bishops Stortford which was extended to Oxford Circus, and marked with a 'T' in the timetable. A footnote says: 'This service is run for the convenience of passengers visiting West End amusements and seats on this coach should be reserved in advance.' The return journey was at 11.30 pm and the same conditions applied as those to the departure mentioned above.

By 7 December 1929, twenty-two journeys were being worked from London to Bishops Stortford of which eight were extended to Newmarket via Saffron Walden and

Gilford 1680T coach of Strawhatter Coaches Limited on stand at Park Square, Luton. (J. F. Higham).

Gilford 1660T coach of Acme Pullman Services Limited on their London – Bishops Stortford service. (J. F. Higham). →

Pampisford.

As an experiment for a short period in the summer of 1930, alternate journeys were diverted at Woodford to run via Whipps Cross, Lea Bridge Road, Clapton and Dalston. They did not produce the traffic expected, and returned to the normal route via Wanstead and Stratford when the route was extended from Liverpool Street to Charing Cross, (Embankment) on 26 August 1930.

The timetable commencing on that date shows a basic half-hourly service between London and Bishops Stortford, which was stepped up to every fifteen minutes in the morning and evening peak hours on Mondays to Fridays. The provision of eight daily journeys to Newmarket had not produced the traffic expected, and north of Stortford, twelve journeys were extended to Stansted, of which three on Mondays–Fridays and five on Saturdays and Sundays were further extended to Newmarket. In addition, an extra journey was worked from London to Saffron Walden on Sunday evenings at 5.45 pm.

The company was well-organised and gave a very good service to the public. Booking offices and waiting rooms were established at Newmarket, Bishops Stortford and Epping, also in London at Bishopsgate (near the terminus). This office and waiting room was still retained in use after the route was extended to Charing Cross.

North of Epping the route covered by Acme was badly served by local buses at that time, and the Company built up a very useful local traffic by charging fares on a lower scale than normal on a coach service, both for single and return tickets. At first fares were charged from village centre to village centre, but later, fare stages were introduced between the towns and villages, the final fares list giving a total of 55 stages for single fares, return fares still being charged from centre to centre. Some of the names of these stages make very colourful reading, amongst which were: Bungalows (this locality is not mentioned); Six Mile Bottom (between Bungalows and Pampisford); Sandpits (between Ugley and Stansted); Red White and Blue (presumably a public-house between Stansted and Stortford) and White Post (the first farestage after leaving Bishops Stortford).

The 1928 timetable even shows local fares south of Epping, these being single fares only, the last of them being from Wanstead to Mile End, 5d, and Liverpool Street, 6d. These fares were evidently intended to compete with the 'General' route 100 which also covered the Acme route from Woodford to Mile End. By December 1929, these fares had been withdrawn, and there were no local fares south of the 'Wake Arms', and, on the inward journey, coaches only stopped to set down passengers between Epping and London. However, when competition began to be experienced from both Green Line and Associated-Lion between London and Epping, fares to London were introduced from Bell Common, Epping Forest (Wake Arms) and Loughton (The Robin Hood) with a minimum of 1/- (5p) single and 1/6 (7½p) return.

At all times, conductors were carried on the coaches, despite the Company having its own booking offices as well as agents along the line of route.

The company prospered, and it was therefore very surprising when Acme sold out to the London General Omnibus Company in September 1932. Possibly, like many other operators at this time, Acme preferred to sell out on its own terms rather than wait for compulsory acquisition when the London Passenger Transport Board was formed in the following year.

Strange to say, although the company was handed over to the L.G.O.C. subsidiary, London General Country Services, to operate as part of the Green Line network, it was never allocated a route letter and although the subsequent timetable folders were issued in the style then used by Green Line, they were headed 'ACME PULLMAN SERVICES LIMITED' and printed in black and not green. The route was also shown on Green Line maps as 'ACME' and presumably the fourteen Gilford coaches were left with the Acme fleet name and livery until London Transport took over. This may be due to the fact that the Road Service Licence was still held in the name of the Acme company.

No alterations were made to the route or fares until the London Passenger Transport Board took over on 1 July 1933, when all journeys were curtailed at Bishops Stortford,

and the Newmarket operations were passed to Varsity Motors Limited. Until Varsity were ready to take over and merge it with their Cambridge service, the Bishops Stortford – Newmarket section was operated by Eastern National on hire to Varsity.

When Acme was placed under Green Line control, all the facilities such as the booking offices and waiting rooms were maintained until the Green Line network was revised on 4 October 1933, when the waiting rooms and booking offices at Epping and Liverpool Street were closed down, and both the Acme service and Green Line Route O were merged into a new Green Line Route V running half-hourly between Bishops Stortford and Liverpool Street (Eldon Street), which was extended to Horse Guards Avenue on Saturday afternoons and Sundays.

BIRCH BROTHERS LIMITED:

The above organisation was one of the oldest in the passenger transport industry, and had started running horse-buses in London in 1846, placing their first two motor-buses in service in 1904, and by 1907, had sixteen of these vehicles in service, but, owing to the unreliability of the early motors, plus the fact that drivers and mechanics experienced in handling them were in short supply, the buses tended to spend as much time off the road as in service, and the company suffered financial losses. The last motor-buses ran on 30 November 1907, and then Birch Bros. concentrated on their horse-drawn vehicles until the last of these was withdrawn at the end of July 1912. The company then concentrated its efforts on its taxicabs of which it had a large fleet, coachbuilding and its mail contracts.

When the independent buses commenced running in London in 1922, Birch Brothers built many of their bodies, and observing the success which many of the proprietors were achieving, Birch Brothers decided to return to the London bus business themselves, placing their first two Leyland buses on the Highgate – Brockley route 536, which they worked jointly with City and United, and by the time they decided to enter the short-stage express service world, had twelve buses working in the London area.

The coach service commenced operation in November 1928 from Aldwych (Bush House) to Bedford via Kings Cross, Highgate, Barnet, Potters Bar, Hatfield, Welwyn, Codicote, Hitchin, Henlow and Shefford. Six daily round trips were worked, and a minimum fare of 1/- single; 1/9 return applied from Aldwych to Potters Bar, after which the fares went from town centre to town centre, the lowest fare being threepence between Welwyn and Codicote, and also from Henlow to Shefford. Return fares only applied from London to country towns and Bedford, and similarly from Bedford to country towns and London, there being none between intermediate points. Reduced single and return fares were introduced for the through journey to and from Bedford to London on 1 July 1929 in order to meet the competition from other operators on the same route.

From 25 September 1929, a new route was introduced when one journey in each direction was introduced from Aldwych to Kettering via St. Albans, Luton, Clophill, Bedford, Rushden, Wellingborough and Burton Latimer, which by January 1931, had been increased to three journeys to Rushden and one to Kettering.

By July 1931, this route had been diverted via Hitchin and Henlow and the times incorporated with the existing London – Bedford service. There were now nine journeys on weekdays (eight on Sundays), of which three operated to Rushden, and of which one was extended to Kettering. The Rushden and Kettering journeys were operated to Oxford Circus, with the Bedford times still using the Aldwych terminus in London.

Birch Brothers were successful in obtaining a Road Service Licence to continue operating their services under

the Road Traffic Act, but had to withdraw their London terminals from Oxford Circus and Aldwych to Kings Cross from 4 October 1933, as per instructions from the Ministry of Transport.

The Beaumont-Safeway timings to Bedford were acquired on 30 November 1932, which left the company without any opposition on this route, and they now had ten departures on weekdays and eleven on Saturdays and Sundays, of which three were extended to Rushden, and one beyond that point to Kettering.

An hourly service to Bedford was introduced from October 1933, at the same time as the cut back to Kings Cross mentioned above. The hourly service to Bedford had no effect on the number of journeys operated north of this point until May 1934, when the service as far as Rushden was increased to two-hourly, with two return journeys to Wellingborough, one of which continued to Kettering. At the same time, local bus fares were introduced between Welwyn Church and Hitchin (Bancroft), as there was no local bus service along this road north of Codicote.

As the Birch service served areas well beyond the agreed boundary of London Transport's operating area, it was not acquired by them, and, as Birch was only allowed to pick-up passengers at Highgate (Junction Road); Finchley (Tally Ho Corner); Barnet Church; Ganwick Corner and Potters Bar, after which there were no restrictions, there was very little competition with Green Line, especially as they followed a different route between Welwyn Church and Hitchin.

With the advent of National Service in 1938, there being two large Royal Air Force stations at Cardington and Henlow on the Birch route, passenger traffic grew up very rapidly, especially on weekends. This was met by the operation of as many relief coaches as the vehicle situation would allow. After the outbreak of the Second World War in 1939, the service continued as normal until both fuel and rubber became scarce in 1942. Owing to shortages in 1942, on 29 September, all Green Line routes ran for the last time, but as Birch operated as a local bus over some sections of its route, it was allowed to carry on between Hatfield Station and Bedford only. For some time Birch had been operating a number of local bus services in the Luton, Hitchin and Bedford areas using route numbers from 204 to 211, so the shortened operation of the coach route took the number 203.

Operation between Kings Cross and Rushden was resumed with an hourly service from March 1946, the route number remaining as 203. Double-deck buses were now in use on the service, but, despite the use of these larger vehicles, the writer, who became a Green Line Inspector in 1949, well remembers weekends on duty at Kings Cross supervising the operation of Luton route 727, and watching the seemingly endless procession of relief buses full of airmen and airwomen on each Birch departure on Route 203.

When the M1 motorway opened in 1959, Birch Brothers seized the opportunity to provide a fast non-stop service to Bedford, numbered as 203M. Running approximately every two hours, the coaches on this route made no stops between Barnet Church and Westoning. This was the last highlight in development by Birch, as traffic started to decline during the 1960's. The local bus service in the Luton, Hitchin and Bedford areas ceased operations on 14 October 1968, and the two London services were sold to United Counties on 14 September 1969, marking the end of Birch Brothers stage carriage operations. The motorway route is still in existence at the time of writing. Now numbered 250 by United Counties, it commences its journey at Marylebone Station and runs two-hourly to Rushden and Kettering.

HILLMAN SALOON COACHES LIMITED:

December 1928 saw the commencement of operations by this company, when they started in a very modest way from Stratford Broadway to Brentwood. Serving as it did

Gilford 1680T coach of Hillman's Saloon coaches Ltd. en route to London at Romford Market Place. (J. F. Higham).

Gilford 1680T coach of Hillman's Saloon Coaches Ltd. at Stratford. (J. F. Higham).

the three very important shopping areas at Stratford, Romford and Ilford at fares which compared very favourably with those charged on the much slower bus service that had been operating over the same route since 1921, it is not surprising that a heavy passenger traffic was built up very quickly.

By 1931, Hillman had opened a coach station at 133 Bow Road (near to Bow Church), and was running every five to ten minutes to Brentwood, every fifteen minutes to Chelmsford, and from hourly to two-hourly to Colchester. Extra coaches, making a 2½–5 minute service to Romford were operated in rush hours and on Saturday afternoons. Commuters were well catered for, season tickets being issued for monthly and quarterly periods, and there is no doubt that, despite the competition later experienced from Green Line and Sunset Pullman Coaches between Bow and Brentwood, Hillman had captured the cream of the traffic.

The Bow – Brentwood section was acquired by London Transport on 1 January 1934, Hillman carrying on with the operations beyond Brentwood until 13 August 1934, when they were disposed of to the Eastern National Omnibus Company, who extended their Route 10 (Chelmsford – Brentwood) right through to Bow (Tomlins Grove) in place of the Hillman Chelmsford service. The Colchester journeys were merged into the Clacton express route of Eastern National.

SKYLARK MOTOR COACH COMPANY LIMITED:

This company commenced operation on 14 December 1928 with an hourly service from Oxford Circus to Guildford. Unlike the present 715, Skylark operated via Hyde Park Corner and Kensington to Hammersmith, and then through Barnes to the Kingston By Pass, Esher and Cobham.

In the advance publicity distributed in Guildford to advertise the new facility, it stated that, in order to popularise and advertise the new service the first twenty single tickets; ten return tickets and ten weekly tickets will be complimentary and free of charge. The handbill also stated that an hourly service would be worked. Passengers were only picked up at Ripley and Cobham en route, and the journey time to Oxford Circus from Guildford was given as 90 minutes.

The proprietor, Charles Dobbs, who had also operated buses in London for a time, was a very astute man, and despite the fact that the Aldershot and District Traction Company very soon jumped on the bandwaggon with an hourly service from Guildford which did not stop after Burpham until reaching London, he got the Guildford route operating quite successfully before attempting to introduce other services.

Gilford 1680T coach of Skylark Motor Coach Company (after acquisition by Green Line) taking its layover opposite Poland Street Coach Station. (J. F. Higham).

Gilford 168SD coach of Skylark Motor Coach Company (after acquisition by Green Line) outside Green Line Coach Station at Poland Street and working Green Line Route S. (J. F. Higham).

The next two routes commenced operation on 14 September 1929, both of them from Oxford Circus, and each running hourly. One route ran westwards to High Wycombe via Shepherds Bush, Ealing, Uxbridge and Beaconsfield, whilst the other went northwards to Hertford via Finsbury Park, Wood Green, Westbury Avenue and the Great Cambridge Road to Wormley.

Skylark became the pioneer operator of cross-London coach services on 4 December 1929, when they joined the Guildford and Hertford services into one long route and extended the High Wycombe route to Dorking via Tooting, Sutton and Reigate instead of using the more direct route via Morden, Epsom and Leatherhead.

The Company's timetable booklet dated September 1930, carries a timetable for a London (Oxford Circus) to Guildford service to be operated via Tooting, Epsom, Leatherhead, Effingham, Horsley and Clandon, which although advertised was never actually operated. Similarly, there was a leaflet giving a timetable covering an extension of the High Wycombe – Dorking route to Horsham via Beare Green and Capel, which never ran, as, in actual fact, the section between London and Dorking already working was withdrawn on 19 December 1930. The reason for this withdrawal is not known, as the handbill informing passengers of its withdrawal simply states that the route will be withdrawn temporarily. It is possible, however, that, as Green Line had started a direct half-hourly service from Dorking as well as one from Reigate with a slightly lower farescale than Skylark, Dobbs decided to withdraw before he lost too much money on the service.

The remaining routes carried on quite successfully, but once again, like other operators, Dobbs was aware that it would only be a matter of time before the London Passenger Transport Board would become an actual fact, and decided it would be better to sell out on his own terms. In consequence, the company passed to Green Line Coaches Limited from 6 February 1932.

The new owners kept Skylark as a separate operation, even retaining the Ledbury Mews (North Kensington) garage as a base for some of the coaches on the Guildford and High Wycombe routes, as well as stabling vehicles for private hire work which were also readily accessible for use as relief coaches on busy weekends and Bank Holidays. The vehicles required at the country end of the Skylark routes to provide early starts and late finishes were then stabled as follows:

High Wycombe: At the Amersham and District bus garage in Queen Victoria Road.

Hertford: At the National Omnibus and Transport Company's garage at The Old Town Hall, Ware.

Guildford: At the London General Country Services garage in Leas Road.

At the same time, through operation from Hertford to Guildford was discontinued, the coaches on these routes terminating at Oxford Circus once more. Any layover time at this end of the route was taken by the coaches proceeding to the Green Line Coach Station in Poland Street.

Although the company was kept as a separate organisation, Green Line allocated route letters to the Skylark routes from 27 April 1932, these being: AF (Hertford Heath); AQ (High Wycombe) and BG (Guildford). From 25 March, despite the differing fares, Green Line and Skylark return tickets were inter-available for the return journey, except on Route AQ, where the Green Line service Q terminated at Uxbridge and the equivalent Skylark return ticket was available beyond that town to Denham Cross Roads.

Like its parent, Skylark was transferred to London Transport on 1 July 1933, but no change was made to the operation until the Green Line network was revised on 4 October in the same year, when the Skylark Hertford and Guildford routes were merged into a new route AM from Hertford via Hertford Heath and Great Cambridge Road to Esher, being extended to Guildford on Saturday afternoons and Sundays. The High Wycombe route was re-lettered as Q, and the only alteration made was a diversion of the outward journeys to run via Portland Place, Marylebone Road and Sussex Gardens to Bayswater Road, the inward journeys using Bayswater Road, Oxford Street and Regent Street to terminate opposite the B.B.C. in Langham Place.

AMALGAMATED OMNIBUS SERVICES AND SUPPLIES LIMITED:

The above somewhat long-winded title was the name of a company owned by Charles William Batten of 439 Barking Road, East Ham, who operated his coaches under

A.E.C. 426 coach of Batten's Luxury Coaches at Barking en route to Grays. (J. F. Higham).

the fleet name of 'Batten's Luxurious Coaches'.

On 8 March 1929 he commenced operating a service from East Ham Town Hall to Grays (War Memorial) with eleven daily journeys, of which six on weekdays and the whole service on Sundays, were extended to Tilbury Dock Station, running via Barking, Dagenham, Rainham and Aveley. A few months later, the service had become half-hourly to Grays, with most of the journeys extended to Tilbury. In addition, one coach every two hours was extended westwards from East Ham via Poplar and Aldgate to Charing Cross (Embankment), but this operation did not last for very long. Also at this time, the route had been withdrawn from Aveley, and was now running via Purfleet Station and Village between Rainham and Grays.

By 24 April 1931, the route had settled down to a 20-minute service between Aldgate (Met. Station) and Grays (Queens Hotel) with eleven journeys on weekdays and seven on Sundays extended to Tilbury Dock Station (this is the station now known as Tilbury Town). In view of the large number of industrial areas served by this route, the service started much earlier in the morning on weekdays than most coach routes. The first coach departed from East Ham Town Hall at 5.20 am for Grays, reaching there fifty minutes later and departing for Aldgate at 6.20 am. The last coach left Aldgate for Grays at 10.35 pm, arriving there at 11.50 pm. It departed from Grays at midnight for East Ham, arriving there at 12.50 am.

Batten had been the proprietor of a large fleet of buses which he mainly worked on Route 15 under the name 'Atlas'. These he sold to the L.G.O.C. in 1926, remaining as manager after the take-over, as 'Atlas' was retained as a separate operating entity by the larger company. Batten even acquired further independent bus concerns for the L.G.O.C. and when the larger company finally took over both management and operation in January 1927, the bus fleet had grown to 36 vehicles.

The original Batten garage at 439 Barking Road had not passed to the L.G.O.C. and Batten used this for a fleet of coaches which he started after leaving the 'General', and which he had built up to twelve vehicles when he started the Grays and Tilbury operation.

It is said that Batten operated the Grays service on behalf of the L.G.O.C. and in view of his former association with that company, it is quite possible that this was the case. Another factor that adds further strength to the story is that, although Green Line introduced a fairly intensive service along the Brentwood route to compete with Hillman and Sunset, it made no attempt to provide a like service on the Grays and Tilbury road.

A very good traffic was built up, no doubt due to the very reasonable fare scale. To cater for the heavy industrial traffic, cheap daily return tickets at single fare for workmen were issued on all journeys up to 8 am on weekdays, and for those commencing work at later times, weekly, monthly and quarterly season tickets were obtainable. For the housewife wishing to visit the large shopping centres of East Ham and Whitechapel, cheap day return fares were issued between 10 am and 4 pm from Grays, Purfleet and Rainham to East Ham or Aldgate.

Competition was experienced between East Ham and Wennington by Price's Super Coaches from an unknown date in 1929, and from 1930 over the whole route from the Gordon Omnibus Company and Tilbury Coaching Services, although Gordon lost the right to operate when the Traffic Commissioners refused them road service licences, having decided that an adequate service was being provided by the remaining operators.

The Batten route passed to London Transport on 23 December 1933, becoming Green Line Route Z on that date. At the time of the take-over, London Transport was already issuing the timetable folders and operating the service with former Premier Line coaches labelled 'GREEN LINE. ON HIRE TO BATTEN'S'.

Once again Batten retained his East Ham garage, as the London service was transferred to Grays Garage for operation by the new owners. He continued in the business of operating summer coastal services, excursions and private hire until the organisation was disposed of to Grey-Green Coaches Limited in the early sixties.

PRICE'S SUPER COACHES:

Before leaving the Grays and Tilbury area it would be as well to discuss the operations of the above company.

J. H. Price of Ranelagh Road, East Ham owned three Gilford 1660T coaches, which from an unknown date in 1929, he worked on a route from East Ham Town Hall every 45 minutes to the 'Ship Inn' at Aveley, a village which at that time was not well served by public transport, only having a somewhat irregular bus service to Romford or Grays. The Price route, whilst working at a rather odd frequency, at least gave the local people a chance to travel towards London, even if they did have to change vehicles at East Ham.

The fares charged were extremely reasonable, being more like bus fares than those usually charged on a coach service. A minimum fare of 6d (2½p) single was charged between East Ham and Dagenham, whilst from the next farestage at South Street (between Dagenham and Rainham), a penny (½p) minimum applied right through to Aveley. In common with Batten, Price issued cheap workman return tickets at single fare from Aveley to Dagenham and East Ham, although there were only two journeys in each direction on which these tickets could be purchased.

Despite the fact that Price suffered from competition from the Gordon Omnibus Company whose Tilbury route ran via Aveley, he carried on and was rewarded by being granted a Road Service Licence to continue operation whilst Gordon was refused.

The Price service was acquired by London Transport on 1 December 1933, becoming Green Line Route AZ. His

A.E.C. 'Reliance' coach of Batten's Luxury Coaches at Barking en route to Grays. (J. F. Higham).

Gilford 1660T coach of Price's Super Service at Barking on their East Ham – Aveley route. (J. F. Higham).

three Gilford 1660T coaches were transferred to Grays Garage which then worked the service until 18 July 1934, when it was withdrawn and Aveley lost its direct connection towards London until June 1935, when the operation of Route Z was revised to include operations via Aveley.

WEST HERTS MOTOR SERVICES LIMITED:

The above company was a local bus operator in the town of Hemel Hempstead, working jointly with the National Omnibus and Transport Company on a route to Watford, plus a Sunday and Bank Holiday route from Boxmoor Station to Dunstable.

In September 1929 the company decided to try a coach service to London, which commenced operating on 22nd of that month. Five daily trips were worked via Boxmoor, Apsley, Kings Langley, Watford-by-Pass, Edgware and Cricklewood. A timetable bill has been seen for this service, and from the list of booking agents on the back, it would seem that no passengers were picked up north of West Hendon on the outward journey or south of Kings Langley on the inward runs, giving a very fast journey to and from London.

In these circumstances it is not surprising that traffic soon built up, and the service was increased to a 90-minute frequency, whilst on Wednesdays and Saturdays, a late theatre coach was operated, leaving Oxford Circus at 11.30 pm.

During the latter half of 1930, H. B. Slade, the West Herts proprietor, was approached by the Premier Omnibus Company of Watford with a very advantageous offer to purchase the business with the result that Premier took over from 1 January 1931.

The company carried on under the fleet name of West Herts for a while, although the application to continue operating under the Road Traffic Act was made in the name of the Premier Omnibus Company Limited. The writer has a timetable for the service headed 'PREMIER MOTOR COACH SERVICE' which is undated and shows that the new management have diverted the route at Kings Langley to run via Kings Langley Station, Abbots Langley and Garston to join the Watford-by-Pass at North Watford roundabout. Fares are quoted from these points to London,

thus giving this area a direct service to London for the first time.

Surprisingly, the Premier bus route in Watford and the whole of the West Herts organisation were amongst the first acquisitions to be made by the new London Passenger Transport Board, the date of takeover being the same day as

---

PREMIER MOTOR COACH SERVICE.
TELEPHONE 3590. WATFORD.

LUXURIOUS COACHES.   FAST & COMFORTABLE.
DAILY SERVICE

London (Oxford Circus) & Hemel Hempstead

The shortest & quickest route via Boxmoor, Apsley, Kings Langley Abbotts Langley, Leavesden, Garston & the Bye Pass Road.

	Single	Day Return	Period
Hemel Hempstead	1/6	2/3	2/6
Boxmoor	1/6	2/-	2/6
Apsley	1/3	2/-	2/6
Kings Langley	1/3	2/-	2/6
Abbotts Langley	1/3	2/-	2/6
Leavesden	1/3	2/-	2/6
Garston	1/3	2/-	2/6

Departure Times (Weekdays & Sundays)   W.S.O.

	a.m.	a.m.	a.m.		P.M.	P.M.	P.M.
Hemel Hempstead (Pellings)	7.30	9.0.	10.30.		7.30	9.0.	10.30.
Boxmoor (Hollicks)	7.35	9.5.	10.35.		7.35	9.5.	10.35.
:y (Wildings)	7.40	9.10.	10.40.		7.40	9.10.	10.40.
Kings Langley	7.45	9.15.	10.45.	THEN	7.45	9.15.	10.45.
Abbotts Langley (Dazeley)	7.55	9.25.	10.55.	EVERY 90 MINS.	7.55	9.25.	10.55.
Leavesden Mental Hos. (Higgs)	8.0	9.30.	11.0.		8.0	9.30.	11.0.
Garston Three Horse Shoes. (Wiltshire)	8.5	9.35.	11.5.		8.5	9.35.	11.5.
Stanborough Park (Hoad)	8.7	9.37.	11.7.		8.7	9.37.	11.7.

From London (Oxford Circus) to Hemel Hempstead. W.S.O.

	a.m	a.m	a.m	p.m	p.m	p.m	p.m	p.m	p.m	p,m	p,m	p,m
LONDON Highways Ltd. 281 Regent St.	9,0	10,30	12,0	1,30	3,0	4,30	6,0	7,30	9,0	10,30	11,30	
KILBURN Makenzie & Co. 241 High Rd	9,10	10,40	12,10	1.40	3.10	4,40	6.10	7,40	9,10	10,40	11,40	
CRICKLEWOOD 124, Broadway, Ash Grove.	9,15	10,45	12,15	1,45	3,15	4,45	6,15	7,45	9,15	10,45	11,45	
HENDON C. V. Hamilton, 236 Br'dw'y.	9,20	10,50	12,20	1,50	3,20	4,50	6,20	7,50	9,20	10,50	11,50	

W.S.O. – Wednesday & Saturday   P.T.O.

the new Board commenced operations, 1 July 1933. In addition to their cash settlement, the Premier organisation also received the excursion and coastal licences formerly operated by London General County Services Limited from Watford. Premier is still in existence today, and operates an extensive coastal and excursion programme from both Watford and St. Albans, having acquired the Albanian coach organisation in the latter town.

The Premier (former West Herts) coach service carried on under the control of the Board's Green Line section, remaining unaltered until the October 1933 revision, when it was cut back from Oxford Circus to a new terminal at Portman Square. It was withdrawn after the last journeys on 10 July 1934, being partly replaced on the following day by the extension of Green Line Route I from Watford (Leavesden Road) to Abbots Langley via Garston.

BUCKS EXPRESSES (WATFORD) LIMITED:

The proprietor of this company was Thomas Edward Greenwood, who was also operating a small fleet of buses on the London Route 14. He was also the owner of three 24-seat Maudsley coaches which he had been running on a service from London to Ilfracombe under the fleet name 'Enterprise', the title which he used on his London buses.

Greenwood had also acquired an interest in the Bucks Garage, which stood in Watford High Street near the Pond Cross Roads (a cinema now covers the site). Early in September 1929, he transferred his coaches to this garage in readiness to start a service to London. This commenced running on 26 October from the Bucks Garage (Watford) to Oxford Circus. Evidently some further coaches had also been delivered before the service started, as a half-hourly service was worked from the start, stepped up to every quarter-hour during the weekday rush hours, which in those days, included the midday period on Saturdays, as most people worked on Saturday mornings at that time. The route followed was via Bushey, Bushey Heath, Stanmore, Edgware, Cricklewood, Kilburn, Edgware Road, Seymour Street and Wigmore Street.

After about two months of operation as Enterprise Coaches, Greenwood decided to separate them from the London business, and in November 1929, a new company was set up to operate them under the title of Bucks Expresses (Watford) Limited, the coaches then bearing the fleet name 'Bucks Express' on the side. The writer, seeing one of the coaches for the first time at Oxford Circus in 1930, and not then knowing of the existence of the Bucks Garage in Watford, could not help wondering why the company was called Bucks Express when the town to which it operated was in Hertfordshire.

Fares were reasonable, 1/6 (7½p) single; 2/- (10p) return being charged for the 16 mile journey from Watford to London, and in order to compete with the 'General' bus route 142, the fare from Watford to Stanmore was 6d (2½p) single; 9d (roughly 4p) return. The single fare was the same on bus or coach, but the buses did not issue return tickets. For commuters there was the choice of weekly tickets or monthly and quarterly seasons, and the journey to Oxford Circus was scheduled to take 55 minutes.

Greenwood sold the company to the L.G.O.C. on 19 February 1932, passing the original three Maudslays, five Gilfords and two very handsome A.E.C. Regals with bodywork similar to that of the Green Line fleet, but beautifully painted in a teak-coloured livery, to the new owners.

Although placed under the control of the Green Line organisation for supervision and administration, Bucks Express retained its separate identity and no alteration was made to the timetable. The fare from Stanmore to London however, was reduced from 1/3 single; 1/9 return to 1/- single; 1/6 return to coincide with the fare charged on the parallel Green Line service.

For administrative purposes the route was allocated the route letters AW in the Green Line series from 27 April, and five days later on 2 May 1932, Bucks Express return tickets were available for return by Green Line Route W, but, as Green Line only issued weekly tickets and quarterly seasons from Watford and Bushey, the Bucks Express monthly seasons, plus all seasons from Stanmore were not available

Gilford 1680T coach of Bucks Express Limited on stand at Oxford Circus. (J. F. Higham).

for return on Green Line.

The Bucks Express service remained in operation until the last journeys on 3 October 1933, after that date being superseded by the new Green Line routes I and J, which gave a 15-minute service to Oxford Circus and Charing Cross on their way to Crawley and Reigate respectively. The company was absorbed into London Transport on 1 July 1933.

REGENT MOTOR SERVICES:

It will be remembered that Arthur Priest sold the timings of his Kings Cross to Hertford service to J. S. Ray of Harringay in October 1929. Ray traded as Regent Motor Services using four Gilford 1660T coaches to operate the service. Ray was not satisfied with the London terminal at King's Cross, considering it to be too far from the centre of London to be of any use in generating traffic, and by November 1930, had extended the route to Oxford Circus, the coaches working from Kings Cross via Euston Road, Great Portland Street, Devonshire Street and Portland Place. Although Regent followed the Great Cambridge Road from Wood Green, this road was only used as far as Bullsmoor Lane, where the route turned right to serve Waltham Cross and Cheshunt.

Although Priest had only worked five daily return journeys, by April 1930, Ray was working an hourly service daily, although by the time the route was running to Oxford Circus, the hourly service was only worked on Saturdays, Sundays and Mondays, nine journeys only being worked for the rest of the week. A new timetable came into operation in January 1931 which gave nine journeys on Mondays–Fridays and Sundays, with an hourly service on Saturdays. This timetable, which was printed on stiff card folded in the centre, also shows a full faretable for the route. Whilst return fares were restricted to fares from Hertford and the towns en route to London, the single fares show a 2d (1p) minimum fare between Hertford and Wormley and then a 9d (roughly 4p) minimum from Cheshunt into London, including a 9d fare from Edmonton (Church Street) to Oxford Circus.

The timetable publicity issued by the Company continually exhorted the public to patronise Regent, and reminded them that the Company had been the first to provide a service to London, and that they have maintained cheap fares since commencement of the service. As a further inducement to people to travel, on the reverse side of the March 1931 timetable, Regent stated that £3 would be paid to the person using and producing to the Regent office the number of Regent tickets (single or return) amounting to the greatest cash value, and which had been issued and used during the month of March. £2 was also to be paid to the person doing likewise with shortstage tickets (1d to 5d) which had been issued and used during the same month.

Evidently the exhortations had been successful, as the timetable issued in January 1932 showed that an hourly service was being worked throughout the route every day.

Despite the competition experienced from Skylark and Green Line, Ray managed to survive, and was granted a Road Service Licence to continue operating by the Traffic Commissioners in 1931. Like everyone else in the shortstage carriage and bus business in the London area, Ray realised it would only be a matter of time before his company was acquired by the new Transport Board, and sold out on his own terms to Green Line Coaches Limited, the take-over date being 26 February 1932.

Once again, probably because of the licensing regulations in those days, Regent Motor Services retained its separate identity, as the timetable leaflets, although printed in green on white paper and obviously produced by the Green Line organisation, were headed 'REGENT MOTOR SERVICES'. The writer has checked this with the last Regent handbill in his collection, and, except for an extra journey on Sunday nights at midnight from Oxford Circus to Hertford, there has been no alteration to the times. The fares have been considerably altered however. The local fares between Waltham Cross and Hertford have been withdrawn, as has the 9d minimum between Waltham Cross and London. Although Green Line and Skylark return tickets were interavailable for the return journey, this was not the case with the return tickets issued on Regent coaches.

The Gilford coaches owned by Regent at the time of acquisition were not retained on the Regent route, but were transferred elsewhere, probably as spares at Ledbury Mews Garage, as the writer has a photograph depicting Green Line A.E.C. Regal coach T262 bearing the Green Line fleet name on the side and carrying route boards for Route CF (the route letters allocated to the Regent service). The illuminated sign under the destination indicator has been altered from 'GREEN LINE' to 'REGENT'.

Although the company passed to London Transport on 1 July 1933, Route CF remained unaltered until 4 October 1933, when it was replaced by the new operations on Green Line Routes M, AM and BM, and the peculiar route between Finsbury Park and Oxford Circus was dropped.

LEDBURY TRANSPORT LIMITED:

The above was the title of a company owned by Robert Thackray, a very astute businessman from the Reading area who controlled a taxi, car hire and garage business in North Kensington. He added the operation of a small fleet of buses in London to those interests in 1924. Being unable to expand the bus business owing to the Restricted Streets Order introduced by the Ministry of Transport in 1926, he sold the bus side to the London Public Omnibus Company in October 1927, and concentrated for a while on the rest of his various business activities. In 1929, he formed Ledbury Transport Limited and purchased a fleet of red and cream Gilford coaches bearing the fleet name 'Thackray's Way', and in September, commenced an hourly service from Oxford Circus to Reading via Slough and Maidenhead.

By January 1930 a 40-minute service was in operation on weekdays, the Sunday service remaining hourly, and a local service from Newbury to Reading was in operation on which through single and return tickets to London could be purchased.

In June 1930, the London service was increased to half-hourly and, although retaining a garage at Ledbury Mews, North Kensington, the head office of the company had been moved to Reading, where a large area was acquired in London Road. The office address was quoted as follows in the timetable in issue at that time: 'Registered Office: 5 and 6, Crown Colonnade, London Road, Reading. Garage accommodation for 100 coaches and large parking ground and garage. Waiting Rooms and a Restaurant for 150 people open day and night will be opened shortly. Well-equipped breakdown service always available for any distance, day or night. Repairs of every description undertaken'. From this, and advertisements in the booklet itself, it

Gilford coach of Ledbury Transport Company (Thackray's Way) at Maidenhead on the London – Reading route. (J. F. Higham).

Gilford 1680T coach of Ledbury Transport Company (Thackray's Way) en route to London. (J. F. Higham).

THACKRAY'S WAY

READING — LONDON via Maidenhead.

London to Reading.					Reading to London.				
London	Coln- brook	Slough 56 High St	Maiden- head	Reading	Reading	Maiden- head	Slough Town Hall	Coln- brook	London
A.M.	A.M.	A.M.	A.M.	A.M.	A.M.	A.M.	A.M.	A.M.	A.M.
a 7.30	8.36	8.47	9.3	9.42	a 7.15	7.54	8.10	8.21	9.26
8.30	9.36	9.47	10.3	10.42	8.0	8.39	8.55	9.6	10.12
9.30	10.36	10.47	11.3	11.42	8.30	9.9	9.25	9.36	10.42
10.0	11.6	11.17	11.33	12.12	9.0	9.39	9.55	10.6	11.12
10.30	11.36	11.47	12.3	12.42	9.30	10.9	10.25	10.36	11.42
11.0	12.6	12.17	12.33	1.12	10.0	10.39	10.55	11.6	12.12
11.30	12.36	12.47	1.3	1.42	10.30	11.9	11.25	11.36	12.42
12.0	1.6	1.17	1.33	2.12	11.0	11.39	11.55	12.6	1.12
12.30	1.36	1.47	2.3	2.42	11.30	12.9	12.25	12.36	1.42
1.0	2.6	2.17	2.33	3.12	12.0	12.39	12.55	1.6	2.12
* 1.30	2.36	2.47	3.3	3.42	12.30	1.9	1.25	1.36	2.42
2.0	3.6	3.17	3.33	4.12	1.0	1.39	1.55	2.6	3.12
2.30	3.36	3.47	4.3	4.42	* 1.30	2.9	2.25	2.36	3.42
3.0	4.6	4.17	4.33	5.12	2.0	2.39	2.55	3.6	4.12
* 3.30	4.36	4.47	5.3	5.42	* 2.30	3.9	3.25	3.36	4.42
4.0	5.6	5.17	5.33	6.12	3.0	3.39	3.55	4.6	5.12
* 4.30	5.36	5.47	6.3	6.42	* 3.30	4.9	4.25	4.36	5.42
5.0	6.6	6.17	6.33	7.12	4.0	4.39	4.55	5.6	6.12
5.30	6.36	6.47	7.3	7.42	4.30	5.9	5.25	5.36	6.42
6.0	7.6	7.17	7.33	8.12	5.0	5.39	5.55	6.6	7.12
6.30	7.36	7.47	8.3	8.42	5.30	6.9	6.25	6.36	7.42
7.0	8.6	8.17	8.33	9.12	6.0	6.39	6.55	7.6	8.12
7.30	8.36	8.47	9.3	9.42	6.30	7.9	7.25	7.36	8.42
c 8.0	9.6	9.17	9.33	10.12	7.0	7.39	7.55	8.6	9.12
8.30	9.36	9.47	10.3	10.42	c 7.30	8.9	8.25	8.36	9.42
c 9.0	10.6	10.17	10.33	11.12	8.0	8.39	8.55	9.6	10.12
9.30	10.36	10.47	11.3	11.42	9.0	9.39	9.55	10.6	11.12
10.30	11.36	11.47	12.3	12.42	10.0	10.39	10.55	11.6	12.12
11.30	12.36	12.47	1.3	1.42	b 11.0	11.39	11.55	12.6	1.12

a Mondays only.   b Sat. & Sun. only.   c Sundays only.
* Sundays excepted.

PRIVATE HIRE A SPECIALITY.

is evident that Ledbury Transport were agents for other long-distance coach operators, whose coaches used the coach station as well as the Ledbury vehicles. They were also involved in the garaging and repair of private cars.

Although the London service also picked up at the Coach Station, it carried on via London Road, Southampton Street and St. Mary's Butts to a parking ground in Cheapside (Reading), where connection was made with the Newbury service, which terminated there and not at the Coach Station.

A second London service, hourly via Bracknell, Ascot, Egham and Staines commenced operation on 31 July 1930, and this route terminated at the Colonnade Coach Station and not in the town centre. This did not cause great inconvenience to the passengers, as Reading Corporation Transport provided a very frequent service of trams (later trolleybuses) to the centre of Reading.

A feature of the Thackray services was the fact that, despite the provision of booking offices by the Company at Reading and in London, and use of booking agents along the line of the various routes, conductors were always employed, and tickets could be purchased on the coaches.

The Road Service Licence to continue operation of the London via Ascot route was refused by the Traffic Commissioners and the service was withdrawn on 25 August 1931.

The London service via Maidenhead was granted a licence to continue in operation, but the Committee of Enquiry into London Motor Coach services recommended that an alternative terminus should be found in London, as it felt that the short section of Regent Street between Oxford Circus and Cavendish Place was too congested to remain as a terminal for all the coach services then using it as such. As a result of this decision, the route was diverted at Marble Arch via Edgware Road, Marylebone Road and Euston Road to Kings Cross Coach Station from 4 October 1933. On the same day, fixed stopping places were introduced between Kings Cross and Colnbrook, and the coaches were no longer allowed to pick up and set down at any other points inside the Metropolitan Police area.

The services remaining then carried on quite successfully, but Robert Thackray decided to leave the coaching world and turn to property investment, so Ledbury Transport was sold to the Thames Valley Traction Company, who took over on 19 December 1935. Although the Reading to Newbury service was merged into Thames Valley route 10, the London route was still operated as 'Thackray's Way' by Ledbury Transport as a subsidiary company of the Thames Valley organisation.

Like other coach routes, the operation was withdrawn from September 1942 until 1946, and when service was resumed, the route was diverted in London to Victoria Coach Station and operated by Thames Valley vehicles bearing slips reading 'On Hire to Ledbury Transport Limited' and showing the route letter B in the destination box to distinguish it from Thames Valley route A via Ascot. This state of affairs lasted until 1949, when the Ledbury Transport company was wound up, and the hire slips removed from the double-deck buses now working the service.

The route still exists today, but in a different form. It follows the old Thackray route from Reading to the 'Plough Inn' at the western end of Colnbrook and then runs via the Colnbrook-by-Pass and Bath Road (Heathrow Airport North), then operates into the Airport Central Bus Station, after which it returns to the M4 motorway and Great West Road to Hammersmith. Now numbered as Route 310, it operates on an hourly headway with one-man operated vehicles and forms part of the Alder Valley network of routes to London.

CURTIS AND THOMPSON
SUPERWAYS LIMITED
LION COACHES LIMITED
ASSOCIATED COACHES (ONGAR) LTD:

In November 1929, Messrs Curtis and Thompson commenced running a service from Liverpool Street (Finsbury Circus) to Ongar via Dalston, Clapton, Leyton, Walthamstow, Chingford, Epping New Road, Epping and North Weald, on which they worked fifteen daily journeys in both directions. They were followed a month later, by a company known as Superways Limited, based in Loughton, who also started from Finsbury Circus but ran out of London via Aldgate, Stratford, Wanstead, Woodford, Buckhurst Hill and Loughton to Epping. This company operated 17 journeys to and from London, plus three to and from Loughton for garage purposes.

The combined service of the two companies amounting as they did to 32 daily workings to and from London was far too generous a service for such a rural area as that which exists between 'The Wake Arms', Epping Forest and Ongar, but despite that fact, they were joined by another operator, Lion Coaches Limited, who had the temerity to provide competition on the Curtis and Thompson route to Liverpool Street and on the Superways route as far as Stratford. Lion provided twelve weekday and eleven Sunday trips to Liverpool Street and eight daily trips to Stratford, both routes commencing operation on 15 February 1930.

The operation by Lion over the Superways service had a quick effect on the Superways timetable which was reduced to nine weekday and four Sunday round trips, plus one journey on weekdays and two on Sundays from London to Epping. There is also no doubt that the Liverpool Street operation by Lion also affected the operations of Curtis and Thompson.

Superways abandoned their route in June 1930, and Curtis and Thompson sold out to Associated Coaches (Ongar) Limited in the same month, whilst, having seen Superways abandon their operation, Lion also withdrew its Stratford route at the end of June, at the same time increasing their service on the Liverpool Street route, now running approximately every half-hour.

A feature of all the three operators on the Ongar road was the local fares charged between Ongar and the 'Wake Arms', Epping Forest. The road from Ongar as far as Epping was only served by four journeys a day on the National Omnibus and Transport Company's Route N9 from Bishops Stortford to Brentwood, so there is no doubt that the coach companies acquired a very useful local traffic by providing fares as low as one penny ($\frac{1}{2}$p) minimum over this section of the route. Even the section between 'Wake Arms' and Chingford enjoyed a threepenny minimum fare, and at Chingford Mount, Lion and Associated met up with the joint London County Council and Walthamstow Corporation Tramways route to Liverpool Street. The trams took 54 minutes for the journey as compared to 32 minutes by the coaches. The coach fare table shows a fare of 7d (3p) single; 1/- (5p) return against the tram fare of 6½d (2·75p) single; 11d (4·75p) return. The coach companies maintained a booking office adjacent to the tram terminus and no doubt milked off quite a fair proportion of through passengers from the tramcars. The single coach fare was evidently not so popular as the return as it was withdrawn by December 1930.

Although conductors were provided and tickets were sold on the coaches, booking offices were maintained at Ongar, Epping and Chingford, as well as the one mentioned in the last paragraph and booking agents were also appointed along the line of the route, as it states at the foot of the timetables that intending passengers between Copt Hall Road (Bell Common) and London, travelling in either direction were requested to obtain their tickets from booking agents before boarding the coach.

Associated Coaches and Lion continued in competition with each other until 12 January 1931, when a merger of the two companies took place, and a half-hourly service was introduced between Ongar and Liverpool Street, with short journeys giving a more frequent service in peak hours between Chingford and London.

The Lion-Associated organisation sold out to Green Line Coaches Limited on 31 March 1932, three Leyland PLSC3 and seven Gilfords of differing types, plus the garage opposite the 'Two Brewers' at the bottom of Ongar High Street passing to the new owners. Operation of the service, later lettered AO, continued unchanged until 4 October 1933, when the route was re-lettered as Route W, and a standard half-hourly service without Chingford short workings was introduced. The London terminus was also shifted from Bishopsgate round the corner into Eldon Street. The coaches continued to operate from the Ongar depot until they were transferred into the new garage at Epping when it opened in the latter half of 1934.

EVANS COACHES/EASTWARD COACHES
WOODGRANGE COACHES
UPMINSTER SERVICES LTD:

Evans Coaches commenced operating eleven daily journeys from Mile End to Chelmsford in November 1929, which were acquired by Eastward Coaches in January 1930.

Gilford 1680T coach of Upminster Services Limited at Hornchurch en route to Upminster. (J. F. Higham).

In October of that year, they also acquired the Stratford – Brentwood workings of Benjamin Davis, which he had started seven months earlier in March. Davis then joined the board of Eastward Coaches, who carried on working both routes. Later in the year they set up another company entitled Woodgrange Coaches Limited, under which name they commenced a 20–30 minute service from Aldgate to Upminster via Mile End, Stratford, Ilford, Becontree Heath, Rush Green and Hornchurch on 1 December 1930. Although this route was more successful than the Brentwood and Chelmsford operations, the company ran into financial difficulties, and could not maintain the hire-purchase instalments on their vehicles. The Gilford Motor Company seized the fleet and Hillman Saloon Coaches volunteered to operate them for the Gilford Company. In January 1932, a new organisation entitled Upminster Services Limited was set up, Edward Hillman becoming one of the directors. The Brentwood and Chelmsford workings of Eastward were merged with those of Hillman, and the new company then concentrated on building up the Upminster route.

The population of the areas served by Upminster Services Ltd. contained many workers in the newspaper world as well as market workers from Smithfield and Billingsgate, and these were well catered for by the company. The first coach left Upminster at 3.30 in the morning daily, and the last coach left Aldgate at 1 am, and for most of the day a 5–7 minute service was operated. Fares were very cheap, and workman return tickets were issued on weekdays on all coaches up to 7 am in both directions, whilst Cheap Day Return tickets on weekdays on all coaches from 9.30 am to 4 pm allowed the housewives to shop in the cheap markets at Ilford and Stratford.

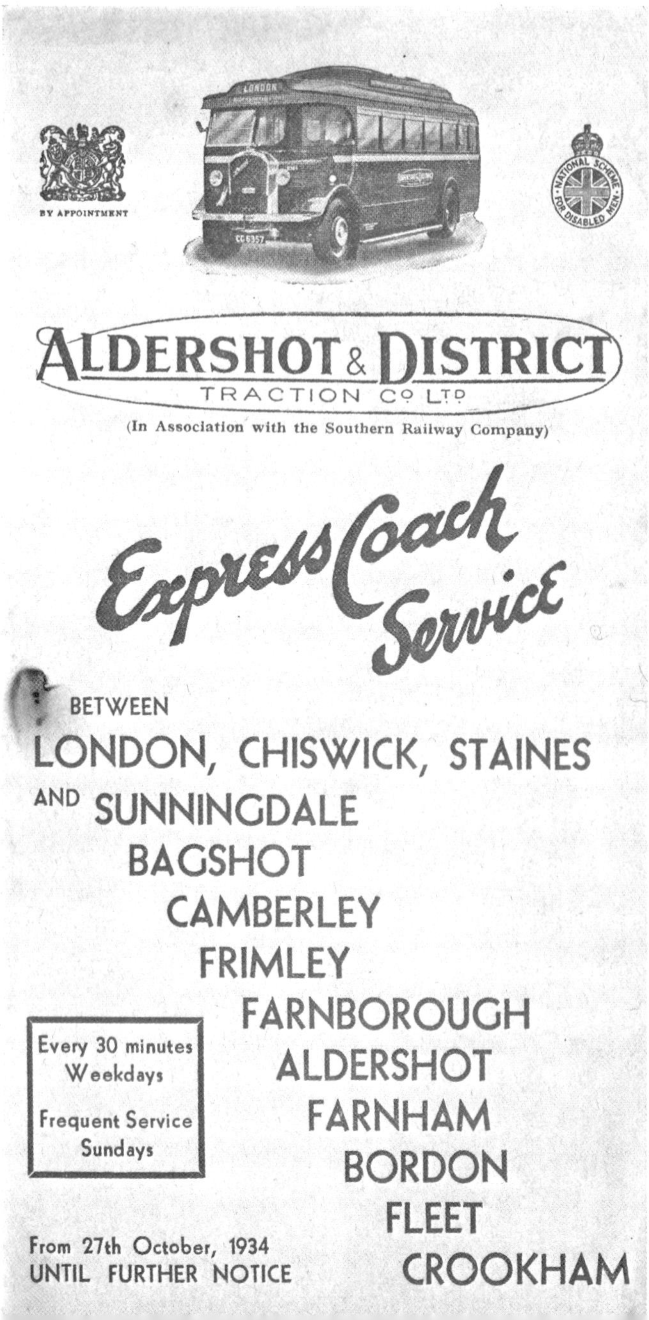

Unfortunately, the company's route lay entirely within the London Transport area, and it was acquired by the Board on 10 January 1934, thirty Gilford coaches being added to their fleet. The route became Green Line Route AY, and to the credit of the new owners, no alteration was made to the timetable, and the route carried on serving the area very well until it was withdrawn due to war circumstances on 2 September 1939, but that is a story for another chapter.

FARNHAM BLUE COACHES
ALDERSHOT AND DISTRICT TRACTION
COMPANY LTD:

In January 1929 Farnham Blue Coaches commenced a service of four weekday and three Sunday journeys from Farnham (Town Hall) to London (Aldwych) via Heath End, Aldershot, Farnborough to Frimley, where it ran via Portsmouth Road (avoiding Camberley) to Bagshot, from whence it operated express to Chiswick, Hammersmith, Kensington, Victoria and Charing Cross.

By May 1929, six weekly and four Sunday round trips were being worked, the route had been diverted via Camberley and was also picking up passengers at Sunningdale. One morning journey was now commencing its journey at Bordon (High Street), whilst two evening journeys were now extended from Farnham to Bordon, all these extensions operating daily.

The route was worked on the 'book in advance' principle, but the timetable handbills state on the front page, that, in the event of booking offices being closed, tickets will be issued on the coaches.

The Aldershot and District Traction Company (the local bus operator) was now running an hourly service from Farnham (Castle Street) to London (Great Scotland Yard) covering the same route as Farnham Blue, who retimed their coaches so that they ran 15 minutes in advance of the Traction Company's service from Farnham and ten minutes in front of them on the return journeys from London. At the same time they increased their service to ten return trips on weekdays. On Sundays, the Traction Company operated seven journeys each way spaced out at intervals of two to three hours between 8 am and 9 pm and Farnham Blue ran five journeys all spaced out to operate between the Traction Company timings.

By August 1930 Farnham Blue were working an hourly service on weekdays, with seven Sunday trips, and were timed from Farnham so that, together with the Aldershot and District operations, a half-hourly service was available on weekdays. The Bordon journeys had been increased to two up to London in the mornings and three down at night, one of which was the last coach from London departing at 11.45 pm and arriving at Whitehill, to which point the Bordon journey had been extended, at 2.20 am in the morning. In addition, the picking-up area had been extended, and fares were available to London from Virginia

Water, Egham and Staines, no doubt due to the presence of the Green Line service from Sunningdale to London.

Conductors were introduced on the coaches in 1931, which meant that the drivers were now relieved of the job of handling tickets and fares, and there was less delay to the service, and from June 1932, the Egham and Staines fares were withdrawn from the faretable, and the coaches ran express from Virginia Water to Chiswick.

Both the Aldershot and District Traction Company and Farnham Blue were granted Road Service Licences to continue their operations by the Traffic Commissioners in 1931, and the two companies carried on with their operations until Farnham Blue finally sold out to the Traction Company on 27 October 1934. The new owners diverted the Farnham Blue service into Victoria Coach Station and continued to maintain a half-hourly service. Although the pre-booking system was retained, conductors were still carried on the coaches, and they would sell tickets to passengers, providing that their journey chart indicated that there would be sufficient seats left after the pre-booked passengers had boarded. These conductors worked in a very unique way. The general rule was for them to board the London coach at Bagshot when they could check the tickets issued from Farnham up to Camberley, these being tickets of the paper type issued either by agents or at the Company's offices at Farnham, Aldershot and Yorktown. They would withdraw single tickets and the forward half of returns, issuing a pre-printed Bell Punch exchange ticket clipped at the fare value of the withdrawn ticket, also at the destination of the passenger. They would also collect any odd fares from Bagshot and points up to Egham, which was the last boarding point towards London. They then travelled with the coach through to Victoria and repeated the process on the return journey, alighting at Bagshot to pick-up the next London-bound coach. The last pick-up on outward journeys was fixed at Egham (Station Road) as in those days, the Traction Company ran an hourly bus service from Egham to Aldershot, and this explains why there were no local fares on the coach service.

After the withdrawal of Green Line 702 from Sunningdale in July 1973, the operation of the Farnham coach service was altered. It then became a one-man operated service on which double-deck vehicles have been introduced for some journeys. The pre-booking facilities were withdrawn, whilst the Egham-Aldershot bus service was withdrawn and replaced by a service to Basingstoke, and a bus-style fare table has been introduced between Aldershot and Staines, the driver issuing tickets from an Almex machine. Season tickets were introduced for commuters, a service which is greatly appreciated by workers at Heathrow Airport, who comprise a fair number of the passengers from Camberley and Bagshot. Now numbered as Route 320 by Alder Valley, an hourly service is provided on weekdays, widened to two-hourly on Sundays.

THE PREMIER OMNIBUS COMPANY LIMITED PREMIER LINE LIMITED:

The Premier Omnibus Company was a London bus operator based on the Shepherds Bush area and which had tried to extend its bus interests in the metropolis by the purchase of smaller companies desirous of selling out. It had also approached the Ministry of Transport with suggestions for routes it wished to operate in the Kingston and South-West Surrey area, but had met with little success. Finally it decided to enter the short-stage express coach field, ordering nine Leyland coaches which were to become the first of a large fleet. The first of these were delivered in January 1930, enabling the company to start a service from the 27th of that month from Bush House (Aldwych) to Windsor via Hammersmith, Chiswick, Great West Road, Harmondsworth, the Colnbrook By Pass and Slough every forty minutes. Following the delivery of more coaches, the service was stepped up to half-hourly from 6 February, to every twenty minutes from 7 April and after the introduction of the L.G.O.C. coach service over the same route, to every quarter-hour from 12 May. Operation along the Colnbrook-by-Pass did not last for long, being diverted via Colnbrook Village from 19 February.

The coach operations were divorced from the bus side of the business from 1 October 1930, when a new company to operate them was formed with the title 'Premier Line Limited'. It was decided to letter the routes, and the Windsor route took the letter 'A'. The new company started another service on the day it was formed, this being over the Windsor route to Slough, then via Bath Road, Salt Hill, Farnham Road and Farnham Royal to Farnham Common (Hedgerley Corner) every half-hour. This took the letter 'B' and gave a combined service with the Windsor route of six coaches an hour from London to Slough.

Further coaches were ordered from Leyland, and when the first of these were received, the service on Route 'B' was stepped-up to every 15 minutes. Sixteen days later, on 22

Leyland TD1 coach of Premier Line Limited on Route A on stand at Windsor. (J. F. Higham).

Leyland TS3 coach of Premier Line Limited on Route A (London – Windsor). (J. F. Higham).

February 1931, Route 'E' to Sunbury Common was started with one coach running from Bush House (Aldwych) via Hammersmith, Barnes, Richmond, Petersham, Kingston and HAMPTON Court. Following the arrival of more coaches, Route E was stepped up to a fifteen-minute service by 2 April 1931.

Premier Line now turned its attention to the Aylesbury road, and four days after the Sunbury Common road was opened, one coach was placed in service on Route 'D'. Starting from Aldwych and travelling via Charing Cross (Trafalgar Square) and Piccadilly and Park Lane to Marble Arch, it competed with Red Rover Saloon Coaches by following the same route to Aylesbury. The service was increased to hourly from 6 March 1931, followed by a further increase to half-hourly from August.

The reader may wonder why there has been no mention of a route lettered 'C'. This route started on the day following the introduction of the Aylesbury route, and consisted of one coach at first, which followed Route 'B' to Farnham Common and then continued via Birtley Corner to Beaconsfield, where it crossed the main Oxford road to terminate in the area then known as Beaconsfield New Town. For a week from 8–16 May, the route was experimentally extended to Knotty Green in order to fully serve the built-up area of the New Town, but the terminal arrangements were less satisfactory. In the meantime, Route 'B' had been extended from Farnham Common to Beaconsfield Station every fifteen minutes, and after the extension to Knotty Green was withdrawn, the letter 'C' was put into cold store and not used again.

Premier Line then turned its attention to providing two routes which, although worked by coaches, charged local bus fares through their length. Route 'F' was a long cross-country route from Aylesbury (Market Square) to Windsor (Lord Raglan) via Wendover, The Missendens, Amersham, The Chalfonts, Gerrards Cross, Stoke Common, Slough and Eton, running every half-hour. The other route, lettered 'G' also started at 'The Lord Raglan' in Windsor and ran via Eton, Slough, Chippenham and Taplow to Maidenhead Bridge, competing from Slough with the main road journeys on Thames Valley Route 22, as Premier Line ran every ten minutes. These two routes were introduced in the early summer of 1931, and, at the same time as they appeared on the scene, Premier Line introduced an early form of Rover Ticket for 5/6, which allowed the passenger to travel on any of the services all-day. In connection with the introduction of this ticket, a tour was suggested by the company by taking Routes 'A' or 'B' to Slough, Route 'F' to Aylesbury, and returning to London via Route 'D'.

Later on, a local service was introduced in Slough from William Street via Stoke Road, Elliman Avenue, Stoke Poges Lane, and Granville Avenue to terminate at Hatton Avenue. The service was the predecessor of the present 446 and 446A routes, except that Granville Avenue is no longer served by buses.

Having got its routes established, the company now had to apply to the Traffic Commissioners appointed under the Road Traffic Act for Licences to continue their operation. They were successful with Route 'A' (London – Windsor), being granted a licence for a twenty-minute service, which, on appeal to the Minister and the Committee of Enquiry, was increased to every quarter-hour. Route 'B' was granted a licence to operate every half-hour from London to Farnham Common, and the section between there and Beaconsfield was withdrawn on 14 October 1931. The Committee of Enquiry did not approve of the Aldwych terminus in London, however, and the two services were then terminated in Cockspur Street outside America House.

The application to continue operating Route 'D' to Aylesbury on a half-hourly basis was dismissed by the Commissioners and Premier Line appealed to the Minister, who passed the appeal to the Committee of Enquiry, the service being withdrawn on 22 October 1931 pending the result of the appeal. At the hearing, Red Rover Saloon Coaches, Green Line and the Metropolitan Railway raised many objections and the Committee upheld the Traffic Commissioners decision.

Route 'E' to Sunbury Common met the same fate. Premier applied to continue the fifteen-minute service, but the Traffic Commissioner, whilst granting Green Line a half-hourly service, refused Premier Line a licence, stating that, in his opinion, the Green Line service was sufficient to meet the needs of the area. The company appealed against this decision and the matter went to the Committee of Enquiry. After hearing the objections raised by Green Line and the Southern Railway, and the evidence of need for the service from Ham Urban District Council and Hampton District Council, the Committee in their report to the Minister of Transport stated that they had not been satisfied that the portion of the route between Kingston and Sunbury Common required more than the service granted to Green Line, and upheld the Commissioner's decision to dismiss the Premier application. In consequence of this, Route 'E' was withdrawn in June 1932.

Premier Line also had trouble with the Southern Area and East Midland Area Commissioners over the road service licence to continue operating Route 'F' from Aylesbury to Windsor, both areas deeming the service operated by the Amersham and District bus company between Great Missenden and Windsor as sufficient to meet the needs of the area concerned. However, after fresh evidence of need was submitted by various councils on line of route, the matter was solved by granting Premier a two-hourly service from Aylesbury to Slough only, and the Amersham company a two-hourly service from Great Missenden to Windsor, and a co-ordinated timetable having been agreed between the two operators, Route 'F' continued in operation. Route 'G' to Maidenhead and the local bus service in Slough seemed to present no problems, and Premier obtained licences to continue their operation without any trouble.

So we find that, at the end of 1932, the company was working the following routes:

Route A. Trafalgar Square – Great West Road – Slough – Windsor.
    B. Trafalgar Square, then as Route A – Slough – Farnham Common.
    F. Aylesbury – Wendover – Great Missenden – Amersham – The Chalfonts – Gerrards Cross – Stoke Poges – Slough.
    G. Windsor – Eton – Slough – Chippenham – Taplow – Maidenhead.

Local Bus Route:
    Slough (William Street) – Stoke Road – Elliman Avenue – Stoke Poges Lane – Granville Avenue – Manor Park Estate (Hatton Avenue).

However, the Company's operations were wholly inside the area of the new London Passenger Transport Board, as, although its main boundary was set at Salt Hill (The Three Tuns), the Board was allowed outworkings to Maidenhead, and in consequence, Premier Line was acquired on 20 December 1933. Routes 'A' and 'B' immediately became Green Line routes 'O' and 'P'; Route 'F' became Country Bus Route 19 (later renumbered to 369); Route 'G' was renumbered to 473, but was diverted from Windsor to Datchet, and the Manor Park route took the number 444. The section between Slough and Maidenhead on Route 473 was passed to the Thames Valley Traction Company at some date between May and August 1934, but Route 369 soldiered on until bus routes in the Amersham area were revised in May 1936, when it was withdrawn in favour of a slightly increased service on Route 353 (Berkhamsted – Windsor).

At the date of acquisition, Premier Line handed over to the Board a fleet of 39 Leyland coaches and a garage in London Road, Slough on the east corner of Upton Court Road, which took the running code letters 'SU' and remained in use until 1937.

SUNSET PULLMAN COACHES LIMITED:

Such was the title of a company formed by Jean Pierre Hensman of Brook Street, Brentwood, a native of the Grand Duchy of Luxembourg.

Hensman started a service in January 1930 from Brentwood to Charing Cross (Embankment) via Harold Wood, Gidea Park, Romford, Ilford, Stratford and Aldgate. Nine daily return journeys were worked at first, but a half-hourly service was soon in operation, which was increased to quarter-hourly early in 1931. The writer has a timetable for the service dated 15 July 1931 which shows the first coach leaving Brentwood at 6.50 am on weekdays (9.19 am on Sundays) and the last coach to London at 10.15 pm (five minutes earlier on Sunday nights), whilst the last coach left London at 11.30 pm on weekdays and five minutes earlier on Sundays.

Eight coaches were required to work the service, these all being Gilfords of the 1680T type, although an Albion was purchased early in 1933. They were painted in a handsome dark purple livery, and had light-coloured curtains at each window. Fares compared very favourably with those of other operators working the same road, and Hensman introduced Cheap Day Returns on Mondays to Fridays on all coaches leaving Brentwood from the 9.42 am departure for the rest of the day. From the London end, they were available on all coaches from 8.10 am to 4.10 pm being then suspended for the evening peak, but were resumed later in the evening.

A feature of the service was the extension of certain journeys on Sunday afternoons to Highwood Hospital (about a mile outside the town on the Ongar Road) for the convenience of visitors.

The operation was quite successful despite the heavy service provided by Green Line and Hillman Saloon Coaches over the same route. Hensman was granted a licence to continue operating by the Traffic Commissioners, but as the company's route was inside the London Transport area, it was acquired by the Board on 27 January 1934, passing over thirteen coaches, none of which was more than four years old, and which joined other vehicles of the same make on Green Line Route Y.

LEWIS'S CREAM LINE COACHES LIMITED:

This company commenced operating eight journeys mainly during weekday peak hours from Brookman's Park (Corner of Mymms Drive) and Charing Cross (Embankment) via Little Heath, Potters Bar, Barnet, North Finchley, Golders Green and Oxford Circus from September 1930. The first coach left Brookman's Park at 8 am and then there was an hourly service until 10 am. The next departure was at 12 noon, and then two-hourly until 4 pm, after which there were departures at 6 pm and hourly until the last coach at 8 pm. From London, the first coach left at 9.15 am and hourly to 11.15 am, then 1.15 pm, and two-hourly until 7.15, with

Albion PV coach of Sunset Pullman Coaches Limited at Brentwood. (J. F. Higham).

Gilford 1680T coach of Sunset Pullman Coaches Limited at Charing Cross on Brentwood route. (J. F. Higham).

Gilford coach of Lewis's Cream Line Coaches, Ltd., at Brookman's Park on London route. (J. F. Higham).

two more departures at 8.15 and 9.15. The fare was very cheap for the mileage covered, being 1/- (5p) single and 2/- (10p) return.

Another timetable dated October 1931, shows a service varying from hourly to half-hourly, the first departure from Brookmans Park now being 7.55 am and the last on Mondays to Fridays at 7.10 pm. The Saturday service, however, has been considerably curtailed by this time. The weekday timetable operates up to the 11.30 am departure from Brookmans Park, after which there is only one coach to London at 3 pm. The fares have also been altered, and from Brookmans Park to London is now 1/3 single; 2/- return; from Potters Bar, 1/- single; 1/9 return and from Barnet, 1/- single; 1/6 return. Weekly seasons available from Mondays to Saturdays cost 10/- (50p) from Brookmans Park and Potters Bar, and 9/- (45p) from Barnet to London. It might seem strange that a Sunday service was not operated, but at the end of the timetable a note says 'On Sundays these coaches run to various seaside resorts at cheap return fares. Particulars of these trips are issued from time to time'.

When applying for his road service licence to continue in operation under the Road Traffic Act, Lewis asked for twenty journeys. The Traffic Commissioner granted a licence for the operation of ten round trips only and Lewis appealed, the application being considered by the Committee of Enquiry into London Motor Coach services, the objectors at the appeal being Green Line Coaches Limited and the London and North Eastern Railway. There seemed to be some doubt what services Lewis was working on 9 February 1931 (the deadline date on which all services existing would be considered for continuance of operation). It was stated on his behalf that he was running 20 services daily at that time, but the timetable accompanying his application to the Traffic Commissioners dated 24 March shows only 14 services, with three fewer on Saturdays and none on Sundays. The Committee felt that the difference between 14 and 20 journeys was probably accounted for by the operation of duplications. They were unable to accept the application for 20 journeys, and assumed that it stood at 14 trips as per the timetable submitted. After further consideration, they could not find any grounds for interfering with the Traffic Commissioner's decision to grant ten journeys only, and this was confirmed.

These ten journeys were then worked by Lewis at approximately hourly intervals, and were curtailed at Portman Square, as per the Committee of Enquiry's instructions.

The London service was acquired by London Transport on 1 August 1933, two Gilford coaches passing to the new owners. The route continued as Green Line Route BR, being withdrawn on 4 October 1933 when the Green Line network was revised.

BLUE BELLE MOTORS LIMITED:

The above company, based on a headquarters at 43–45 Acre Lane, Brixton were the operators of a fleet of coaches mainly used on summer coastal services, excursions and private hire when they decided to enter the short-stage carriage scene.

The first two services commenced operations on 1 October 1930 from the R.A.F. Memorial on the Victoria Embankment and consisted of twelve journeys which

Gilford 1680T coach of Lewis's Cream Line Coaches Limited at Oxford Circus. (J. F. Higham).

A.E.C. 'Regal' coach of Blue Belle Coaches (after the route had passed to Green Line) at Paddington terminus. (J. F. Higham).

shared a common route via Victoria, Clapham Road Coach Station, Brixton, Thornton Heath, Purley Way, Whyteleafe and Caterham to Godstone, where six journeys carried on to Godstone and East Grinstead, while the other six diverted via Oxted and Limpsfield to Westerham. A note at the bottom of the timetable handbill states that 'these coaches do not ply for hire in the Metropolitan Area, and cannot pick up passengers between the Caterham boundary at Whyteleafe Station and Charing Cross unless they have booked previously or hold Season Tickets, which can be obtained from the Company's Head Office or any of their Authorised Agents'. Another note states: 'The present route via Caterham and Croydon-by-Pass (Purley Way) has been chosen by the Company after actual tests of alternative routes. Besides being the safest, the route chosen proved itself to be the most expeditious owing to entire lack of excessive traffic.' The writer feels that this would hardly apply at the present time.

The restriction on picking up north of the Caterham Boundary seems to have been solved by the granting of Metropolitan Stage Carriage plates by the Police Authorities, as, when the company introduced a new route to Caterham-on-the-Hill on 15 December 1930, the restriction does not apply to that service, nor is it included on the revised timetable for the East Grinstead and Westerham services.

The new Caterham-on-the-Hill service followed the same route as the others to Thornton Heath, where it stayed on the main road through Croydon to Purley, joining the other routes there to Whyteleafe, where it turned up Whyteleafe Hill and served Kenley R.A.F. station on its way to Caterham-on-the-Hill. This service consisted of six trips to London and five to Caterham in the first timetable, running at three hourly intervals.

A fortnight later on 29 December 1930, there was a slight reorganisation of the services. The London terminal was switched to Spring Street, Paddington, where the coaches stood outside Messrs. Charles Rickards office at No. 12. The new terminus was reached from Clapham Road Coach Station via Victoria, Hyde Park Corner, Marble Arch and Sussex Gardens. At the same time, the Oxted and Westerham route was withdrawn and replaced by a new service to the latter town which ran hourly and followed a most unusual route. Leaving the other two routes at Brixton, it then travelled via Tulse Hill, Norwood, Crystal Palace, Penge, Beckenham, Shortlands, Bromley, Keston Mark, Biggin Hill and Westerham Hill to Westerham (Kings Arms). Every alternate coach, making a two-hourly service, carried on via Hosey Common and Crockham Hill to end its journey at Edenbridge (The Crown Hotel).

In addition to the issue of Season Tickets, Workman tickets were issued on all routes up to 8.30 am and were available for the return journey after 12 noon. Of course, these tickets were issued on weekdays only.

The Westerham, Edenbridge and Caterham-on-the-Hill operations were withdrawn in December 1931 by order of the Traffic Commissioners, leaving Blue Belle with just the hourly operation from Paddington to East Grinstead.

The route, together with six A.E.C. Regal coaches, was

sold to Green Line Coaches Limited on 20 July 1932. As Blue Belle was staying on in the coach world with its summer coastal routes, excursions and private hire, the East Grinstead service was merged into the Green Line organisation becoming Route 'AU', but as the former Blue Belle fare scale had several single and return fares which were lower than those charged on Green Line Route U from Poland Street to East Grinstead, return tickets were not interavailable. Also, with the change of ownership, Workman Return Fares and Season tickets were also withdrawn.

No alteration was made to the timetable or fares and the route carried on operating until the last journeys on 3 October 1933, when the Purley Way routeing was transferred to Green Line Route G from Caterham to Horse Guards Avenue, and the East Grinstead route became a half-hourly service as Route H to Harpenden and AH to Dunstable. None of these routes however, served the Clapham Road Coach Station or the former Blue Belle route to Paddington.

TILBURY COACHING SERVICES:

This company, as its title implies, operated from a garage at 35 Dock Road, Tilbury, and in October 1930, started a service of twelve daily journeys between that town and East Ham via Grays, Purfleet Station, Rainham, Dagenham and Barking. This service was increased to eighteen journeys at a later date, and despite the competition received from Batten's Coaches and the Leighton Coach Company, the company managed to survive, and when applying for a road service licence to continue operating the route, also asked for permission to extend the service to Aldgate on Sundays, but although the Commissioners were prepared to grant a licence for twelve journeys only, they would not grant the service to Aldgate.

Feeling that twelve journeys were better than nothing, the company introduced the new timetable from 1 January 1932. The journeys were spread over the day, sometimes operating at hourly intervals, with gaps at times of 90 minutes and 120 minutes between departures.

The company was acquired by London Transport on 23 March 1934, the new owners acquiring three more Gilfords to add to their already extensive fleet of this make of vehicle.

FLEET TRANSPORT SERVICES LIMITED:

The above company with headquarters in Tramway Avenue, Stratford, was registered in 1928 and by December 1930 was working a service from Stratford to Chatham via Blackwall Tunnel on which they operated four daily journeys. In addition to this, they operated an all-night coach service from Aldgate (Mansell Street) to Romford (Market Place) via Stratford and Ilford at 45-minute intervals, the first coach leaving Aldgate at 11.35 pm, and the last at 7 am on weekdays and 5.20 am on Sundays. Despite the fact that it was a night service, the fare scale was very reasonable, in fact even cheaper than those charged on the day-time services operated by Green Line and Sunset Saloon Coaches. From Romford to Ilford the fare was 4d single; to Stratford, 7d single and the through fare to Aldgate was 9d single; 1/3 return. In addition weekly and monthly season tickets were issued from Romford to Stratford and Aldgate.

The service was worked with two Gilford 1680T coaches, and evidently there was sufficient need for the service, as they obtained a Road Service Licence from the Metropolitan Traffic Commissioner without any trouble.

As the route lay well within the London Transport area, the company was acquired by London Transport on 22

THE AMERSHAM & DISTRICT MOTOR BUS & HAULAGE COMPANY, LIMITED.

Reg. Office: BROADWAY, AMERSHAM. 'Phones: Amersham 36.   High Wycombe 32.

Express Coach Service
AMERSHAM, UXBRIDGE & LONDON

Commencing THURSDAY, 22nd OCTOBER, 1931.

	A M	P M			A M	P M		Booking Offices.
AMERSHAM (A. & D. Gar.)	7 30	7 30	......	LONDON (Oxford Circus)...	9 2	9 2	......	
Chalfont St. Giles (Pheasant) ..	7 38	7 38	......	Shepherds Bush (R. & A.)	9 20	9 20	......	Mr. R. Wright, Chesham Broadway.
Chalfont St. Peter (Church)....	7 43	7 43	......	Acton (Six Bells)	9 30	9 30	......	Tel. No. 32 Chesham.
Gold Hill (Jolly Farmer)	7 45	7 45	......	Ealing Bdy. (Church)............	9 35	9 35	......	Bucks Insurance Bureau Ltd., Oakfield Corner
Gerrards Cross (Orchehill Av.)	7 49	7 49	......	Hanwell (Lloyds Bank)	9 39	9 39	......	Tel. No. 77 Amersham.
Uxbridge (Garretts)	8 2	8 2	......	Southall (Goodman's)............	9 44	9 44	......	A. & D. Office, The Broadway, Amersham.
Uxbridge (Eight Bells)	8 4	8 4	......	Hayes (P.O.)	9 49	9 49	......	Tel. No. 36 Amersham.
Hillingdon (Bews)	8 10	8 10	......	Hillingdon (Bews)	9 52	9 52	......	Post Office, Chalfont St. Peter.
Hayes (P.O.)	8 13	8 13	......	Uxbridge (Eight Bells)	9 56	9 56	......	Garrett, Uxbridge. Tel. No. 642 Uxbridge.
Southall (Goodman's)	8 17	8 17	......	Uxbridge (Garretts)	9 58	9 58	......	Wallpaper & Homecrafts Co., Uxbridge Rd.,
Hanwell (Lloyds Bank)	8 22	8 22	......	Gerrards Cross (Orchehill Av.)	1010	1010	......	Hayes. Tel. No. 320 Hayes.
Ealing Bdy. (Church)............	8 25	8 25	......	Gold Hill (Jolly Farmer)	1012	1012	......	Bews Booking Office, Uxbridge Rd., Hillingdon Heath. Tel. No. 663 Uxbridge.
Acton (Six Bells)	8 32	8 32	......	Chalfont St. Peter (Church) ...	1014	1014	......	Roadways & Airways, Ltd., 5 Uxbridge Rd.,
Shepherds Bush (R. & A.)	8 42	8 40	......	Chalfont St. Giles (Pheasant)...	1019	1019	......	W.12. Tel. No. Shepherd's Bush 1200.
LONDON (Oxford Circus)...	9 0	9 0	......	AMERSHAM (A. & D. Gar.)	1028	1028	......	The District Messenger Office, 279 Regent St. Tel. No. Mayfair 0509.

Passengers will not be picked up between Gerrard's Cross (Orchehill Avenue) and Uxbridge on the journey to London, and will not be set down between Uxbridge and Gerrard's Cross (Orchehill Avenue) on the return journey.

SUNDAYS.—First Coach leaves Amersham 9.30 a.m. and Oxford Circus 11.2 a.m. and then hourly as weekdays.

FOR FARES SEE OVERLEAF.

Southall Saloon Coach Booking Agency, 15 Broadway. Tel. 1409 Southall.
Vine's Library, 164, The Broadway, West Ealing. Tel. No. Ealing 4667.

Bedford WLB coach of Sunshine Saloon Coaches Limited at Ashford Station en route to Kingston operated on behalf of Bentall's Stores. (J. F. Higham).

February 1934. The Stratford – Chatham route was passed to Maidstone and District, while the Aldgate – Romford night service was merged in Green Line Route Y (Aldgate – Brentwood) until 13 June 1934, when the timings were transferred to Central Buses, who extended their night route 617 (Charing Cross – Seven Kings) to Hornchurch Garage to cover the former Fleet operations. At the same time, they introduced a Saturday night and early Sunday morning service on 617 between Aldgate and Hornchurch as the Fleet service had operated every night. Only one of the Fleet Gilford coaches passed to London Transport, the others being handed over to Maidstone and District.

AMERSHAM AND DISTRICT OMNIBUS AND HAULAGE COMPANY LIMITED:

This company had been started in September 1919 to operate local bus services in the countryside surrounding Amersham, and by August 1929 when the London General Omnibus Company had acquired a controlling interest, was operating a fleet of over thirty buses in an area which stretched from Aylesbury and Berkhamsted to Windsor, plus a small network of routes servicing the villages in a triangle formed by a line drawn just north of the Oxford road between High Wycombe and Gerrards Cross, plus a line drawn just west of the road between Amersham and High Wycombe and one drawn east of the road from Amersham to Gerrards Cross.

In November 1930, the Green Line organisation applied to the local councils at Chesham and Amersham for licences to operate services to London both via Rickmansworth and Gerrards Cross, but fortunately for the coach operators already established in the area, the respective councils refused the Green Line application.

The L.G.O.C., of which Green Line was a subsidiary, were not to be deterred, and transferred five A.E.C. Regal T-type Green Line coaches to the Amersham company's fleet which were repainted in that Company's livery, an application being made by the Amersham and District to operate an hourly service from Chesham Broadway to London (Oxford Circus) via Amersham, Gerrards Cross, Uxbridge and Ealing. The Amersham council having granted a licence, the service started on 26 January 1931 from Amersham (Oakfield Corner), being extended to Chesham Broadway from 1 February, Chesham Council having given their approval in the meantime.

Having now got the service started before the deadline of 9 February, the company now had to apply to the respective Traffic Commissioners to continue operating. The Metropolitan Commissioners granted a licence in respect of their area, but the Southern Area Commissioner only granted a licence to operate from the Company's garage at Amersham, stating that the West London company already provided an adequate service for the needs of Chesham people. He also stipulated in the licence granted to the Amersham company that they should not pick-up or set down passengers between Gerrards Cross (Orchehill Avenue) and Uxbridge High Street, stating that the needs of that area were adequately provided for by Skylark Motor Coaches.

The service then continued under Amersham and District control until the last journeys on 3 October 1933, being replaced on the following day by Green Line Route R covering the same route. The bus section of the company carried on as a separate organisation until 24 November 1933, when it was merged into London Transport (Country Buses).

SUNSHINE SALOON COACHES LIMITED:

The above company was a small organisation with a depot at 37 Birkenhead Avenue, Kingston-on-Thames, who had for some years operated a service from Kingston Station to Ashford (Middlesex) Station, via Hampton Court, Kempton Park, Sunbury and Lower Feltham, which was sponsored by the famous Bentall store in Kingston.

A service running every 80 minutes was operated using one coach, the first vehicle leaving Kingston at 9.0 am, and the last one at 7.20 pm on Mondays to Fridays, with a later bus on Saturdays at 8.40 pm. No Sunday service was operated, as the coaches were used for other purposes on that day.

A minimum fare of 3d (1½p) was charged throughout the route, and the through fare from Kingston to Ashford was 9d (roughly 4p) single; 1/2 (6p) return, return tickets being issued for all fares from 4d upwards.

It was granted a licence to continue operating by the Traffic Commissioners in July 1931, as the route was operated as a bus service charging bus fares, whereas both Green Line and Premier Line from Sunbury Common were considered to be short-stage express carriages, and, as has been mentioned before, Premier Line lost their right to operate over this road.

The company used two Bedford WLB-type 20-seater buses and a 32-seat Gilford 1660T coach on the service, and these were acquired by London Transport when they took over the operations on 30 December 1933. The new owners passed the operation of this service to the Central Bus Section, it becoming Route 198 (renumbered to 216 on 3 October 1934) and was immediately extended from Ashford Station to Staines over the route used by 216 today.

LONDON GENERAL OMNIBUS COMPANY LTD
EAST SURREY TRACTION COMPANY LIMITED
AUTOCAR SERVICES LIMITED:

It may well be wondered why there has been no mention of the L.G.O.C., East Surrey and Autocar operations which were started in 1929 and 1930. As they were the direct

Gilford 1660T coach at Ashford Station en route to Kingston operated by Sunshine Saloon Coaches on behalf of Bentall's Stores. (J. F. Higham).

ancestors of the Green Line company, it is appropriate that their activities precede the chapter on Green Line Coaches Ltd.

East Surrey entered the scene on 7 August 1928 with two routes to London, both terminating at Charing Cross (Northumberland Avenue). One route commenced at Redhill Town Hall and ran via Reigate, Kingswood, Sutton, Tooting and Clapham. The other, commencing its journey at Reigate, operated via Redhill, Merstham, Croydon and Brixton. Each route operated every three hours on weekdays only, giving a 90-minute service to the two towns. One fare was charged on either route, this being 2/6 (12½p) single; 3/6 (17½p) return. Tickets were not issued on the coaches, being purchased in advance from the Company's offices in Bell Street, Reigate or at the Enquiry Offices at Redhill Market Place or the Old Town Hall at Reigate. In London, passengers booked at The District Messenger's office on the corner of Whitehall and Northumberland Avenue. Though there were no intermediate fares en route, passengers could book at agencies en route, provided they were travelling right through to London or the Surrey terminals.

These arrangements were soon altered, and seats could be booked either on the coaches or at agents outside the Metropolitan Police area, but only in advance from agents inside that area.

A Sunday service from Reigate via Redhill and Croydon was introduced on 10 November 1928, and, in an attempt to stimulate an increase in traffic on both routes, the fare was reduced by 6d (2½p) on both single and return fares. However, passengers were only allowed to board between Charing Cross and Brixton or Clapham on the outward journey, and between Reigate and Merstham or Redhill and Kingswood on the inward journeys.

Both services were withdrawn on 3 March 1929, as there was insufficient through traffic to justify their continuance, and it was over twelve months before East Surrey decided to enter this field again.

The London General Omnibus Company had been watching events in the coaching world since the commencement of short-stage carriage express operations in 1927, particularly watching the effect it was having on their outer area bus services. They finally decided to enter the

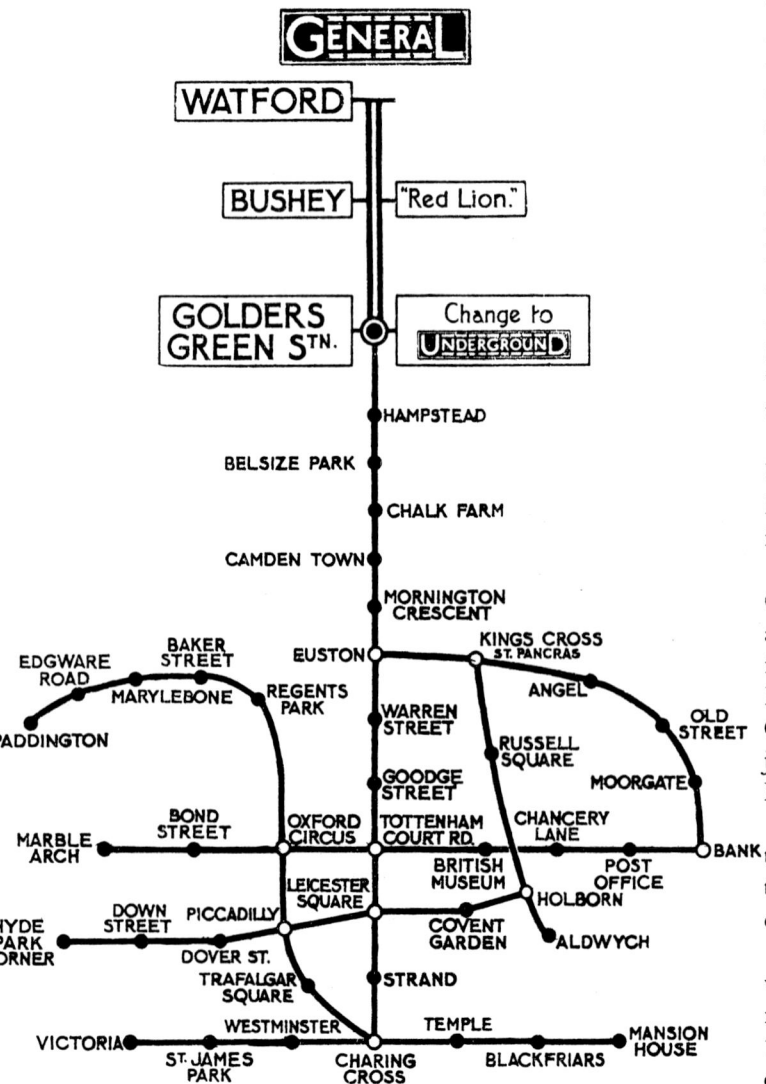

AUTOCAR SERVICES LTD.

OPERA HOUSE BUILDINGS, TUNBRIDGE WELLS. 'Phone: Tun. Wells 1267

EXPRESS COACH SERVICE
LONDON (OXFORD CIRCUS)
NEW CROSS—LEWISHAM—CATFORD—BROMLEY—SEVENOAKS—TONBRIDGE
TUNBRIDGE WELLS

EVERY 60 MINUTES

Commencing FRIDAY, 6th JUNE, 1930.

TIME OF DEPARTURE.

FROM LONDON (OXFORD CIRCUS)

	a.m.					p.m.									
LONDON (Oxford Circus)	9 0	10	11	12	1	2	3	4	5	6	7	8	9	10	11 30
LONDON (Gt. Scotland Yard)	9 14	10 29	11 29	12 29	1 29	2 29	3 29	4 29	5 29	6 29	7 29	8 29	9 29	10 29	11 44
LONDON (Elephant & Castle) Planet House, St. George's Rd.	9 20	10 35	11 35	12 35	1 35	2 35	3 35	4 35	5 35	6 35	7 35	8 35	9 35	10 35	11 50
NEW CROSS (193, New Cross Road)	9 33	10 48	11 48	12 48	1 48	2 48	3 48	4 48	5 48	6 48	7 48	8 48	9 48	10 48	12 3
LEWISHAM (22, Lewisham High Road)	9 40	10 55	11 55	12 55	1 55	2 55	3 55	4 55	5 55	6 55	7 55	8 55	9 55	10 55	12 10
CATFORD (171, Rushley Green)	9 44	10 59	11 59	12 59	1 59	2 59	3 59	4 59	5 59	6 59	7 59	8 59	9 59	10 59	12 14
BROMLEY (113 High Street)	9 58	11 8	12 8	1 8	2 8	3 8	4 8	5 8	6 8	7 8	8 8	9 8	10 8	11 8	12 23

FROM TUNBRIDGE WELLS. (COACH STATION, LIME HILL ROAD)

	a.m.					p.m.									
TUNBRIDGE WELLS (Coach Station, Lime Hill Road)	7 0	8 15	9 15	10 15	11 15	12 15	1 15	2 15	3 15	4 15	5 15	6 15	7 15	8 15	
SOUTHBOROUGH (Post Office)	7 6	8 21	9 21	10 21	11 21	12 21	1 21	2 21	3 21	4 21	5 21	6 21	7 21	8 21	
TONBRIDGE Auto Car Services, High St.)	7 12	8 27	9 27	10 27	11 27	12 27	1 27	2 27	3 27	4 27	5 27	6 27	7 27	8 27	
SEVENOAKS (Market Place)	7 29	8 44	9 44	10 44	11 44	12 44	1 44	2 44	3 44	4 44	5 44	6 44	7 44	8 44	
BROMLEY (118, High Street)	8	9 17	10 17	11 17	12 17	1 17	2 17	3 17	4 17	5 17	6 17	7 17	8 17	9 17	

FARES.

	TUN. WELLS.		TONBRIDGE.		SEVENOAKS.		BROMLEY.	
	Adult.	Child.	Adult.	Child.	Adult.	Child.	Adult.	Child.
	Single / Return	Single / Return	Single / Return	Single / Return	Single / Return	Single / Return	Single / Return	Single / Return
BROMLEY	3/6 / 3/10	3/3 / 3/6	3/6 / 3/10	3/3 / 3/6	2/- / 2/6	1/- / 1/9		
LEWISHAM	3,6 / 3/10	3/3 / 3/6	3/6 / 3/10	3/3 / 3/6	2/- / 2/6	1/- / 1/9	1/- / 1/6	9d. / 1/-
NEW CROSS	3/6 / 3/10	3/3 / 3/6	3/6 / 3/10	3/3 / 3/6	2/- / 1/4	1/4 / 1/4	1/- / 1/6	9d. / 1/-
LONDON (Oxford Circus)	3/6 / 3/10	3/3 / 3/6	3/6 / 3/10	3/3 / 3/6	2/- / 1/4	1/4 / 1/4	1/- / 1/6	9d. / 1/-

All Children, except infants in arms, must be paid for.

BOOK YOUR SEATS ON THE COACH OR AT ANY OF THE BOOKING AGENTS OVERLEAF.
CONDITIONS.—The Company will make every effort to maintain the scheduled Service, but cannot accept any responsibility for inconvenience, loss, damage or breakdown, or anything arising from any unavoidable causes. **Small hand luggage carried free at owner's risk.**

EAST SURREY TRACTION Co. LTD.

BELL STREET, REIGATE. 'Phone: Reigate 593

EXPRESS COACH SERVICE
LONDON (OXFORD CIRCUS)
KENNINGTON—CLAPHAM—TOOTING—MITCHAM—SUTTON—KINGSWOOD
REIGATE (MARKET PLACE)

EVERY 60 MINUTES

Commencing FRIDAY, 6th JUNE, 1930

TIMES OF DEPARTURE

FROM LONDON (OXFORD CIRCUS)

	N.S. a.m.					p.m.									
LONDON (Oxford Circus)	8 30	9 30	10 30	11 30	12 30	1 30	2 30	3 30	4 30	5 30	6 30	7 30	8 30	9 30	10 30	11 30
LONDON (Gt. Scotland Yard)	8 44	9 44	10 44	11 44	12 44	1 44	2 44	3 44	4 44	5 44	6 44	7 44	8 44	9 44	10 44	11 44
STOCKWELL (231, Clapham Rd.)	8 54	9 54	10 54	11 54	12 54	1 54	2 54	3 54	4 54	5 54	6 54	7 54	8 54	9 54	10 54	11 54
CLAPHAM COMMON (9, South Side)	8 58	9 58	10 58	11 58	12 58	1 58	2 58	3 58	4 58	5 58	6 58	7 58	8 58	9 58	10 58	11 58
BALHAM (1, Station Parade)	9 3	10 3	11 3	12 3	1 3	2 3	3 3	4 3	5 3	6 3	7 3	8 3	9 3	10 3	11 3	12 3
TOOTING (38, Tooting High St.)	9 8	10 8	11 8	12 8	1 8	2 8	3 8	4 8	5 8	6 8	7 8	8 8	9 8	10 8	11 8	12 8
MITCHAM (The Cricketers)	9 15	10 15	11 15	12 15	1 15	2 15	3 15	4 15	5 15	6 15	7 15	8 15	9 15	10 15	11 15	12 15
SUTTON STATION	9 25	10 25	11 25	12 25	1 25	2 25	3 25	4 25	5 25	6 25	7 25	8 25	9 25	10 25	11 25	12 25

FROM REIGATE (MARKET PLACE)

	N.S. a.m.					p.m.									
REIGATE (Market Place)	7 5	8 5	9 5	10 5	11 5	12 5	1 5	2 5	3 5	4 5	5 5	6 5	7 5	8 5	9 5	10 5
KINGSWOOD (The Fox)	7 15	8 15	9 15	10 15	11 15	12 15	1 15	2 15	3 15	4 15	5 15	6 15	7 15	8 15	9 15	10 15
SUTTON STATION	7 30	8 30	9 30	10 30	11 30	12 30	1 30	2 30	3 30	4 30	5 30	6 30	7 30	8 30	9 30	10 30
MITCHAM (The Cricketers)	7 40	8 40	9 40	10 40	11 40	12 40	1 40	2 40	3 40	4 40	5 40	6 40	7 40	8 40	9 40	10 40
TOOTING (38, Tooting High St.)	7 47	8 47	9 47	10 47	11 47	12 47	1 47	2 47	3 47	4 47	5 47	6 47	7 47	8 47	9 47	10 47

N.S.—Not Sundays.

FARES

REIGATE.		KINGSWOOD (The Fox)		SUTTON.	
Single.	Return.	Single.	Return.	Single.	Return.
1/-	—	—	—	—	—
2/-	3/-	1/-	—	—	—
2/-	3/-	2/-	3/-	1/-	1/6

BOOK YOUR SEATS ON THE COACH OR AT ANY OF THE BOOKING AGENTS OVERLEAF.
CHILDREN'S FARES.—Children under 14 years of age half price. All Children, except infants in arms, must be paid for.
CONDITIONS.—The Company will make every effort to maintain the scheduled service, but cannot accept any responsibility for inconvenience, loss, damage, or breakdown, or anything arising from unavoidable causes. **Small hand luggage carried free at owner's risk.**

express field, setting up an Express Coach section in 1929. They still held the lease on the garage in Leavesden Road (Watford) which had been used as a base for expansion of their London bus operations into the West Hertfordshire countryside during the 1920–1921 period, and this was to become one of the depots for some of the 'General' express services.

On 2 October 1929, a fifteen-minute service worked by the light green and cream A.E.C. Reliance all-weather coaches from the Private Hire fleet commenced operation between Watford and Golders Green via Bushey, Bushey Heath, Watford Way, Mill Hill and Hendon Central. There were boarding restrictions in Watford, where passengers could only board the coaches at Leavesden Road Garage or the Pond Cross Roads.

It might be wondered why Golders Green was chosen as the London terminal for the new venture in preference to one in Central London, but it will be remembered that the

---

GREEN LINE

MOTOR COACH AND RAIL SERVICE

WATFORD AND
BUSHEY, MILL HILL
LONDON via GOLDERS GREEN
EVERY 30 MINUTES

Departure Points.	WEEKDAYS AND SUNDAYS.		
	First Coach. a.m.	Then at minutes past each hour	Last Coach. p.m.
To GOLDERS GREEN from			
Watford, Leavesden Road	7 35	5 35	11 5
Pond Cross Roads	7 38	8 38	11 8
Bushey, Aldenham Road	7 41	11 41	11 11
Bushey, "Red Lion" Hotel	7 43	13 43	11 13
Bushey Church	7 46	16 46	11 16
GOLDERS GREEN arr.	8 8	38 8	11 38
To WATFORD from			
Golders Green Station	8 23	53 23	11 53
Hendon Central Station	8 28	58 28	11 58
Mill Hill Broadway	8 35	5 35	12 5
WATFORD arr.	8 58	28 58	12 28

FARES

Fare Stages.	WATFORD		BUSHEY		MILL HILL	
	Single	Return	Single	Return	Single	Return
MILL HILL	9d.	1/3	—	—		
HENDON CENTRAL	1/-	1/6	—	—		
GOLDERS GREEN	1/-	1/6	9d.	1/3	—	—
*LONDON	1/6	2/-	1/3	1/9	1/3	1/9

WEEKLY TICKETS.	SEASON TICKETS (Quarterly).
WATFORD & LONDON 10/-	GOLDERS GREEN & BUSHEY... £3/7/6
BUSHEY & LONDON 8/6	Ask coach conductor for application form.

*Passengers change at Golders Green Station and travel by UNDERGROUND to any of the Stations shown on map overleaf.

Passengers may hail and board the coach at any point en route, except in the Watford area, where passengers can only board and alight at the garage (Leavesden Road) or the Pond Cross Roads.

CHILDREN'S FARES. Reduced fares for Children under 14 years of age. All children (except infants in arms) must be paid for.

CONDITIONS. The Company will make every effort to run according to Time Table, but cannot accept any responsibility through any inconvenience caused by late arrival at destination, breakdown, fire, or anything arising from unavoidable cause.

LIGHT LUGGAGE ALLOWED FREE.   ONLY LAP DOGS CARRIED.

TICKETS CAN BE OBTAINED ON THE COACH—OR AT ANY OF THE ADDRESSES MENTIONED AT FOOT OF PAGE OVERLEAF.

GREEN LINE COACHES. July, 1930.   P.T.O.

'General' company was part of the Underground group of companies, and it was an easy matter to arrange for through coach and rail single and return tickets to travel by coach to Golders Green and thence by Underground to any of the stations in an area which stretched from Marble Arch, Paddington and Hyde Park Corner in the west to Aldwych, Bank and Mansion House in the east.

The coaches took only 35 minutes for the journey from Watford to Golders Green, with the rail journey taking a further 20–25 minutes, and with complete coverage of all the central area tube stations for the same fare as the competing Bucks Express service, which suffered to some extent from traffic congestion from Cricklewood inwards, the new 'General' service compared very favourably with its competitor.

Tickets could be purchased on the coaches or from the many agents on line of route, whilst they were also sold in London at Charing Cross, Victoria and Hendon Central Underground Stations, and at a large number of booking agents in the City and West End.

I feel that this operation was in the nature of an experiment to test the potential market, as it was withdrawn on 12 November after about six weeks of operation.

The withdrawal was only temporary, as operation recommenced on 18 December with a half-hourly service (hourly on Sundays until May) and was accompanied by the introduction of a service direct to Charing Cross via Bushey, Stanmore, Edgware, Cricklewood, Kilburn and Oxford Circus, to compete with the Bucks Express service. This route ran every forty minutes on weekdays and hourly on Sundays. The Sunday service to Golders Green was increased to half-hourly, whilst the Charing Cross service became half-hourly daily from May 1930.

A facility to encourage commuters was introduced with the newly increased service, this being the issue of weekly 12-journey tickets from Watford and Bushey to London on both services. The coach-rail tickets, of course, could only be used on the Golders Green route, and were not available for return on the direct London service. Later, quarterly season tickets were introduced on the direct route from Watford and Bushey to Charing Cross and between Bushey and Golders Green only on that service.

Both routes were fairly successful, and in due course, the Private Hire coaches were replaced by the new A.E.C. Regal T-type coaches painted in the red livery used on the 'General' buses.

The next service to commence operation was that to Windsor from Charing Cross (Embankment) via Hammersmith, Chiswick, Great West Road, Colnbrook, Slough and Eton. It commenced on 20 April 1930 on an half-hourly basis, being worked by six of the new A.E.C. Regal T-type coaches based on a new Coach Depot in Alpha Street, Slough.

To compete with the Premier service which covered the same route, after leaving the terminal on the Embankment the coaches proceeded to the Premier terminal at Aldwych (Bush House) to pick up passengers on their way to Windsor. The frequency was stepped up to every 15 minutes on 8 May, now requiring 12 coaches to work the service, followed by an increase to every 10 minutes (18 coaches) on 1 July, although it dropped back to a 15-minute service from 6 August.

Between Windsor and Colnbrook there was a 3d (1½p) minimum fare, and return tickets were only issued at that time from Windsor, Slough, Colnbrook and Harmondsworth to London, and from the latter point there was only one fare for any distance, this being 1/3 (6½p) single; 2/- (10p) return. From June 1930, passengers from Windsor were able to change at Hammersmith to the Underground and travel on the District Line to Charing Cross or the Piccadilly Line to Leicester Square, and were allowed to carry on to Oxford Circus on the Bakerloo or Tottenham Court Road on the Northern Line. From late June, weekly, monthly and quarterly season tickets were issued from Windsor, Slough and Colnbrook to London.

As mentioned in the paragraph dealing with the Watford services, the new coaches were in a red and black livery with the fleet name 'General' in smaller gold lettering than used on the company's buses. At that time, the 'General' bus route 81 ran through to Windsor daily, and it has been said that there were many arguments between coach conductors and their passengers in the Slough and Langley areas, when the passengers, thinking it was some new form of local bus service, asked for a penny fare, and got somewhat annoyed when told by the conductor that the minimum fare was threepence. This was said to have been the reason for setting up Green Line Coaches Limited and changing the fleet name and livery.

A fleet of the new coaches, also in the red and black livery, but bearing the fleet names of East Surrey and Autocar were delivered to the two companies during May 1930, and after crew and route training, East Surrey commenced three hourly services from Oxford Circus to Reigate via Tooting, Mitcham, Sutton and Kingswood; Redhill via Brixton, Croydon and Merstham, and Dorking via Tooting, Morden, Epsom and Leatherhead. On the same date, Autocar Services started a service from Oxford Circus to Tunbridge Wells via Lewisham, Bromley, Sevenoaks and Tonbridge, also hourly. More coaches were delivered to the two companies during the next fortnight and all four services became half-hourly from 24 June.

Meanwhile, the 'General' themselves had not been idle, and had opened a new depot at Staines, and crew training had commenced in readiness for the new services to be operated from that depot. The first of these commenced on 10 July 1930 from Charing Cross (Embankment) to Windsor, via Bush House, Oxford Circus, Shepherds Bush, Chiswick, Hounslow, Bedfont, Staines, Egham, Englefield Green and Old Windsor. The service was half-hourly, requiring seven coaches to operate it. The fare from Windsor to London was exactly the same as that for the Slough and Windsor route, and return tickets were inter-available, except for passengers using the Underground facility, as the interchange point on the service via Staines was at Shepherds Bush, whilst that on the route via Slough was at Hammersmith.

Although this was the last service to be introduced before the Green Line company was set up, it was not to be the last service started by either the General or East Surrey companies.

Meanwhile, Green Line Coaches Limited had been registered as a company on 9 July 1930, and although some independent operators were still setting up new services, it was Green Line Coaches who were responsible for the majority of developments over the next two years, and all of these will be discussed in the next chapter.

Green Line Builds Up
CHAPTER THREE

1930-1934

Green Line Coaches Limited was registered as a company on 9 July 1930, its head office being at 55 Broadway, Westminster, S.W.1, with a capital of £20,000. Lord Ashfield, Frank Pick and Daniel Duff were the directors, whilst John Christopher Mitchell was appointed Secretary of the Company, which was a subsidiary of the London General Omnibus Company (see introduction). At the same time, three other companies were also registered: Red Line Coaches Limited, Yellow Line Coaches Limited and Blue Line Coaches Limited, each with a capital of £100 in order to secure the copyright of the names, but operation under these titles was not contemplated, and they were dissolved in February 1935.

At the time of formation of the company it was officially announced that it had been formed for the purpose of convenience in operation and in order to distinguish from the ordinary single-deck buses of the London General Omnibus Company Limited.

Arthur Henry Hawkins, the dynamic Managing Director of the East Surrey Traction Company (another L.G.O.C. associate) was also appointed as the Operating Manager of Green Line, and the day-to-day operations of all coaches were placed under his control. New vehicles were now painted in the Green Line livery, although many of them were licensed by East Surrey, Autocar Services and the National Omnibus and Transport Company. The original A.E.C. Regal T-types of East Surrey, Autocar and the London General Omnibus Company were also repainted in the new livery at a later date. The first coach to appear in green livery was T119, which appeared with an elliptical name device, but before entering service, this was replaced by the legend 'GREEN LINE' in gold block letters.

The company commenced operation of its first service on 17 July, eight days after it had been registered. This was the route from Charing Cross (Embankment) to Guildford via Hammersmith, Barnes, Kingston-by-Pass, Esher, Cobham and Ripley. This route also ran out from Charing Cross via Oxford Circus in order to compete with the Skylark route, which commenced at that point, but ran hourly, whilst Green Line maintained a half-hourly service. Seven coaches were needed to work the route at this time, and, as neither Green Line nor its associated companies had a garage at Guildford in those days, the coaches were based at Rice and Harper's Garage and Filling Station in London Road, Guildford. These premises had a very large asphalted yard in London Road on the corner of York Road, which today is used as a depot for the vehicles of the Post Office Telephone service. Green Line used it as a base until the present garage in Leas Road (off Woodbridge Road) was opened in 1932.

On the same day as the Guildford services commenced operation, the two original services operated by the L.G.O.C. from Watford to Charing Cross and Golders Green were taken over by the new company, the 'General' vehicles being transferred elsewhere and their place taken by coaches in the Green Line livery.

From this point onwards, other developments began to take place which to the public eye appeared to be Green Line developments, and to all intents and purposes they were, there being various reasons such as licensing, ownership of vehicles and staff agreements which prevented immediate official transfer to Green Line, although as will be seen later, the Green Line fleet name was used extensively.

The first of these took place on 23 July, when Green Line started a route from Charing Cross (Embankment) to Brentwood, which competed with Sunset Saloon Coaches throughout and with Hillman Saloon Coaches from Stratford (later Bow). It was started with a 20-minute service, but by February 1931, a 15-minute service was worked until midday, then every 12 minutes (10 minutes on Saturdays) until close of traffic. Extra coaches were also worked between Charing Cross and Gidea Park during weekday peak hours. Once again, Green Line had no depot on line of route, and the coaches were garaged at the Lincoln Works, Eastern Avenue (near the Gidea Park roundabout) for a period, and were later transferred to the Romford Ice and Cold Storage depot in North Street, Romford until the Hillman company was acquired by London Transport.

On the same day the parent 'General' company introduced a new route from the Staines depot. This was an hourly service from Charing Cross (Embankment) to Sunningdale, via Piccadilly, Hammersmith, Chiswick, Kew, Hounslow, Bedfont, Staines and Egham, which was later stepped up to half-hourly with vehicles released from the two Watford routes. They followed this on 2 August by the introduction of a half-hourly service to Maidenhead, which, after leaving Charing Cross, ran via Oxford Circus in order to compete with the Thackray's Way Reading service, which also ran via Maidenhead. This service required seven coaches to work it and was based on the Slough (Alpha Street) depot.

The next development was also initiated by the 'General', once again from Staines depot, and consisted of an hourly service from Oxford Circus to Ascot which competed with the other Thackray route to Reading, which ran via Ascot also. To provide the coaches for this route, the Sunningdale service was reduced to hourly, but, as both the Ascot and Sunningdale routes met up at Hyde Park Corner, a joint half-hourly service was maintained between that point and Virginia Water. This operation commenced on 1 September 1930.

A week later on 8 September, Green Line commenced its third new service from Charing Cross (Embankment) to Tring, following the same route as the Charing Cross – Watford service, then continuing via Kings Langley, Apsley, Boxmoor, Berkhamsted and Northchurch, terminating at 'The Britannia' public-house at the end of Western Road, Tring. A half-hourly service was worked, requiring eight coaches based on the Leavesden Road (Watford) depot, as the Tring garage in those days, was the property of E. Prentice and Sons Ltd., who operated buses on the Aylesbury – Watford route, and who remained independent until they were acquired by London General Country Services in May 1933.

When starting this service, Green Line were refused licences by the Watford Council to ply for hire in the Borough of Watford, and, in consequence, the service did not pick up passengers nor set them down between Bushey (Aldenham Road) and Grovemill Lane, running express over this section. This also applied to coaches running to and from Leavesden Road Garage, which ran to Bushey only from London and to Grovemill Lane from Tring.

It was evident that Green Line envisaged operating a much larger network, and over a much larger area than that which finally emerged by the time the Road Traffic Act came into operation. Between September and November 1930, applications were made for licences in no fewer than 57 local authorities in the Home Counties, and, if they had all been successful, routes would have operated out as far as Gravesend (they ultimately reached there in 1933); Woking, Godalming, Farnham, Aldershot, Reading, Henley, Marlow, Bedford, Cambridge (via Royston and also via Saffron Walden) and Chelmsford. (See Appendix B.)

The first East Surrey-owned coach appeared in the Green Line livery on 13 September, and was followed four days later by the introduction of a new service by the National Omnibus and Transport Company as operating agents for Green Line, in whose livery the coaches appeared. This was a half-hourly service from Charing Cross to Welwyn Garden City via Oxford Circus, Golders Green, Barnet and Hatfield. The six coaches for this service did not operate from the 'National' garage at Hatfield, but were based on a depot set up in the yard of the gasworks at Welwyn Garden City. Although the coaches ran through to Charing Cross, passengers could alight at Golders Green and continue their journey by Underground, using the same ticket.

Three days later on 20 September, Green Line started another new route on its own account, this time from Charing Cross to Harpenden every half-hour. This took the same route as the Welwyn Garden City route to Golders Green, where it diverged to Hendon Central, Mill Hill, Brockley Hill, Elstree, Radlett and St. Albans. As neither Green Line nor its associates had a garage in either St. Albans or Harpenden, Green Line came to an agreement with the local bus company, Comfy Cars Limited, to stable the seven vehicles required for the service in their garage in Luton Road, Harpenden. Passengers on this service were also allowed to change at Golders Green and complete their journey on the Underground if they so wished.

The next new service was started by East Surrey on 29 September with A.E.C. all-weather Regal coaches normally used for private hire, coastal trips and excursions, bearing labels to inform passengers that it was a Green Line service. The route ran half-hourly from Oxford Circus to Godstone Green via Brixton, Streatham and Croydon to Purley and then through the valley road via Kenley and Whyteleafe to Caterham. Tickets were issued on the coaches or at booking agents on line of route. Six coaches worked the route, based on the East Surrey garage at Godstone. In order not to abstract traffic from the local bus services of the East Surrey and 'General' between Croydon, Caterham and Godstone, a higher minimum fare applied on the coach service between these points.

East Surrey followed this four days later with the introduction of another new route from Oxford Circus, this time to Great Bookham. This ran every half-hour between the Dorking coaches and gave a 15 minute service to Leatherhead. Six coaches were required to work the service, and these, like the Dorking route, were based on the East

Surrey garage at Leatherhead, as the Dorking Garage was not opened until 1932.

1 October 1930 was a day of great activity for the Green Line company. First of all, the Autocar route from Tunbridge Wells, plus the three original East Surrey routes from Reigate, Redhill and Dorking became Green Line services, although still operated by the two companies as operating agents. In addition to this, the Staines depot together with the routes to Ascot, Sunningdale, and Windsor via Staines passed from the L.G.O.C. to Green Line Coaches Limited.

On that day also, another operation was started by National, this being a route from Bishops Stortford to Charing Cross, half-hourly. Like the 'Acme' service from the same town, this route followed the A11 road from Bishops Stortford to Epping Forest (Wake Arms), where it diverged to run via Loughton, Woodford, Forest Road (Walthamstow), Tottenham Hale, Finsbury Park, Camden Town, Southampton Row and Kingsway. Passengers were allowed to change at Finsbury Park (later Camden Town) and complete their journey by Underground, although they could not alight at as many stations in the Central area as the scope allowed to passengers changing at Golders Green. Eight coaches were required to work this service, these being based in the 'National' garage in South Street, Bishops Stortford, although later they were transferred to the Acme garage in Station Road.

A week later on 8 October, East Surrey commenced an hourly operation from Oxford Circus to Westerham which followed the Tunbridge Wells route to Oakley Road, Bromley Common, diverging there via Keston Mark, Leaves Green, Biggin Hill and Westerham Hill, and which ten days later was extended to Sevenoaks via Brasted, Sundridge and Bessels Green. The four coaches for this service were based at the East Surrey Garage at Dunton Green, garage journeys to and from Sevenoaks not being worked in service at that time.

Green Line started another route on its own account from 11 October, this time from Charing Cross (Embankment) to Chertsey, via Piccadilly, Hammersmith, Barnes, Richmond, Kingston, Thames Ditton, East and West Molesey, Walton-on-Thames, Weybridge and Addlestone. Once again, passengers who held tickets to or from London were enabled to change at Hammersmith and continue by Underground, the stations to which the ticket was available being stated on the back of the ticket. Neither Green Line nor East Surrey had a garage in the area at that time, and the coaches for this route were stabled at the Metro-Cammell-Weymann coach works at Addlestone until the present garage was opened.

The 'General' coach depot at Slough (Alpha Street) together with the coach services to Maidenhead and Windsor via Slough, passed from the L.G.O.C. to Green Line Coaches Limited on 18 October, and four days later a combined timetable for the Maidenhead and Windsor routes was introduced, giving a regular ten-minute service from Slough to London, of which four coaches went to Charing Cross and two to Oxford Circus and Poland Street Coach Station. Both routes of course, had interchange to the Underground for London passengers. Those on the Windsor route changed at Hammersmith, and those on the Maidenhead route at Shepherds Bush (Central Line) station.

At this time the company was becoming a little concerned about the number of coaches which terminated their journeys in the section of Regent Street between Mortimer Street and Oxford Circus. Admittedly, they were not the only company which terminated there, but they had more services operating through that point than other operators, in addition to which they had further services on the drawing board, some of which, if terminated in London, would also have to use Oxford Circus as their terminal point. Although the Charing Cross terminal on the Embankment was free of traffic congestion, it was an unpleasant spot for passengers awaiting coaches, especially on wet and windy days.

The company purchased an old brewery site in Broadwick Street, south of Oxford Street, it being on an island site formed by Broadwick Street, Lexington Street and Ingestre Place, on which a coach station was erected.

Plans were also made at the same time to link as many routes as possible to form cross-London services and thus avoid the problem of terminating in London. A list of these proposed routes will be found in Appendix 'C' at the end of the book, but the writer would like to discuss some of the proposals as they incorporated several ideas, some of which came into operation at a later date but in a different form. It was proposed that the Windsor via Staines route would be extended from Oxford Circus to Dartford, opening up a new link in the South-Eastern suburbs.

The Windsor via Slough service was to be extended from Charing Cross, giving a fifteen minute service as far as Lewisham (a proposal which did not come into effect until 1946). After Lewisham, two coaches an hour were proposed to Orpington. The choice of this point as a terminal is very interesting for two reasons. Presumably, Orpington would have been reached via Eltham, Chislehurst and Petts Wood, as the road through Farnborough would have been served by two coaches an hour to Tunbridge Wells, plus two coaches an hour to Sevenoaks under the new proposals. The second reason was, where would the terminal be at Orpington? Admittedly, there was not the vehicular traffic through the town that there is today. The coaches could have turned at the War Memorial and stood in the High Street facing north, but the High Street is none too wide at that point. The East Surrey buses on Route 407 ended their journeys at that time at 'The Maxwell Hotel' by the railway station bridge, but the writer has the feeling that the Southern Railway would not have taken too kindly to a competing coach service from London using its forecourt to reverse its vehicles.

The other two coaches from Lewisham are shown as proceeding to Sidcup hourly and Farningham hourly. The separation of these terminals in the proposals seems to indicate that they would take separate routes as far as Sidcup. The writer presumes that the coaches to Sidcup would proceed via the 21 bus route and terminate at 'The Black Horse', whilst the Farningham coaches would turn off from Eltham Road along the Sidcup-by-Pass to speed the journey up a bit.

It was proposed that the Maidenhead service should continue from Oxford Circus as a half-hourly service to Westerham Hill (Fox and Hounds) and hourly to Sevenoaks. This proposal was evidently intended to operate come what may, as the tickets for it were printed and used on the two separate services.

The service from Tunbridge Wells was to have been projected from Oxford Circus to Uxbridge with a half-

A.E.C. T-type coach in East Surrey Traction Company livery on Victoria Embankment on the Dorking route. (W. N. Jackson).

A.E.C. T-type coach at Charing Cross (Embankment) en route to Windsor. (W. N. Jackson).

↑ A.E.C. T-type coach at Charing Cross (Embankment) at the commencement of the service to Windsor. Note the makeshift crew uniforms. (W. N. Jackson).

A.E.C. T-type coach in the livery of Autocar Services Limited, at Oxford Circus on their route to Tunbridge Wells. (C. F. Klapper).

A.E.C. T-type coach at Golders Green Station on Route V to Watford. (J. F. Higham).

A.E.C. T-type coach in the livery of the East Surrey Traction Company at Redhill on the London route. (McCall Collection).

First A.E.C. T-type coach to appear in Green Line livery outside 55 Broadway, S.W.1, for inspection by Lord Ashfield and senior officials of the Company. (E. N. Osborne).

Ex-L.G.O.C. A.E.C. 'Reliance' all-weather coach in Green Line livery. (J. F. Higham).

← *A.E.C. 'Regal' coach, formerly owned by East Surrey, now in Green Line livery. Taking its layover near Poland Street Coach Station. (J. F. Higham).*

A.E.C. T-type coach en route to Edenbridge to Great Scotland Yard. (C. F. Klapper).

A.E.C. T-type at Great Scotland Yard on Route A to Dartford. (E. G. P. Masterman).

A.E.C. T-type coach leaving Poland Street Coach Station for Hertford. (McCall Collection).

← A.E.C. T-type coach at Bush House (Aldwych) en route to Guildford. (McCall Collection).

A.E.C. 'Regal' coach, formerly owned by East Surrey, now in Green Line livery. At Sunbury Common on Route S. (J. F. Higham).

hourly service, and also strengthened from Sevenoaks with a further half-hourly service which would go on beyond Uxbridge to divide at Gerrards Cross to form an hourly service to Amersham via The Chalfonts and an hourly service to High Wycombe and West Wycombe.

The Uxbridge area would also have received a further three coaches an hour under the proposals, as an hourly service terminating at Uxbridge was proposed from Caterham-on-the-Hill, plus the route from Edenbridge, which it was proposed to run hourly to Chelsham Garage, then half-hourly to Gerrards Cross, where it would divide as an hourly service to Amersham and Beaconsfield respectively.

The Redhill service, which at that time, had not been extended to Crawley, was to open a new facility in the North-West, the proposal being to extend it half-hourly to Northwood (Maxwell Hotel), with one coach an hour carrying on to Chesham via Rickmansworth, Chorleywood and Chalfont Station. If this proposal had become effective, it would have been a most useful facility for Chesham people, as, whichever way they went to London at that time, they always had to change at one point or another. The town was on a branch line of the Metropolitan Railway, and it was necessary to change trains at Chalfont & Latimer, whilst the West London Coach service serviced Chesham by a shuttle coach, passengers changing coaches at Amersham.

An interesting proposal for a coach service in the North West sector was the proposal for an hourly service from Caterham-on-the-Hill to Harrow Weald, an area which never was served by a Green Line route. Presumably, the terminus would have been at Harrow Weald bus garage, but the route it would have followed from London remains a mystery lost in the mists of time. The writer favours the Harrow Road, Wembley, Sudbury, Harrow and Wealdstone, although an alternative would have been along the Edgware Road, Canons Park and Stanmore.

The East Grinstead route was to have been combined with the Tring route, providing a half-hourly service to Two Waters, where one coach an hour would proceed to Hemel Hempstead, the other running via Berkhamsted and Northchurch to Tring. Arriving here, one coach every two hours would be further extended to Wendover, serving the R.A.F. station at Halton on the way. It is strange to think that part of this plan was subsequently introduced many years later. East Grinstead – Hemel Hempstead was the route of Service 708 from 1946 to 1977, when it was extended to Tring and Aylesbury, not Wendover.

Watford was to be served by two half-hourly services, both running through to Surrey. One was to be more like an express bus route through London to Belmont Station in Surrey. The other, also half-hourly, would have made a 15-minute service with the above route as far as Kennington Oval, where it would have turned off through Brixton and Croydon to Chelsham Garage, where one coach an hour would have carried on to Oxted, which would have given that town a half-hourly service together with the proposed hourly coach from Edenbridge to Amersham. No mention is made in the report of the fate of the Watford – Golders Green coach service, and it is presumed that this would have operated in addition to the two routes mentioned above.

The Dorking route was to have been extended to St. Albans every half-hour, where the service would have diverged hourly to Dunstable and hourly to Wheathampstead. The reason for such a strange terminus as Wheathampstead is that Harpenden and Luton were already well served by Strawhatter Coaches and Venture Transport. The route between St. Albans and Dorking was finally brought into operation when Green Line routes 712 and 713 were started in 1946.

The Reigate route was to be combined with the Welwyn Garden City route and extended half-hourly to Stevenage, where one coach per hour would have gone on to Baldock via Hitchin and Letchworth, while the other coach would also have gone to Baldock, but via Graveley and the A1 road. The route via Hitchin and Letchworth would have competed with the Queen Line service and when it finally came into operation was half-hourly to Hitchin only.

At first, it was proposed that the Guildford route should be extended from Oxford Circus to Hertford with a half-hourly service to Ware, where one coach per hour would go to Hertford, the other would have proceeded to Royston via Wadesmill, Collier's End, Puckeridge, Westmill, Buntingford, Chipping, Buckland and Reed. This would have been a most useful facility, since many communities in that area were some distance from a railway station. However, after some reflection, it was decided that the Guildford service should be linked with that to Bishops Stortford, and Royston and Hertford were to have been linked with the Chertsey route, which had originally been intended to run to Bishops Stortford.

A new cross-London route serving areas which at that time had no service by Green Line was the proposal to link Ongar with West Byfleet.

Tickets were printed and a timetable folder produced for a new cross-London route from Uxbridge to East Grinstead, which seems to show that the routes listed in Appendix 'C' were only tentative proposals.

Five routes have not been mentioned in the above proposals, these being, Ascot, Sunningdale, Great Bookham, Brentwood and the Watford – Golders Green service. Presumably, the first three were intended to end their journeys in the new coach station, and the Brentwood service would remain at its old terminus outside Charing Cross (now Embankment) station.

With six coaches per hour proposed to run from Watford to the centre of London, presumably the Watford – Golders Green service was considered to be unnecessary and would have been withdrawn, whilst with only three services to find terminals for in central London, one wonders why it was necessary to build the coach station. Of course, it is possible that, bearing in mind the fact that the company had applied for licences in towns as far away as Cambridge, Bedford and Reading, there would have been some need for it. Also, it is quite possible that the cross-London routes would have been worked through Poland Street.

All this, of course, is pure speculation, and when the first cross-London routes came into operation, only one of the original proposals came into operation, this being the Hitchin – London – Reigate route.

To turn to events which actually happened, another service was introduced by East Surrey on 22 October 1930. The route ran from Oxford Circus to Chelsham Garage half-hourly, with a coach every two hours continuing via Botley Hill and Titsey Park to Oxted. The route followed the Godstone service to South Croydon, where it diverged via Selsdon, Sanderstead and Warlingham to Chelsham. Operation was started with L.G.O.C. all-weather Reliance coaches bearing the Green Line fleet name.

The winter was now approaching, and whilst the East Surrey, Autocar and National operations were crewed by staff wearing the uniforms of those undertakings, the staff at depots directly controlled by Green Line were merely issued with dustcoats and uniform caps with a small metal badge bearing the letter 'G', which had formerly been issued to staff in the L.G.O.C. Private Hire section. Timekeepers and inspectors wore ordinary civilian suits with an armband reading 'Green Line', plus a small circular badge in their lapel bearing the legend: 'GREEN LINE – OFFICIAL' and a number as well in case passengers wished to lay a complaint against the official in question. All this was altered on 12 November, when drivers, conductors and inspectors were issued with a smart new uniform in green worsted, plus badges of two different types according to the rank of the wearer. By this time also, most of the coaches were now in Green Line livery.

On the same date as the uniform issue, East Surrey extended alternate coaches on the London – Redhill route to Crawley via Salfords, Horley and Lowfield Heath, giving an hourly service along this stretch of road. In addition to this, an hourly service was commenced from Oxford Circus to East Grinstead, which, unlike the present route which follows the valley road through Kenley and Whyteleafe to Caterham, ran via Purley, Stoats Nest Road, Coulsdon Common and Caterham-on-the-Hill. This route was worked by Green Line coaches from the commencement, and required five coaches to work it, these being stabled in the East Surrey garage in Garland Road, East Grinstead.

The National Omnibus and Transport Company was responsible for the next new operation, which comprised an hourly service from Charing Cross (Embankment) to Hertford. Started on 22 November, it followed the same route as the Bishops Stortford service as far as Manor House, where it turned along Green Lanes through Wood Green and Palmers Green to Enfield and Ponders End, where it joined the main Hertford Road. The hourly service did not last for long, and when further coaches became available, it was stepped up to half-hourly (every 20 minutes during weekday rush hours) before the end of the year.

Alterations were made to the Ascot and Sunningdale routes on 29 November, when the Ascot route was withdrawn between Hyde Park Corner and Oxford Circus and diverted to Charing Cross, thus sharing a common terminal with the Sunningdale route, and giving a joint half-hourly frequency as far as Virginia Water. In addition, both routes were diverted between Hounslow Heath and Staines to run via Feltham and Ashford (Middlesex) to rejoin the main road at the Stanwell Road junction and leaving the Windsor via Staines route to service the Bedfont area.

From 6 December, the Oxted route underwent a change. The half-hourly service was retained between London and Chelsham Garage, but, instead of a two-hourly service to Oxted, a coach every hour now served that town, and in addition, was extended via Limpsfield, The Chart, Kent Hatch and Crockham Hill to Edenbridge, where they terminated at 'The Star' public house.

Four days later the first through-London operations were introduced, when the Harpenden – Charing Cross service was combined with the Oxford Circus – Great Bookham route and the Welwyn Garden City – Charing Cross route was linked with the Oxford Circus – Reigate route. All the coaches on these two services now bore the Green Line fleet name, and a peculiarity in the working of this type of route at that time was the fact that coaches from the southern terminals showed 'LONDON' as their destination until they reached Clapham Common, when the blind was altered to show the respective northern terminals. In the opposite direction, 'LONDON' was shown until the coach reached Golders Green, where the blind was altered to show the Surrey terminal.

Christmas Day seems to be a strange time of the year on which to introduce new ideas, but the new Coach Station in Poland Street was opened on that day in 1930, the Guildford and Windsor via Staines routes being the first to use it.

Hitherto, the T-type A.E.C. Regal coaches used by Green Line had all been 27-seat rear-entrance vehicles, but, on the same day as the new coach station opened, a new 30-seat front-entrance A.E.C. Regal coach also classified as T-type, made its appearance on the road.

Whilst we are talking about Christmas Day, it is interesting to note that in the early days of Green Line operation it was the practice to operate a service all day, and not just until 4 pm only, as was the case on most local bus services in the London area at that time. Later, coaches ran up to 4 pm, after which there were only one or two journeys operated in the late evening, usually terminating in Central London.

These Christmas Day innovations marked the end of the Company's activities for 1930, and it is a good point at which to take stock of what it had achieved in the five months it had been in existence. It now had no fewer than 24 routes in operation, requiring 160 coaches to cover the daily scheduled requirements, and, allowing for two spare vehicles at the very least to be held at each garage to cover docking and emergency requirements, the fleet strength was over 200 vehicles. This was not enough, particularly on summer weekends when relief coaches were needed to carry the heavy traffic, and it was usual to see Autocar, National and East Surrey buses pressed into service, bearing labels reading 'On Hire to Green Line Coaches Limited'.

After the passing of the Road Traffic Act (1930), a date was set by the Minister of Transport (9 February 1931), after which no new service should start without a Road Service Licence, and only those routes which had been established before that date could plead an established facility as a basis for their application to the Traffic Commissioners for such a licence.

In November 1930, an agreement was made with the Maidstone and District Motor Services for joint operations on the Gravesend route, and as far as Farningham on the Maidstone road; traffic beyond Farningham was to be left to the Maidstone company. In actual fact, this agreement does not seem to have been followed up.

Two cross-country routes were planned at this time, one from Dartford to Guildford via Hawley, Sutton-at-Home, Farningham, Eynsford, Otford, Sevenoaks, Westerham, Oxted, Godstone, Redhill, Reigate, Dorking, Shere, Newlands Corner, and Merrow. The other was to start at Guildford and run via Woking, Chertsey, Staines, Egham, Windsor, Uxbridge, Denham, Rickmansworth, Watford and Garston to St. Albans. Local licences for these routes were granted, but lack of coaches prevented opera-

T-type A.E.C. coach (T69) in Amersham & District livery at Oxford Circus on London – Amersham route. (D. W. K. Jones).

A.E.C. T-type coach on layover at Oxford Circus in 1930. (E. G. P. Masterman).

A.E.C. T-type coach in the livery of the Amersham and District Omnibus Company outside Amersham Garage. (J. F. Higham).

Ex-L.G.O.C. All-weather A.E.C. coach in Green Line livery outside Brixton Hill Coach Garage (E. G. P. Masterman).

A.E.C. T-type coach on Route Z at Windsor. The present Windsor Garage is under construction in the background. (J. F. Higham).

A.E.C. T-type coach (on hire to Regent Motor Services) taking its layover near Poland Street Coach Station. (J. F. Higham).

tion being introduced prior to the February 1931 deadline, and the project was not pursued thereafter. When Green Line resumed operation after the war, in 1946, the number 719, which was vacant until 1956, was to have been used for a cross-country route from Guildford to Luton which would have followed the route mentioned above.

1931 started with a rush to get new services on the road before the Ministry of Transport deadline date.

On 4 January, the Maidenhead route was diverted into Poland Street Coach Station, followed a week later by the Chertsey, Ascot and Sunningdale routes.

14 January was a busy day for the road officials of Green Line. The Dorking, Edenbridge, East Grinstead, Hertford, Sevenoaks and Tunbridge Wells routes were diverted into Poland Street, where a one-way system had been adopted for coaches entering and leaving the station. Coaches coming in ran via Great Marlborough Street and Poland Street and outwards via Broadwick Street, Berwick Street and Oxford Street. No less than 25 coaches per hour followed these routes and the congestion caused in the narrow streets around the coach station must have been the despair of the local police authorities.

Experimental double-deck A.E.C. coach at Charing Cross (Embankment) en route to Bushey. (J. F. Higham).

A.E.C. T-type coach in Northumberland Avenue (Charing Cross) en route to Great Bookham. (W. N. Jackson).

Leyland PLSC3 coach, formerly owned by Associated Coaches (Ongar) Limited now owned by Green Line, but on hire to Skylark Motor Coach Company, and working their Wycombe route. (J. F. Higham).

Dennis 'Arrow' coach, formerly owned by Red Rover, at Marble Arch on Route AT to Aylesbury. (J. F. Higham).

A.E.C. T-type coach on Route D to Sunbury about to depart from Horse Guards Avenue. Note the original type of Green Line stop-post and sign. (C. F. Klapper).

Ex-Regent Motor Services Gilford 1660T coach at Kings Cross on Route CF to Hertford. (J. F. Higham).

Maudslay coach, formerly owned by Bucks Express, leaving the Bucks Garage, Watford High Street for London. (J. F. Higham).

On the same date the East Grinstead route was diverted at Purley to run via Kenley and Whyteleafe to Caterham, and three more cross-London services commenced operation. The Godstone Green – Oxford Circus and the Charing Cross – Tring routes were combined to form a through route, whilst the Crawley – Oxford Circus route was extended to Bushey Station via Kilburn, Edgware and Stanmore.

The third cross-London route provided a completely new facility, running as it did from Caterham Station to Hemel Hempstead via Caterham-on-the-Hill, Croydon, Streatham, Brixton, Charing Cross, Oxford Circus, Kilburn, Edgware, Bushey, Kings Langley and Two Waters every hour. Like the Tring service, it ran express from Bushey Station to Grovemill Lane, owing to the Watford licensing difficulties, and was operated by two coaches from Godstone Garage and four from Watford (Leavesden Road).

A further cross-London service was introduced on 28 January, when the Ascot and Sunningdale routes were withdrawn between Piccadilly Circus and Poland Street and extended via Charing Cross, Elephant and Castle, New Cross, Blackheath, Shooters Hill, Welling, Bexleyheath and Crayford to Dartford. From the western end, this route was worked by the Staines depot, but, as neither Green Line or East Surrey had a garage at Dartford, the coaches starting work from the eastern end were based on the East Surrey garage at Swanley until the L.G.O.C. garage and local bus services in the Crayford area were handed over to the East Surrey company later in the year.

On the same date, the Windsor via Staines route, which had been running between Isleworth and Gunnersbury via Syon Lane and the Great West Road, was diverted through Brentford for some unknown reason.

Three days later on 31 January, four new routes were introduced. The first, operated by East Surrey, was an hourly operation from Farningham to Poland Street via Swanley Junction, Sidcup, Eltham, Lewisham, New Cross and Elephant & Castle. The other three were started by Green Line itself and consisted of three half-hourly services from Poland Street Coach Station to Rickmansworth, Sunbury Common and West Byfleet respectively.

The Rickmansworth route followed the Harrow Road through Kensal Green, Harlesden, Wembley and Sudbury to Harrow-on-the-Hill and thence via Pinner and Northwood, competing with West London Coaches whose Aylesbury service followed the same route. The Rickmansworth Council had refused Green Line licences to ply for hire within their area, and passengers could not board coaches unless they had obtained their ticket from a booking agent in the town beforehand. Six coaches were required for the operation of this route, these being based at Watford (Leavesden Road) garage, the coaches running to and from the garage out of service.

The West Byfleet route was interworked with the Guildford route from Poland Street Coach Station, and jointly they gave a 15-minute headway to Cobham (Paines Hill), where the Byfleet coaches diverged to run via Byfleet Road, Byfleet High Road and Parvis Road to terminate at West Byfleet Corner. It was intended for this route to have gone on to Woking via Old Woking and Maybury, but the Woking Urban District Council refused the necessary licences. The vehicles for this service, which required six coaches, were based at the Metro-Cammell Weymann works at Addlestone, and worked in service to Byfleet via New Haw, and a minimum fare of 1/- (5p) was charged over this section.

The Sunbury Common and Chertsey routes were interworked from Poland Street Coach Station to Kingston, giving a 15-minute joint service to that riverside town. From Kingston, the Sunbury Common route then ran via Hampton Court, Hampton, Kempton Park and Sunbury Cross to terminate at 'The Black Dog' at Sunbury Common. As Green Line did not have a garage nearer than Staines, the six coaches for this service were stabled in a yard at Cantrell and Cochrane's mineral water works in Hanworth Road, Sunbury.

Two days before the Ministry deadline of 9 February 1931, a new service was started from Poland Street Coach Station to Uxbridge. It had been intended for this route to provide a half-hourly service to Beaconsfield, which had been advertised as such in the advance publicity. Unfortunately, the necessary coaches were late in delivery and it was decided to work the service as far as Uxbridge only, in order to get it into operation before the deadline. Once again, Green Line had no operating base in the area and the five coaches for this route were based at the A.E.C. works at Southall, it being the duty of one of the depot clerks from Watford High Street garage to motor-cycle over to Southall every day to collect and bank the previous day's takings.

The deadline date had now been reached, but despite this fact, Green Line carried on with the programme it had decided upon. On 18 February, the Godstone Green – Tring route was extended to Aylesbury, still on an hourly basis, and three days later, a new hourly service was introduced between Charing Cross and Upminster via Aldgate, Poplar, East Ham, Barking, Becontree Heath and Hornchurch. The Upminster terminus was at 'The Bell Hotel', a somewhat congested point, and a week later, the route was extended eastwards to terminate at 'The Thatched House' and the service increased to half-hourly. It had been proposed that an alternative service was to be introduced, also between Charing Cross and Upminster, but via Stratford, Ilford and Romford, and this was advertised to commence operation on 25 February, but never materialised, and the writer suspects that the coaches for this proposed service were used to increase the service on the route via Poplar.

In the meantime, Green Line had decided that it was high time that some method of distinguishing the various routes should be introduced for the convenience of the public and staff alike, and, accordingly, each route was lettered from 21 February 1931. These route letters were shown on all timetable publicity, and later, on the route boards carried on the sides of the coaches. The allocation of letters to routes is shown in Appendix 'D'.

This was the last of the new developments for the time being, as Green Line now had to concentrate on preparing applications for Road Service Licences to continue operation of its existing services. How their applications were received and dealt with by the Traffic Commissioners and the subsequent Committee of Enquiry into London Motor Coach services will be discussed in the next chapter, and it is proposed to continue this one by discussing the remaining events in the story of Green Line as a private company up to its takeover by the London Passenger Transport Board on 1 July 1933.

At the end of February 1931, the Company announced that it had 28 routes in operation, requiring 196 coaches for the day-to-day operation, and that its fleet strength was 226 coaches.

On 1 April 1931, the recent extension of Route T from Tring to Aylesbury, plus the new Route AV from Charing Cross to Upminster were both withdrawn pending the decision of the Traffic Commissioners on the Company's application to operate them. The Ministry of Transport had issued an order that, as these two operations had started after the deadline date, they should be withdrawn after 31 March 1931.

A useful facility for ramblers was introduced on 21 June 1931, when return tickets issued from London were accepted for the return journey on any route and from any farestage of the same or lower fare than the ticket held by the passenger.

Hitherto all vehicles operated by Green Line had been single-deckers, except on busy weekends, when double-deck buses owned by the various companies responsible for the operation of Green Line were used on reliefs to help clear the queues, but on 22 September 1931, an experimental double-deck vehicle was brought into operation on Route E (Bushey – London – Crawley). Numbered LT 1137, it was an A.E.C. 'Renown' six-wheel vehicle, which, with the luxury body it carried, seemed to the writer to be even larger than its contemporaries which were in service on the London bus routes, although it only seated 50 passengers. It had a front entrance, but the staircase to the upper deck was situated at the rear of the vehicle. It stayed on Route E until that route was withdrawn in October 1933, after which it worked for a time on Routes I and J from Leavesden Road (Watford), before being transferred to St. Albans for use as a Country bus.

Green Line received further valuable publicity when coach T 219 appeared in the Lord Mayor's Show on 9 November 1931. It is interesting that when it was decided to preserve a Green Line coach from the early days in London Transport's historical vehicle collection, T 219 was chosen to be preserved, and is now in the London Transport Collection.

The first independent operators to be acquired by Green Line Coaches Limited were taken over during February 1932. The Skylark Motor Coach Company Limited was acquired on the sixth of the month, bringing 19 coaches (all Gilfords; 14 of the 166SD type and 5 168SD), and three routes, all commencing their journeys at Oxford Circus, running at hourly intervals to High Wycombe, Guildford and Hertford Heath. This was followed on 20 February by the takeover of Bucks Expresses Limited of Watford, bringing in the route between Oxford Circus and Watford. This route was worked half-hourly (every 15 minutes during weekday peaks) and gave Green Line seven departures every hour (nine in peaks) from Oxford Circus and Bushey Station. A very mixed bag of coaches were taken over from the company, there being ten in all. Three were Maudslay MLB3 24-seat coaches purchased in 1929; two Gilford 1660T 29-seat vehicles also purchased in 1929; three 1680T Gilfords purchased in 1930, and two A.E.C. Regals with Dodson bodywork seating 30 passengers and acquired in 1931.

Although all future publicity was to be produced in the Green Line style and the Head Offices of the two companies were transferred to 55 Broadway, they were retained as separate operating entities from the Green Line Company, probably to avoid the necessity to apply to the Traffic Commissioners to transfer the Licences to Green Line.

The Regent Motor Service route from Oxford Circus to Hertford was the next independent to be acquired, the takeover date being 2 March 1932. An hourly service was worked to Hertford over a different route to both Green Line and Skylark, and purchase of Regent gave Green Line complete control of that route with four coaches per hour (2 Green Line; 1 Skylark and 1 Regent) operating over three differing routes from London. Four Gilfords 1660T coaches passed to Green Line, all purchased in 1929, and, although they were all vehicles of the same make, each one had a differing seating capacity, varying between 27 and 32 seats.

Once again the company was retained as a separate operating entity, although in the case of Regent, the vehicles were transferred for operation elsewhere, and replaced by standard A.E.C. T-type coaches.

Green Line commenced a new service on its own account on 24 March 1932. It had been granted a Road Service Licence for a limited stop service from Baker Street Station to Whipsnade Zoo, picking up only at Golders Green Station and Barnet Church. Three departures were operated from London on Mondays to Fridays and five on Saturdays, Sundays and Bank Holidays, and, as Whipsnade Zoo had not been open for very long, and was somewhat inaccessible from London by rail, the coach route (lettered BH) was an instant success. Through Underground and coach return tickets could be purchased at 14 of the most Central area tube stations for travel by train to Golders Green, where people could change to the coach to continue their journey. The London terminus at Baker Street Station was not a very satisfactory loading point, and from 29 March, it was transferred to Marylebone (Harewood Avenue).

The first benefits to the public of the acquisition of Skylark Motor Coaches by Green Line was felt from 25 March 1932, when return tickets on the Guildford and Hertford routes became interavailable for the return journey, despite the differing fares charged by the two companies. Strange to say, although Regent Motor Services had also been taken over by this time, and also charged differing fares, Green Line and Regent return tickets did not become interavailable for the return journey.

The month of March ended with the acquisition by Green Line of Associated Coaches (Ongar) Limited, which, it will be remembered, operated a Liverpool Street – Ongar route, thus expanding the Green Line network into Leyton, Chingford, North Weald and Ongar, and giving the company a new depot in the town of Ongar.

Although all the independent companies taken over so far had retained their titles and remained separate operating entities under Green Line control, and still continued to do so, they were allocated route letters in the Green Line series from 27 April, and details will be found at the end of Appendix D.

From 2 May 1932, return tickets issued on Green Line Route W became interavailable for the return journey on Bucks Express Route AW, with the Bucks Express tickets being accepted on Route W. Weekly and quarterly seasons from Watford and Bushey to London were also interavailable, but the monthly seasons from Watford and Bushey

Gilford 168SD coach (formerly belonging to Skylark Motor Coach Company) taking its layover outside Poland Street Coach Station. (J. F. Higham).

Maudslay coach with Strachan body (formerly owned by the Great Western Railway, but now in the Green Line fleet. On layover outside Poland Street Coach Station. (J. F. Higham).

London Transport Museum preserved coach T219 leaving Historical Commercial Vehicle Rally at Brighton.

and all types of seasons issued from Stanmore by Bucks Express were not accepted for the return journey by Green Line, as they did not issue monthly seasons at that time, neither did they have any season ticket facilities from Stanmore.

Premier Line Route E, which had competed with Green Line Route S between Sunbury Common and London was withdrawn from 13 June 1932, the Traffic Commissioners having refused a Road Service Licence for its continuance. The withdrawal was announced as temporarily pending the result of the Premier Line appeal to the Committee of Enquiry into London Motor Coach services, but, in the event, the appeal was refused, leaving the Sunbury Common road as undisputed Green Line territory.

July 1932 saw a further acquisition by Green Line. This time, it was the Blue Belle Motors route from East Grinstead to Paddington (Spring Street). The route, which was taken over on 20 July, differed from Green Line Route U, in that, between Purley and Thornton Heath it ran via Purley Way and Thornton Road, and, in London served Victoria, Hyde Park Corner and Marble Arch en route to Paddington, whereas Green Line Route U ran from Croydon into London via Brixton, Westminster and Charing Cross to Poland Street. As the Blue Belle company was continuing in the coach business with coastal trips and private hire, the Road Service Licence was transferred to Green Line, the route becoming Route AU. The farescales charged by the two companies only differed very slightly, although Blue Belle had issued early workman returns and season tickets. These facilities were withdrawn after Green Line took over, but although Green Line and Skylark return tickets were interavailable despite differing fares, return tickets issued on Routes U and AU were not interavailable.

This was followed on 22 September by the takeover of Acme Pullman Services Limited of Bishops Stortford. The company was actually acquired by the London General Omnibus Company, and handed over to its subsidiary for operation and control. The company, however, retained its separate identity, and was not even allocated a route letter in the Green Line series. This could have been due to the fact that it operated several journeys beyond Bishops Stortford as far away as Newmarket, which was well beyond the area normally served by Green Line and London General Country Services, but, on the other hand, the L.G.C.S. timetables included two Eastern National routes (13, Bishops Stortford – Saffron Walden; 13A, Bishops Stortford – Henham) over the timetables for which it stated that they were operated by L.G.C.S., so boundary difficulties could not have been the reason for retaining Acme as a separate company.

As Acme and Green Line followed differing routes into London from Epping, interavailability of return tickets was not introduced.

Green Line achieved its ambition to possess a regular service to Aylesbury when it acquired the Aylesbury – London (Marble Arch) route of Red Rover Saloon Coaches on 29 November 1932. Like Blue Belle Motors, Red Rover was continuing operation in the Aylesbury area with its route to Buckingham, and consequently the London service was merged into Green Line becoming Route AT.

A further ambition was fulfilled, that of a service to Baldock, when the Queen Line service from that town to London was taken over by Green Line from 26 April 1933. Once again, the Queen Line company was remaining in business with other coaching activities, so the Road Service Licence was transferred to Green Line, the route becoming AR in the Green Line series.

This was the last acquisition by Green Line as a private company, and, on 1 July 1933, together with all the associated companies it had acquired in the past twelve months, it became part of the new London Passenger Transport Board.

Central London Terminal Points.

(1) Marylebone (Harewood Avenue):—
Terminating – BH.

(2) Poland Street Coach Station:—
Terminating – C.D.F.G.I.
J.L.M.N.P.Q.S.U.X.Y.

(3) Bishopsgate (Hamilton House):—
Terminating – AO
ACME route to Bishops Stortford &
Newmarket also picks up in this
thoroughfare.

(4) Charing Cross (Embankment):—
Terminating – B.O.W.Z.ACME.

(4) Great Scotland Yard:—
Picking-up – A.D.E.H.I.
J.K.L. R.T.U.X.

(5) Oxford Circus:—
Terminating – AF CF BG AQ AW.
Picking-up – C.D.E.F.G.H.I.J.K.L.M.N.P.Q.R.S.
T.U.W.X. and Y.

(6) Paddington (Spring Street):—
Terminating – Route AU.

Green Line – October 1932

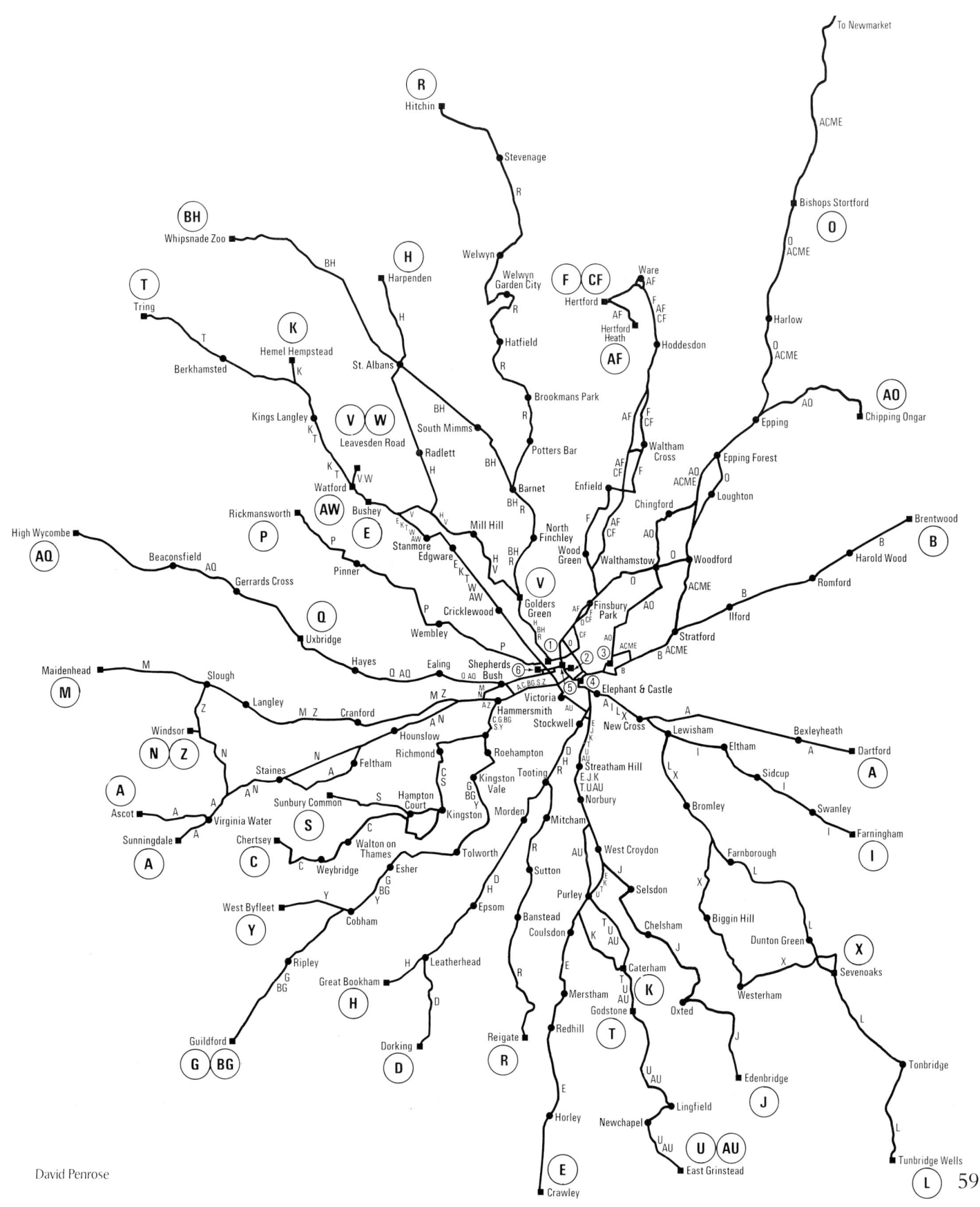

David Penrose

LICENSING SYSTEMS
CHAPTER FOUR

Before launching into the effect which the Road Traffic Act had upon the operations of Green Line and its contemporaries, it is essential to consider the Licensing system both before and after the Act became law later in 1930.

When the various coach operators commenced their operations there were two licensing systems in operation in the areas served. The first and most important was that which applied in the Metropolitan Police District, and which had its origins in the Metropolitan Stage Carriage Act of 1832, together with its subsequent amendments.

The system was administered by the Metropolitan Police, and in the opinion of the writer, was the best in existence at that time. Vehicles were given a thorough examination by a police officer from the Public Carriage Office, and if satisfactory, a licence to ply for hire was granted for twelve months (fee £2), and upon expiry of that licence, the vehicle had to be withdrawn from service, overhauled, and re-submitted to the Public Carriage Office before a further licence would be granted. Vehicles approved by the Public Carriage Office carried a square enamel-iron plate on the rear of vehicle bearing the Royal Coat of Arms and the licence number, which, by law, also had to be painted on another part of the vehicle, the position for which would be indicated by the officer inspecting the vehicle.

The Metropolitan Police were also responsible for licensing the drivers and conductors who operated the vehicles. The application form for these licences had to be accompanied by a recommendation from the proprietor or company proposing to employ the person in question, and in addition, the man himself had to satisfy the police that he was a man of good character before the licence would be granted. The licence was then renewable every year, the fee at that time being 5/- (25p).

In addition to all this, the proposed list of fares to be charged on any route the proprietor or company wished to operate, had also to be submitted for approval by the Public Carriage Office, and all copies of the fares list, which by law, had to be displayed on every vehicle working the route, bore a rubber stamp mark showing the date of approval, and the word 'Approved', together with the initials of the Commissioner of Police.

Outside the Metropolitan Police District, things were arranged much differently. In the larger towns, the municipal authorities would issue licences through the Watch Committee for the vehicles to ply for hire within their boundaries, issuing small metal plates bearing the name of the town and the licence number which were also fixed at the rear of the vehicle, and the author well remembers, in his youth, seeing coaches of the Maidstone and District and East Kent companies passing through the South London suburbs literally festooned with enamel-iron plates at the rear of the coach. However, licences were not considered to be necessary in many of the smaller towns, as will be seen from the list in Appendix 'B'.

The position was somewhat similar as far as conductors and drivers were concerned, most large towns requiring them to be licensed, while most small towns did not. Some insisted on issuing badges (the writer has seen badges issued in Reigate and Aylesbury), whilst others issued licences but no badges, particularly in the Home Counties, where, if the crew to be licensed were already in possession of a badge and licence issued by the Metropolitan Police, the display of that badge was considered sufficient evidence of their capability to be in charge of a bus or coach.

It was the usual practice for L.G.O.C. and Green Line crews to pay for their own Metropolitan Police Licence and badge, but, for any licence to be held in the outside areas, it was usual for the company to pay for such a licence which had to be held by the staff working on the route in question, and only crews holding such a licence would be allowed to work on that route. A typical example in the London area was the L.G.O.C. bus route 86 (Stratford and Brentwood), where the crews had to be licensed in the Romford Council area as well as in London. Only crews holding Romford licences at Seven Kings Garage would be allowed to work Route 86.

One thing the two licensing systems had in common was the fact that, although the vehicles and crews were licensed, no control was exercised over the routes to be operated, other than a survey to ensure that it was suitable for the type of vehicle the operator proposed to work thereon, and this lack of control led to unbridled competition, particularly on the more remunerative routes.

The Road Traffic Act (1930) was designed to clear up all these anomalies in the licensing system and to institute a firmer control over the operation of buses and coaches throughout the country, which was to be divided into Traffic Areas. Commissioners were to be appointed in these areas who would be responsible to the Minister of Transport for the issue of licences to ply for hire (to be known as Public Service Vehicle Licences), this section involving the inspection and approval of such vehicles; the issue of Road Service Licences to work bus and coach routes. These licences being split into sections according to the type of service they covered, as follows:

Stage carriage licences: These were to cover the normal city, suburban and country bus routes working at a low minimum fare.

Short stage express carriage licences: These were to cover the operations of routes of the Green Line type, where the minimum fare at that time was usually 6d (2½p) in the country areas, and a compulsory minimum fare of 1/- (5p) in the Metropolitan area of London.

Express Service Licences: These were to cover the operations of long-distance coach services, such as those which are operated from Victoria Coach Station, and which are mainly pre-booked services and do not sell tickets on the vehicles.

All these types of licences would be issued by the Traffic Commissioners concerned, and a route running through more than one area needed an application for a Road Service Licence in each area, although usually the licence issued in the other area would be known as a 'Backing Licence'. No licence would be issued without a survey of the proposed route for suitability (particularly as to the type of vehicle to be operated), and a timetable had to be submitted showing the frequency of service to be worked, also a fare table showing the fares to be charged, both of which had to be approved by the Commissioner before the licence was issued. The siting of stopping places and the licensing of crews to work the vehicles was also the responsibility of the Commissioner, although, unlike the previous system, if a conductor or driver was licensed in one Traffic area, he could also work in other traffic areas without the need to display a different badge or purchase a separate licence.

Traffic courts were to be set up at which all applications for Road Service Licences to operate the various routes would be considered, and where objections to the proposed operations could be raised, such matters being considered by the Traffic Commissioners before the licence was issued or refused. Appeals against refusal could be made to the Minister of Transport, whose decision for or against was final. This, of course, is the system which is in operation at the present time, and which has proved to be a protection both to the operator and the travelling public.

Obviously, time had to be allowed for the system to be set up, and the Traffic Commissioners and their staff to be appointed. The various operators also needed time to prepare their applications for the new Road Service Licences necessary to continue their existing services, and the Minister of Transport set a date (9 February 1931) after which no new route could start without a Road Service Licence, and only routes established before that date could plead an established facility as a basis for their applications to the Commissioners for a licence to continue operating the route in question.

Having read the previous chapters dealing with the build-up of operations by Green Line and its contemporaries, the reader will have realised that the number of coaches running in the Metropolitan Police District had grown very rapidly. The police stated that 347 coaches had been licensed to ply for hire in the district in 1928. By 1929, the figure had more than doubled to 811. It more than doubled again in 1930 when 1,762 coaches were licensed.

When the Metropolitan Stage Carriage Act was introduced in 1832 it only applied to vehicles which plied for hire along the London streets and whose passengers paid their fares on the vehicles. It will be remembered that railways were in their infancy at that time, and that communication between London and the provinces was by stage coach whose passengers had to purchase their seats and tickets in advance from a booking office. These coaches therefore, were not subject to the provisions of the 1832 Act.

The last regular stage coach service was in operation from London in 1895, but whilst motor coaches had been operating summer daily services to the coast since 1921, as the tickets were purchased from a booking-office and not on the coaches, they also were not subject to the 1832 Act, so it is possible that the actual number of coaches operating in the Police District was much higher, especially as many of the earlier operators who commenced short-stage express coach services from London to the Home Counties in the period between 1928 and 1930, did not sell tickets on the vehicles in the London area, thus avoiding the necessity for Stage Carriage plates. The Road Traffic Act cleared up this ambiguity, and brought 'express carriages', as coaches conveying passengers at separate fares of not less than 1/- (5p) within the licensing procedure.

A further census was taken in London in September 1930, which showed that over 3,500 coaches were operated in each direction in the central area of the metropolis on the two Saturdays in the period during which the census was taken, and two months later, the Minister of Transport gave notice that he proposed to make restrictive practices in order to alleviate the situation. Naturally, much opposition to the proposals was generated among the operators, and, as a result, the Minister gave general directions to the Metropolitan Traffic Commissioner appointed under the 1930 Act. On 5 January 1932, the Commissioner stated his future policy in which he said that the proper function of motor coaches was to supplement the railways and serve places which were unserved by train. He also said that coaches should run to the fringe of the central area of London, where passengers could change to other forms of transport.

There was another outcry, particularly from Green Line and the other short-distance coach operators, many of whom terminated their routes at points such as Oxford Circus, Aldwych and Charing Cross (Embankment), and whom, in so doing, gained much of their revenue and traffic from the fact that they traversed the main shopping and theatre areas of Central London.

On 30 January 1932 the Minister appointed a Committee of Enquiry into London Motor Coach Services under the chairmanship of Lord Amulree, which heard evidence from the operators and also from those persons who objected to the operation of coach services in the central area. Two reports were issued, the first in June 1932, which recommended the Minister to restrict coaches from the more congested central areas, urging the provision of coach terminals off the streets, as a result of which the present routes followed by coaches to and from Victoria Coach Station, and those traversed by Green Line through Central London, were introduced. The second report, issued in August, mainly dealt with the Appeals against refusal and modification of Road Service Licences by the Traffic Commissioners which had been passed to the Committee for consideration and for recommendations to be made to the Minister, to whom the Appeals had been made in the first instance.

Grey Coaches Limited of Peckham, who operated a daily service from King's Cross to Brighton, crossing the Central Area via Charing Cross and Victoria, appealed to the Minister against a decision of the Metropolitan Traffic Commissioner in respect of their route, the Appeal being dismissed without a hearing. The Motor Hirers and Coach Services Association, of which Grey Coaches was a member, took the matter to High Court, and were granted a rule nisi against the Traffic Commissioner and the Minister to show cause why the Grey Coaches appeal should not be heard.

This Appeal against a decision of the Traffic Commissioners and the method in which it was heard, was intended as a test case regarding the validity of the action of the Ministry of Transport in dealing with Appeals of motor coach operators in the London District.

In view of the rule nisi the Minister abandoned his intention to make formal decisions on the lines recommended by the Amulree Committee of Enquiry effective on 19 September 1932, and coach services operating on that date were confirmed as continuing to operate as before.

Therefore the proposals made by the Traffic Commissioners and the Committee of Enquiry did not come into operation until October 1933, three months after the London Passenger Transport Board had been formed and had taken over the Green Line organisation and its associated companies.

Although the original decisions made by the two bodies did not come into effect until the date stated above, and then in a different route network to that which had been decided originally, the writer feels that they are of interest and will discuss them in the next chapter.

Q-type Green Line coach held up in rush-hour traffic in Oxford Street. Traffic congestion caused havoc with timetables.

THE ROAD TRAFFIC ACT:

The short distance coach operators, including Green Line Coaches Limited, set about preparing their applications in the latter half of 1930. For most of them it was a simple matter, as they only operated one route, and it was merely a matter of submitting a copy of the existing time and faretables, plus details of any relief services they wished to work at busy periods, but Green Line had 26 routes in operation at the time. In addition, they had not completed the full network which they had intended to operate, and they proposed several alterations to some of the existing routes. No change to the route or frequency of service were proposed to the following routes (for their destinations and frequencies see Appendix D):

Routes A. B. C. D. F. G. I. J. K. L. M. N. O. S. U. V. W. and Z.

Alterations were proposed to the following routes:

Route E: Crawley – London – Bushey: It was proposed to extend this route from Bushey Station to Watford (Leavesden Road).

Route H: Great Bookham – London – Harpenden: It was proposed to alter this route at both ends. At the southern end, it was proposed to extend it to Guildford via Effingham, The Horsleys and Merrow half-hourly. At the northern end, it was proposed that the half-hourly service should operate to St. Albans, where it would split to form an hourly service to Luton and Dunstable respectively.

Route P: London (Poland Street) – Rickmansworth: A half-hourly service was proposed as far as Rickmansworth, with one coach per hour continuing via Chorleywood,

Chalfont Station, Amersham-on-the-Hill and Chesham Bois to Chesham Broadway.

Route Q: London (Poland Street) – Uxbridge: It was proposed that Route Q should be extended half-hourly to Gerrards Cross, where one coach per hour would carry on via Beaconsfield to High Wycombe, with the other timing running via The Chalfonts and Amersham to Chesham. Presumably, if permission had been granted for this operation, the associated Amersham and District company would have withdrawn its service over the same route.

Route R: Reigate – London – Hitchin: This service was running as a half-hourly operation throughout, and Green Line proposed a 30-minute service to Stevenage, where one coach per hour would continue to Hitchin, with the other running to Baldock via the Great North Road and Graveley.

Route T: Godstone – London – Tring: Green Line applied to resume the operation of this route to Aylesbury. It will be remembered that Route T had been extended to this point on 18 February 1931, but the extension had been withdrawn by order of the Ministry of Transport as it had started nine days after the deadline date.

Route X: London – Sevenoaks (via Westerham): This route was operating at an hourly frequency, and Green Line applied to vary the frequency and to provide a half-hourly service from London to Westerham Hill, with one coach per hour projected to Sevenoaks.

Route Y: London (Poland Street) – West Byfleet: This route was operating on a half-hourly frequency, and Green Line applied to operate a half-hourly service from London to Esher, where one coach per hour would proceed via Cobham, Paines Hill and Byfleet to Woking, whilst the other hourly service would also proceed to Woking but via Hersham, Weybridge and Byfleet.

Green Line were granted Road Service Licences for only seven routes without modifications, these being:

Route A. Ascot or Sunningdale – London – Dartford.
B. Brentwood.
D. Dorking.
J. Edenbridge.
S. Sunbury Common.
U. East Grinstead.
W. Watford – Charing Cross.

Road Service Licences were refused for no fewer than eleven routes, two of which were cross-London services:

Route K. Hemel Hempstead – London – Caterham.
T. Tring – London – Godstone Green.
F. Hertford.
G. Guildford.
I. Farningham.
M. Maidenhead.
N. Windsor (via Staines).
P. Rickmansworth.
Q. Uxbridge.
V. Watford – Golders Green.
Z. Windsor via Slough.

From the above list it will be seen that Green Line would have lost the lucrative routes to Windsor, Maidenhead, Hertford and Guildford. In view of the Metropolitan Traffic Commissioners statement on 5 January 1932 (see Chapter Four), the writer fails to see why he reversed his policy by refusing licences for Routes G and I. In the case of Route G, after leaving Esher it served communities which were a considerable distance from a railway station. In the case of Route I, after leaving New Eltham, the only railway station it passed was Swanley Junction, as the station at Sidcup was some distance from the town itself, whilst Farningham was nearly two miles from Farningham Road Station. He was also reversing his policy when refusing a licence for Route V (Watford – Golders Green), which did not penetrate the congested Central area of London.

Eight routes were granted Road Services Licences with some form of modification, as under:

Route C: Chertsey: Green Line had applied for continuance of the half-hourly service on this route. The Commissioner varies this to a half-hourly service to Weybridge, with one coach per hour proceeding to Chertsey, the other to Woking via Weybridge Station, Byfleet, West Byfleet and Maybury, an action which could not have pleased the Southern Railway.

Route E: Crawley, London, Bushey: It will be remembered that the Company when applying for continuance of this service had also asked to extend the route to Watford (Leavesden Road), presumably to avoid the necessity for 'dead' mileage to and from the garage when entering service. The southern section from Crawley to London was granted a licence, but the section from London to Bushey, plus the proposed extension to Watford, was refused.

Route H: Great Bookham, London, Harpenden: When applying to continue the operation of this route, Green Line had applied to extend it at the southern end over bus route 408 to Guildford, and at the northern end to split the half-hourly service at St. Albans, one timing to proceed to Luton, the other to Dunstable. A licence was granted for the northern end for an hourly service to Dunstable, plus an hourly service to Harpenden only. The whole of the southern end, including the proposed extension to Guildford, was refused a Licence, the Commissioner considering that the railway and bus facilities between Great Bookham and Guildford were quite sufficient to meet the public need.

Route L: Tunbridge Wells: Here, the company had applied to continue the existing half-hourly service on this route. The competing company (Redcar Services Limited) had been granted a licence for an hourly service, and accordingly, the Commissioner, in granting a licence to Green Line to continue operating, reduced the service to hourly.

Route O: Bishops Stortford: Once again, Green Line had applied for the continuance of the half-hourly service on this route, which followed a different route between Charing Cross and Woodford Green, and again between that point and 'The Wake Arms', Epping Forest to that followed by the competing service operated by Acme Pullman Services Limited. Whilst the Commissioner took this fact into consideration, he only granted Green Line a licence for a half-hourly service to Epping, deeming the Acme service to Bishops Stortford as sufficient to meet the needs of the public between Epping and that town.

Route R: Reigate, London, Hitchin: At the time Green Line was preparing its application to continue this operation, it was working a half-hourly service throughout the length of the route, which was more than adequate beyond Stevenage, bearing in mind that Hitchin was also served by Birch Brothers Limited, Baldock Transport and Beaumont Saloon Coaches. In view of this, when asking for continuance, Green Line proposed to vary the operation by maintaining a half-hourly service to Stevenage, with one coach per hour proceeding to Hitchin, and the other operating to Baldock via Graveley and the Great North Road to avoid competition with the Baldock Transport Service which ran via Letchworth. The Commissioner thought differently however, considering that there was no public need for the Green Line service north of Welwyn Garden City, to which point he granted Green Line a half-hourly service from Reigate.

Route X: Sevenoaks (via Westerham): In applying for the continuance of this service, Green Line applied to vary the timings to give a half-hourly operation to Westerham Hill (instead of hourly), with alternate journeys operating to Sevenoaks, except in the early mornings and late evenings when the service would be increased to half-hourly to Sevenoaks in order that the coaches could return to Dunton Green Garage without the necessity to operate excessive 'Dead' mileage. The Traffic Commissioner granted a licence for the service to continue, but as an hourly service from London to Westerham Hill only.

If all these decisions had been accepted by Green Line without any protest, the number of destinations served by the Company would have been considerably reduced, and the writer estimates that, instead of the 226 coaches needed to work the existing services, approximately 150 vehicles (including spares) would have been sufficient to work the remaining network. At least 76 coaches would become surplus to the fleet, whilst there would have been a considerable number of redundant crews, this being a serious matter as unemployment was fairly rife at that time.

Fortunately, Green Line had the resources of a large organisation behind it, and was prepared to fight the decisions made by the Commissioners. Appeals were made to the Minister of Transport against them and these, together with those made by other operators, were passed on to the Committee of Enquiry into London Motor Coach Services, the cases being heard by them in June and July 1932.

The Committee of Enquiry was set up in the first place to enquire into the operation of motor coach services in Central London, including the congestion caused by increasing numbers of them in the streets in the Central Area, particularly in the West End areas of Oxford Street, Charing Cross and Piccadilly. The Committee was to hear evidence from the operators, and their objectors and make recommendations to the Minister of Transport which would alleviate the situation. They presented their report and recommendations on these matters to the Minister in June, evidently considering that their task was ended.

The Minister had received a spate of appeals by the coach operators against the decisions made by the Traffic Commissioners, and he re-convened the Committee to consider the various Appeals and report back with their recommendations. This second report was sent to the Minister for his consideration in August 1932.

It is not the intention of the writer to bore his readers with all the evidence submitted for or against the Appeals, but he feels that a precis of the report, plus the recommendations made in respect of the Green Line services and those of the independent suburban coach operators will help the reader to understand the reasons for the revised Green Line network which came into operation on 4 October 1933.

Thirty-five specific Appeals from operators of short distance coach services were presented to the Committee, twenty-three of which concerned Green Line Coaches Limited, and the other twelve were from the independent suburban coach operators.

The Committee divided the area covered by the Appeals into eight sectors as follows:
1. Dartford to Redhill and Crawley.
2. Reigate to Woking and Chertsey.
3. Sunbury Common to Farnham Common.
4. High Wycombe to Chesham.
5. Aylesbury to Hemel Hempstead.
6. Dunstable to Baldock.
7. Hertford to Ongar.
8. Chelmsford and Brentwood to Tilbury.

The services which Green Line operated as cross-London routes were considered by the Committee as constituting two services with central terminals, and dealt with each half in its appropriate sector.

The only evidence allowed at the Appeal hearings was that which was submitted to the Traffic Commissioners at the original hearings, and all evidence and figures in respect of periods later than 31 December 1931 was not admitted.

The report states that the short distance services referred to in it were reported to have carried 25,000,000 passengers during 1931, and that the present Enquiry was only to consider the decisions of the Traffic Commissioner relating to restriction of the services in question.

It also stated that where the Committee have recommended that certain applications should be granted, it was intended that the grant should be subject to any modifications as to route, terminal points and picking up points as outlined in their First Report to the Minister, also that such grant should have regard to any local evidence respecting Traffic Areas other than the Metropolitan Traffic Commissioners Area.

The Committee were guided throughout the hearings by the needs of the public as they saw them, and also by the comparative value to the public of alternative transport facilities where they existed. The reader will best be able to judge whether this was so or not after perusal of the brief summary of the recommendations which appear in the following paragraphs. Briefly, in nearly all the eight groups of services which were the subject of appeals, an increase of service was made, but *only* to Green Line services, and despite the weight of evidence submitted by the independent operators, both in support of their Appeals against the Traffic Commissioners decisions, and also against the grant of licences to Green Line, it cannot be said that such evidence was not considered in a fair manner having regard to the recommendations made.

In dealing with the recommendations, the writer proposes to deal with Green Line Appeals first and sector by sector and not in route letter order.

Sector 1. Dartford to Redhill and Crawley:

Route I. London and Farningham. Continuation refused by Traffic Commissioner. The Committee recommended that a licence for an hourly service be granted.

Route L. Tunbridge Wells. Appeal for half-hourly service. The Committee recommended that a licence be granted for half-hourly service to Sevenoaks with hourly extension to Tunbridge Wells. On Saturday afternoons and evenings and Sundays the alternative services which during the rest of the week would stop at Sevenoaks, should also be extended to Tunbridge Wells. This recommendation had complete disregard to the evidence of an established and frequent service operated by Redcar Services.

Route X. Sevenoaks via Westerham. Appeal for half-hourly service to Westerham Hill and hourly (with additional journeys morning and evening) to Sevenoaks. It was recommended that the application be granted (including the additional journeys) and also that the outer terminal should be in Sevenoaks itself unless there were strong objections locally which the Committee were unaware of.

Route T. London – Godstone section: Appeal for hourly service. The Committee recommended that the decision of the Traffic Commissioner NOT to grant the licence be upheld.

Route K. London – Caterham section. Appeal for an hourly service. The Committee recommended that the application be granted.

Sector 2. Reigate to Woking and Chertsey:

Route H. London – Great Bookham – Guildford Section. Half-hourly service refused by Traffic Commissioner. The Committee recommended that half-hourly service be granted to Great Bookham only.

Route G. Guildford via Cobham. Appeal for half-hourly service. The Committee considered that, subject to suitable arrangements to avoid congestion in Guildford, that an hourly service be granted to Green Line, which, in conjunction with the hourly service granted to Skylark Motor Coach Company, will give a half-hourly service to this point. They also recommended that an additional service every hour should be run to Guildford on Saturday afternoons and evenings and Sundays which should be provided by the extension of the service which terminates during the rest of the week at Esher.

Route Y. Woking. Proposed half-hourly service (hourly via Esher, Cobham and Byfleet, and hourly via Esher, Weybridge and Byfleet). It was recommended that an hourly service be granted via Esher and Cobham and to terminate at West Byfleet. The Committee also recommended that there was no need for the other service from Esher to Woking via Weybridge, and therefore this service would be run to Esher, but on Saturday afternoons and evenings and Sundays, this timing should be extended to Guildford via Cobham as recommended under Route G.

Route C. Chertsey via Kingston and Weybridge. Appeal for half-hourly service to continue. The Committee recommended that an half-hourly service to Weybridge via Kingston be granted with hourly extensions to Chertsey and to Woking via Byfleet.

Sector 3. Sunbury Common to Farnham Common:

Route N. Windsor via Staines. Appeal for half-hourly service. Recommended that the application for this service be granted.

Route Z. Windsor via Slough. Appeal for 15-minute service. Recommended that Traffic Commissioners decision NOT to grant licence be upheld.

Route M. Maidenhead. Appeal for half-hourly service. Recommended that the Traffic Commissioners decision NOT to grant licence be upheld.

Sector 4. High Wycombe to Chesham:

Route Q. Uxbridge. Proposed half-hourly service to be extended to Gerrards Cross, with hourly coach alternately to High Wycombe and Chesham. Appeal against refusal by Traffic Commissioner. The Committee considered that, despite the operation by Skylark of an hourly service to High Wycombe plus that of the Amersham and District to Chesham hourly, there was public need for a extra service as far as Uxbridge, and recommended that a licence be granted accordingly.

Route P. Rickmansworth. Proposed continuance of this service as half-hourly with hourly extension to Chesham refused by Traffic Commissioner. The Committee recommended that an hourly service to Rickmansworth only be granted. The extension to Chesham was considered to be unnecessary as West London Coaches was already operating a service to that town.

Sector 5. Aylesbury to Hemel Hempstead:

Route T. London – Tring section. Proposed that existing hourly service be continued, also extended to Aylesbury. Refused by Traffic Commissioner. The Committee recommended that an hourly service be granted as far as Tring on condition that Route T did not operate through Watford.

Route K. London – Hemel Hempstead section: Appeal to continue hourly service. The Committee recommended that this service be granted a licence on condition that Route K did not operate through Watford.

Route E. London – Bushey section. Continuance of half-hourly service refused by Traffit Commissioners. The Committee recommended that the Commissioners decision NOT to grant a licence be upheld.

Route V. Watford – Golders Green. Half-hourly service refused by Traffic Commissioner. The Committee felt that this service was unique amongst those to which their attention had been drawn because it had been designed to feed the tube railway at Golders Green instead of bringing the passengers into Central London by coach. They considered that this was a type of coach service which ought to be encouraged. They felt that, in spite of the comparatively small receipts recorded on this service (which however required to be considered, for their proper appreciation, in conjunction with the receipts on the tube derived from the service), they were not satisfied that there was no public need for the service on the route which it followed. They therefore recommended that the application for this service be granted and facilities for co-ordination with the tube railway being afforded by means of through tickets, such as were being issued on the present service.

Sector 6. Dunstable to Baldock:

Route H. London – Harpenden section. Green Line, in applying for the continuance of the half-hourly service, also applied to vary the route beyond St. Albans by operating one coach per hour to Luton and one coach per hour to Dunstable. The Commissioner granted a licence for the hourly service to Dunstable, plus an hourly service to Harpenden only. W. D. Beaumont appealed to the Committee against the grant of a licence for an hourly service to Dunstable, stating that his service of six journeys in the summer and three in the winter adequately served the section of route between St. Albans and Dunstable. He had found that the increase in service he made in the summer season, which he had started in 1930, had not resulted in any increase in receipts per car mile, and it was argued that this showed no further increase in service to be necessary. The Committee did not consider that the existing Beaumont service supplied all the public needed, and recommended that the Commissioners decision to grant a licence to Green Line for an hourly operation to Dunstable and Harpenden only be upheld.

Route R. London – Hitchin section. Appeal by Green Line

to operate half-hourly to Stevenage, with hourly extensions to Hitchin and Baldock via Graveley. The Committee recommended that the half-hourly service to Welwyn Garden City approved by the Traffic Commissioner be confirmed, but with an hourly extension to Hitchin, but that there was no public need for the proposed service to Baldock. It was submitted in evidence that nine services a day were operated between London and Hitchin by Messrs. Birch Brothers plus an hourly service between London and Baldock by Messrs. Queen Line Coaches and Baldock Transport, but, in spite of this evidence, the Committee considered that there was still 'public need' for the additional services to Green Line.

Sector 7. Hertford to Ongar:

Route F. Hertford. Appeal by Green Line for a half-hourly service, increased to every twenty minutes at peak hours. The Committee recommended that a half-hourly service be granted.

Route O. Bishops Stortford. Appeal for a half-hourly service. In considering the Appeal, the Committee felt that the difference in route between the Green Line service and that of Acme Pullman Services as far as Epping as affording adequate justification for the operation of both services up to that point, but they were not satisfied as to any public need for more than a half-hourly service beyond Epping, such as is being operated by Acme Pullman Services. They recommended that the Traffic Commissioners decision to grant Green Line a half-hourly service to Epping only be upheld.

We now come to the Appeals lodged by the independent surburban coach operators, the largest of which was from Premier Line, covering four routes from London.

Premier Line Route A. Windsor via Slough. Appeal for fifteen minute service. The company had applied to continue the existing fifteen minute service from London (Aldwych) to Windsor. Despite the fact that the Traffic Commissioner had refused a licence for Green Line Route Z, which covered the same route, in granting a licence to Premier Line, he reduced the frequency to every twenty minutes. The Committee of Enquiry felt that there was sufficient public need for a fifteen minute service on this route, and recommended that this be granted by the Traffic Commissioner.

Premier Line Route B. Farnham Common. Appeal for fifteen minute service. The company had applied for continuance of the existing service every fifteen minutes from London (Aldwych) to Farnham Common, the application for the whole operation being dismissed by the respective Traffic Commissioners. The Committee of Enquiry, after hearing all the evidence submitted, were satisfied that there was sufficient public need for a service to Farnham Common to justify a half-hourly frequency, though not for a service every fifteen minutes, and recommended that the Commissioners decision be reversed and a licence for a half-hourly service be granted.

Premier Line Route D. Aylesbury. Appeal for half-hourly service. This service had been started by the company on 26 February 1931, after the deadline date set by the Ministry of Transport for the commencement of new services without a road service licence. The application to continue operating this service was refused by the Traffic Commissioners, and Premier Line lodged an appeal with the Minister of Transport, withdrawing the route pending the result of the Appeal, which was considered by the Committee of Enquiry. At the hearing, objections to the granting of a licence to Premier Line was heard from Green Line Coaches Limited, Red Rover Saloon Coaches and the Metropolitan and London and North Eastern Railways. After hearing all the evidence, the Committee found that the Premier Line service was not necessary in addition to the service by Red Rover already allowed by the Traffic Commissioner, and the recommendations they had made in respect of Green Line Routes K (Hemel Hempstead) and T (Tring). They therefore recommended that the Traffic Commissioners decision NOT to grant a licence to Premier be upheld.

Premier Line Route E. Sunbury Common. Appeal for fifteen minute service. Again, this service had been started by Premier Line on 27 February 1931, after the deadline date set by the Minister of Transport for the commencement of new services. When the Traffic Commissioners refused a licence for continuance, Premier Line withdrew the service in June 1932, and immediately lodged an Appeal against the refusal of a licence with the Minister of Transport, which was referred by him to the Committee of Enquiry for consideration. In support of the Appeal, fresh evidence was heard on behalf of the Ham Urban District Council, whilst Premier Line submitted a written communication they had received from the Hampton Urban District Council also in support of the Appeal. The Committee however, were not satisfied that the portion of the route which lay between Sunbury Common and Kingston required more than the half-hourly service on Green Line Route S which the Traffic Commissioner had allowed, whilst on the other portion of the route on which public need for a service existed, namely the portion between Kingston and Richmond, the Traffic Commissioner had allowed, besides Route S, another half-hourly service of Green Line Coaches, namely Route C, both of which had been operating prior to the introduction of Premier Line Route E. Accordingly, they recommended that the Traffic Commissioners decision NOT to grant a licence to Premier Line be affirmed.

To work the above four routes, plus Routes F (Aylesbury) and G (Windsor – Maidenhead) before the Traffic Act came into operation, Premier Line had needed 50 coaches on the road, plus spares. After Road Service Licences had been refused for Routes D and E, and the service on Route B had been halved to half-hourly, whilst Route G was reduced from every ten minutes to half-hourly by the Southern Traffic Commissioners, only 28 coaches were required for service. Eleven coaches were retained for engineering spares and to cover duplications on busy weekends, leaving approximately twenty coaches redundant. Fortunately, at this time Premier Line had gained control of the Aylesbury Bus Company, whose fleet was in need of replacement, and so these coaches found a new home. The redundant Premier Line crews were not so fortunate however, and found themselves without work at a time of high unemployment.

Highways Limited. Appeal for an hourly service. This company was the first operator to start a service from London to Windsor, providing an hourly service between the two towns from November 1929. It was withdrawn in July 1930, no doubt due to the heavy competition received from Green Line and Premier Line, but was resumed with an hourly service on 14 November 1930. This frequency was altered to half-hourly on Saturdays and Sundays only from Easter 1931, but was again withdrawn after the Traffic

Commissioner had refused a licence for its continuance. An appeal was made to the Minister of Transport, and referred by him to the Committee of Appeal. The Committee however recommended that the decision of the Traffic Commissioner NOT to grant a licence be affirmed.

Bucks Expresses Limited. Appeal for extra journeys at peak hours. Bucks Expresses applied to the Traffic Commissioner for continuance of their service between London and Watford, presenting the existing timetable, which consisted of a basic half-hourly service, stepped up to quarter-hourly during weekday rush periods. Although the Traffic Commissioner granted a Road Service Licence, it was only for the basic half-hourly service, and Bucks Expresses were now appealing for the peak hour extras. The Committee recommended that the half-hourly service should be confirmed and that Traffic Commissioners decision not to grant the additional peak hour services be upheld.

Lewis's Cream Line Coaches. This company had been operating a service between London and Brookman's Park Estate since 1925, and the service had been gradually increased since September 1930. In its application for a Road Service Licence the company had applied for fourteen daily journeys, but was granted a licence for ten journeys only, and was now appealing for an increase to the fourteen originally asked for. At the hearing, fresh evidence in support of the Company's appeal was submitted on behalf of the Barnet Urban District Council. The Committee stated that it seemed to be a matter of some doubt what services the Applicant was operating on 9 February 1931 (the deadline date). It was stated on his behalf that he was then operating 20 services daily each way; but the timetable accompanying his application to the Traffic Commissioner, dated 24 March 1931, clearly shows only 14 services daily, with three fewer on Saturdays and none on Sundays. The difference between 14 and 20 was possibly accounted for, in part at least, by duplications. They also stated that they were unable to accept the application made before them for twenty services, and assumed that it stood at 14 services as in the original application. They found no ground however, for interfering with the Traffic Commissioners decision to grant a licence for ten services only, which should be affirmed.

P. and S. Motor Services Limited. Appeal for 12 daily services. This operator had commenced a service between Hertford and London (Liverpool Street) before the Green Line and Skylark services had been commenced. At first, ten daily journeys were operated, but this was increased to twelve journeys long before the deadline date of 9 February 1931. The Traffic Commissioner had refused a licence for the continuance of this service. Evidence was given on behalf of the Urban District Councils of Enfield, Cheshunt and Hoddesdon in support of the Company's Appeal. The only objector to the granting of the licence was the London and North Eastern Railway, whose lines paralleled the route followed by the coach service. After hearing all the evidence, the Committee stated that it did not find any ground for interfering with the decision of the Traffic Commissioner NOT to grant a licence for the service, which should be affirmed by the Minister.

Batten's Coaches, East Ham. Appeal for fifteen minute service. This operator had started an East Ham – Tilbury service in March 1929 at a lower frequency and it was gradually increased so that by November 1930, a 20 minute service was being operated between Aldgate and Tilbury, with additional coaches at peak hours. In its application to continue the service, the company asked for a fifteen minute service but the Traffic Commissioner reduced this to every 20 minutes when granting the licence to continue operation. The Committee felt that the public need was being adequately met by the 20 minute service granted by the Commissioner, and recommended that his decision be upheld.

Tilbury Coaching Services. Appeal for 18 daily services and extension to Aldgate on Sundays. This company had commenced their operations between Tilbury and East Ham on a lower frequency in October 1930. This had been increased to the present frequency of 12 daily journeys on 1 January 1931. The company applied to continue operation, but with an increase in the number of journeys to eighteen, and to extend the route to Aldgate on Sundays, but the Metropolitan Traffic Commissioner refused to grant the Road Service Licence. The Eastern Traffic Commissioner, in whose area the major portion of the route lay, had granted a licence for 12 daily journeys, and having regard to the fact that only a small portion of the route was within the Metropolitan area, the Committee recommended that a backing be granted by the Met. Traffic Commissioner for the operation of this route as far as East Ham. They did not recommend the extension of the route to Aldgate on Sundays.

Gordon Omnibus Company Ltd. This organisation had been operating on a route between Tower Hill and Tilbury via Aveley and Grays since October 1929, and, by the time it was necessary to apply for a Road Service Licence to continue operation, was running every forty minutes between the two terminals. In their application to continue in service, the company asked for the existing forty minute service plus additional journeys during peak hours. This application was dismissed by the Traffic Commissioner, and the company were now appealing against the decision. In connection with the Appeal, the Committee heard fresh evidence on behalf of the Purfleet Urban District Council for the continuance of this service through Aveley. The two services which the Met. Traffic Commissioner had granted licences to operate through Aveley gave 30 services daily to and from East Ham and 12 services daily to and from Tilbury. In these circumstances, the Committee recommended that the Met. Traffic Commissioners decision NOT to grant a licence to Gordon be affirmed.

Having received the Report together with the Committee's decisions and recommendations quoted in the previous paragraphs of this chapter, the Minister of Transport declared that the Report would become effective from 19 September 1932, and it looked as if the revised Green Line network, and the services outlined for the other operators would come into operation on this date.

However, as has been stated in a previous chapter, a rule nisi was granted in the High Court against the Traffic Commissioners and the Minister to show cause why a certain motor coach company's appeal against a decision made by the Traffic Commissioner should not be heard.

As a result of the rule nisi, the Minister decided that the formal decisions of the Amulree Committee should not become effective on 19 September 1932, and the status quo of existing coach services should be maintained until further notice.

LONDON TRANSPORT
CHAPTER FIVE

1934-1936

After a long and stormy passage through the Houses of Parliament, the London Passenger Transport Act received the Royal assent on 13 April 1933, and the Act was to come into force on 1 July 1933. Its object was to bring under one common ownership the municipal and company-owned tramways; the Underground and Metropolitan Railways; The London General Omnibus Company; London General Country Services Limited and Green Line Coaches Limited, together with the associated coach proprietors acquired by Green Line during the previous year, which, because of various factors, had remained nominally independent after acquisition. The Board also had powers to take over the various independent bus and coach operators then working within the London Passenger Transport area boundaries whose services operated entirely within the area.

On 1 July 1933 all the undertakings mentioned in the first part of the last paragraph immediately passed to the new Board, and there were several immediate changes to the Green Line services. Route A (Ascot or Sunningdale to Dartford) was extended to Gravesend, and the former Maidstone and District route serving that town was diverted via the A2 road away from the town. Route I (Poland Street to Farningham) was extended to Wrotham and the Maidstone and District coaches from London no longer picked up north of Wrotham Heath on London-bound journeys. On the same day, the undertaking of the Premier Omnibus Company of Watford was acquired, and its Hemel Hempstead – London route became Green Line Route AK.

It will be remembered that Acme Pullman Services, which was one of the nominally independent companies controlled by Green Line, worked certain journeys to Newmarket, of which the section beyond Bishops Stortford was now outside the Board's area of operation. This section was therefore passed to Varsity Motors, but as this company had not yet received its Road Service Licence to operate the extra journeys, Eastern National took over the operation on a temporary basis from 1 July 1933.

The next acquisition was the business of Lewis's Cream Line Coaches who operated a route from Brookman's Park to Portman Square on weekdays only. London Transport acquired this business on 1 August, two Gilford coaches being taken over, whilst the route became Green Line Route BR for the short period in which it continued operating.

In the meantime, the Minister of Transport had decided that the recommendations made by the Amulree Committee of Enquiry would become effective from Sunday, 1 October 1933. As the Green Line working week ran from Wednesday to Tuesday, Wednesday thus being the day on which any route or timetable alterations were introduced, Green Line were given a dispensation to introduce their alterations from Wednesday, 4 October.

Accordingly, Poland Street Coach Station was closed as a terminus after the last departure on 3 October, it then

Ex-Premier Line Leyland TD1 coach on Route A at Ascot.
(J. F. Higham).

Ex-Maidstone and District Leyland TS2 coach on Route A at Staines.
(J. F. Higham).

Ex-Premier Line Leyland TD1 coach at Gravesend on Route A.

being used as a garage for coaches laying over in London between the peak hours, and also served as the office for the District Superintendent, until it was closed on 19 February 1934. On 3 October, the Maidenhead and Windsor via Slough services also operated for the last time.

On the following day a new network of 29 routes came into operation, of which only ten terminated in Central London. The route letters were now arranged in a clockwise system, commencing with Route A (Gravesend) and ending with Route Y (Brentwood). Certain letters of the alphabet were not used immediately, being reserved for the independent routes to be acquired by London Transport at a later date. A list of the new routes and letters will be found in Appendix 'E' at the end of the book.

Three weeks later, on 25 October 1933, a new route made its appearance between Gidea Park (Gallows Corner) and Aldgate. Lettered X, it opened up new territory by operating from Romford along Eastern Avenue to Wanstead and thence via Leytonstone, Leyton, Hackney Wick, Victoria Park and Bethnal Green to Aldgate. On Saturdays after 12.30 pm and all day on Sundays, it was extended to Charing Cross (Horse Guards Avenue). At first an hourly service (half-hourly from Romford Market Place) was provided, but the new service, with its sixpenny (2½p) minimum fare over the section between Hackney (Mare Street) and Gidea Park, attracted such a good passenger traffic that a 15-minute service was introduced within a few weeks.

Three of the remaining independent coach operators were taken over in December 1933. Price's Super Coaches, who operated an East Ham – Aveley service every 45 minutes with three Gilford 1660T vehicles, was acquired on the first of the month, followed by one of the larger companies (Premier Line) on 20 December. Premier Line handed over 19 Leyland TD1 and 20 Leyland TS3 coaches, five routes and a large garage in Bath Road, Slough. The two London services, from Windsor (Route A) and Farnham Common (Route B) passed to Green Line, becoming Routes O and P respectively, whilst the other three routes became part of the Country Bus network. By the acquisition of Premier Line, Green Line once again acquired access to Windsor via Slough.

Batten's Luxurious Coaches were taken over on 23 December. They operated a 20-minute service from Aldgate to Grays, certain journeys of which were extended to Tilbury Dock (now Tilbury Town) Station on weekdays. This acquisition brought Green Line into the Grays and Tilbury area for the first time. Unlike most coach operators whose fleets usually seemed to consist of either Gilfords or Leylands, the thirteen coaches taken over from Batten's consisted of three A.D.C. 426 and ten A.E.C. Reliances.

The New Year of 1934 commenced with a short extension of Route D from Sunbury Common to Staines, probably introduced in order to have the coaches for that route operating from the garage in Staines rather than stabled in the yard in Hanworth Road, Sunbury which had been their base since operation commenced in that area. This extension came into operation from 3 January.

A week later, on 10 January, the Bow – Brentwood section of the Hillman organisation, plus the Aldgate (Mansell Street – Upminster) route of the Hillman-associated company, Upminster Services, passed to London Transport. The two fleets added no fewer than 65 Gilford coaches to the Green Line fleet, all of the 1680T type, and included in the purchase was the Hillman garage in London Road, Romford. The Bow – Brentwood workings were merged into the existing Route Y, with the Upminster route becoming Green Line Route AY. These two routes then became the most frequent of all the Green Line services. The frequency on Route Y on weekdays was: Aldgate – 10 – Bow – 5 – Romford – 10 – Brentwood. This was further increased in peak hours to: Aldgate – 5 – Bow – 2½ – Romford – 5 – Brentwood. On Saturdays, the Bow – Romford short workings were extended to Brentwood, giving a 5-minute service over that section. On Sundays, part of the service was extended to Horse Guards Avenue, the frequency being: Horse Guards Avenue – 15 – Aldgate – 7/8 – Bow – 3 – Romford – 7/8 – Brentwood. On the Upminster route a 30-minute service was worked from 3.30 am to 5 am then every 15 minutes until 6 am, then every 5 minutes (rush hours); 7 minutes (slack hours) until 9.30 pm, after which a 15-minute service operated until 11.30 pm, with a last coach to London at midnight.

The next acquisition on 17 January brought in a more leisurely service, with West London Coaches Limited, whose Victoria Coach Station – Aylesbury route operated eight weekday and six Sunday return trips at intervals which varied from hourly to every 2½ hours on weekdays and every 2–3 hours on Sundays. There were eight coaches in the fleet, including two Saurers, two T.S. Motors, three Gilford 1680T and a Daimler DH6.

This was followed a week later on 25 January by the take-over of Sunset Saloon Coaches, who operated a Charing Cross – Brentwood service. The company handed over twelve Gilford 1680T coaches, plus an Albion PV70 which had only entered service during the past twelve months. As the service on Route Y was already extremely frequent, the Sunset timetable, except for the operations to Highwood Hospital on Sundays, was abandoned.

Green Line achieved its ambition to reach Luton when the Strawhatter Coaches from that town to Kings Cross was taken over on 1 February 1934. A service varying from half-hourly to hourly was being worked at that time, requiring five coaches for the basic operation. The company handed over 24 coaches (all Gilfords) to London Transport, plus the garage in Park Street West, which then became the base for the Board's local bus services as well as the coach route. It might be wondered why Strawhatter possessed such a large fleet, but, in addition to the London route, they operated express services from Luton to Bournemouth, Portsmouth and Southsea, Margate and Great Yarmouth, as well as tours and excursions from Luton. As London Transport could not participate in these activities, these licences were passed to Eastern National, who were the principal bus and coach operators in the area at that time. Nine of the coaches were also sold to Eastern National at the same time.

Green Line received its first and only all-night service when the route between Aldgate and Romford Market Place operated by Fleet Transport Services of Stratford every 45–50 minutes was acquired on 22 February. The timetable for this service was merged with that of Green Line Route Y and the one Gilford 1680T coach which changed hands joined the others of the same type at Romford Garage.

There now remained only one independent coach operator to be taken over by the Board, the Tilbury Coach-

Ex Maidstone and District Leyland TS2 en route to Sunningdale (Route A2). (J. F. Higham).

Ex-Maidstone and District coach (Leyland TS2) at Gravesend on Route AA to Sunningdale. (J. F. Higham).

↓ Leyland TS2 coach (ex-Redcar Services) at Victoria (Eccleston Bridge) on Route C to Tunbridge Wells. Still carrying Redcar-type side route boards. (J. F. Higham).

Ex-Blue Belle A.E.C. coach at Rickmansworth on Route B from ↑ Wrotham. (J. F. Higham).

Experimental Leyland TF-type coach at Tunbridge Wells Coach Station in 1938. (McCall Collection).

A.E.C. T-type coach en route to Tunbridge Wells on Route C c.1936. (McCall Collection).

Ex-Prince Omnibus Company Leyland TS1 coach on forecourt of Staines Garage (Route D). (J. F. Higham).

ing Service, who operated between that town and East Ham 12 times daily. The company was taken over on 24 March 1934, adding another four Gilford 1680T coaches to the Green Line fleet, whilst the timings were merged into Route Z.

The way was now clear for the Country Bus and Coach section to start making adjustments to the enlarged bus and coach network they had inherited, and this was the task that was to occupy the next two years.

The first alteration took place on 16 May 1934, when, as part of the Dartford and Swanley area re-organisation, bus route 485 (Farningham and Wrotham) was withdrawn, its place being taken by the introduction of bus fares on Route B which covered the same route.

The night service acquired from Fleet Transport and now operating as part of Route Y, followed the same route to Seven Kings as the Central Bus night route 617 (Charing Cross – Seven Kings). It was obvious that there was no real need for two services covering the same route, so the night service on Route Y was replaced by the extension of 617 from Seven Kings to Hornchurch Garage from 13 June 1934. The night service on Route Y had operated every night, and in consequence, 617 was given a Saturday night and early Sunday morning service from Aldgate to Hornchurch Garage.

Three of the former independent coach services operating from Central London terminals made their last journeys on 10 July 1934, these being AF (Portman Square – Hemel Hempstead); AS (Marble Arch – Aylesbury via Tring) and S (Victoria Coach Station – Aylesbury via Amersham). On the following day, they were replaced by alterations to cross-London routes B, E, F and I. Dealing with Route AF first, we find that this route was replaced by the extension of Route I (Crawley – Watford) to Abbots Langley, the section from that point to Hemel Hempstead being withdrawn. Route AF had operated every 90 minutes, but the replacement service gave a half-hourly frequency at first, and this soon proved to be more than adequate, and was reduced to hourly from 5 December 1934. Turning now to Route AS, this route was replaced by adjustment of Route E, which was withdrawn between Edenbridge and Chelsham Garage at the southern end and extended from Tring to Aylesbury at the northern end, an hourly service being provided to Tring, with a coach every two hours being extended to Aylesbury. To replace the southern end of Route E, the coach on Route F which terminated at Chelsham was extended to Edenbridge, so that F ran alternately to Tatsfield and Edenbridge, 15 coaches being required to work the two routes. We now come to Route S, the former West London route from Victoria Coach Station to Aylesbury, which had been working its original timetable, together with the shuttle coach from Chesham to Amersham. To replace it with a more regular service, Route B was extended from Rickmansworth hourly to Amersham (Oakfield Corner), where alternate coaches ran to Chesham or Aylesbury. Eight coaches were needed to work the new Route B, and the operation from the northern end was now transferred from Watford (Leavesden Road) to Amersham.

The programme now switched to the Grays area on 18 July 1934. On this date Route AZ between East Ham and Aveley was withdrawn and replaced by a new hourly bus service 375 from Rainham (White Post Corner) to Grays, whilst the service on Route Z was revised to give a 15 minute service during Monday–Friday peak hours, Saturday afternoons and evenings and Sundays (20 minutes Monday–Friday slack hours) to Grays, with a regular hourly service to Tilbury which was now extended through the town via Civic Square and Feenan Highway to terminate at the junction of St. Chad's Road.

Epping was the next area to receive attention on 5 September, when Country Bus route 9 (Bishops Stortford – Warley) was renumbered 339, and withdrawn north of Potter Street, being replaced by the introduction of bus fares on Route V between Epping and Bishops Stortford. In addition to its withdrawal north of Potter Street, the frequency on Route 339 was widened and bus fares introduced on Route W between Epping and Ongar.

Traffic had increased on the Aylesbury journeys of Route E at weekends, and to meet the demands, the service was increased to hourly on Saturday afternoons and evenings and Sundays from 15 September. Four days later, the hourly service on Route H to Harpenden was extended to Luton, whilst the operation intermediately was altered to run between Radlett and Mill Hill (Apex Corner) via Elstree Village, Brockley Hill and Edgware Way.

Fare scales on Green Line services now received some attention from the powers that be, and from 10 October, those coach routes which had not received lower bus fares due to the withdrawal of bus services, now received lower fares at 6d and 9d single in the country districts, this being followed on 18 November by the issue of weekly and four-weekly season tickets on all routes (with the exception of Routes BH, T and U). The new tickets gave unlimited journeys for the period in which they were issued, and passengers were allowed to board and alight intermediately between the points the tickets were covering. On Route BH, special weekly tickets were issued from Luton to London (10/–; 50p) and London Colney to London (8/–; 40p) which were not available intermediately, although monthly tickets could be purchased which carried this facility. On Route T (Watford – Golders Green), six-day tickets through to London by Underground still continued to be issued, but were restricted to one return journey each day, and no four-weekly tickets were issued on this route. Route U, being the express service to Whipsnade Zoo, was exempted from the issue of either class of ticket.

Bus fares were introduced on parts of two more Green Line routes during December 1934. A re-organisation of bus services in the St. Albans area caused the withdrawal of bus route 374 to Dunstable on 5 December, the service being replaced by the introduction of bus fares from St. Albans to Dunstable on Route AH. The second route to receive them was Route F between Oxted Station and Edenbridge from 19 December, as the bus route covering these two points only operated every two hours.

Road traffic was on the increase in the Upminster area, particularly in the St. Mary's Lane area, where Route AY had its terminus. For coaches to stand facing towards London, they had to cross to the wrong side of the road, then carry out a reversing movement into Sunnyside Gardens, thus causing heavy congestion at that point, especially in peak hours when the five minute service operated. To alleviate the situation, the route was extended along Corbets Tey Road to terminate at Little Gaynes Lane, where they could circle a roundabout and stand without interference to traffic. This extension was only a temporary measure, as the

A.E.C. T-type coach on Route D at Lewisham en route to Sevenoaks. (McCall Collection).

A.E.C. T-type coach with experimental body at Horse Guards Avenue in 1936. (A. Duke).

Leyland TS3 coach (ex-Premier Line) at Caterham on Route G to Windsor. (McCall Collection).

A.E.C. T-type coach at Caterham on Route G to Windsor (McCall Collection).

A.E.C. T-type coach at Golders Green en route to Baldock. (J. F. Higham).

A.E.C. Regal coach at Watford on Route I to Crawley. (J. F. Higham).

A.E.C. Regal coach (ex-Aston of Watford) at Hadley Highstone en route to Dorking on Route K1. (J. F. Higham).

A.E.C. T-type coach at Crawley (The George) on Route I to Abbots Langley. (McCall Collection).

A.E.C. T-type coach en route to Guildford on Route M. (Pamlin Prints).

route was extended along Corbets Tey Road to the 'Huntsman and Hounds' in Corbets Tey village on 8 May 1935.

A re-organisation of bus services in the Grays area took place on 5 June 1935 which also resulted in changes to Green Line Route Z, on which bus fares were introduced between Dagenham (The Chequers) and Purfleet (Stonehouse Corner) to cover the withdrawal of bus route 371. One coach per hour was diverted between Rainham and Stonehouse Corner via Wennington and Aveley as Route Z2 to replace bus route 375 which now became a local service in Rainham Village. Bus fares were applied on Route Z2 between the same points as those on Route Z, which was now re-lettered as Z1. This new combination of letters and numbers was to be gradually applied to the rest of the network, as routes or timetables changed, and the process did not end until the middle of 1936. A list of the new route lettering and numbering will be found in Appendix F at the end of the book.

There were several minor alterations during the summer and autumn of 1935. On 26 June, alternate coaches on Route AY (now re-lettered as Y2) were terminated at Hornchurch Station from the London direction, and Route Y to Brentwood was re-lettered as Y1. From 3 July, the Saturday pm and Sunday service on Route P was diverted from Farnham Common (Hedgerley Corner) to Burnham Beeches for the summer season. On 31 July, the former Redcar service to Tunbridge Wells, which for the past few months had been operated by Maidstone and District, was now taken over by Green Line and run as an extra hourly service from Victoria on Route C. This was followed on 14 August by a revision of bus services in the Hertford area which resulted in the withdrawal of the bus route across Hertford Heath. To cover it, the hourly service on coach Route BM was diverted at Hoddesdon Clock Tower across the Heath, bus fares being introduced between Broxbourne (Station Road) and Hertford on Route BM only. Surprisingly enough, Routes M, AM and BM were not re-lettered at this time. Meanwhile passenger traffic had been steadily building up on weekends between Epping and Bishops Stortford, and from 7 September, Route N (Epping – Windsor) was extended hourly on Saturdays pm and Sundays to help out.

Traffic congestion in the central area of London had been causing trouble for some time, resulting in bad timekeeping, particularly between 9 am and 7 pm on weekdays, and revised timetables incorporating extra running time during this period were introduced on 8 January 1936. The opportunity was also taken to re-letter some routes into the new system combining letters and numbers, as follows: A to A1; AA to A2; H to H1; AH to H2; M to M1; AM to M3 and BM to M2. In addition some route adjustments were made at the same time, the first of these being to Route B, on which the Chesham journeys were withdrawn and diverted to Wendover, giving an hourly service to that point, which, with its close proximity to Halton R.A.F. Station, now needed extra coaches. The service to Chesham was improved from two-hourly to hourly by the extension of Route R from Amersham. The hourly ex-Redcar service to Tunbridge Wells was withdrawn and replaced by the extension of Route AC (now re-lettered as C2) from Sevenoaks daily instead of on weekends only, whilst Route C from Chertsey was now re-lettered as C1.

Route H was re-lettered as H1, being withdrawn through Elstree Village, returning to its old route via Allum Lane, Borehamwood and Stirling Corner, giving a half-hourly service over this section with Route H2. Its place through Elstree Village was taken by an adjustment on Route T (Watford – Golders Green), this half-hourly service being divided into two separate hourly services as follows:
T1 Watford – Golders Green via Watford-by-Pass and Edgware Way.
T2 Watford – Golders Green via Elstree Village, Barnet Lane, Stirling Corner and Barnet Way.

At the same time, a minimum 3d (1·25p) fare was introduced on both routes in addition to the 6d (2½p) and 9d (3·75p) fares already in operation, although the 3d fare only applied between Watford and Mill Hill (Apex Corner).

The largest alteration was to Routes K and AK. Route K, which had been operating half-hourly from Dorking to Welwyn Garden City with an hourly extension to Hitchin, was now re-lettered as K1 and divided into two separate hourly operations as follows:
Dorking Garage – Welwyn Garden City (Longcroft Green).
Leatherhead Garage – Baldock (White Lion).

The operation of this service required 16 coaches on weekdays (14 on Sundays, which were divided between four garages as follows: Hitchin (5 daily), Hatfield (3 daily), Leatherhead (3 weekdays; 2 Sundays) and Dorking (5 weekdays; 4 Sundays). Route AK was withdrawn and its place taken by a new route K2 from Welwyn Garden City Station (Hitchin on Saturdays pm and Sundays) to Horsham, breaking into new territory between London and Leatherhead by running via Putney, Kingston, Surbiton, Hook and Chessington and also with the extension beyond Dorking to Horsham. The new route also broke another record by becoming the longest route on Saturdays and Sundays, the mileage between Hitchin and Horsham being 80 miles, whilst the running time for the journey was 4 hours 7 minutes. The frequency of service was hourly from the northern terminals to Dorking, from whence a coach every two hours (hourly on Saturdays and Sundays) ran on to Horsham. This operation required eight coaches on Mondays to Fridays and ten on weekends, five of which came from Dorking Garage daily and three from Hatfield, increased to five on Saturdays and Sundays.

It was observed that the operation of Route Z1 right through Tilbury to Feenan Highway was not necessary as most Tilbury passengers alighted in the town centre, and accordingly, the route was curtailed at Civic Square from 5 February 1936. This was followed on 8 April by the resumption of a daily service to Whipsnade Zoo on Route U, which had been running on Sundays only for the winter.

The first series of area re-organisations ended with the one for the Amersham area introduced on 13 May. Bus routes 369 (Aylesbury – Slough) and 369A (Great Missenden – Chesham via Amersham) were both withdrawn and replaced by the introduction of bus fares on route B between Great Missenden and Amersham (Oakfield Corner), the coach route being diverted through Little Missenden village to replace the withdrawn buses. It might be wondered why bus fares were not introduced right through to Aylesbury, but Eastern National operated a bus route between that town and Great Missenden, and there were also buses provided by two independent operators between Aylesbury and Halton Camp, some of which ran via Wendover Vil-

T-type A.E.C. Regal coach passes 'The Hut Hotel' at Wisley on its way to Hertford in 1934. (London Transport).

A.E.C. T-type coach on layover at Hertford Car Park (J. F. Higham).

A.E.C. T-type coach in light-green livery at Windsor Coach Station forecourt (1936). (J. F. Higham).

lage.

The Summer programme for 1936 was spread over the four months from May to August, starting with the diversion of Route P to Burnham Beeches on weekends from 30 May. On the same day, Route L (Great Bookham – Uxbridge) was extended hourly to Chesham as L1 and High Wycombe hourly as L2. Both operations ran on Saturdays pm and Sundays. This route reverted back to the letter L when the summer weekend extensions were withdrawn on 7 October. The beautiful countryside around Dorking was always a great attraction to Londoners in the summer, and to help deal with the increased passenger traffic, the hourly Baldock – Leatherhead section of K1 was extended to Dorking on Sundays only from 26 July. This was followed on 2 August by a new Sunday cross-London service from Brentwood to Windsor, running half-hourly as Route Y3. An increased service from Luton to Kings Cross on Route BH was introduced daily from 29 July, the route being re-lettered H3 at the same time. The summer weekend operations of Routes K1, P and Y3, plus the weekday operation of Route U were all withdrawn on various dates in October, but were repeated each summer until the declaration of war in 1939 put a temporary end to Green Line operations.

A new travel facility for passengers to Whipsnade Zoo was introduced from Wednesday, 29 July 1936. Through railway and bus returns from St. Pancras and intermediate stations to Whipsnade Zoo were introduced by the L.M.S. Railway. Passengers changed at St. Albans City Station to a new direct bus service 368. These tickets were not available on coach Route U, but passengers holding coach return tickets were able to return to St. Albans by bus, and upon surrendering their Green Line tickets to the booking clerk at City Station, were given special single tickets to St. Pancras, enabling them to travel home by train. This was a useful facility as the bus and train service was more frequent than that provided on Route U.

For some unknown reason, probably due to a fall in passenger traffic, Route X was withdrawn between Gidea Park and Romford Market Place from 19 August 1936, whilst, with the introduction of the winter programme on 7 October, the Sunday morning service on Route N to Bishops Stortford was withdrawn for the winter season.

The Summer programme for 1937 was introduced on Sunday, 2 May, when the usual extensions to Routes P and K1 were introduced, also Route Y3 reappeared. In addition Route G from Caterham to London was diverted at Purley Fountain to run via Purley Way and Thornton Road to serve the Croydon Airport, the frequency being stepped up from hourly to half-hourly. It was also extended from Horse Guards Avenue to Windsor via Slough to supplement Route O.

An adjustment was made to Routes M1/2/3 between Enfield and Waltham Cross, M1 being diverted at the Southbury Road/Great Cambridge Road junction to run via the Cambridge Road and Bullsmoor Lane, whilst M2/3 were diverted at the same junction via Southbury Road, Ponders End and Enfield Highway in place of M1.

Route L was withdrawn completely, the London – Great Bookham section being replaced by the extension of Route O from Trafalgar Square. The northern half to Uxbridge was replaced by an increased service from Oxford Circus on Routes Q and R. The revised timetable on these two services gave an even 15-minute service to Uxbridge, a 30-minute service to Gerrards Cross, and then hourly alternately to Chesham and High Wycombe. On summer Saturdays and Sundays, the 15-minute service was extended to Gerrards Cross and then half-hourly to High Wycombe and Amersham, with an hourly service to Chesham.

Route T2 from Watford – Golders Green via Elstree Village was withdrawn, T1 being re-lettered as T and the service stepped up from hourly to half-hourly.

Passengers to and from Whipsnade Zoo were given revised methods of travel from 15 May 1937 as follows:
(1) Direct to and from the Zoo by Green Line Route U.
(2) From Underground stations in the central area to Marylebone or Golders Green by tube, changing to Route U at either station.
(3) From Underground stations in the central area to Kings Cross St. Pancras, thence via L.M.S. train to St. Albans and bus 368 to the Zoo.

The passengers travelling by Underground and Green Line received paper vouchers at the station booking office which were exchanged on the coach for a standard Bell Punch ticket, whilst those travelling via St. Pancras and St. Albans were issued normal railway two-portion return tickets. On the return journey from Whipsnade, coach return tickets were available for return by coach throughout; by coach and Underground, or by bus and train via St. Albans, whilst the return halves of railway tickets were accepted for return by coach.

With the winter programme of 1937, introduced on 6 October, the extensions of Route V from Liverpool Street and Routes X and Y1 from Aldgate to Horse Guards Avenue on weekends were withdrawn.

A programme of alterations to routes was introduced on 9 February 1938. Route D was withdrawn between Westerham (Kings Arms) and Sevenoaks, the garage journeys to Dunton Green being worked in service as part of bus route 403. The frequency on Route D now became: Staines – 30 – Victoria – 30 – Westerham Hill – 60 – Westerham, requiring twelve coaches, six each from Staines and Dunton Green Garages. Route G from Caterham to Windsor had its service increased over the London – Windsor section due to the withdrawal of Route O, the frequency now becoming: Caterham – 30 – Horse Guards Avenue – 20 (Mon–Fri and Sat/Sun mornings; 15 minutes Sats/Suns pm) – Windsor. Route P was extended from Trafalgar Square to Horse Guards Avenue, and a combined timetable was worked with Route G as far as Slough, the whole operation requiring five coaches from Godstone Garage on Route G, and 16 from Windsor on Routes G and P combined. The withdrawal of Route O between Victoria and Great Bookham affected the operations on Routes K1/K2. Route K1 retained its two separate hourly workings, but instead of running direct from Stanborough (The Bull) to Hatfield Station along the old Great North Road, it was now diverted at Oldings Corner via the Barnet-by-Pass, Stonehouse Corner and St. Albans Road to serve the growing community of New Hatfield. Route K2 was completely revised, losing its Hitchin – Welwyn Garden City weekend extension, plus the Dorking – Horsham section daily, becoming an hourly service from Welwyn Garden City Station to Dorking. In addition, it was diverted away from the Barnet-by-Pass at Cecil Road (South Mimms) to run via Cecil Road and

Leyland TS3 coach ex-Premier Line on Route O at Windsor outside Garage. Coach is still in Premier Line livery with temporary Green Line transfer on side. (J. F. Higham).

A change in the method of displaying Public Service Vehicle Licences became effective from 1 July 1939. Hitherto, a small oval enamel-iron plate bearing the initial letter of the traffic area and the licence number allocated to the vehicle was displayed on the rear of the vehicle. Now a new regulation stated that the actual licence was to be displayed, and the present system of a paper disc was introduced, which was now displayed with the Road Fund Licence and Certificate of Insurance in the driver's cab.

On 31 August 1939, it became obvious that a declaration of war against Germany would be made in a matter of days, and all Green Line coach routes with the exception of Routes X, Y1 and Y2 (on which service carried on for a few days longer), were withdrawn after the last journeys on that date, in order that the coaches could be converted to ambulances.

By 2 September 1939, all the coaches available had been converted, and were ready to evacuate patients from the hospitals in Central London, and also to deal with casualties, as it was expected that air attacks on London would be made within hours of the declaration of war.

Mutton Lane to Potters Bar, where it joined Route K1 to London. The southern end of the route was also altered, being diverted at Victoria over Route K1 to cover the withdrawal of Route O. Its former route to Horsham via Putney, Kingston and Chessington was taken up by a new Route K3 from Baker Street with an hourly service to Dorking, which was extended to Horsham every two hours on Mondays to Fridays (hourly on Saturdays and Sundays).

The new frequencies on Routes K1/2/3 required no fewer than 27 coaches to work the three services, these being divided among the respective garages as follows:
K1/K2 – Joint Service: Hitchin – 4; Hatfield – 7; Leatherhead – 7; Dorking – 3. Total 21 coaches.
K3 – New route: Dorking – 6 coaches.

Daily service on Route U was once again resumed on 13 April for the summer, followed on 5 June by the usual weekend extensions of K1 and P; the increased services on weekends on Routes Q and R and the re-appearance of Route Y3.

The main network of routes had now settled down, and, apart from the introduction of the usual summer weekend adjustments mentioned in the last paragraph on 28 May 1939, remained undisturbed until it became evident that war was imminent.

Leyland TD1 coach on Route O at Windsor. Taken soon after Premier Line was acquired by L.P.T.B. Coach is still in Premier livery with Green Line transfer on side. (J. F. Higham).

Leyland TS3 coach (ex-Premier Line) on Route O at Windsor. (J. F. Higham).

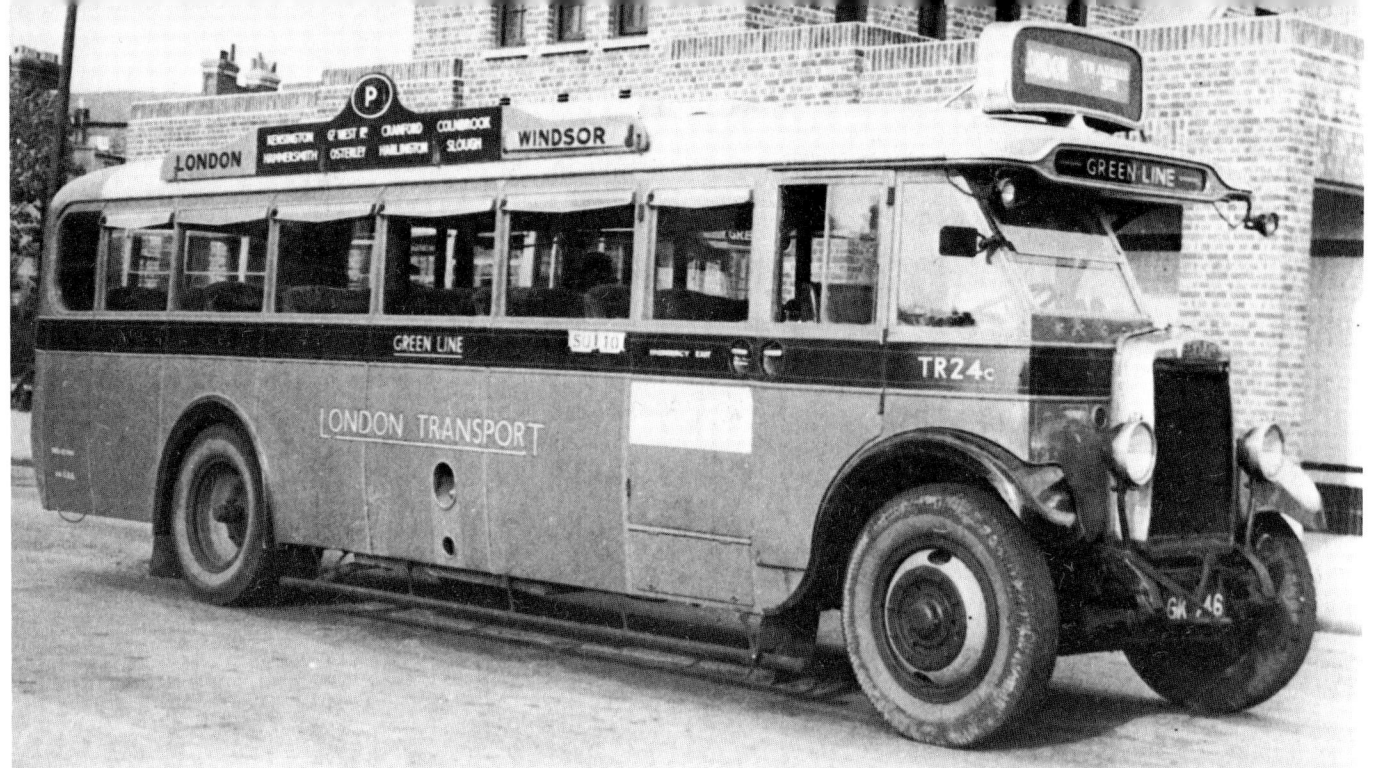

Leyland TS3 coach (ex-Premier Line) at Windsor Coach Station. (J. F. Higham).

Leyland TS3 coach (ex-Premier Line) at Windsor Coach Station. Side routeboards have been altered to Route P, onto which route this coach will transfer on arrival in London. (J. F. Higham).

Ex-Amersham and District A.E.C. 'Regal' coach on Route R outside Amersham Garage. (McCall Collection).

Ex-Bucks Express A.E.C. 'Regal' coach on Route T at Golders Green. (J. F. Higham).

A.E.C. Regal T-type coach at Golders Green on Route T to Watford. (J. F. Higham).

A.E.C. T-type coach en route to Watford at Mill Hill (A. Duke).

Gilford 168MOT type coach (ex-Hillman's Saloon Coaches) outside Romford London Road Garage. (McCall collection).

Saurer 2AD coach (ex-West London Coaches) used to cover the 'shuttle' service from Chesham to connect with the London coach at Amersham. (J. F. Higham).

Former Blue Belle coach rebodied to Green Line standards on Green Line relief duty at Victoria (Eccleston Bridge). (McCall Collection).

Central London Terminal Points.

(1) Kings Cross Coach Station:—
Terminating — BH AK.

(2) Oxford Circus:—
Terminating —Q R
Picking-up — I J M AM and BM

(3) Marylebone Stn (Harewood Avenue):—
Terminating — U.

(4) Liverpool Street (Eldon Street):—
Terminating — V W.

(5) Aldgate (Minories Layby):—
Terminating — X Y AY Z

(6) Charing Cross (Horse Guards Ave):—
Terminating — G, also V
X and Y (Mon-Fri late evenings,
Saturdays p.m. and Sundays.)

Trafalgar Square (America House):—
Terminating — O P.

Victoria (Eccleston Bridge):—
Picking-up — A AA
B C AC D E F H AH K and L.

Green Line – July 1934

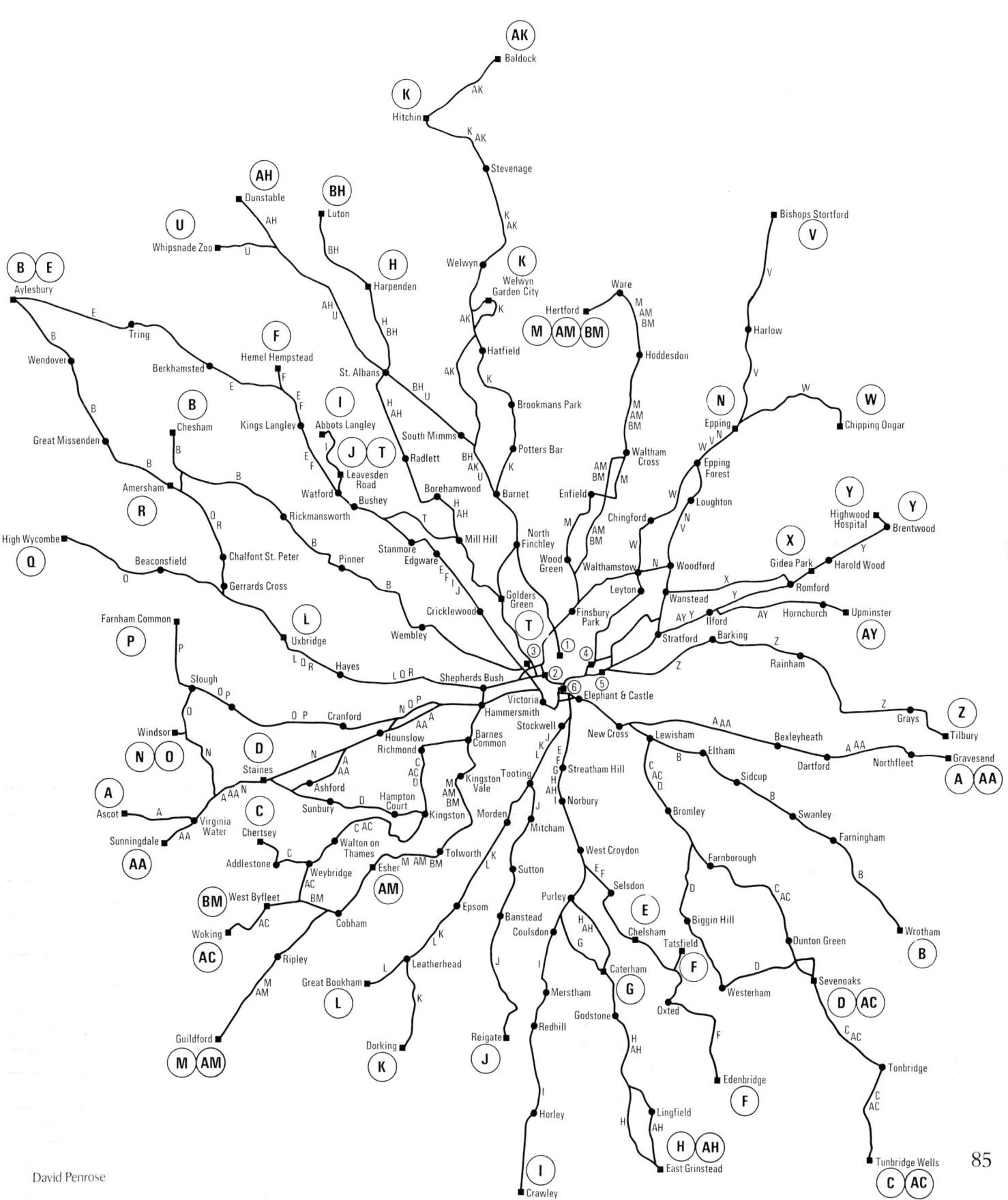

David Penrose

THE WAR YEARS
CHAPTER SIX

1936-1938

When Germany attacked Poland at the end of August 1939, it was obvious that, sooner or later, Great Britain was going to be involved in another war. As has been stated in the previous chapter, the majority of the Green Line services were withdrawn on the night of 31 August and converted to ambulances in order to evacuate patients from some of the London hospitals. Panel bills were hastily posted at all coach stops which explained that the routes had been suspended until further notice, as the coaches had been requisitioned for war service, the consequence being that the public had to find alternative means of travel.

The hardest hit sections of the community were those resident on the sections of Green Line routes where bus services had been withdrawn and replaced with lower fares on Green Line coaches. The Board had obviously given some thought to the matter, as, on 1 September, three new bus routes were introduced, of which two covered the two sections of withdrawn route B which were affected, as follows:
478. Swanley Junction – Wrotham.
393. Amersham (Oakfield Corner) – Great Missenden.

The third new route, numbered 380A, was introduced between Hertford and Broxbourne Station to replace the withdrawn section of Route M2 via Hertford Heath. This left nine sections of former routes working on bus fares uncovered. It is believed that as a temporary measure, buses were worked on these, operating to the former coach timetable and bearing some indication that they were covering the withdrawn services. The local paper in Sevenoaks reported that although the service to London had been discontinued, a half-hourly service was in operation to Tunbridge Wells worked by London Transport red buses.

This state of affairs existed until 25 September, when the following new bus services were introduced to cover the former bus fare sections operated by Green Line coaches:
369. St. Albans – Dunstable, replacing Route H2.
371. Grays – Aveley – East Ham, replacing Route Z2.
371a. Grays – Purfleet-by-Pass – East Ham, replacing Route Z1.
392. Ongar – Woodford Wells, replacing Route W.
396. Bishops Stortford – Epping, replacing Route V.
403c. Warlingham Green – Tatsfield, replacing Route F.
403d. Sevenoaks – Tunbridge Wells, replacing Routes C1/2.
465. Warlingham – Edenbridge, replacing Route F.

Route 380a was absorbed by the extension of Route 342 from Hertford on 8 November 1939; 392 was withdrawn between Epping and Woodford Wells from 6 December, whilst Route 478 was withdrawn between Swanley Junction and Farningham and diverted to Horton Kirby in January 1940.

A partial resumption of Green Line operation commenced on 1 November 1939, when Route Y1 (Aldgate – Brentwood) was reinstated with a 6–10 minute service to Romford, coaches continuing every 30 minutes (20 minutes on Saturdays pm; 15 minutes Sundays) to Brentwood. Bus routes 371/A were withdrawn, and operations on Routes Z1 and Z2 between Aldgate and Grays were resumed on the same date, a half-hourly service being worked on both routes. These operations were resumed with double-deck STL-type buses of both front and rear entrance types operating from Romford and Grays garages respectively.

Route Y2 resumed operation on 13 December with a 6–10 minute service from Aldgate to Hornchurch Station, with a coach every half-hour being extended to Corbets Tey. Unlike Route Y1, this route was operated with single-deck coaches.

Contrary to the expectations of the Ministry of Defence, the expected air-raids had not materialised, and it began to release some of the coaches which had been converted into ambulances, allowing for the resumption of Green Line services on a limited scale, commencing with four routes on 17 January 1940, these being:

A1. Gravesend – 120 – Victoria – 120 – Ascot.
A2. Gravesend – 120 – Victoria – 120 – Sunningdale.
Q. High Wycombe – 60 – Oxford Circus.
R. Chesham – 120 – Amersham Garage – 60 – Oxford Circus.

More coaches were released during January, allowing for the partial resumption of service on Routes H1 and M1, as follows:

H1. Luton – 30 – Victoria (Eccleston Bridge).
M1. Hertford – 30 – Shepherds Bush.

This was followed on 13 March by resumption of service on Route C and partial resumption on Routes E and F:

C. Tunbridge Wells – 30 – Weybridge – 60 – Chertsey.
E. Victoria (Eccleston Bridge) – 60 – Tring – 120 – Aylesbury.
F. Victoria (Eccleston Bridge) – 60 – Hemel Hempstead.

On the same date, Route H1 was extended from Victoria to East Grinstead via Felbridge. It had been intended to re-introduce Route H2 from Luton instead of Dunstable, so that the service would have been hourly via Felbridge (H1) and hourly via Baldwins Hill (H2), but evidently it was felt that operation via Baldwins Hill might prove to be unremunerative.

The last route to be resumed was a half-hourly service from Portman Square to Epping on Route N, which was extended to Bishops Stortford on Saturdays and Sundays, this service commencing operation on 8 May.

There was no further resumption of Green Line services for the time being, but two minor adjustments were made to Routes M1 and N, the former being withdrawn between Shepherds Bush and Oxford Circus on 4 September 1940, whilst the latter lost its Epping – Bishops Stortford section from 2 October. The cross-London services A1, A2, C and H were divided at Victoria (Eccleston Bridge) from 23 October, as the London blitz was now at its height, and this, combined with the black-out was causing considerable late and irregular running to the cross-London operations.

Green Line, of course, was not the only service to suffer disruption from this cause, the main-line railways being very badly interrupted. To alleviate the situation, the Government decided upon a more or less complete resumption of Green Line operation, with the exception that the services would terminate in London.

As a result, the fourteen lettered routes already in operation made their last journeys on 3 December 1940, being replaced on the following morning by seventeen new numbered routes, to which had been added a further seven to new destinations, three of which started their journeys at Victoria, another three at Oxford Circus and one from Aldgate.

Seven more routes made an appearance on 18 December, six of which ran to Victoria and one to Aldgate, but, although the network could now boast of 31 routes in operation, the following pre-war destinations were not being served: Westerham, Tatsfield; Edenbridge; Horsham; West Byfleet; Woking; Dunstable; Baldock; Ongar and Tilbury.

A word now about the new route numbers used on the revised wartime network. The routes were allocated numbers between 2 and 59, working clockwise in sequence round the country terminals, starting from Gravesend (Route 2) and ending at Grays (Routes 59/59A). The allocation of numbers to routes was worked out so that the number used on any Green Line route did not conflict with the Central bus route bearing the same number. A list of the routes, together with their route numbers and frequencies will be found in Appendix 'G' at the end of the book.

There are two alterations to be discussed, however. A route 40B (Watford, Leavesden Road Garage – Victoria) had been proposed to start on 4 December 1940, its timetable being published in the Watford area timetable booklet, which would have given a ten minute service from that town to London with Services 40 and 40A, but for some unknown reason it failed to operate, leaving Routes 40/A working at an uneven 10 and 20 minute interval until the timetable was revised on 9 April 1941. Route 58 (Aldgate – Corbets Tey) was originally to have been numbered as 56, but when it was realised that it would meet Central bus route 56 at Mile End Station, it was decided to number it as 58.

The network rapidly settled down and was well patronised, so much so, that the single-deck coaches used on the majority of the routes proved to be inadequate to deal with the crowds wishing to travel, and while some duplication could be provided, the fuel situation would not permit too many of these to be worked. However, route withdrawals and service cuts on the Central bus services had left about 180 STL-type buses standing idle, and these were repainted into Green Line livery, and allocated to those coach routes where there were no low bridges or other obstructions. This action nearly doubled the seating capacity on the routes on which the double-decks were used, thus saving the need for excessive duplications. These vehicles were introduced to the network on 11 June 1941.

After this, the network settled down to providing a useful and reliable service to the countryside around London, the population of which had greatly increased since the blitz had caused many Londoners to move into the country around London in order to avoid sleepless nights in air-raid shelters. In addition, at this time, most of the southern and eastern coastal towns were inside a special defence area, and thus were not available for holidaymakers, and these made great use of the Green Line services during the summer months.

By 1942 however, fuel supplies were getting down to a dangerously low state due to heavy shipping losses, in addition to which, rubber supplies had been cut by the loss of the plantations in Malaysia. The fortnightly Traffic Circular issued to the operating staff dated 1 May 1942 pointed

A.E.C. T-type coach en route to Upminster on Route Y2. This route was operated by T-type coaches when replaced in the early part of World War II. (J. F. Higham).

Green STL-type bus at Oxford Circus on war-time route to High Wycombe. (J. G. S. Smith).

STL-type bus transferred to Green Line duty in November 1939. Bus is on layover at Aldgate (Minories) Bus and Coach Station. (C. F. Klapper).

Green STL-type bus at Tunbridge Wells Coach Station on war-time route to London. (J. G. S. Smith).

out to drivers that a serious shortage of both commodities had been created, and that effective measures must be taken to ensure economies. They were asked to avoid driving at excessive speeds; unnecessary brake applications; to avoid striking curbs and pavements with their tyres and leaving engines idling at terminals, as well as many other suggestions for the avoidance of wastage.

Despite all these precautions the situation still remained critical, and as the blitz on London had now abated somewhat, and the main-line railways had more or less returned to normal, the Ministry of War Transport now decided that the operation of Green Line coach services could be dispensed with, and they were withdrawn for the second time after the last journeys on Tuesday, 29 September 1942, thus saving 1½ million miles per annum. Where the withdrawal of a Green Line coach route would have left passengers without means of travel to a railway station, existing bus routes were extended to provide the necessary connections, as follows:

Route 25B. Extended from Becontree Heath to Hornchurch Station during weekday peak hours to cover Green Line 58.

Route 72. Extended from Tolworth to Esher daily to cover part of Green Line 18.

Route 86. Reinstated daily from Romford to Chadwell Heath to cover part of Green Line 55.

Route 310. Alternate journeys diverted via Bullsmoor Lane and Great Cambridge Road between Enfield and Waltham Cross, replacing 49.

Route 340. New route from New Barnet to Hatfield (Birchwood Avenue) via Mutton Lane and Barnet-by-Pass, replacing 47A.

Route 355. Extended southwards from Radlett to Borehamwood (Red Lion) replacing part of Route 45.

Routes 345/346. Extended from Northwood to Harefield to provide a service to Batchworth Heath, replacing part of 35.

Route 359. New route jointly operated by London Transport and Eastern National between Amersham and Aylesbury, replacing Green Line 35.

Route 370. Extended from Grays to Purfleet, covering Green Line 59.

Route 371. New route Grays – Rainham via Chandlers Corner, replacing Green Line 59.

Route 371A. New route Grays – Rainham via Aveley, replacing 59A.

Route 402. Extended from Sevenoaks to Tonbridge Station to replace Green Line 5. It was proposed to extend Route 403 to Tunbridge Wells, but the proposal was dropped.

Route 443. New route from Staines Station (SR) to Ascot, replacing Route 23.

Route 478. Withdrawn between Horton Kirby and Farningham and diverted to run Swanley Junction Station – Wrotham replacing Route B.

This time, the withdrawal of Green Line services was more permanent, and they did not return to serve London until nine months after the war had ended, and when they did, it was with a very much altered network to that which had existed hitherto.

Central London Terminal Points.

(A) Victoria (Eccleston Bridge):—
Terminal — 2 3 5 8 14 15 20 21 23 23A 26 26A 35 40 40A 45 46 47 47A.

(B) Oxford Circus:—
9 10 18 33 34 49 52.

(C) Aldgate (Minories Layby):—
53 54 55 58 59 59A.

Note:— There were no through services across London during the war period.

Green Line – January 1941

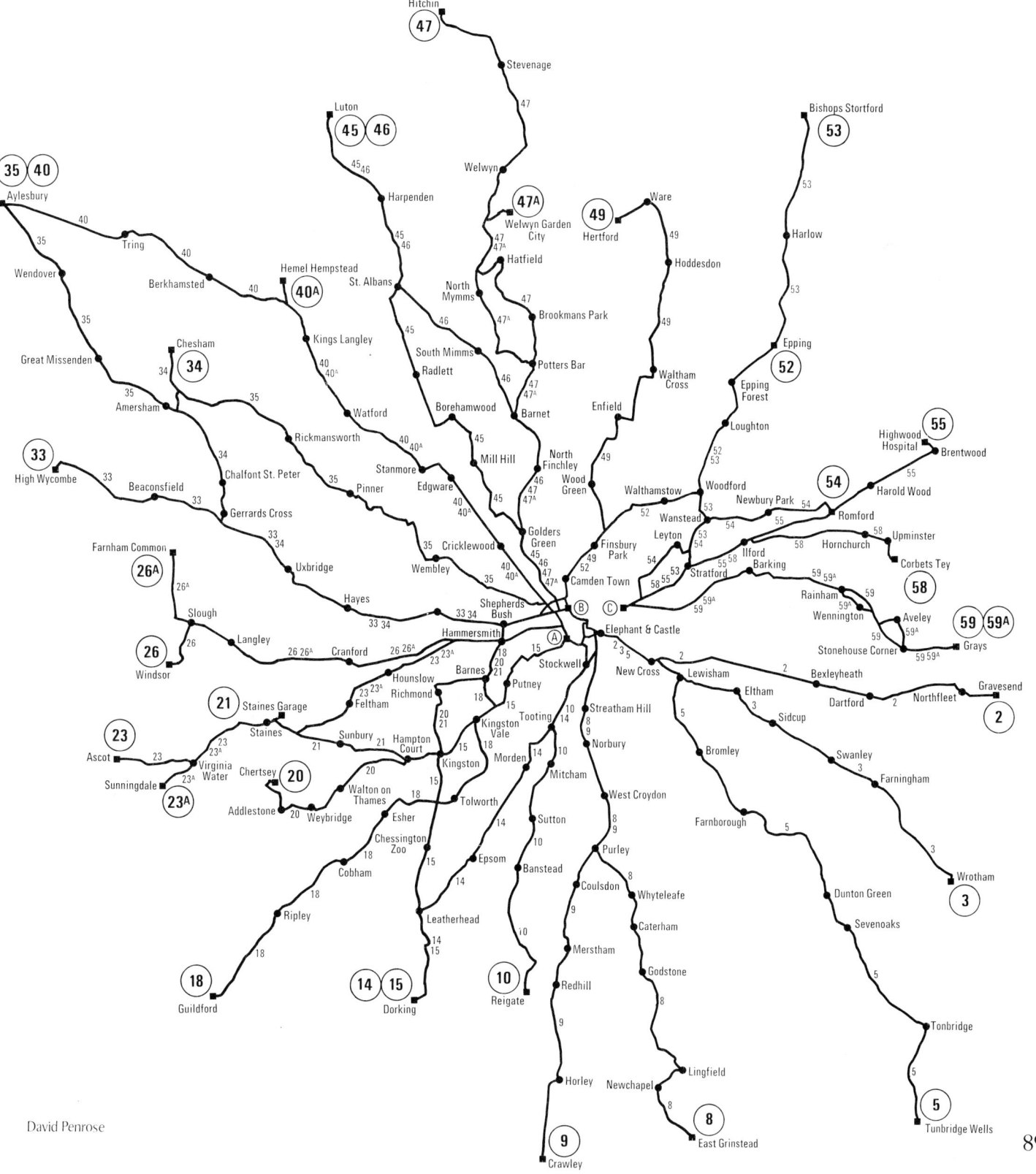

David Penrose

Back Again
Chapter Seven

1938-1953

Although the war in Europe ended on 8 May 1945, an immediate return to peacetime conditions was not possible. Whilst fuel and oil supplies had become more plentiful, they were still rationed, and although by the end of the year bus service levels had been increased, it was still not possible to reinstate Green Line services.

This was partially due to a shortage of suitable vehicles. When Green Line services had been withdrawn for the second time in September 1942, more than a hundred of the single-deck coaches had been handed over to the United States Army for use as troop carriers and mobile canteens, whilst many more of the fleet, although still in London Transport garages, were fitted out as ambulances and were maintained as such in case they should be needed by the Government or Civil Defence Authorities.

By the end of 1945, however, they started to trickle back to the Chiswick Works, where work started on removing the wartime equipment; replacing seats; mechanical overhaul and repainting those returned by the U.S. Army into the Green Line colours.

When the reinstatement of services finally commenced on 6 February 1946, the speed with which the network was replaced (the job was completed in just over five months) indicates that much thought and planning had taken place during the 3½ years Green Line had been off the road.

Although a spoked-wheel arrangement whereby routes radiated outwards from central London was retained, several of the cross-London routes were re-arranged. With the exception of the Whipsnade Zoo route, all of the new services were to operate daily throughout the year, and there were to be no minor deviations on line of route such as had happened in pre-war days. (See Routes F, H1/2, M1/2/3 and Z1/2 in Appendix 'F').

The new services were to be numbered in the 700 series, the numbers being allocated in a clockwise sequence, starting at Gravesend and ending at Tilbury, but it would seem that there must have been a change of plan at some time, as, having started at Gravesend with 701 and carried on clockwise to Windsor (718), the numbering jumped to the Eastern sector, recommencing at Bishops Stortford with 720 and carrying on to Tilbury (723), whilst the self-contained services from High Wycombe and Chesham to Oxford Circus, which, if the clockwise system was to be maintained, should have been numbered 719 and 720, were numbered 724 and 725 instead. The Whipsnade Zoo route, which should have taken the number 721 was numbered 726, which perhaps was logical in a route which operated in the summer only, and the Luton – Kings Cross route became 727 instead of 722.

The first of the new routes was introduced in February 1946, and thereafter groups of routes were introduced at approximately monthly intervals until the network was finally completed at the end of June. The dates of introduction were as follows:

6 February. Routes 715 and 720.
27 February. Route 716.
6 March. Routes 704, 709, 710, 721 and 723.
3 April. Routes 703, 711, 718, 722 and 724.
1 May. Routes 708, 714 and 717.
29 May. Routes 705, 712, 713, 726 and 727.
19 June. Routes 702 and 725.
22 June. Route 701.
26 June. Routes 706 and 707.

A full list of routes, showing the frequencies of service and the new terminals is given in Appendix 'H' at the end of the book.

Before carrying on with the story of the post-war network, it might be as well to compare it with the one which existed up to 1939. The best way of doing this is to work round in a clockwise direction.

There were no changes intermediately to the routes taken by the Gravesend, Wrotham or Tunbridge Wells sections of Routes 701/2, 703 or 704, neither were the pre-war frequencies of service altered.

Westerham was better served than it had been pre-war by Route D, which had consisted of two coaches per hour to Westerham Hill, one of these carrying on to Westerham itself. The post-war service on Route 705 via Bomley gave two coaches per hour, both of which continued via Brasted to Sevenoaks, a facility which had been withdrawn in 1938. There was also an additional service to Westerham every hour by Route 706 via Croydon.

The pre-war terminus at Tatsfield was no longer served, but this state of affairs was corrected in May 1948, when all journeys on Route 706 were diverted to make a double-run into the village.

The pre-war operation to Edenbridge was not resumed in the post-war network, but connections were made by Route 707 at Oxted to bus route 464.

When post-war operation was resumed to East Grinstead, the whole service was routed via Felbridge and Newchapel to Lingfield, and the pre-war alternate journeys via Baldwins Hill and Felcourt were not resumed, but an hourly service on bus route 428 gave access to the coach service at Lingfield.

The principal difference between post-war route 709 and its predecessor, Route G, lies in the route 709 follows from Old Coulsdon to Thornton Heath Pond. Route G had always operated via Coulsdon Court and Stoats Nest, thus missing Coulsdon Town Centre, whilst 709 ran via Meadway and Marlpit Lane to join 710 in Coulsdon, thus providing the pre-war half-hourly headway to London and saving the necessity of providing such a service from Redhill, as had happened in pre-war days. In addition, whilst Route G had operated via Purley Way to Thornton Heath Pond, 709 ran via Croydon Town Centre, thus retaining the pre-war frequency of six coaches an hour from that town to London.

Turning now to the Dorking group of routes, there was no resumption of service between Dorking and Horsham, but that town now enjoyed a good train service.

Nowadays, however, with the stations between Dorking and Horsham only open during Monday–Friday peak hours, there might be some case for the extension of Route 714.

No service was now provided to Leatherhead Garage as had been the case in pre-war days, and this garage, which had operated Green Line routes from their inception until 1939, no longer participated in their workings.

Route 714, which was the post-war replacement for Route K3, took the same route to Kingston, but ran into London via Richmond and Hammersmith instead of the K3 route via Roehampton, Putney and Chelsea.

The service from Guildford was exactly the same as in pre-war days, but there were no extra coaches from Byfleet joining the route at Cobham, nor was there the coach which turned at Esher pre-war to boost the service to London to four coaches per hour. This was soon corrected when passenger traffic increased rapidly over the Esher – London section and the service was increased from two to three coaches per hour from 17 April 1946.

West Byfleet came off pretty badly when the post-war network was planned, as it lost both of its coach services. Admittedly, the area had had no Green Line service since 1939, and presumably the former coach passengers had transferred their allegiance to the railway, on which trains only took 35–40 minutes to reach London.

The service to Woking was restored, but followed a different route, now working from Weybridge via Addlestone, New Haw and Woodham instead of Weybridge Station, Byfleet, West Byfleet and Maybury.

Both 716 and 717 took a different route between East Molesey and Kingston, using the direct road through Hampton Court rather than the more circuitous route through Thames Ditton taken by pre-war C1 and C2. The route through Hampton Court allowed for the operation of double-deck vehicles on relief journeys, whereas the low railway bridge at Thames Ditton had precluded the use of these types of vehicles.

Routes 701 and 702 followed the main road through Hounslow Heath and Bedfont to Staines, leaving Feltham and Ashford without coach facilities, although Ashford did get a Green Line service from November 1964 when orbital route 725 was diverted that way.

Turning now to the Slough area, coach operation was not resumed to Farnham Common, but this area was now adequately served by buses to and from Slough, which gave good connections to Routes 704 and 705.

Aylesbury lost its service to London via Amersham, but gained a half-hourly service via Watford, which was a much more direct route.

On the other hand, Watford lost out in the post-war network. Pre-war it had enjoyed eight coaches per hour (two to Victoria; four to Oxford Circus plus two to Golders Green with through tickets to London on the Underground). Now it had to make do with four coaches per hour to Victoria on Routes 706/7/8, although for a period in the winter of 1946/7, two extra coaches per hour were provided between Watford and Victoria on Route 708, and ten years later, Route 719 appeared on the scene. North of Watford, Garston and Abbots Langley were no longer served, and it was to be another ten years before this area saw a Green Line service.

Routes 712 and 713 followed a different route between Radlett and St. Albans to that of their predecessors, running via Shenley and London Colney instead of Colney Street and Park Street. Although operation via Shenley slightly increased the running time between London and St. Albans, it allowed for the operation of double-deck vehicles as relief coaches, whereas a low railway bridge on the pre-war route

10T10 coach at Victoria en route to E. Grinstead (L. Norris).

RF-type coach at Rickmansworth en route to Wrotham. (J. G. S. Smith).

TF-type coach at Morden en route to Dorking (Alan B. Cross). (J. G. S. Smith).

had restricted all operations to single-deck vehicles.

Between Potters Bar and Hatfield there was no post-war service of Green Line coaches via Mutton Lane, Water End and the Barnet-by-Pass, but this was a sparsely populated area, and in 1946 was adequately served by bus route 340.

Hertford started off with a half-hourly service on Route 715, which was increased to every 20 minutes from 17 April, but this route followed the roads served by pre-war Route M1, but the pre-war route along the Great Cambridge Road between Turnpike Lane Station and Southbury Road, plus Ponders End to Waltham Cross via Enfield Wash was not resumed, nor was the section across Hertford Heath.

The pre-war service to Ongar from Liverpool Street was not included in the new network, although the author has the feeling that it was intended for Route 718 to operate beyond Epping to Ongar, but the work on extending the Central Line out to Epping and Ongar had now resumed, and, in these circumstances, a coach service might have proved to be superfluous. These remarks also apply to the reinstatement of the route between London and Romford along Eastern Avenue. The tube railway under that thoroughfare had been completed in pre-war days, except for the tracks, and it was used as a factory during the war. It was only a matter of time before trains would be running to Newbury Park, so the resumption of a coach service was unnecessary.

On the Grays route the operation from Rainham via Chandlers Corner and the A13 road which avoided Wennington and Aveley villages was not resumed, but as this route was practically devoid of human habitation, very few people were inconvenienced.

The new network soon settled down, and passenger traffic built up fairly quickly. Petrol was still rationed, new cars were unobtainable, and even a modest fare increase introduced on 1 July 1946 did nothing to stem the flow of passengers.

Hitherto only single tickets were issued on the coaches, but from 1 October 1946, a limited scheme of Cheap Day return tickets to and from Central London was introduced. These tickets were only available on Tuesdays, Wednesdays and Thursdays. Tickets from the country areas were only available on the forward journeys on coaches scheduled to arrive in London after 10.30 am and could not be used for the return journey between 4.30 and 6.30 pm. On the other hand, tickets from Central London could be purchased on any coach before 4.30 and after 6.30 pm and the return journey could be made at any time on the day of issue.

In order to encourage more commuter traffic, Weekly (6-return journey) tickets were issued from Monday 30 September. These were available for use from Monday to Saturday, and were issued for fares from 1/4 single giving 12 journeys for the price of 9 single fares. They were issued on any coach on any route, with the exception of Route 726 (Whipsnade), and could be purchased between intermediate farestages, except for cross-London trips such as New Cross to Kensington High Street or Brixton to Cricklewood.

Routes 724 (High Wycombe) and 725 (Chesham) made their last journeys on Tuesday, 11 November 1947, being replaced on the following day by three cross-London routes as follows:

709. Chesham – 60 – Oxford Circus – 60 – Caterham. Journeys extended to Godstone Garage.

710. Amersham Garage – 60 – Oxford Circus – 60 – Crawley.

711. High Wycombe – 30 – Oxford Circus – 30 – Reigate.

Strangely enough, the introduction of cross-London operation on 711 revived the old Skylark Motor Coach company operation of 1929 which covered the same route, but on an hourly headway.

Green Line returned to Tatsfield from 19 May 1948, when all trips on Route 706 were diverted to double-run into the village.

From 1 June 1948 the issue of Cheap Day Return Tickets was extended to include Mondays and Fridays, which helped to stimulate traffic on those two days.

From 1948, all London Transport operations had come under the control of the British Transport Commission and it was now possible to ascertain the passenger loadings on Green Line as the Commission's Annual Report for 1948 revealed that 26 million passengers had been carried in that year, whilst in 1949 that figure had dropped by one million despite the fact that there had been a very fine and hot summer season.

Green Line service was restored to the Chingford area from 10 May 1950 when Route 718 was diverted at Walthamstow via Chingford Mount. To avoid the unremunerative section via Epping New Road followed by the pre-war Ongar service, 718 turned off at 'The Bull and Crown' along Whitehall Road to rejoin its original route at Woodford Wells.

Another fare revision was introduced on 1 October 1950, and for the first time, Green Line fares were charged on a strict mileage basis, many additional farestages being introduced on all routes, which had the effect of reducing the distance covered by the 1/- minimum fare charged in the Metropolitan Police District. The Cheap Day Return fares to and from London were withdrawn except on Routes 716 and 717 between London and points from Potters Bar to Welwyn Garden City and Hitchin, where they were in competition with Birch Brothers and on Route 721, where the return fare from Brentwood to Aldgate was retained.

The passenger returns for 1950 showed a further drop in passengers carried, the drop being from 25 millions in 1949 to 23 millions in 1950. Petrol rationing had ended on 1 May 1950, and this may well have been the cause of the drop.

A new L.C.C. estate had been under construction for some time at Belhus Park, Aveley, and there was now a demand for transport facilities to East Ham and Dagenham. From 4 July 1951, alternate coaches on Route 723 were diverted at Aveley Village via Stifford Road, Ford Place and North Stifford. This diversion was numbered 723A and provided the first example of a suffix-lettered Green Line route.

During the middle of 1951, the L.C.C. informed the company which controlled the operaton of the temporary Kings Cross Coach Station that it would be shortly needing the site for housing purposes. This meant that another terminus had to be found for Route 727, the problem being solved by linking it up with Route 714 to form a new cross-London route from Luton to Dorking via Kings Cross and Baker Street. The new service took the number 714 and commenced operation on 30 September.

1951 was the year of the Festival of Britain, the major events of which took place in London, bringing in many

TF-type coach en route to Baker Street at Kingston. (Alan B. Cross).

RF-type coach at Hertford about to depart for London (Marble Arch). (J. G. S. Smith).

![RF-type coach]

RF-type coach bound for London (Aldgate), in Epping High Street. (J. G. S. Smith).

Post-war Daimler Double-Deck coach in Aldgate Bus and Coach Station. (J. F. Higham).

provincial and foreign tourists to the capital. The B.T.C. Annual Report for that year revealed that Green Line had carried 27 million passengers, an increase of four million over the previous year.

1952 was an uneventful year and ended with a small alteration to Route 717 which was diverted through the Sheerwater Estate on its way to and from Woking. Once again passenger traffic showed an increase, rising to 30 millions for 1952.

The next year was Coronation Year, and was also noted for the introduction of the first orbital route from Windsor to Gravesend. Numbered 725, it commenced operation between Windsor and Gravesend on 1 July, providing useful cross-country connections between Dartford, Bromley, Croydon, Sutton and Kingston every hour. All of these connections had hitherto necessitated the use of slow local buses, or if attempted by rail, had meant travelling into Central London and out again.

33 million passengers were carried in Coronation Year, a rise of three millions over the 1952 figure. Obviously the traffic carried in the Coronation period had much to do with this, but when it is compared with the increase achieved in the Festival of Britain year, the result seems a little disappointing.

The next two years started a period of much change as the housing estates in the outer suburban areas and the New Towns started to receive the first of their new residents. The orbital route 725 introduced in July 1953 had been an undoubted success and much duplication had been necessary, mainly from both ends of the route to Croydon, and it was decided to increase the frequency from hourly to half-hourly between Windsor and Dartford. The revised service was introduced on 28 April 1954, bringing Green Line operation to Dartford Garage for the first time since 1935, as this garage lost its workings on Routes A1/A2 when the new garage at Northfleet opened.

This was followed on 19 May by a revision to Route 726 (Whipsnade), which was extended from Baker Street to Romford. The service remained as a limited stop route and only picked up at certain points between Romford and Aldgate, running express from that point to Baker Street. Single tickets only were issued and in order to compete with local excursions operated by private coach operators the fare from Romford to Whipsnade was the same as that from Baker Street.

A revision to the operation of Routes 723/A was introduced on 30 June. The passenger traffic on these two routes had increased to such an extent that double-deck operation with RT-type vehicles was introduced. Route 723A was withdrawn between Grays and Tilbury, and Route 723 now ran to that town via Chadwell St. Mary, whilst the former journeys via East Thurrock and Dock Road were renumbered 723B. A new terminal was introduced at Tilbury Ferry (Riverside) Station and an hourly frequency was provided by each route.

On the same date, a new hourly service numbered 720A was brought into operation to Harlow New Town. This route supplemented 720 to the outskirts of Old Harlow and then ran via First Avenue to The Stow.

The latter half of 1954 was beset by staff problems which resulted in the temporary withdrawal of two routes and the partial withdrawal of another. From 3 October, Routes 710 and 720A were withdrawn and 705 lost its Windsor – Victoria section. Normal working was restored on 705 and 720A on 20 October, followed a week later by 710.

Hatfield and Stevenage were the next areas to see changes to their coach services when 717 was diverted at Valley Road Corner to run to Stevenage as new route 716A. To serve Welwyn Garden City, a new hourly 717 was introduced from Victoria which diverged from 716/A at Little Heath Church to serve Brookmans Park and Welham Green. These alterations were started on 5 October 1955.

There was a railway strike during May and June 1955, and the B.T.C. Annual Report for that year showed that Green Line carried 35 million passengers, two million more than the previous year.

1956 was a year of much change to Green Line services. The New Towns were growing rapidly, whilst the South Hatfield area and the large estate at Borehamwood were both demanding fast and direct transport to Central London. To serve the South Hatfield area, 717 was diverted at Welham Green to run via Dixons Hill Road, Barnet-by-Pass and Bishops Rise, this diversion applying from 18 April. A further programme of alterations was introduced on 11 July, when 712 and 713 were diverted at Borehamwood to run through the new L.C.C. estate and Theobald Street to rejoin their original route just south of Radlett village. Route 718 was extended to Harlow New Town, running from Potter Street through the Southern Way and Tillwicks Road area to the bus station. In addition, 720A was diverted at Potter Street over the same route, giving three coaches an hour to London with a choice of travel to either the West End or City.

On the same date a new service was introduced to Hemel Hempstead from London (Victoria), which, in addition to serving the New Town Centre, also operated through the eastern suburbs of Adeyfield and Leverstock Green. Allocated the number 719 (in use for the first time), it ran hourly, restoring the pre-war Green Line facility to Garston and Abbots Langley as well as opening up new territory between Stanmore and Kilburn by running through Queensbury, Kingsbury, Neasden and Willesden.

A few weeks later on 8 August, Hertford received a new service to Marble Arch. Numbered 715A, it ran hourly, restoring the pre-war service to Hertford Heath and Ponders End, and breaking new ground by running through Edmonton to Tottenham and Manor House.

Despite all these praiseworthy attempts to encourage new traffic to Green Line, when the figures for 1956 were announced, they showed a drop of one million passengers, probably due to the fact that, as 1956 drew to a close the Suez crisis occurred, resulting in the rationing of petrol and diesel oil, which caused the introduction of reduced services on some Green Line routes from 17 December. Route 709 lost its Amersham – Chesham section outside the peak hours on Mondays–Fridays and on Saturday and Sunday mornings. Route 712 lost its Dorking – Leatherhead and St. Albans – Luton sections during the same periods as 709; 716 was withdrawn between Addlestone and Chertsey and 718 between Epping and Harlow New Town was reduced to hourly at certain periods of the day. Outside the peak hours on Mondays–Fridays and all day on Sundays, Route 722 became half-hourly from Aldgate to Hornchurch and hourly to Corbets Tey, and 725 was withdrawn between Dartford and Gravesend in the mornings after the early

Offside front view of TF-type coach at Aldgate (J. F. Higham).

journeys, and in off-peak hours on Mondays–Fridays became an hourly service between Staines and Windsor. Although the rationing of fuel continued until May 1957, normal services were restored on these Green Line routes from Monday, 1 April.

As a result of the fuel rationing and the general uncertainty when it would end, a major Summer Programme was not introduced for 1957 but some minor alterations came into operation on Green Line, starting with an increase in frequency from hourly to half-hourly on 719 from 29 May. This was followed on 12 June by a slight extension to 717 in Welwyn Garden City from the Station to Cole Green Lane. From 28 July, certain journeys on 721 were extended in Brentwood to Highwood Hospital on Sunday afternoons, thus restoring another pre-war facility. Five days later on 2 August, Route 710 was diverted at Horley along the new section of the A23 road, passing the entrance to Gatwick Airport, but now leaving Povey Cross and Lowfield Heath unserved.

Passenger figures for 1957 reached the highest total they had ever achieved when it was announced that 36 million passengers had been carried in that year. There is no doubt that the petrol shortage in the early part of the year had brought many motorists back to public transport even if it was only for their journeys to and from work.

A further attempt to attract off-peak traffic on Mondays–Fridays was made when, for the first time since their withdrawal in 1950, Cheap Day Return tickets were issued on certain routes. Introduced from 8 April 1958, they were issued on Mondays–Fridays only between 9 am and 4 pm from London *only* to Tunbridge Wells, Dorking and Guildford. They were planned as an experiment for the summer and it was intended to withdraw them after 24 September, and it was unfortunate that the experiment was spoiled by the fact that the coaches were off the road for eight weeks in May and June due to the crews being on strike. They were withdrawn on the appointed date and the experiment was not repeated.

The strike mentioned in the last paragraph was an event which marred the whole of the operations for the rest of the year. The reason for the strike is now academic but suffice to say that neither London Transport nor the crews gained anything from it, and when the passenger statistics were published in 1959, they showed a drop of six million passengers in 1958. It has been said that the strike accelerated the fall in passengers which continued during the following years, but while this may have been so as far as the general bus services were concerned it was not the case with Green Line, as a peak of 36 million passengers was once again achieved in 1959.

There was little alteration to the routes during this period, but Route 722 was diverted between Rush Green and Romford (Roneo Corner) from 8 January 1958 in order to provide a service to Oldchurch Hospital. Route 705 was diverted at Bromley South via Hayes Village in an effort to tap new sources of traffic, whilst a half-hourly service was provided to Highwood Hospital daily on Route 721, both of these alterations commencing on 15 October 1958.

An attempt was made to break new ground in the Romford area in the autumn of 1959. It was planned that part of the service on Route 722 would be diverted at Oldchurch Hospital to run via Waterloo Road, Mawney Road, Eastern Avenue and Collier Row to terminate at North Romford (Chase Cross). This was a cleverly designed route, which would have given the residents of that area a direct service to London, and it was to have operated from 14 October. Unfortunately, there were two Central bus routes from Chase Cross which more or less covered the same route as the proposed Green Line service as far as Becontree Heath, and the crews working them felt that the new service would lead to abstraction of traffic from their buses, which might ultimately lead to their withdrawal. In consequence of this, they opposed its introduction and the Union intervened on their behalf, and Route 722A never operated.

Since the diversion of Routes 712 and 713 at Borehamwood had been introduced there had been a fall-off in passengers over the section between London Colney and Radlett. This was partly due to the somewhat roundabout route they took south of that point, while the heavy traffic congestion being experienced along Finchley Road and Watford Way had destroyed the reliability of the timetables. There was however, enough traffic left on the Shenley section to support an hourly service, so this route left to 713 and 712 was diverted at Radlett via Colney Street, Park Street and St. Stephens to St. Albans from 23 November 1960.

On the same date adjustments were made to Routes 716 and 717 in order to give a better service to Welwyn Garden City and its growing suburbs. Route 716 was diverted at Stanborough (The Bull) to run via Longcroft Green, Pear Tree Village, Welwyn Garden City Town Centre, Knightsfield and Digswell to Welwyn Village, leaving 716A to cope with the traffic along the Great North Road. 717 was diverted at Hatfield in an easterly direction to operate via Mill Green and Howlands to terminate once again at Welwyn Garden City Station. The introduction of this operation caused a certain amount of confusion in Hatfield for a time until intending passengers got used to 716/A running along St. Albans Road in an easterly direction to London, while 717 ran in a westerly direction to go to the same destination.

When the traffic figures for 1960 were announced they had once again reached 36 million, but it will be seen that there was no increase over the 1959 total. Green Line had been holding its own since the strike but this was the last year in which it was to do this, and the decline started in the following year.

Central London Terminal Points.

(A) Baker Street Station:—
Terminating — 709 710 711 714 726.
Picking-up — 712 713 716 717 718.

(B) Kings Cross Coach Station:—
Route 727 terminates here.

(C) Aldgate (Minories Layby):—
Terminating — 720 721 722 723.

(D) Oxford Circus:—
Terminating — 724 725.
Picking-up — 709 710 711 715.

(E) Victoria (Eccleston Bridge):—
Picking-up — 701 702 703 704 705 706 707 708 712 713 718.

Green Line – May 1946

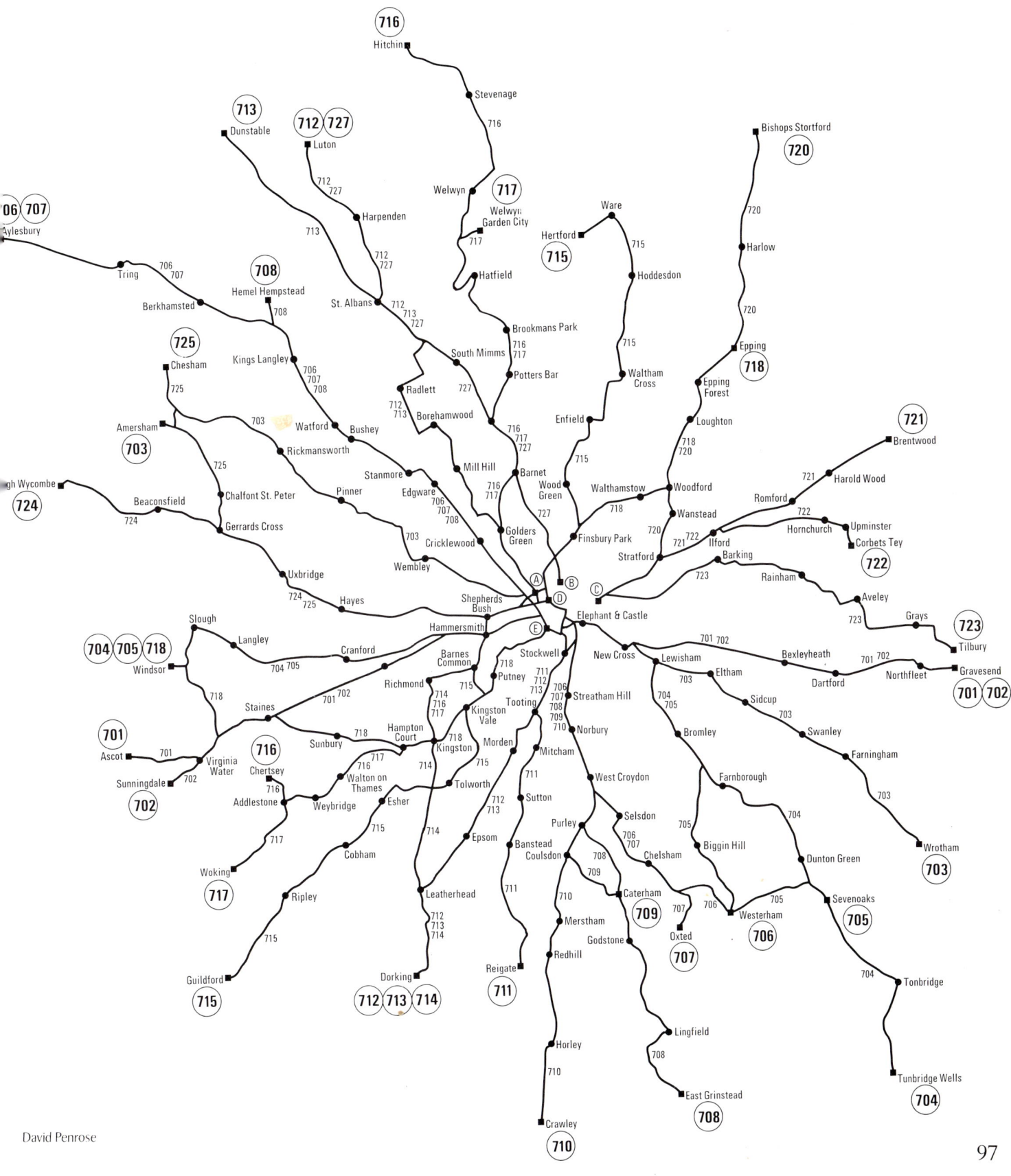

David Penrose

DECLINE SETS IN
CHAPTER EIGHT

1953-1966

From the time they returned to serve London and its countryside in 1946, except for a slight decline in 1949 and 1950, the Green Line services of London Transport had enjoyed an ever increasing passenger traffic which reached its peak in 1959 and 1960. From then onwards, the loadings started to fall, and in this chapter we shall discuss the various methods that were tried in order to stem the decline.

Several factors had contributed to their success, among the most important of which was the high standard of service performance. The timetables allowed for a scheduled speed of 18·4 m.p.h. to be maintained throughout the routes, which compared favourably with the 11·3 m.p.h. on ordinary bus services. In addition, before staff shortages arose in certain areas, it was the practice to employ only the more senior staff on the Green Line duty rotas, thereby ensuring a high standard of courtesy, experience, and efficiency.

The slight decline in 1949 and 1950 can be attributed in part to a drop in traffic on Routes 721 and 722, due to the electrification of the railway from Liverpool Street to Shenfield in the late summer of 1949. The main traffic losses occurred west of Romford, where the railway stations and Green Line stops were in close proximity. As either train or coach deposited their passengers on the edge of the City at either Aldgate or Liverpool Street, necessitating a further bus or Tube journey to reach their destinations, the faster electric train won the day over the coach. The loss of traffic on Route 721 was later balanced by increased loadings from Harold Wood and Gidea Park when the Harold Hill L.C.C. estate built up, and where the coach was more convenient than the train.

Green Line was fortunate in that five of the six New Towns that were established to take the overspill population from London, were inside its operating area. As they grew up, fresh sources of traffic were tapped with trips to London for shopping and entertainment, as well as visits to friends and relatives still left in the metropolis. In the reverse direction, visitors came out from London to see friends and relatives in the New Towns, and many of these, especially older people without cars, used the Green Line, resulting in the operation of many relief coaches on Sundays, especially in the evenings when it was usual to see one and sometimes more double-deck buses operating on each departure to London. Before the central shopping areas built up in the New Towns there was also a good off-peak traffic, especially on local market days and Saturdays, to the nearest large town possessing full shopping facilities. Much of this traffic was carried by local buses, but Green Line came in for a fair share, particularly at Harlow, where the nearest large shops were at Walthamstow or Stratford, bringing much useful traffic to Routes 718 and 720.

In retrospect, the writer feels that an opportunity was

RF-type coach in last Green Line Coaches Ltd. livery at Colindale. (J. G. S. Smith).

RF-type coach at Colindale en route to Oxted, passing site of Colindale trolleybus depot. (J. G. S. Smith).

RF-type coach at Kings Langley. (J. G. S. Smith).

RF-type coach outside Ealing Town Hall en route to Crawley. (J. G. S. Smith).

RF-type vehicle in Country Bus livery on Green Line duty at Beaconsfield. (J. G. S. Smith).

RF-type in last Green Line livery at Park Street (near St. Albans).

missed at this time by not introducing double-deck vehicles sooner on the New Town coach routes. Admittedly, neither the Routemaster bus nor coach had been thought of at this time, but passengers travelled quite happily for long distances on the RT-type double-deck buses used on Green Line relief duties on weekends, and if some of these vehicles had been fitted with platform doors and luggage racks on both decks, running costs would have been reduced, especially later on when Green Line crews had their pay brought up to the same rate as that paid on Central Buses in London.

1959 saw the commencement of the elimination of steam operation on the main-line railways North of the Thames. In May, the lines from Kings Cross to Hertford North and Hitchin were converted to diesel multiple unit operation with more frequent and faster trains, but the line from Hertford North followed a different route to London than that used by Route 715, whilst Route 716 from Hitchin, due to competition with Birch Brothers between that point and London, ran at fares which were lower than those charged on the railway, so there was little traffic loss to the Green Line.

In January 1960 the line between St. Pancras and Luton went over to complete diesel operation, causing some loss of traffic on the outer sections of Routes 712 and 714. Later, in November, the Hertford East and Bishops Stortford lines from Liverpool Street were electrified. At first, this made little impact on Route 715 from Hertford, but once the Victoria Line tube came into service with an exchange station to the main-line at Seven Sisters and through tickets were issued from stations on the Hertford East Line to the West End, long distance traffic on 715 began to fall off. The route which suffered the most from this electrification was 720, which lost most of its long distance traffic from Bishops Stortford.

After the 1958 bus and coach strike there was a great increase in the level of private motoring for journeys to work. Apart from taking passengers away from public transport, it also increased traffic congestion in urban areas, thereby destroying the credibility and reliability of Green Line timetables, thereby losing more passengers from public transport.

Green Line had suffered several fare revisions without any real loss of passengers, but this trend was reversed from 1961 onwards. In that year, two fare increases were introduced, the first in January and the second in July. The first was on a progressive scale, starting with a penny increase of fares between 11d and 1/11, then building up in progressive penny steps, so that the increase on higher fares was as much as 1/4. The second increase added an extra penny to all fares. Passengers who were fortunate enough to reside on routes where the service to London was shared with another operator working the same type of service, did not suffer either of these fare increases, as the other operators had not revised their fares due to lower running costs in most cases.

There was evidently a great deal of resistance to the 1961 fare increases, as, when the traffic figures for 1961 were published in the B.T.C. Annual Report, the figure quoted showed a drop of two million passengers, and now a fight was on to stop the decline.

For a month from the first of January 1962, Cheap Day Return Tickets were issued to London on Mondays to Fridays after 9.30 am on Routes 703, 709, 710 and 711 from Chesham, Amersham and High Wycombe and intermediate points en route to London in an effort to attract traffic to the London Sales. Conductors on inward journeys were asked to inform the inspectors at Victoria (Route 703) and Oxford Circus (for the other three routes) of the number of tickets at each value they had issued. Evidently, the experiment was not a success as it was not repeated in the following year.

A further effort to attract traffic was made in April, when Ranger Tickets valid for seven days were introduced, giving 25/- (£1·25) of travel on Country Buses or Green Line routes for £1. They were available for use after 9.30 am on Mondays to Fridays and all day on weekends. Surprisingly enough, these tickets were not sold on the vehicles, but had to be obtained from enquiry offices or bus garages, which did not help to increase their sales. The experiment ended on the last day of September and was not repeated in subsequent years.

The first of the new Routemaster double-deck coaches made their appearance on Routes 715/A from 29 August 1962, and an attractive poster appeared on bus shelters, garages and Underground stations to draw attention to their introduction. Unfortunately, the service on 715 was reduced from every twenty minutes to half-hourly on the basis of increased seating on the double-deckers, but, if passengers just missed a coach, they were not happy about waiting a full half-hour for the next, and loadings started to drop away. More Routemasters were delivered in September and the whole 68 vehicles ordered were in service by December on the busiest routes, namely those serving the New Towns, although in the case of Hemel Hempstead they only appeared on Route 719. All this sounds more like growth than decline, but the truth is that these new coaches had arrived too late. Car use had increased; the modernised railway services had started to take the longer distance passengers, whilst in the New Towns, although their populations were on the increase, the need to travel to outside areas for shopping and entertainment had decreased, as these facilities were now available in the New Town Centres.

1962 was the last year in which any separate traffic figures for Green Line were shown in the B.T.C. Report, as that organisation was abolished under the Transport Act (1962) and London Transport was now an independent Board responsible to the Minister of Transport, and from 1963, lumped the traffic figures of all bus and coach services together in one total in their Annual Reports. The figures for 1962 were very depressing, 32 million passengers having been carried, once again two million less than the previous year.

It had been noticed that for the past few summer seasons, the loadings on Route 726 to Whipsnade Zoo had been falling, and it was thought this might be due to the fact that the Baker Street picking-up point was too far away from the usual tourists' haunts. To remedy this an experiment was tried for the 1963 season by the introduction on 22 May of Route 712A from Dorking, although the majority of the Zoo journeys started from Victoria, picking up at Hyde Park Corner and Marble Arch as well as Baker Street. This operation was very successful, and a similar operation on Route 712 was repeated in subsequent summer seasons. Although it lost some journeys, Route 726 was not withdrawn, and from May 1964 was speeded up by a diversion along the M1 motorway between Mill Hill and Flamstead

RF-type coach and RF Country Bus in the coach park at Whipsnade Zoo. (J. G. S. Smith).

RF-type coach at South Mimms (Bignells Corner) en route to Dorking. (J. G. S. Smith).

Central Buses RTL-type bus used as a substitute for a Green Line coach breakdown. At Egham en route to Windsor. (G. Mead).

(Friars Wash).

Express operation between Victoria and Windsor was introduced on Route 705 on 28 August 1963, reducing the running time from 79 to 60 minutes by serving only 14 out of the 44 stops on this section of route, also by using the Great West Road extension from Hammersmith to Ealing Road (Brentford) and avoiding the narrow road through Colnbrook by using the by-pass.

The new Thames Tunnel between Purfleet and Dartford opened for use on 18 November 1963, and on the same day, Route 722 was extended from Corbets Tey to Dartford. The extension was not a great success as 722 was subject to heavy congestion throughout the day which played havoc with the timetable. Loadings on the extension were light, as the population on both sides of the river at this point had no real affinity with each other. It lasted for just under a year, being withdrawn on 4 October 1964.

Further fare increases were introduced in June 1963 and July 1964, the first being on the usual progressive scale, starting with a penny increase on fares up to 2/9, then proceeding in penny steps to a maximum of 10d on higher fares. The second was more selective, applying in the lower ranges to a penny increase on 1/3, 1/11 and 2/2 fares, with fares from 2/4 upwards increased by twopence. Birch Brothers also increased their fares at this time so Routes 716/A/717 did not escape an increase on the northern half of their routes. Naturally, neither of these increases helped to stem the decline in passenger traffic.

There were several adjustments to services in the Winter Programme for 1964, introduced on 4 November. The electrification of the Metropolitan Line from Rickmansworth to Amersham in 1960 had eroded the passenger loadings on the northern half of the route 703, so it was now withdrawn. To cover the southern end of the route, 717 was extended from Victoria to Wrotham, at the same time being converted from RF-type single-deck coaches to Routemasters. These were released from Harlow Garage, as Routes 720/A were now converted to single-deck crew operation. There was no reduction in frequency on Route 717, as it was already an hourly service.

On Route 709, passenger loadings had been falling for some time on the western end of the route, but not enough to justify withdrawal. Instead the section between Amersham Garage and London was converted to express operation, serving only 17 stops between these two points. It was also diverted along Western Avenue between Uxbridge and Shepherds Bush in order to speed up the service and perhaps attract some new traffic. On Sundays, 709 was withdrawn west of Baker Street, and the service to Chesham was provided by the extension of 710 from Amersham.

Timetable and journey adjustments were made at the northern ends of Routes 712/713. Certain 712 journeys were renumbered 712B and ran to Dunstable and some 713 journeys ran to Luton as 713A. This move evidently caused some confusion amongst crews and passengers, and the numbering system was altered once more from 14 April 1965. The route number now indicated the route followed by the coach and not the destination. All 712 journeys ran via Park Street between Radlett and St. Albans, with all 713 timings running via Shenley and London Colney.

The Fenchurch Street – Grays – Tilbury electric train service had now been running for two years, and had been steadily acquiring passengers from Routes 723/B, both of which ran parallel with the railway for most of their journey. On the other hand, the loadings on Route 723A through Belhus Estate were still very buoyant. In view of this, 723 was diverted at Aveley to help out, still retaining its workings to Tilbury via Chadwell St. Mary. 723B remained running parallel to the railway once per hour, but lost its Grays – Tilbury section via Dock Road, which was transferred to Route 723A.

A new express route was introduced from Tring to Victoria at this time, numbered 727. In addition to providing a direct service between Tring and the new Hemel Hempstead Town Centre, it ran non-stop along the M1 motorway for 14 miles to Mill Hill. There were only 19 stops on the whole route, but the roads followed from Mill Hill to Victoria undid all the good the fast-running along the motorway had achieved. The section of the M1 between Mill Hill and Staples Corner had not been completed at this time, and 727 had to use Watford Way, a road which was heavily congested in peak hours, also at that time there were extensive road widening works going on along Finchley Road. On reaching Baker Street, 727 ran to Victoria via Oxford Circus, Charing Cross and Westminster, a route which was no help to drivers trying to make-up lost time.

There was a proposal by London Transport to increase fares yet again in 1965, and this time the Government intervened. The Transport Minister stated in the House of Commons that the Government felt an examination of the conditions under which the Board operated was necessary. They were anxious that, while this was being carried out, the attractiveness of the Board's services should not be impaired by a further fare increase, at the same time giving an assurance that the Board would not have to bear the loss in revenue. A sum of £3,850,000 was paid to the Board in compensation for not raising fares, but there was still a loss of passengers in 1965, and London Transport incurred a deficit of £1 million when the final accounts for the year were presented.

The express operation on Route 705 to Windsor had shown itself to be a great success during its first full summer of operation in 1964. This was only to be expected, as Windsor is very popular with both tourists and Londoners, especially on fine days. The heavy loadings experienced during most of the summer necessitates the operation of many relief coaches, which are worked by crews on overtime. To cut running costs, it was decided that all relief coaches would emulate the example of Route 705 by running express between Hammersmith and Langley, using the M4 motorway instead of coming down on to the Great West Road at Brentford. This working commenced with the Easter Holiday programme on Good Friday, 16 April 1965, and continued throughout the next two summers.

A further attempt was made to increase off-peak traffic on Mondays to Fridays from 26 April 1965 by the introduction of Cheap Day Return Tickets on Routes 709/710 and 711 between London and Amersham, Chesham and High Wycombe, also on Routes 712/713/714 between London and Luton or Dunstable. The tickets were issued after 9.30 am in both directions and were also available to and from intermediate points en route. They were issued from country districts for the rest of the day, but from London, they could not be purchased between 4.30 and 6.30 pm, neither were tickets from the country accepted for the return journey during these times.

RF-type coach bound for Bishops Stortford at Potter Street in the Harlow New Town. (J. G. S. Smith).

RF-type on special Sunday journey from London to Leavesden Hospital. (J. G. S. Smith).

RF-type coach en route to High Wycombe in St. Albans Road, Garston. (J. G. S. Smith).

The RT-type double-deck vehicles used at Romford and Grays on Routes 721, 722, 723 and 726 had now been running for almost fifteen years and were nearing the end of their useful lives, so an order was placed for 43 new Routemaster coaches with a larger seating capacity than those introduced in 1962. The 1962 vehicles seated 57, whereas the new coaches were to have a new half-window bay in the centre of the body in both saloons, giving an extra eight seats. These were to be known as the RCL-type to distinguish them from the original fleet, which were known as the RMC-type.

It had been proposed to allocate 29 of the new vehicles to Romford Garage and 14 to Grays, but at the last minute it was discovered that there was a problem on Route 723B which passed under a railway bridge at South Stifford. There was a dip in the road at this point, and it was thought that the RCL-type coaches would have insufficient clearance, so five of the new coaches went to Hertford Garage for Route 715A, whose five RMC-type coaches came to Grays for use on 723B. The new coaches were delivered to their various garages during June 1965.

A small extension to Route 707 on Sundays was made on 3 October 1965, when it was extended from Oxted via Hurst Green to Holland, replacing bus route 464 on that day of the week. Bus 464 was one-man operated, and the extension of 707 saved the cost of operating a bus and paying two drivers, as the journey from Oxted to Holland and back used up the time wasted in lay-over by Route 707 at the Oxted terminal.

The winter programme for 1965 was introduced over the last weekend in October. There was a great deal of alteration to Green Line services, nine routes being affected, these being: 701, 702, 709, 710, 714, 718, 720, 722 and 727. Traffic congestion was still on the increase and was seriously affecting the running on Routes 701, 702 and 714, so, in an effort to restore some reliability to their timetables, it was decided to split them in London on Mondays to Fridays. On Routes 701/702, it was not possible to make the break at Victoria from the Gravesend direction as there was a fair amount of carry-over traffic to Kensington High Street and Hammersmith, so the routes were split as follows:
(1) Gravesend – Hammersmith (all journeys numbered 701).
(2) Victoria – Ascot (701); Victoria – Sunningdale (702).
Route 714 was split at Baker Street, working to this point from both Luton and Dorking. Although the route was split, it was still possible to purchase tickets for journeys across the Baker Street terminal, changing coaches at that point.

The expresss operation on 709 between Chesham and Oxford Circus had now been running for nearly a year. It had not come up to expectations however, and the route was withdrawn west of Baker Street. Traffic on the southern half to Godstone was still fairly good, and an hourly service continued to operate daily over this section. To retain a service between Amersham and Chesham, 710 was extended daily instead of on Sundays only.

Things were not too happy on Route 718 at this time. While passenger loadings were very good throughout the summer season, the previous winter traffic figures had revealed that loadings were good during Mondays to Fridays in peak hours, and on Saturdays during shopping hours, but they fell away at other times. To meet this, a new timetable was introduced on 31 October 1965, which gave a basic hourly service on Mondays–Fridays, Saturdays (early and late) and Sundays. To step up the service in peak hours extra coaches operated between Harlow and Baker Street and Windsor and Victoria giving a half-hourly service over these two sections. During Saturday shopping hours a half-hourly service was worked right through from Harlow to Windsor.

Loadings had also been falling on Routes 720 and 720A and to alleviate the situation and still provide a service through the Tillwicks Road area of Harlow, Route 720 was diverted via 720A to the bus station, regaining the main route to Bishops Stortford via First Avenue. Route 720A was withdrawn, leaving only the service on 720, which was adequate to handle the reduced passenger loadings.

Off-peak and weekend loadings on Route 722 had been falling off for some time, and in consequence, the operation of this route was now reduced to Mondays–Fridays peak hours only. In order to keep the commuter traffic, a new 5-day (10-journey) ticket was introduced at a rate of $7\frac{1}{2}$ times the single fare rounded off to the nearest threepence above. 722 ran for the last time on weekends on Saturday, 30 October.

Express Route 727 (Tring – Victoria) was not justifying its existence and made its last journeys on 30 October.

Another drastic fare increase was made on 16 January 1966 when 1/4 fares were increased to 1/6; 1/6 fares to 1/9 and 1/9 to 2/-. All fares above 2/- were increased by threepence, and there was now a minimum fare of 1/6 for journeys up to five miles in the outer areas and 2/- up to seven miles inside the Central Bus area. As usual there were sections of routes where fares remained unchanged where other operators worked the same type of service, while the Cheap Day Return Tickets which were introduced on certain routes in 1965, were also unaffected by the fare increase. Evidently, the issue of these tickets had been a great success, as it was decided to extend the issue to other routes.

From 6 June 1966 the Cheap Day Return Ticket scheme was revised. The original 1965 scheme was scrapped, and a new one introduced which was to apply on all routes with the exception of peak-hour route 722, orbital route 725 and Whipsnade route 726. Cheap Day Return Tickets were now to be issued from country destinations to London all day on Mondays–Fridays after 9.30 am. There was only one restriction, and that was they could not be used for the return journey from London between 4.30 and 6.30 pm. The only Cheap Day Return Tickets exempted from the scheme were those issued in both directions on Route 716/A over the section of route between London and Hitchin where they were in competition with Birch Brothers Limited.

The Summer Programme for 1966 was introduced on 15 May, and apart from a revised timetable on Route 718, giving a daily 30-minute service right through from Harlow to Windsor for the summer season, there was no further effect on Green Line operations.

A month later on 12 June, Route 704 was converted to double-deck operation using RCL-type vehicles, seven of which came from Hertford (Route 715A converted to single-deck) and nine from Romford which had been working on Route 722. As this route was now a Monday–Friday peak operation, it was considered to be rather wasteful to use brand-new vehicles on such a route, and it was now worked by RT-type coaches.

July 1966 saw the introduction of Green Line's second orbital route. Introduced on 10 July and numbered 724, it operated between High Wycombe and Romford via Amersham, Watford, St. Albans, Welwyn Garden City, Hertford, Harlow, Epping, Abridge, Chigwell Row and Collier Row. Running hourly, it was an express service, there being only 26 stops throughout the whole route. It had the distinction of being the first Green Line service to be one-man operated, also it was the second time that High Wycombe had seen a route numbered 724.

On the same day as 724 was introduced, a service was also provided for visitors to Winston Churchill's historic home at Chartwell, which was now open to the public. Journeys on Route 706 were extended from Westerham via Hosey Common to the house on Wednesdays, Thursdays, Saturdays and Sundays, an operation which was repeated during subsequent summer seasons.

On 2 October 1966, Route 718 was reduced for the winter, the same pattern of service used during the previous year being introduced.

A large programme of alterations involving changes to six Green Line routes was introduced on 31 December. Off-peak and weekend traffic on Route 709 had fallen off to such an extent that there were only two Monday–Friday peak journey and two Sunday journeys at hospital visiting times which did any real business. Accordingly, the service was reduced to the two Monday–Friday peak journeys, plus the two Sunday workings for visitors to St. Lawrence's Hospital at Caterham. At the same time, the single-deck vehicles were withdrawn and replaced with RCL-type double-deck coaches which could handle the peak traffic without need for duplication. Now being a peak-hour operation on weekdays, the issue of Cheap Day Return Tickets was withdrawn on this route, and to retain the commuter traffic, 5-day (10-journey) tickets were introduced replacing the former 6-day (12-journey) ones formerly issued.

With this programme, Routes 711, 714 and 718 were the subject of intermediate diversions. 711 was diverted at Belmont via Sutton Lane, Downs Road, Banstead Village and Garratts Lane in the hope of drumming up some new traffic. 714 resumed through operations daily between Luton and Dorking, but was diverted at Great Portland Street to run via Oxford Circus to serve the West End shopping area. 718 was also diverted via Oxford Circus for the same reason, with the peak hour extras from Harlow terminating at this point instead of Baker Street.

Routes 723A and 723B were also altered at this time. 723A was withdrawn completely, leaving the operation through Belhus Estate to Route 723, while 723B was withdrawn between Aldgate and East Ham Town Hall, running from there to Grays in peak hours on Mondays–Fridays, and with a reduced service on Saturdays and no Sunday service. Tilbury was now only served by Route 723 via Chadwell St. Mary, the operation via Dock Road having been withdrawn with 723A.

When Route 724 was introduced it had been routed between Theydon Bois and Epping via Piercing Hill, Theydon Road and Bell Common (Epping Road). The Epping Road, being the main A11 road to and from London was heavily trafficked in both directions all day, and drivers on 724 found it a difficult job to get out of Theydon Road on northbound journeys to High Wycombe. To alleviate this situation, the route was diverted through Ivychimneys, Centre Drive and Station Road to Epping High Street, where the cross-roads were controlled by traffic lights.

Since the introduction of the revised service on Route 709, the peak hour journeys from London after the morning peak, and those up to Town in the afternoons, had been running out of service. It was now felt that, if they covered these journeys in service they might pick up a few passengers. Accordingly, running in service in both directions was put into operation from 25 February 1967.

The traffic on orbital route 724 was being watched very closely and it was discovered that loadings were generally very good from Romford as far as St. Albans, but they were not so good from there onwards to High Wycombe. To encourage people on the eastern half of the route to explore new territory at the western end, a maximum adult fare of 10/- single was introduced from Romford to High Wycombe, together with a Cheap Day Return Fare of 15/- issued after 9.30 am on Mondays to Fridays, and all day on Saturdays and Sundays (also Bank Holidays). These new facilities were introduced from 24 March 1967.

The Summer Programme for that year was introduced on 13 May. Once again, the timetable on Route 718 was revised for the summer but in a different form to that of the previous year. On Mondays to Fridays the service pattern was: Windsor – 30 – Victoria – 60 – Harlow. The service to Harlow was stepped up to half-hourly from Oxford Circus during the peak hours, while a 30-minute service operated throughout the route on weekends.

This programme also saw the introduction of the third orbital route, which was also the second Green Line route to be one-man operated. This was the hourly express service 727 from Crawley to Luton Station via Gatwick Airport, Reigate, Epsom, Kingston, Heathrow Airport, Uxbridge, Watford Junction Station and St. Albans, serving only 25 stops in a route nearly 80 miles long. Serving as it did the two airports, and running directly into the forecourts of Watford Junction and Luton railway stations, great play was made of this fact on the posters and timetable leaflets advertising the service. By arrangement with the London Midland Region of British Rail, passengers holding Rail/Air or Rail/Road tickets could travel from Luton or Watford stations to Heathrow Airport without payment of fare upon production of a special London Transport pre-paid exchange ticket covering the journey in question. These tickets were issued by the booking offices at Luton and Watford Junction, and in the reverse direction by the British Rail hostesses at Heathrow Airport.

When the winter programme was introduced on 7 October, the service on Route 718 was reduced to hourly permanently, and as peak hour loads had been considerably reduced, there was now no build-up of service either from Harlow or Windsor.

Another large programme of alterations to Green Line services was made on 2 December, affecting Routes 704, 705, 716A and 717. As the changes to 716A were less involved, we will deal with them first. 717 was withdrawn between Welwyn Garden City and Baker Street, being replaced by 716A which was diverted at the junction of Great North Road and Valley Road via Bridge Road to Welwyn Garden City centre, where it followed the former

RF-type coach bound for Romford proceeding through the snow at Cole Green (Herts). (J. G. S. Smith).

RF-type coach bound for High Wycombe at Beamond End (between Amersham and Hazlemere). (J. G. S. Smith).

RCL-type Routemaster coach in Whipsnade Zoo Car Park. (J. G. S. Smith).

Coach running at speed along the M1 motorway. Taken from bridge taking the A414 over the M1 near Hemel Hempstead. (J. G. S. Smith).

London-bound coach at Bunkers Lane (between Leverstock Green and Bedmond). (J. G. S. Smith).

Coach on the first Road-Rail-Air Link at its first terminus at Luton (Midland Road) Station. (J. G. S. Smith).

717 route via Howlands, South Hatfield, Welham Green and Brookmans Park, rejoining its original route to Woking at Little Heath Church.

After 37 years of supplying coaches for Green Line services to London and beyond, Tunbridge Wells garage closed its doors for the last time on Friday, 1 December 1967. During that night the coaches were driven up the road to Dunton Green Garage, and henceforth Route 704 was operated from that depot. This reorganisation gave London Transport the opportunity to revise the operations on both 704 and 705. Taking 705 first, the RC-type single-deck coaches were replaced by double-deck RCL-type vehicles rendered redundant by timetable adjustments on Route 723. Traffic had fallen off between Sevenoaks and Tunbridge Wells, so the service on that section of route 704 was reduced to one coach per hour, increased to two during Monday–Friday peak hours and Saturday shopping periods. Although there were still two coaches per hour on 704 between Sevenoaks and Windsor, these did not run every half-hour, but at alternate intervals of 20 and 40 minutes between coaches in order to provide an even 20-minute service jointly with 705 (which had been reduced to hourly) from Bromley South to Windsor. The RC-type coaches from Route 705 were sent to St. Albans and Reigate Garages for use on the orbital route 727. Incidentally, with the conversion to double-deck operation, the express service on Route 705 between Windsor and London was now withdrawn and it served all stops over this section.

A fortnight later on 15 December, the Minister of Transport and the Leader of the Greater London Council made a joint announcement that the G.L.C. was to become the statutory transport planning authority for London, including the provision of public passenger transport services. A new London Transport Executive was to be formed, the members of which would be appointed by the Council, who would have effective control over policies, finance and the broad lines of operations, with the Executive being responsible for the day-to-day management of the bus and Underground services in the Greater London area. The future of the Country Bus and Green Line services outside the G.L.C. boundary was left for further discussion.

The year ended with the conversion of Routes 717 and 719 from RMC-type Routemasters to single-deck RF-type coaches, still crew-operated. These were introduced on 30 December, and the Routemasters were transferred to Hemel Hempstead and East Grinstead garages for use on Route 708. In view of the increased seating capacity, the service on 708 was reduced from half-hourly to hourly.

Alterations were made to the operation of Routes 701 and 702 on 18 May 1968. The split-service arrangement which had existed since November 1965 was withdrawn, and 701 now provided a through hourly service on weekdays from Ascot to Gravesend daily, with extra coaches in peak hours between Victoria and Gravesend. Route 702 now provided an hourly service from Sunningdale to Victoria during Monday–Friday peaks, and a through hourly service from Sunningdale to Gravesend on weekends, although no service was provided in the early morning or late evening.

On the same date, summer route 726 which hitherto had operated express from Aldgate to Baker Street via Holborn, Grays Inn Road, Kings Cross and Euston Road was now diverted at Holborn via Oxford Street, Oxford Circus and Portland Place, and an additional picking-up point was introduced at Oxford Circus. This was in Portland Place, some distance away from the Circus, and evidently did not produce many extra passengers. Since the operation to Whipsnade by Route 712 had been introduced, the need for 726 had gradually decreased, and, as it was worked from Romford Garage, involving spreadover duties, the running costs were high. In consequence of this, the 1968 season was the last in which it was operated, the last day of operation being Friday, 6 September.

For some time, work had been going on to widen the Kingston Road at Putney Heath, both to accommodate the increasing commuter car traffic into London, and at the same time, to provide an underpass at Tibbetts Corner. This work was now completed, but the widening and provision of the slope for the underpass had necessitated the closing of the Old Portsmouth Road across the middle of the heath. This road had been used en route by 718 on its journey to Windsor, and from 8 June 1968, the route was now diverted via Roehampton Village.

Passenger loadings south of Chelsham to Oxted and Holland had been practically non-existent for some time, and on 15 June 1968, Route 707 lost its Sunday service. To compensate for its withdrawal a half-hourly service was introduced on Route 706 from Aylesbury to Chelsham Garage, with alternate coaches carrying on to Westerham, some journeys of which were extended to Chartwell.

Evidently the peak hour loadings formerly enjoyed by Route 722 had found quicker means of travel to and from London, so this peak-hour route made its last journeys on Friday, 2 August. One may well wonder how a service which had been operating for 38 years could lose its attraction for the public, but, when it started, the coaches were much faster than the slow steam trains which served Upminster. Now the position was reversed, and there were three electric trains per hour in the off-peak, and a much more frequent service in peak hours, taking only 22 minutes for the journey to Fenchurch Street, in addition to which the District Line also offers a service not only to the City, but to the West End by changing at Charing Cross, where the coach was dumping people at Aldgate.

Another fare increase, the first for over two years, was introduced on 7 September. On Green Line routes, fares from the 1/6 minimum up to 2/9 were not increased, whilst between 2/9 and 4/6, fares were increased by amounts between one penny and sixpence, so that single fares now went up in threepenny steps from 1/6 to 5/-. The same principle was applied on fares above 5/-, but there was now a maximum single fare of 10/- on the longer routes, this fare covering in some cases, journeys of more than sixty miles. Fares which were not increased were the Cheap Off-peak day returns to London, and the special day returns on Routes 716, 716A and 724. For the first time, single fares on routes shared with other operators did not escape the increase.

Stage One of the winter programme was introduced on Saturday, 5 October, and Route 723B made its last journeys on the day before, being withdrawn due to decreased passenger loadings.

Stage Two was introduced six weeks later on 22 November, affecting nine Green Line services and bringing one-man operation to some of the routes running through Central London. Routes 701, 702, 714 and 720 were con-

Southbound RF coach en route to Crawley at Childwickbury Lodge, near Harpenden. (J. G. S. Smith).

Redundant RF-type Green Line coach now working as Executive Express coach to Heathrow Airport for BEA.

RF-type coach departing from Watford Junction Station for Luton having just completed one of its Road – Rail – Air Links. (J. G. S. Smith).

verted to this method of operation without any alteration to their routes or frequencies. Route 710 (Chesham – London – Crawley) was altered to run from Amersham Garage to Baker Street only and converted to one-man operation. Instead of running in via Bayswater Road and Sussex Gardens, it was now diverted via Marble Arch and the Baker Street/Gloucester Place one-way system. The former Baker Street – Crawley section was not replaced with another service, but the double-deck relief which had operated from Coulsdon to London in peak hours was replaced by an extra journey on Route 709.

Route 711 was converted to one-man operation, a new timetable being introduced, giving an hourly through service on Mondays–Fridays from High Wycombe to Reigate, stepped up in peak hours to half-hourly with two separate operations from Baker Street to Reigate and High Wycombe respectively. On Saturdays during shopping hours, a half-hourly service ran right through from Wycombe to Reigate, while on Sundays, the service was hourly. In addition, 711 now made a double-run from the Oxford Road to the 'Packhorse Inn' to give additional service to Gerrards Cross.

Route 717 (Baker Street – Wrotham) was withdrawn at this time, and replaced by the extension of 719 from Victoria. This route was now converted to one-man operation, and an hourly service was provided with extra coaches during peak hours and on Saturdays until early afternoons making a half-hourly service between Victoria and Garston Garage.

A further programme of alterations was introduced on 15 February 1969, bringing two route withdrawals and more conversions to one-man operation. Route 707 was withdrawn, and one-man operations introduced on Route 706. A revised timetable was introduced on this route, giving a half-hourly service from Aylesbury to Chelsham Garage to cover the withdrawal of 707. Coaches now only proceeded south of Chelsham during Monday–Friday peak hours and for the Chartwell journeys during the summer. The operation through Tatsfield was now confined to northbound journeys in the morning peak and southbound in the evenings.

Routes 712, 713 and 725 were converted to one-man operation to reduce running costs, while passenger loadings had fallen to such an extent on Route 708 that it was now converted to single-deck one-man operation on the same frequency that had applied when double-deck coaches were operated. The displaced Routemasters were sent to Hatfield and Addlestone garages to be placed on Country Bus routes.

Route 715A from Hertford, which had provided a service across Hertford Heath and through Tottenham and Edmonton had lost most of its traffic to the main-line and the new Victoria Line tube, and was now withdrawn. Traffic from Hertford and places up to Waltham Cross was not greatly affected by the withdrawal as Route 715 still provided a half-hourly service to London, and the section between Waltham Cross and Manor House was well-served by main-line electric trains and a frequent service of Central Buses.

Windsor garage was now suffering from a severe staff shortage, which was affecting the operation of Route 704, so an Emergency timetable was introduced from 19 April 1969. The Windsor – Sevenoaks short-workings were withdrawn when they were due to be worked by Windsor-based crews, leaving a 20/40 minute service (joint with 705) from Windsor during these periods. The spreadover coach on Route 705 from Sevenoaks worked up to London on that route in the mornings, but to cover a 40-minute gap in the evening peak, returned to Sevenoaks via Route 704. This emergency timetable was to last until 4 October, when a new timetable was introduced, reducing the frequency on 704 to an hourly service, which worked jointly with 705 to Bromley South, giving a half-hourly service over that section.

Another fare increase was introduced in September, this time on a strict mileage basis, although to bring single fares on to this scale, certain fares were increased by either threepence or sixpence. Fares started at 1/6 in country districts and 2/- in the Metropolitan Police District, then rising in sixpenny steps to the maximum of 10/- single on the longer routes. This time, the fares on sections of route shared with other operators were not increased. Off-peak Cheap Day Return Tickets, which had not been increased since their introduction in 1966, were now subjected to increases of either sixpence or 1/-, although the 15/- Cheap Day Return fare from Romford to High Wycombe on Route 724 remained unchanged.

It will thus be seen that, over the years since 1961, the traffic officers of the Country Bus and Coach section of London Transport had done their best to combat the continued fall in passenger traffic, reducing services and withdrawing them where necessary. Their task was made harder by the constant need to increase fares to cover the ever increasing running costs. Various schemes for cheap fares in the off-peak periods had been tried in attempts to attract off-peak traffic, but car ownership was still on the increase, and television was a great deterrent to evening travel for pleasure purposes. Also the continuing traffic congestion which caused so much havoc to coach timetables did a lot to deter passengers from using the coaches.

Following the joint announcement by the Transport Minister and the Greater London Council in December 1967, the Bill to set up the new arrangements for public transport in London was introduced to Parliament in November 1968. Known as the Transport (London) Bill, it went through the usual parliamentary procedure during 1969, and when passed, became entitled 'The Transport Act (London) 1969'. Under its terms the London Transport Board ceased to exist, being replaced on 1 January 1970 by the London Transport Executive, now responsible to the Greater London Council and not the Government.

The new Executive was no longer responsible for the Country Bus and Green Line coach services, which were handed over to London Country Bus Services Limited, a subsidiary company of the National Bus Company, specially set up for this purpose, and the story of their development under the new company is the subject of the next chapter.

Central London Terminal Points.

(A) Baker Street Station:—
Terminating — 702 710.
Picking-up — 711 712 713 714 716 716A.

(B) Victoria (Eccleston Bridge):—
Terminating — 702 (Mon-Fri Only)
Picking-up — 701 702 (Sat/Sun) 704 705 706 708 712 713 718 719

(C) Oxford Circus:—
Terminating — none.
Picking-up — 709 711 714 715 718.

(D) Aldgate (Minories Layby):—
Terminating — 720 721 723.

Green Line – January 1970

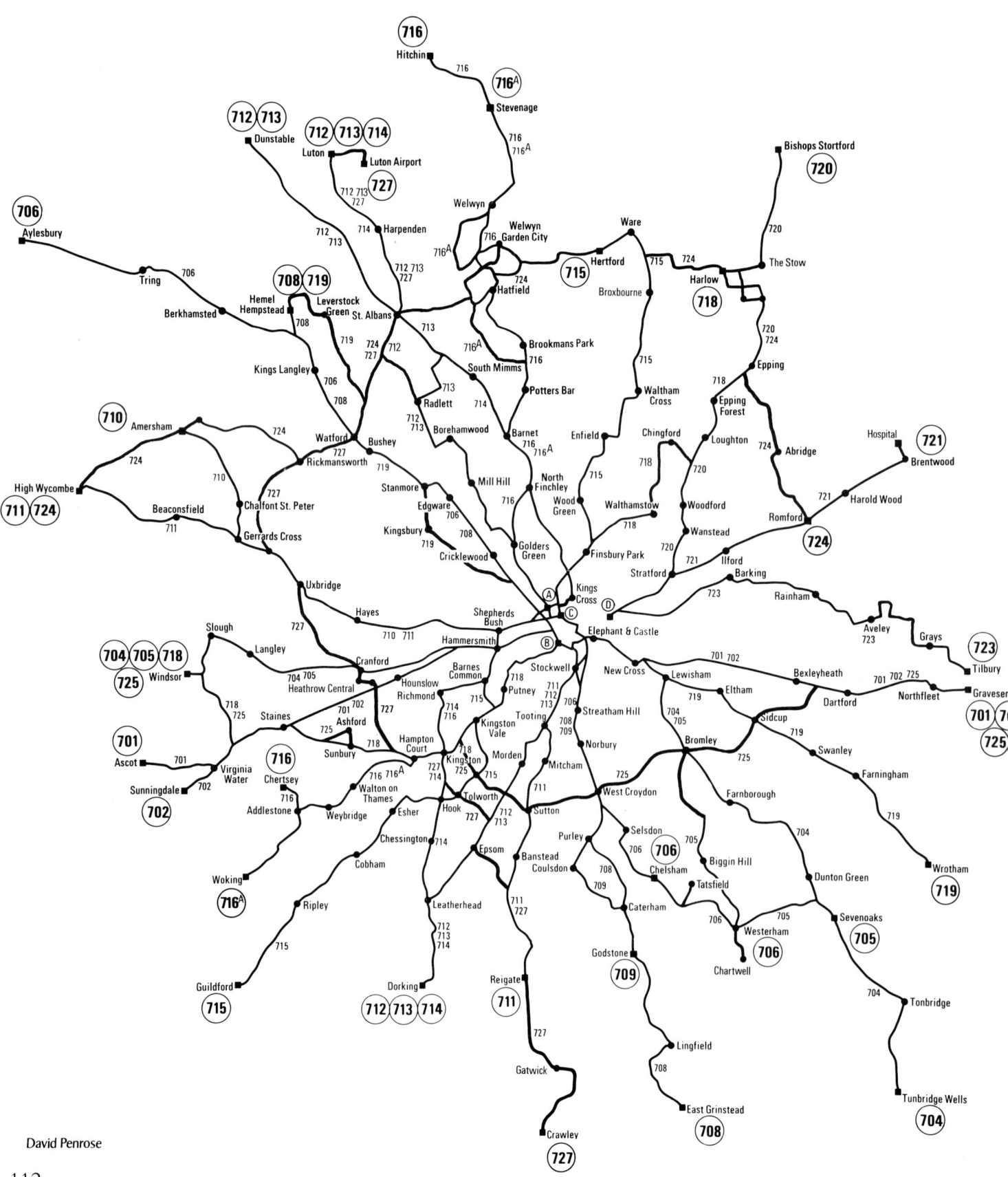

David Penrose

LONDON COUNTRY
CHAPTER NINE

1967-1973

As stated in the last chapter, the Country Bus and Green Line coach services of London Transport were taken over by London Country Bus Services Limited on 1 January 1970.

The new company found itself in possession of twenty-eight garages and roughly 1,200 vehicles of which about 700 were double-deckers, and the rest single-deck, a goodly portion of which were reaching the end of their useful life.

Of this fleet some 210 (130 single-deck and 80 double-deck) were needed to meet the daily requirements of the Green Line routes. The 80 double-deckers were part of the Routemaster fleet brought into service in 1962 and 1965, but the single-deckers were of the RF-type introduced in 1952, and while they were still rendering good service, would soon need to be replaced.

Another fare increase was introduced on 7 August 1970, bringing fares on to a strict mileage basis, and resulting in a penny increase on some fares and sevenpence on others, whilst many were unchanged. Off-peak Cheap Day Return fares were increased in accordance with the above scales, there now being a minimum return fare of 6/- (30p). For the first time, the rate charged for children under 14 years of age was altered, being increased from half-fare to ¾ of the adult fare.

The new company decided that, as it would have to renew the best part of the fleet, the ultimate aim would be to go over completely to one-man operation. Henceforth all new vehicles would be suitable for this type of operation.

The first programme of changes to Green Line services was introduced on 20 February 1971, affecting six routes. Route 702 (Sunningdale – Gravesend) now became a peak-hour Monday–Friday operation only from Victoria to Sunningdale, the route being left at other times to the hourly Farnham service operated by Alder Valley. Route 710 was withdrawn between Uxbridge and Baker Street, thus retaining the only part of the route still carrying any worthwhile traffic. The timetables of Routes 712 and 713 were adjusted, and the Luton journeys, the majority of which were in peak hours, were now withdrawn north of St. Albans. A request had been made for deeper penetration by Route 723 into the Belhus Estate (Aveley), so alternate journeys were diverted via Foyle Drive, Erriff Drive and Daiglen Drive back to Stifford Road, the journeys over this section being renumbered 723A.

With an eye to increasing the usage of the route, and at the same time bringing the three airports useful to London in direct communication with each other, Route 727 was extended from Luton Station to the airport from 20 March.

An interesting experiment was tried with the Saturday service on Route 715 from 15 May 1971. Alternate coaches were diverted at Esher via Hampton Court and Kingston,

RF-type coach en route to Ascot at Victoria. (J. G. S. Smith).

RP-type coach passing the 'Wake Arms', Epping Forest on its way to Walthamstow. (J. G. S. Smith).

regaining the original route at Kingston Vale (Robin Hood Gate), thus restoring for one day of the week only, the connection between the important towns of Guildford and Kingston which had been severed when Central Bus route 215 was withdrawn between Guildford and Ripley in December 1939.

With the introduction of the Summer Programme on 6 June, another alteration was made to Routes 712 and 713. This time the Dunstable road was affected, the service between there and St. Albans being withdrawn during off-peak hours on Mondays to Fridays. To compensate for the withdrawal, through single and Cheap Day Return tickets were issued in both directions, with availability by coach and bus by changing at St. Albans. The operation of the Summer Special journeys to Whipsnade Zoo were not affected by the above alteration and continued to operate.

For some time a Safari Park had been in existence on the outskirts of Windsor on the Winkfield Road. While Green Line had been under the control of London Transport, it had not been possible to run a service to the Safari Park as it was situated outside the Board's area. There was now no such restriction, and Routes 704 and 705 had some journeys extended thereto on Sundays from 4 July.

Towards the end of 1971 the first deliveries of a fleet of 90 A.E.C. Reliance coaches equipped for one-man operation and to be known as the RP-type, were received by the Company, the first being placed in service on Route 727 (Luton – Crawley) on 18 December. This released the experimental RC-type coaches hitherto used on this route, and also signalled the start of the conversion of further Green Line routes to one-man operation.

New Year's Day 1972 saw the first of these conversions when Route 721 from Romford Garage received a fleet of the new coaches, thus releasing their RCL-type Routemasters for bus work, these going to Reigate and Dorking Garages respectively. On the same date, Route 723 from Grays Garage also went over to one-man operation using the RC-type vehicles released from Route 727. The Routemasters formerly used on this route stayed at their home garage for use on bus routes 300, 328 and 370. This conversion also brought a revised pattern of service, as Route 723A was withdrawn, and 723 was diverted in Belhus Estate via Foyle Drive and Daiglen Drive in its place.

This was followed on 5 February by the conversion of Route 718 operated from Harlow and Windsor garages. Here, the Routemasters went to Dartford to replace the remaining RT-type buses at that depot, the remainder going to Grays.

On 29 January, an attempt was made to stimulate weekend loadings on Routes 711, 715, 715A and 723 by the extension of the issue of Cheap Day Return tickets all day on Saturdays and Sundays as well as on weekdays.

Routes 716 and 716A were the next to go over to one-man operation using the new RP-type coaches. This conversion took place on 11 March, the Routemasters going to St. Albans and Two Waters Garages for use on Routes 330 and 330A. This was followed a fortnight later by the conversion of Routes 704 and 705 from Windsor and Dunton Green depots, the RCL-type Routemasters being split between Crawley, Reigate and Grays garages for use on bus work.

For some time off-peak loadings on Route 706 had been falling off, and from 1 April, the service was reduced to hourly between Aylesbury and Chelsham Garage. Extra coaches were worked during Monday–Friday peak hours between Victoria and Tring, and an uneven peak hour service to and from Westerham (two morning up journeys and one evening down journey) also continued to operate, as did the Chartwell journeys during the summer seasons.

Saturday, 29 April, saw the completion of the programme for the conversion of Green Line routes to one-man working when the Routes 715 and 715A from Hertford and

Guildford Garages went over to this method of operation. Some of the Routemasters at Hertford remained there for use on local bus routes, while the Guildford allocation went to Swanley Garage to work on bus route 477.

With this conversion, only one coach route remained as a crew-operated service. This was the Monday–Friday peak hour and Sunday hospital route 709 from Godstone Garage. The peak-hour journeys particularly were heavily used, and it was not practical to convert the route at this time.

It had now become obvious that the High Wycombe – Watford section of Route 724 would never be a paying proposition, but, on the other hand, Route 727 was having a problem coping with the loadings between Watford Junction and Heathrow Airport, necessitating much duplication provided at overtime rates of pay. To relieve the situation and reduce costs, Route 724 was diverted at Rickmansworth to run to Staines via Route 727 to Heathrow Airport Central and then through the Cargo Tunnel and Terminal, leaving the Airport at Stanwell Moor, thus providing a direct service into the Airport for many of its workers resident in the Staines area, this operation commencing on 3 June 1972.

As traffic congestion was still playing havoc with timetables in the Greater London area, more peak-hour loadings were falling, and from 17 June, the service on peak hour Route 702 was reduced to one journey in each direction. On Route 711, the extra peak hour journeys from Reigate to Baker Street were reduced from three to one each way from the same date. This was followed on 15 July by withdrawal of the peak-hour and Saturday extras between Victoria and Garston Garage on Route 719.

The remaining section of 710 between Amersham and Uxbridge had not been paying its way for some time, and the Company withdrew it from 14 October, leaving Amersham without a Green Line service after forty years of operation to that town, and also with no direct connection with Uxbridge by public transport.

The first of what was to be a large fleet of Leyland National coaches made their appearance in 1973. They went to Romford Garage first of all, the first batch appearing on Route 721 on 17 February. This released sufficient RP-type coaches to replace the ageing RF-type vehicles on Route 724 from the same garage. By 3 March, Route 721 had received its full allocation of Nationals, and the remaining RP-types had gone to Harlow to work on Route 720.

It was reported that a Leyland National coach had been seen at work on Route 706 from Tring Garage on 7 April, and by 1 May, the whole allocation from this depot consisted of the new coaches. The operation on 706 from Chelsham could not be changed over at this time, due to space difficulties inside the garage.

On 5 May, Route 723 lost its Grays – Tilbury section, once again due to a fall in passenger loadings.

More Leyland Nationals were delivered in this month, and the allocation from Reigate Garage on Route 711 was worked by this type from 21 May, followed by the High Wycombe allocation on 9 June.

In the meantime, the Company introduced another fare revision on 3 June, there being no change to the single fares, but a new system for return tickets was brought into use. The old system of 'off-peak' Cheap Day Return tickets to London only were withdrawn and replaced with one where Cheap Day Return tickets were available between any two farestages where the adult fare was 20 pence or more. These tickets were available daily, but not before 9.30 am on Mondays–Fridays. A ticket purchased on Saturday could be used for the return journey on Sunday, without extra charge.

The system of 5-day (10-journey) and 6-day (12-journey) tickets was also withdrawn at this time and replaced with weekly and monthly season tickets issued between any two farestages where the adult fare was 15 pence or more. During the period for which they were issued, they were available for unlimited journeys between the points for which they had been issued, or intermediately.

Peak hour services on Routes 701, 702, 706 and 711 were adjusted from 7 July 1973. The Monday-Friday short journeys between Gravesend, Victoria and Hammersmith on Route 701 were withdrawn, together with the last remaining journey on 702, leaving an hourly service between Ascot and Gravesend on Route 701. On Route 706, the peak hour trips to Westerham were now reduced to one up journey (mornings) and one down in the evenings. On Route 711, the remaining peak journeys from Reigate to Baker Street, plus one trip each way between High Wycombe and London were withdrawn, and the Saturday service was reduced to hourly throughout the route at the same time.

There was only one route alteration in 1974, this being the extension of Route 720 to Stansted Airport on 4 May. A service to this point had been proposed in 1967. The route was to have been worked jointly with the Eastern National Omnibus Company on a limited stop basis. It would have started from Victoria (Eccleston Bridge) and 718 to Walthamstow (Bell Corner) from where it would have carried on along Forest Road and through Woodford Green to the Epping New Road up to the 'Wake Arms', where it would have joined the 720 route to Bishops Stortford. Application was made to the Traffic Commissioners for road service licences to operate the route, but for some unknown reason, the application was withdrawn a few weeks later.

The Company received several deliveries of new coaches from Leyland National during the year, and these were allocated to the following routes and garages, replacing RF-type coaches in most cases:

26 January 1974. Route 719. Garston and Swanley Garages.
9 March 1974. Route 714. Luton and Dorking Garages.
6 April 1974. Routes 712/3. St. Albans and Dorking Garages.
3 August 1974. Route 723. Grays Garage.
21 September 1974. Route 701. Staines and Northfleet Garages.

In the case of Route 723, the new Nationals replaced the RC-type coaches, which then went to Hertford for use on local bus routes. The RC-type had been very prone to mechanical troubles, and it was felt that there would be less disruption of service if they were placed on routes nearer to a garage.

There were two fare increases in 1974, the first on 17 March, the second on 1 September. With the March increase, some 10 pence fares were raised by 2p, some 12 pence fares by 3p and about half the higher fares by 5p. Minimum fares on the coaches were now 10 pence in the country areas and 15 pence in Central London. The price of a Golden Rover ticket was now 90 pence (60 pence child), and children now had to pay the full adult fare during peak hours on Mondays–Fridays. With the September increase, one penny was added to the 12 and 15 pence fares while some higher fares were raised by 5 pence, and the maximum fare on the longer routes was now 80 pence, also the minimum single fare in Central London was raised by one penny.

Route alterations in 1975 consisted mainly of reductions in service, withdrawals and adjustments to meet the continuing fall in passengers. From 15 May one of the three peak hour journeys on Route 709 was withdrawn in each direction, followed on 31 May by the withdrawal of all journeys south of Chelsham on Route 706, except for the special journeys to Chartwell in the summer. Route 701 was withdrawn without replacement from 4 October, leaving the route between Victoria and Ascot to the Alder Valley Reading route, which was supplemented as far as Virginia Water by that company's Farnham service.

The major route alteration in 1975 was the adjustment made to Routes 712 and 713 on 31 May. Except for the summer extension of both routes to Whipsnade Zoo, they were both withdrawn north of St. Albans, and in addition, Route 712 now operated on weekdays only. Both routes also terminated at Victoria, the service to Dorking now being covered by a new hourly route from Baker Street numbered 703.

More Leyland National coaches were received during September 1975, and the space problem at Chelsham Garage now having been resolved, the RF-type coaches on Route 706 from this garage were replaced with the new vehicles. The remainder were split between Staines and Romford Garages for use on Route 724, the whole Staines allocation consisting of the new vehicles, but only part of that at Romford.

Fares were increased once again on 19 October and judging by the scale of the increase added to various fares, a new mileage basis seems to have been adopted at this time. The remaining 10 pence fares were unchanged, while 13 pence fares were raised by 3p; 16 pence fares were raised to 20 or 23 pence; 20 pence fares went up to 25 or 27 pence and 25 pence fares were increased to 30 or 35 pence. Existing 30, 35 and 40 pence fares were raised by either 10 or 15 pence, with a maximum single fare of 95 pence. The minimum single fare for which a return ticket was issued was now 23p (45p return), and a Golden Rover ticket now cost £1.20. Although children were still charged the adult fare during peak hours, they now paid half-fare at other times.

Due to a further fall in passenger loadings, the peak hour extras on Route 711 were reduced to one journey in each direction from 29 November, this being the last alteration for 1975.

The first alteration in 1976 took place on 15 May, when Route 716 was altered to operate hourly from Hitchin to Woking, following its normal route to Welwyn Garden City, then taking the 716A route to Woking. 716A was

Routemaster RML-type bus laying over between trips at Harlow London Country Bus Garage.

Country Bus Routemaster on Green Line service in the Bus Station at Harlow New Town Centre. (J. G. S. Smith).

RP-type coach on Woodridden Hill (between Waltham Abbey and 'The Wake Arms') en route to Bishops Stortford. (J. G. S. Smith).

Pair of RT-type Country Buses at the entrance to Windsor Garage on relief duties on Routes 704 and 718. (J. G. S. Smith).

Country Bus RT-type on Green Line Relief duty sets off from Windsor for London with a full load of passengers. (J. G. S. Smith).

RF-type Country Bus on Green Line duty negotiates the level-crossing at Colnbrook on its way to Windsor. (J. G. S. Smith).

Country Bus Routemaster pressed into service as a Green Line relief leaves Biggin Hill R.A.F. Station on the occasion of the annual Air Display. (J. G. S. Smith).

withdrawn, together with the Addlestone–Chertsey section of the former 716. On the same day, the last crew-operated Green Line coaches were withdrawn when the new Leyland National coaches entered service from Godstone Garage on Route 709.

Once again it became necessary to increase fares. The increase was introduced on 3 April and was on a selective basis. Most of the 10 pence fares rose to 12p; and 16 and 20 pence fares were unchanged; 23 pence fares went up one penny, 25 pence by 2p, 27 pence by 3p and 30 pence by 5p. Whilst some higher fares remained unchanged, others went up by 5 pence. The maximum fare of 95 pence was left unchanged, except on Route 727, where new fares of £1·00, £1·05 and £1·10 were introduced. The maximum Cheap Day Return fare was now £1·20 (80 pence single) and passengers asking for a return ticket where the single fare was higher than 80 pence were advised to take a Golden Rover, the fare for which was the same price as the maximum return fare. On Saturdays, if the passenger wished to return on Sunday, a £1·20 return ticket was issued, even if the single fare was higher than 80 pence.

The author remembers wondering on several occasions during 1976 how much longer London Country was going to carry on operating the remaining part of what was becoming a somewhat outdated network, especially where the cross-London routes were concerned. In pre-war days, London Transport had constantly monitored the performance of the coach routes, and on several occasions they had been altered to meet changing traffic patterns, but, except for the introduction of services to the New Towns and the three orbital routes, little change had been made to the post-war network during the thirty years it had been operating. He was, however soon to find out that the traffic department of London Country had also been having some thoughts, and were not only contemplating a revitalisation of the routes, but also the closing of some of the smaller garages in order to reduce running costs.

During 1976 a new type of coach had been ordered, and when the first one was delivered to Reigate, the Company announced to the Press that there were to be 150 of the new vehicles. Delivery would be spread over five years at a rate of 30 coaches per year to replace all existing RP, SMA and SNC-type coaches. The coaches were A.E.C. Reliances, and thirty to be delivered in 1977 would consist of 15 with 49-seat Plaxton Supreme bodies, which would be known as the RS-type, the other 15 being fitted with 53-seat Duple Dominant 2 bodies to be designated as the RB-type. The first five would be delivered in time to inaugurate two new routes on 29 January 1977.

On that date, Luton Garage was closed, Routes 712 and 713 were withdrawn, and Route 714 was altered to run from Dorking to Victoria hourly. To replace all three routes on the northern side, two new routes were introduced from Victoria, not only to St. Albans and Luton Town Centre, but providing for the first time a direct service from London to Luton Airport. New route numbers were given to the services, and the routes to be followed were carefully worked out. Route 707 runs daily, every two hours on weekdays and hourly on Sundays, following the old 714 route from Luton to North Finchley, from whence it travels via Finchley Central, Golders Green, Finchley Road and Baker Street to Victoria. Route 717, which runs two-hourly on weekdays only, follows the same route as 707 to London Colney, also from Golders Green to Victoria, but in between operates via Shenley, Borehamwood, Mill Hill and Hendon Central, also making a double-run to serve the new Brent Cross Shopping Centre, an operation which has been remarkably successful. One journey in each direction is also provided on this route (but missing out Brent Cross) on Sundays for visitors to Shenley Hospital. These new services are worked from St. Albans Garage.

Tring Garage was closed on 2 April, and on the same day Route 706 was withdrawn and replaced by the extension of Route 708 from Hemel Hempstead to Aylesbury. In order to handle the peak-hour traffic, extra journeys were worked between Victoria and Hemel Hempstead to give a half-hourly service over this section.

On the same date, there were also alterations which affected Routes 715, 715A, 718, 720 and 724. Due to a reduction in the subsidy paid by the Surrey County Council to London Transport, that organisation had decided to withdraw their 215 bus route between Esher and Cobham. Since 1971, part of the Saturday service on Route 715 had been diverted via Kingston as Route 715A, an operation which had been fairly successful, and in order to maintain a direct connection between the villages south of Esher with Kingston (where the Surrey County administrative offices are situated), Routes 715 was diverted at Esher over its Saturday route via Hampton Court and Kingston, and to completely replace the withdrawal of 215, it was also diverted to make a double-run into Cobham village centre. A new timetable was introduced giving a basic hourly service from Guildford to Hertford which is stepped up on Mondays–Fridays (except during the late evenings) to half-hourly between Guildford and Kingston and also between Oxford Circus and Hertford. On Saturdays, during the main shopping period, a half-hourly service is maintained throughout from Hertford to Guildford. Observations have revealed that there were two journeys in both directions during the peak hours on the former route via the Kingston-by-Pass which were worth retaining, and to meet this, a new semi-express service was introduced from Guildford to Oxford Circus. To distinguish them from the normal 715 route, they were given the number 710, and they ran express from Guildford to Cobham (White Lion) and also from Hammersmith to Oxford Circus.

The biggest upheaval in the April programme was the change introduced at Harlow. Route 720 was completely withdrawn and 718 lost its Harlow – Victoria section, while 724 was withdrawn between Romford Station and the Market Place and extended from Staines to Windsor Castle, stopping only at Runnymede (Windsor Road), Old Windsor (The Wheatsheaf) and Datchet (Windsor Road), the operation from the eastern end being transferred from Romford to Harlow Garage at the same time. To replace 718 and 720, two new routes were introduced. Both were hourly services from Bishops Stortford, one to Walthamstow Central Station (daily) and covering former routes 720 and 718 to Walthamstow (Bell Corner) and then running via Hoe Street to the station, from which passengers could travel quickly to the West End by the Victoria Line. This route was numbered 702. The other hourly service followed the same roads as 702 to 'The Wake Arms' and then turned off via Woodridden Hill and Waltham Abbey to terminate at Waltham Cross, where a connection was made with 715 to Hertford and London. This route only ran from Monday

RP 77 passes across Harpenden Common on its way to Luton. (J. G. S. Smith).

RF-type coach about to depart from Amersham Garage on much shortened route 710. (J. G. S. Smith).

RF 162 waits outside Amersham Garage to commence its next journey to Uxbridge on now much-shortened Route 710. (J. G. S. Smith).

RC5 pauses at the coach stop at Sutton Station on its way to Reigate. (J. G. S. Smith).

Leyland National single-deck bus covering a Green Line duty at the finish of its journey in St. Albans. (J. G. S. Smith).

RP 11 proceeding along First Avenue, Harlow New Town on its way to Romford. (J. G. S. Smith).

RMC-type Routemaster in Hertford Car Park awaiting departure to Guildford. (F. Mussett).

RF Country Bus covering a Green Line duty passing along Oxford Street on its way to Guildford. (J. G. S. Smith).

RP 74 in the original livery of this type at Cheshunt on its way to Guildford. (J. G. S. Smith).

to Saturday (not late evenings) at first, but from 20 August, an evening service on weekdays and a Sunday service (from midday) was introduced to cover the withdrawal of London Transport bus route 217A between 'The Wake Arms' and Waltham Cross. At the same time, the whole service was diverted along Sharnbrooke Road to serve the lower end of the Ninefields Estate.

Attention was then directed to the Windsor area in the next programme introduced on 21 May. In this case, there were no route withdrawals, but alterations were made to the existing services, and a new route was introduced. This was an hourly express service with no intermediate stops between Victoria and Windsor Castle. Running in the summer only, and scheduled to take 54 minutes for the journey, it runs out via Chelsea Embankment, the Earls Court one-way scheme, the Great West Road and the M4 motorway. This route is numbered 700.

Routes 704 and 705 were re-routed to double-run via Heathrow Airport Central bus station, and also extended to Windsor Safari Park on summer Sundays. At the other end of Route 704 certain Sunday journeys were diverted at Knockholt Station to run via Halstead and Knockholt Pound as an experiment in answer to a request from the Kent County Council. As Route 706 had now been withdrawn, certain journeys on Route 705 on Wednesdays, Thursdays, Saturdays and Sundays during the summer season were re-timed to enable them to make a double-run from Westerham to Chartwell House en route to either Windsor or Sevenoaks.

The operation of orbital route 725 was also altered in this programme. 725 now became an hourly operation from Windsor to Dartford, with some journeys, mainly during Monday-Friday peak hours, extended to Gravesend. A new route 726 was introduced hourly from Gravesend, which, on reaching Dartford, made a half-hourly joint service with 725 as far as Ashford Town Centre, where it turned off to run via Staines Road to Bedfont, then Stanwell Road; the Cargo Terminal and tunnel through to Heathrow Airport Central bus station, from whence it runs express via the M4 motorway to Windsor.

Traffic on orbital route 727 between Gatwick and Heathrow Airports had been steadily growing, especially during the summer season, and to meet the demand, the service was stepped up to half-hourly between Crawley and Heathrow from 21 May to 30 September.

Readers might well be forgiven if they are wondering what was going to serve Whipsnade Zoo now that Routes 712 and 713 had been withdrawn. On 7 May, a new express service numbered 737 was introduced on Sundays and Bank Holidays from Victoria. It consisted of one journey in each direction, and for the 1977 season ran out via 717 to Mill Hill and then express along the M1 motorway to Flamstead (Friars Wash). This service was to operate until the end of September.

With the transfer of Route 724 to Harlow Garage in April, there were only a few vehicles left in Romford Garage, these being for use on Route 721. This route had been losing traffic for some time, and the Greater London Council, in whose area the route operated for the greater part of its length, had refused financial support. In consequence of this, Route 721 was withdrawn after the last journeys on 1 July. Romford Garage was closed for operational purposes and retained as a store for de-licensed vehicles.

For some time it had been known that High Wycombe garage was to close at the end of the summer, and that all London Country operations in that area were to be transferred to Amersham garage, and as a result, many of the staff at Wycombe decided to find other employment. By August, the position had become so bad that it was necessary to introduce an emergency timetable on Route 711. Introduced on the 8th of that month, a two-hourly service was worked daily from High Wycombe to Reigate, which was supplemented on weekdays by an additional two-hourly service from Reigate to Baker Street, giving an hourly frequency over that section.

The winter programme for 1977 was introduced on 1 October. Routes 700 and 737 were withdrawn for the winter, together with the extension to the Safari Park of Routes 704/705, also the extra service to Heathrow on 727. As forecast, High Wycombe garage was closed and Route 711 was withdrawn. To replace it, a new Route 790 was introduced, which operated every two hours to Victoria. The timetable is co-ordinated with that of City of Oxford Motor Services route 290 from Oxford to Victoria, giving an hourly joint service from High Wycombe to London. Five of the journeys from London on Route 790 are extended from High Wycombe to Amersham, with four journeys from Amersham in the reverse direction, these being mainly operated for the convenience of crew changeovers, although passengers are carried. On the Reigate – Sutton section of Route 711 there were a fair number of short-distance passengers, and to cater for these a London Country bus service 422 was introduced, which was later extended to Redhill. It runs on weekdays only, and gives a half-hourly frequency as far as Kingswood with Route 406.

Evidently there had been some requests for a Green Line service to the new Brent Cross Shopping Centre from the Hemel Hempstead area, and nine journeys in each direction on Route 708 were diverted at Staples Corner (Cricklewood) to make a double-run to the new shopping centre, giving an hourly service between 10.30 am and 6.13 pm northbound and 10.22 am and 6.22 pm southbound.

Attention was then turned to Route 716, and from 14 January 1978 it was withdrawn between Hitchin and Marble Arch and diverted to run from Woking to Oxford Circus hourly. Replacing it on the Hitchin section were two new services from Victoria, numbered 722 and 732. Route 722 was a daily service on a hourly basis, although on Mondays–Saturdays, alternate coaches from Victoria between 11 am and 7 pm and from 8.40 am to 4.40 pm from Hitchin are diverted between Golders Green and Finchley Central to provide a service to the Brent Cross Shopping Centre. These journeys bear the route number 732.

The services to Wrotham and East Grinstead came under review in the meantime, and changes were introduced on 1 April, when Route 708 was withdrawn between Victoria and East Grinstead, its place being taken by the diversion of Route 719, now withdrawn between Victoria and Wrotham. There was one journey in each direction in peak hours on the former 719 route to Wrotham which was still producing a worthwhile traffic, and this has been catered for by the introduction of Route 729 from Borough Green to Victoria. To cover the needs of the remaining off-peak traffic, the Maidstone and District Tenterden – London service has been given the number 919 and now

Country Bus RF 50 covering a Green Line duty and almost at the end of its journey. The building now occupied by Mann Egerton was at one time the Hitchin Green Line Garage. (J. G. S. Smith).

Country Bus RT 4514 covering a Green Line duty and travelling around Birchwood Roundabout on the Hatfield-by-Pass on its way to Hitchin. (J. G. S. Smith).

RF 164 (the spare coach carried at Riverside L.T. garage to cover London area breakdowns) leaving Golders Green Station on its way to Stevenage. (J. G. S. Smith).

operates as a Green Line type of service, picking up passengers west of Wrotham for the first time since London Transport was formed in July 1933.

The famous Brands Hatch Motor Racing Circuit is situated on the Wrotham route, and to cater for the traffic on meeting days, a special Green Line service, numbered 739, operates from Victoria. The first occasion on which this route operated was 16 April 1978. In most cases, up to three departures are operated before and after meetings, but in 1978, the British Grand Prix was held at Brands Hatch on 16 July, and to carry the crowds, a frequent service was operated from Victoria from 7.30 am until 12 noon, and in the reverse direction after the meeting.

Although the programme of changes in the Windsor area introduced in May 1977 had been satisfactory as far as the operations between London and Windsor were concerned, it was felt that a few adjustments were necessary for the 1978 season. Express Route 700 was re-introduced for the season on 29 April, but the remainder of the alterations were deferred until 20 May, as approval of the Traffic Commissioners to the new proposals had not been received in time for an earlier introduction. A new hourly daily service was introduced, numbered 701. This was a semi-express service from Victoria to Windsor serving all stops from Victoria to Hammersmith, then running express via the M4 motorway to Heathrow Airport Central bus station. From this point, it runs via the Bath Road and Slough, observing all the normal stops to Windsor Bus Station, being extended during the summer months to Windsor Safari Park daily. Route 704 retained its hourly frequency from Mondays–Saturdays, but was reduced to two-hourly on Sundays, with two 'up' and three 'down' journeys diverted via Halstead and Knockholt Pound. Route 705 was withdrawn on weekdays, but continues to operate on Sundays on a two-hourly frequency and extended from Sevenoaks to Tunbridge Wells to give a joint hourly service with 704 over that section. One journey in each direction is diverted during the summer months to make a double-run to serve Chartwell House. On Sundays, bus route 410 does not operate, and there is no public transport between Bromley Common and Westerham, or from that town to Sevenoaks, so 705 is increased to an approximately hourly service over this section by the operation of short workings between Bromley North Station and Sevenoaks.

On the same date, the Green Line services from Harlow were the subject of some further changes. Traffic congestion at various points along Route 724 were destroying the reliability of the timetable, and in order to restore it, the Harlow – Romford section was withdrawn. Route 703 to Waltham Cross was only moderately successful, the section between Epping and Waltham Cross being more suited to a local bus service rather than Green Line coaches. In these circumstances, it was withdrawn and replaced by bus route 329, also operating daily between Harlow and Waltham Cross. To retain the half-hourly service between Bishops Stortford and Epping on weekdays and at the same time cover the withdrawn section of 724, a new Green Line Route 712 was introduced between Bishops Stortford and Romford, with an hourly service on weekdays and two-hourly on Sundays.

The increased service on Route 727 between Crawley and Heathrow Airport was reintroduced for the summer on 20 May. It was proposed to withdraw it for the winter on 27 October, but there were so many requests for its retention that it now runs throughout the year.

Route 737 to Whipsnade Zoo was reintroduced on 21 May 1978 and consisted of one journey in each direction on summer Sundays and Bank Holidays. Scheduled to operate until 24 September, the route it follows has been altered. Instead of joining the M1 motorway at Mill Hill, it now turns left at Brent Bridge along the North Circular Road to Staples Corner, joining the M1 at its commencement, and reducing its running time for the journey to 76 minutes.

With the changes introduced on 28 October both routes 725 and 726 have been diverted between West Croydon Bus Station and Addiscombe to serve East Croydon Station. At the same time 725 was diverted between Bexley and Crayford to serve Bexleyheath Clock Tower.

This brings us to the end of 1978, and for the time being, to the end of our story of Green Line, its development and later contraction. It has covered nearly fifty years of triumphs and disappointments, but what of the future?

Many people may be of the opinion that Green Line has had its day, and that the attempts London Country are making to bring it back to life are just flogging a dead horse. The writer held this opinion for quite a time, but now he is not so sure. The new coaches introduced in the past two years are the most luxurious ever seen in Green Line service, and when one looks at the vast area served by London Country, one can see quite a scope for further development. Green Line is now no longer hampered by the necessity to stay within certain boundaries as it was in London Transport days. As it is part of the National Bus Company organisation, the writer sees no reason why there should not be some more joint working on the lines of the present 290–790 arrangement, while there is still scope for further orbital routes.

RMC-type Routemaster passing along Howlands (Welwyn Garden City) on its way to Hitchin. (J. G. S. Smith).

Country Bus RT 4176 covering a Green Line duty to Woking and passing through the forecourt of Golders Green Station. (J. G. S. Smith).

RF-type coach picking up passengers at Potter Street en route to Windsor. (J. G. S. Smith).

Leyland Atlantean bus AN90 working as a Green Line relief at Victoria (Buckingham Palace Road). (J. G. S. Smith).

Maidstone Borough Council Leyland bus No. 23 acting as a relief coach on Route 719 to a motor-racing meeting at Brands Hatch. (J. G. S. Smith).

Country Bus RF 120 on Green Line duty passing through Stratford on its way to Aldgate. (J. G. S. Smith).

RMC-type Routemaster en route to Aldgate at Stratford. (J. G. S. Smith).

RCL-type Routemaster stops for passengers at East Ham Town Hall. (J. G. S. Smith).

Romford-bound RF proceeding along Great Gannet (Welwyn Garden City). (J. G. S. Smith).

RMC-type Routemaster rests between journeys at Aldgate Coach and Bus Station. (J. G. S. Smith).

Two RF-type buses working coach duties on route 725. RF221 is at Chislehurst en route to Croydon and later in the day on its way back to Dartford.

Central London Terminal Points.

(A) Victoria (Eccleston Bridge):—
Terminating —
700 701 707 708 714 717 718 722 729 732 737 739 790.
Picking-up — 704 705 719.

(B) Oxford Circus:—
Terminating — 710 716
Picking-up — 709 715.

(C) Aldgate (Minories Layby):—
Terminating — 723.

(D) Baker Street Station:—
Terminating — 709.
Picking-up — 707 717 722 732 737.

Important Out-Town Points.

(E) Brent Cross Shopping Centre:—
Routes 708 717 732.

(F) Heathrow Airport Central Bus Stn:—
Routes 701 704 705 724 726 727.

Green Line – May 1978

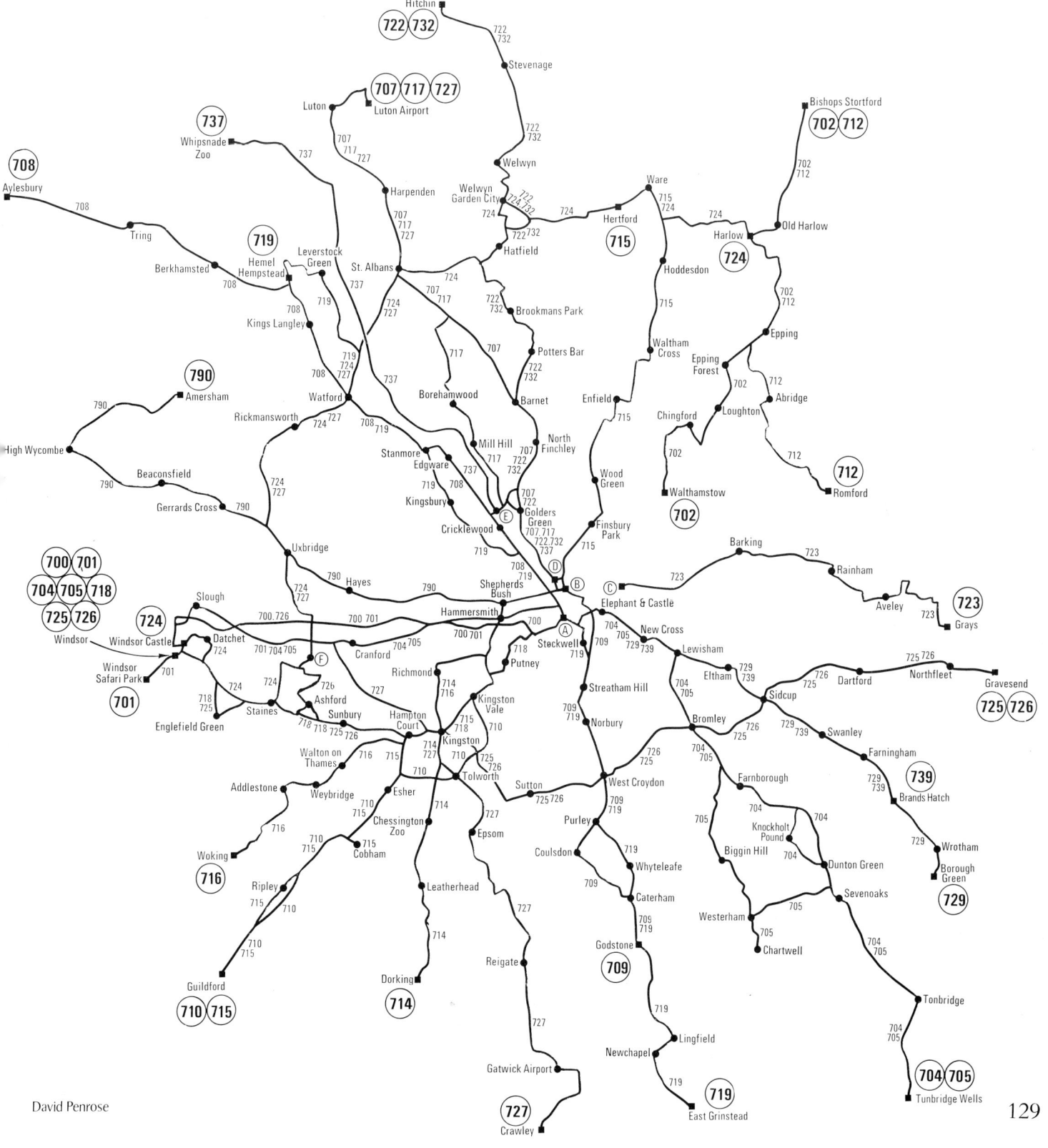

David Penrose

THE VEHICLES
CHAPTER TEN

1973 - 1978

When the first two services started from Watford in November 1929, they were worked by some of the vehicles from the L.G.O.C. Private Hire fleet. These were the A.E.C. Reliance 660 all-weather coaches fitted with 32 seats of a luxury type, servo-assisted brakes and a 6-cylinder petrol engine. The livery was the same colour green as used on the Southdown buses at the time, with cream waistbands and window surrounds. These coaches were known as the R-type, and about fifteen of the 34 were required to work the two services. When the T-type coaches appeared in 1930, the R-type were returned to the Private Hire fleet.

The first T-type vehicles came into service in 1929, but these were fifty rear-entrance 30-seat buses for use on the single-deck bus routes operated by the L.G.O.C. They took the fleet numbers T 1–37, 39–50 and 156. The T-type could well be regarded as one of the largest fleets of single-deck vehicles in the country, and although they were not all in service at the same time, amounted to 798 vehicles in all. The type can also lay claim to being the longest in service with London Transport, the last of the type (T 787) being withdrawn in August 1962.

They were based on the A.E.C. Regal 662 chassis, and, at first, were fitted with 6-cylinder petrol engines but these were changed for 7·7 litre oil engines at a later date. They also had vacuum servo brakes. The first of the coaches was T 38, which appeared on the road for trials in 1929. These trials were evidently successful as a fleet of 150 were ordered by the L.G.O.C. in 1929, delivery commencing in 1930. This first batch were fitted with 27-seat rear-entrance bodies built by three different bodybuilders (L.G.O.C. themselves; Short Brothers Ltd. and Hall Lewis). They were finished from the lower panels to the waistband in the standard L.G.O.C. red. The waistband and window surrounds were finished in black, which was also continued up the wide surrounds of the rear window and on the roof up to about a quarter of the way over the rear entrance. The mudguards and surrounds of the windscreens were also painted black.

This batch was given the fleet numbers T 51–149, 155 and 157–206. It will be observed that there are gaps in the numbering. T 150–154 were five coaches with sliding roofs and 32-seat bodies for the L.G.O.C. Private Hire fleet and were withdrawn and sold by London Transport in 1937. T 156 was a rear-entrance bus to replace T 38 in the L.G.O.C. bus fleet. As delivered, T 52/66/72 – 3/81 – 2/85/90 – 1/100/102 – 3/110/113/116 – 8 bore the fleet name 'EAST SURREY' (an L.G.O.C. subsidiary) and passed to them in order that they could start express coach services to London from Redhill, Reigate and Dorking. T 65/70/77/86/88/98/106/109 and 112 bore the fleet name 'AUTOCAR' and went to Autocar Services Limited of Tunbridge Wells (another L.G.O.C. subsidiary) and enabled them to start a service to London in competition

10T10 A.E.C. Regal coach about to commence its journey to Aldgate from Grays on route 723A. (F. Mussett).

Leyland TF coach on the first route 727 from Kings Cross to Luton, takes its layover in the temporary coach station in Judd Street, Kings Cross in 1950. (F. Mussett).

Former RF556 demoted from passenger service but still doing useful duty as a towing vehicle.

Experimental Bristol coach proceeding along the Victoria Embankment en route to Reigate on a summer day in 1952. (F. Mussett).

RF-type coach in last Green Line livery used by London Transport at Hertford. (J. G. S. Smith).

Country Bus RF 221 covering a Green Line duty on Route 725 at Hampton Wick. (J. G. S. Smith).

with Redcar Services Limited of the same town. The remainder bore the fleet name 'General' and were used to open up that company's services to Windsor (both via Slough and Staines), Ascot, Sunningdale and Maidenhead, and also to replace the Reliances used on the two Watford services.

By July 1930 it had been decided that the coach operations of the L.G.O.C. and its associate companies should be separated from their bus operations and merged into a new company to be known as Green Line Coaches Limited. The first coach in the new livery was T 119, which was shown to Lord Ashfield and officials of the new company a few days after its formation. It bore the name 'Green Line' in an elliptical device on this occasion, but when it appeared in service the more usual underlined block-letters had been substituted.

The first of the next batch of T-type coaches appeared on Christmas Day, 1930, and was part of a batch numbered from T 207–306. They differed from the first batch by having front instead of rear-entrances, and also seated three more passengers. Three of them were fitted with the early A.E.C. oil engines, presumably T 304–306, as the writer remembers that T 305 was involved in an accident with a London United tramcar between Hayes and Uxbridge soon after entering service, and one of the Press reports mentioned that it was an oil-engined coach.

Green Line Coaches had been trying for some time to get licences from the local councils in Amersham and Chesham for a service to London, but had been unsuccessful, but the local bus company, Amersham and District (by that time an L.G.O.C. subsidiary) were granted the necessary licences to operate from Amersham to Oxford Circus early in January 1931. To work the service, five T-type coaches from the Green Line fleet were repainted into a lighter green and given Amersham and District fleet names. These were from the first batch of 150, the fleet numbers being: T 69/71/89/96 and 104. They had cream waistbands and the fleet name was in a style exactly like that of the Aldershot and District Traction Company, which gave the writer, then a tender youth of 19, the impression that the Amersham and Aldershot companies were connected in some way.

The next batch of T-types were eighteen coaches with all-weather 20-seat Hall Lewis bodies for the East Surrey Traction Company, who used them mainly for private hire, tours and excursions, although they did occasional duty as relief coaches on Green Line services. When they were merged into the Green Line fleet, they took the fleet numbers T 307 to 324, but, at a later date, the remaining units left in service were renumbered by London Transport as T 391–402.

T 325–345 were the fleet numbers of a batch which were the same in every respect as those delivered to the East Surrey Traction Company. They went to Autocar Services Limited, once again mainly for tours, excursions and private hire, but they also occasionally appeared as reliefs on the London service. The fleet numbers 325–345 were allotted to them when they were merged into the Green Line fleet. The bus and tour operations of Autocar Services covered routes which lay outside the boundaries of the new London Passenger Transport Board, and when the new Board commenced operations on 1 July 1933, Autocar became a subsidiary of Maidstone and District Motor Services Limited, and for some unknown reason T 325–345 passed to them instead of to London Transport.

During 1932 and the early part of 1933 Green Line Coaches Limited acquired several independent coach operators in the Home Counties. Among the acquired fleets there were twelve A.E.C. Regals of the 662 type with bodies by London Lorries Limited, and as they had the same chassis as the Green Line T-type, were given the fleet numbers T 346–357. In addition to the Regals there were 55 Gilfords which were allocated fleet letters and numbers from GF 1–55. These were the predecessors of what was later to become quite a large fleet of this type of vehicle.

After the formation of London Transport, the new Board acquired a large number of independent bus and coach operators in the country area who contributed a variety of vehicles to the Board's rolling stock. The most important of the makes were the 138 Gilfords, mainly of the 1660T and 1680T types, which, with the 55 already in the Green Line fleet, gave a total of 193 vehicles of this make, the majority of which were employed on Green Line operations. There were also 23 Leyland Titan TD1 coaches which had come from Premier Linc Limited. These were standard double-deck chassis and engines carrying a single-deck body, and were a very powerful and fast coach. There was also a fairly large fleet of double-deck buses on the Leyland Titan TD1 chassis, and both buses and coaches were given the type letters TD with fleet numbers from 1–195. The TD coaches were numbered from 174–191 for the ex-Premier Line vehicles, whilst TD 192–195 were four coaches handed over by Maidstone and District together with the ex-Redcar service from Tunbridge Wells – London in 1935.

In addition, there was a fleet of 36 Leyland TS2 and TS3 type coaches (known as Leyland Tigers), which took the type letters TR and fleet numbers 1–36. The majority of the TD and TR coaches were operated from Slough (Bath Road), Staines, Windsor and Northfleet garages.

Most of these non-standard vehicles were withdrawn from service by 1939, but the last of the A.E.C. Regals acquired from independent operators was not withdrawn from service until 1952.

The new Board was anxious to achieve some degree of standardisation, and the Rolling Stock Department at Chiswick was busy designing new vehicles from 1934 onwards. In 1932, A.E.C. had produced a new chassis numbered as 0762, which carried a 6-cylinder A170 Ricardo oil-engine which was mounted in a slanting position on the offside of the chassis, and which allowed for the whole of the body area to be used for seating, thus giving a higher seating capacity in a single-deck vehicle. This was allotted the type letter 'Q' by the L.G.O.C. Q 1 was a single-deck version with a petrol engine seating 37 passengers, for use on Central London bus routes. This had the passenger entrance in the centre of the vehicle. Q2 and Q3 had double-deck front entrance bodies built at Chiswick Works, and were equipped with self-change Daimler gearboxes. They appeared in service in Central London in 1934, but London passengers did not take to the front entrances, and they were transferred to Country Buses in 1937. Q4/5 were similar double-deckers for Country Buses and had 56-seat Weymann bodies with central entrances. The first production vehicles were 102 single-deck buses numbered Q6–105 and 186/7 for use on Country bus services. These were fitted with 37-seat bodies by the Birmingham Railway Carriage and Wagon Company, and had hand-operated sliding doors fitted just behind the front wheels. These entered service in 1935 and 1936 and were noted for the sloping roof they bore, the slope being from front to back. These were followed by Q 106–185, which were 80 buses for Central Buses, and fitted with 37-seat all-metal Park Royal Bodies. The entrance, which was not fitted with a door, lay in front of the front wheels, a fact that made these buses a danger to those passengers who loved to alight on corners while the bus was still in motion. The writer remembers working on these Q-types as a conductor on a local route in South London. The all-metal bodies were like a furnace inside in the summer, and like an icebox in winter.

The next delivery, known as the 6Q6 type, consisted of 50 coaches for Green Line. These were numbered Q 189–238, and were fitted with 32-seat Park Royal bodies, with sliding door entrances operated by hand and situated just behind the front wheels. They could be distinguished from the Country Bus Q-types, as they did not have sloping routes, and had a dummy radiator fitted at the front. These appeared in service on Routes M1/2/3 late in 1936. When they were withdrawn from Green Line service in 1953, 24 of them went to Muswell Hill Garage and were used on Route 210 until superseded by the RF-type.

Q 188 was a 6-wheeled, double-deck, petrol-driven Green Line coach with Hydraulic transmission. The entrance was situated behind the front wheel, and had a hand-operated sliding door. It entered experimental service during 1937, but was found to be unsuitable, partly because Green Line loadings, especially in midweek, were not sufficient to fill a double-deck vehicle, and it was transferred to Country Bus duties, being withdrawn sometime in 1940.

A new version of the T-type also appeared in 1936. Known in official parlance as the 9T9 type, the maker's reference was A.E.C. 0662. It had a fluid-flywheel clutch, A.E.C. pre-selective 4-speed gearbox, Lockheed servo brakes, leaf spring suspension and was powered with an A.E.C. 7.7 litre oil engine. The bodies were built by Weymann and seated 30 passengers. The livery was a dark Lincoln green up to the waistband, with a lighter green for the window surrounds and up to roof level. Fifty in all were produced, numbered as T 403–452. All of these finished up as Country buses and were withdrawn from service by 1951.

These were followed in 1938 by the 10T10, which was a later development of the 9T9 type built two years earlier. The chassis was still the A.E.C. 0662 type, but the more powerful 8.8 litre oil-engine was fitted, and the braking system was improved over that used on the 9T9. 226 of these coaches were produced, numbered from T 453–718. The 30-seat bodies were built by London Transport at Chiswick Works, and the majority entered service as Green Line coaches, although a few were fitted with 34-seat bodies and used on Country Bus routes. The livery details are exactly the same as for the 9T9 type. During the war many of them were converted either into ambulances, and some were loaned to the U.S. Army for various purposes. All returned to work as Green Line coaches in 1946, and when withdrawn from service in 1951/2, some were painted red and used as buses on Central Area single-deck routes pending the arrival of a fleet of new single-deck vehicles.

T 718 was the last T-type built for Green Line work, but after the Second World War, two further batches were built for bus work, fifty being brought into service at Kingston and Uxbridge Garages during 1946. These had 33-seat Weymann bodies and were numbered T 719–768, and were withdrawn in 1958. The second batch appeared in 1948, and were 31-seaters with Mann Egerton bodies for Country Buses. They were numbered T 769–798 and lasted in service until 1962.

The first of a revolutionary type of chassis and body appeared on the road in 1937. This was a Leyland F.E.C. chassis with the engine mounted under the floor, thus increasing visibility from the driving seat. Instead of entering his cab from the normal off-side position, the driver entered it through a door in the saloon. It was powered by a 6-cylinder oil 8.6 litre flat engine; an A.E.C. fluid-flywheel clutch was fitted, together with a pre-selective air-pressure gearbox, and it carried a 33-seat Park Royal body. The prototype was given the type letters and fleet number TF 1, and was tested on various Green Line routes, and following the tests, twelve further models (TF 2–13) were produced for the Private Hire fleet, also bodied by Park Royal Vehicles Limited. These were followed in 1939 by 75 further vehicles numbered as TF 14–88, which appeared during the year as Green Line coaches from Romford and Grays garages. They had a very short life in service, as when the war started they were converted to ambulances, although the Private Hire fleet were placed in store, all of these (with the exception of TF 9) being destroyed by enemy action.

TF 14–88 returned to Green Line service during 1946 and spent their time working from Dorking, Epping, Grays, Luton and St. Albans garages until they were replaced by the new RF-type in 1951/2. After this, they had a short spell on Country Buses before being sold.

During the wartime period between late 1939 and September 1942 when Green Line coaches were reinstated at the behest of the Government, the two services from Romford Garage were worked by ordinary STL-type buses, and when reinstatement was due to start after the war, it was decided to work these routes with double-deckers once more. At first, the STL-type bus was used, but these were soon replaced by a new fleet of double-deck vehicles on a Daimler CWA6 chassis equipped with A.E.C. 7.7 litre oil engines and fitted with 56-seat bodies supplied either by Duple or Brush. A large number of this type were already in service in the Central Bus fleet, and the new vehicles for Green Line were of a less austere type. The Rolling Stock Department had allocated the type letter 'D' to these vehicles, and the Green Line models took the fleet numbers D 132–181. Twelve of them were fitted with the Daimler 8.6 litre oil engines as an experiment, together with Duple highbridge bodies.

One of the pre-war RT-type buses (RT 97) had been badly damaged during the war, and was converted for a pay-as-you-board experiment on Route 65. The experiment was a failure on Central buses, but it was decided to give it a trial on Green Line Route 721 from Romford Garage for a short period. This also proved unsuccessful, and RT 97 returned to Chiswick Works. It was then completely rebuilt as a luxury double-deck Green Line coach and renumbered RTC 1. The author remembers it working from Windsor Garage on Route 704. The vehicle heating system was an experimental one, and was very temperamental. He remembers one occasion when RTC 1 left Windsor on a fine summer day, and by the time the coach

Line-up of RT-type Green Line coaches in the bus park at Whipsnade Zoo on a busy Bank Holiday in 1952. (F. Mussett).

Green Line RT3231 takes its layover in the Aldgate Bus, Coach and Trolleybus Station in 1952. It is carrying the first type of destination blinds used on these vehicles, the lettering being in yellow on a green background. (F. Mussett).

RMC-type coach at Colindale en route to East Grinstead. (J. G. S. Smith).

Experimental Routemaster coach crossing Westminster Bridge en route to Reigate (Pamlin Prints M 2352).

RMC-type Routemaster coach in Hertford Car Park. (J. G. S. Smith).

Experimental Routemaster Coach en route to Stevenage at Golders Green. (F. W. Ivey).

had reached Colnbrook, passengers were complaining of the heat inside the vehicle. The coach was stopped and the engineering staff from Windsor were called out. They discovered that although the heater switches were in the 'Off' position, the heaters were working. RTC 1 did not stop in service long after that, going to the Country buses first of all, and later to Chiswick for further experimental purposes.

The post-war RT-type double-decker bus was beginning to appear in increasing numbers by 1950, and it was decided to allocate some of this type to Romford Garage for operation on Green Line Routes 721, 722 and 726. The batch chosen was RT 3229–3259. These 31 vehicles were fitted with 56-seat Weymann bodies and were powered by A.E.C. A204 6-cylinder oil engines. They also had air-pressure operated pre-selective 4-speed gearboxes and 18″ fluid-flywheel clutches, and lasted in service at Romford until 1965. The Daimler vehicles they replaced went to Merton Garage for service on Routes 77, 88 and 152, and were later repainted from green to red.

In the meantime, thought was being given to the type of coach which would ultimately replace the 10T10, 6Q6 and TF-types which were nearing the end of their useful lives. Two makers (A.E.C. and Leyland) were asked to submit vehicles for consideration, and both were received in 1949. The Leyland vehicle was an Olympic seating 35 passengers, but as it used a 4-speed constant-mesh gearbox with a dry mesh clutch, it was rejected without a test. The A.E.C. coach was a Regal Mark IV model with an underfloor engine, pre-selective gears and a fluid-flywheel clutch, and carried a 40-seat Park Royal Body. It was not allocated a type letter and fleet number by London Transport, and was always known by its registration number (UMP 227). It underwent trials in the Country bus area, and from the results and experience gained in the tests, the RF-type single-deckers were evolved.

The first of the RF-class to appear were 25 coaches for the Private Hire fleet, to replace the LTC-type vehicles. Numbered RF 1-25, the makers reference was A.E.C. Regal Mark IV 9821 LT. They were powered by A.E.C. A219 6-cylinder 9·6 litre underfloor oil engines and were fitted with 35-seat Metro-Cammell-Weymann bodies. They were painted in Lincoln green livery with red window surrounds, and the fleet name 'London Transport' together with the fleet number, appeared in red lettering instead of the usual gold transfers. In case it became necessary at a later date to use them for universal operation, they were restricted to 27′ 6″ in length. These appeared in May 1951, and the version for use as Green Line Coaches made their appearance in October from Windsor Garage on Route 704. There were 263 vehicles in this batch fitted with the same type of power units as RF 1-25. The bodies were supplied by Metro-Cammell-Weymann, being 30′ long, and seating 39 passengers. This batch was numbered from RF 26 to RF 288, but there was later quite a bit of juggling about between RF-type buses and coaches, with quite an involved renumbering scheme. Also RF 16–25 were later transferred from the Private Hire fleet to Green Line operation.

More double-deck Green Line operation was introduced on 30 October 1954, when Routes 723/A/B from Grays Garage received a batch of 21 RT-type double-deckers numbered from RT 4489–4509. These had the same power units as the rest of the RT-type vehicles, but had 56-seat bodies built by Park Royal Vehicles Limited.

The first Routemaster bus appeared in service from Cricklewood Garage on Route 2 in February 1956, and with passenger traffic growing on the Green Line routes serving the New Towns, plus the fact that a new type of double-decker vehicle would be required at a later date on the services from Romford and Grays garages, it was decided to build and test a Routemaster coach. This was given the fleet number CRL 4 (the letters stood for Coach Routemaster Leyland), and was delivered to Chiswick Works in June 1957. It was carrying an Eastern Coachworks body seating 57 (25 lower-deck; 32 upper-deck), giving extra leg room over the bus version which had 64 seats. The seating itself was of a higher standard than that used on the bus prototypes. It was powered by a Leyland 0600 9·8 litre oil engine and had automatic transmission.

It appeared in the dark Lincoln green livery with light green surrounds to lower-deck windows, and also had a light green central band between lower and upper decks.

The first route to see the new coach was the RT-operated 721 from Aldgate to Brentwood, on which it entered service in October 1957. Moving to High Wycombe on 30 December, it spent a few days there on Route 711 before moving to Reigate for operation on the same route. After further tests on Route 704, it had a spell on Routes 715 and 718. In August 1960 it moved to Stevenage Garage for operation on Routes 716 and 716A, where it stayed until joined by the production models in 1963.

It was now decided to produce a revised version of the Routemaster bus to seat an extra eight passengers by the insertion of a central bay on both decks. This was to be known as the RML-type (Routemaster Long), and to avoid confusion in the Rolling Stock section, CRL 4 became RMC 4, RMC standing for Routemaster Coach.

The first order for Routemaster coaches was for 68 vehicles to be delivered in 1962. The Rolling Stock section at Chiswick had decided that all Routemaster vehicles, whether buses or coaches, should be numbered in one sequence, and the first order took the fleet numbers RMC 1453–1520. Unlike RMC 4, they were powered with A.E.C. 9·6 litre engines, and the layout of the front destination boxes was reduced from three to two apertures, the route number now appearing on the intermediate points blind, instead of in a separate box.

Delivery of the new coaches was spread over the five months between July and December 1962, and with the exception of the allocations to Hertford and Guildford garages for Route 715, all of them went into service on routes serving the New Towns to the north of London. It might be wondered why Route 710 which served Crawley New Town at that time, did not receive an allocation in preference to Route 715. Unlike the northern New Towns, Crawley from its inception, had had the benefit of three railway stations (Three Bridges, Crawley and Ifield) within its area, all of which enjoyed a service of at least two trains per hour to and from London, all of which were electrified, in consequence of which Route 710 did not experience the good loadings seen on the Green Line routes from Hemel Hempstead, Harlow and Stevenage.

The RT-type double-deckers working the routes from Aldgate on Routes 721, 722 and 723/A/B had now seen nearly twelve years service, and it would not be long before replacement would become necessary. The 30-foot long

← *The first of the production batch of Routemaster coaches (RMC 1453) proceeds along a country road en route to Hertford. (London Transport).*

RMC-type Routemaster coach at Golders Green. En route to Woking. (J. G. S. Smith). →

Northfleet-based Routemaster bus loaned to Swanley Garage for Green Line duty on Motor Racing Special Route 739 to Brands Hatch. (J. G. S. Smith).

RC1 pauses to pose for the camera on its way to Sevenoaks. (London Transport).

RC-type coach in original white livery at Victoria. (J. G. S. Smith).

Side view of RC-type coach in original livery. (J. G. S. Smith).

RC-type coach in original white livery at Victoria. (J. G. S. Smith).

version of the Routemaster was chosen for the replacement, and an order for 43 coaches with A.E.C. engines and Park Royal bodies was placed, incorporating the half-width central bay used in the RML-type bus, but in order to give greater comfort and better leg room, the coach version only seated 65 passengers, against the 72 seats on the bus.

Delivered in the summer of 1965, the new long Routemaster coaches were known as the RCL-type, and were allocated the fleet numbers in the Routemaster series from 2218 to 2260. The whole 43 should have gone to Romford (29) and Grays (14), but tests on Route 723B revealed a dip in the road at South Stifford railway bridge which meant that the longer coaches would have insufficient clearance. As a result, five RCL-type were sent to Hertford garage in exchange for a similar number of the RMC-type.

The next question was, what was going to replace the RF-type single deck coach? The Green Line image was beginning to fade in the public mind. Private car use, and late running due to heavy traffic congestion was losing passengers, and the organisation felt that a more luxurious coach capable of a higher turn of speed was required to re-vitalise the service.

As an experiment, it was decided to purchase sufficient new vehicles to completely equip one route for a start, and, if successful, to go on from there. The route chosen was 705 (Windsor – London – Sevenoaks) operated from Windsor and Dunton Green garages. It was a route which had all the necessary features to ensure a successful experiment. It was operated as an express service along the M4 motorway between Langley and Chiswick, and experienced heavy traffic congestion from Hammersmith as far as Bromley. From Bromley onwards the route involved negotiating some very narrow roads, whilst the long and tortuous Westerham Hill was on the line of route.

Fourteen A.E.C. 4U2RA coaches with 36' Willowbrook bodies seating 49 passengers were ordered, these being the first vehicles of this length to be operated by London Transport. They were powered by an A.E.C. AH 691 6-cylinder oil engine with a 5-speed Wilson epicyclic gearbox and fluid-flywheel clutch, and with air suspension on both axles. The bodies incorporated a very luxurious type of seating with headrests, and had panoramic windows. They were painted in a new and very distinctive livery of white, with a wide waistband of Lincoln Green bearing the fleet name 'GREEN LINE' in large gold letters, although they were later repainted in the standard Lincoln green with the waistband in a lighter shade of the same colour.

They were allocated the Type letters RC and fleet numbers 1–14 when they entered service on 28 November 1965. After Route 705 was converted to double-deck Routemasters in January 1967, they were operated for a short while on Route 725, and then had a slightly longer spell on orbital route 727, being transferred to Grays Garage in December 1971 in readiness for the conversion of Route 723 to one-man operation on 1 January 1972. Since the advent of the Leyland National SNC-type on Route 723, they have been relegated to one-man bus work at Hertford.

The RC-type was the last new type of Green Line coach to be introduced by London Transport.

The first new coaches acquired by London Country Bus Services was a fleet of 21 A.E.C. Swifts with 36' bodies by Alexander, and with ramped floors and deep panoramic windows. They had originally been ordered by South Wales Transport as buses, but, in view of the urgent need for new coaches by London Country, the order was diverted to them, and London Country was in time to arrange for them to be equipped to coach specification. On delivery, they went into service on Route 725.

These were followed by 90 A.E.C. Reliances, the first of which was delivered in December 1971, labelled as the RP-type. As delivered, they were painted in the Lincoln green livery with light green waistband as used on the RC-type, but were later repainted in National green to the top of the waistband and white for the window surrounds and roof. The first delivery entered service on Route 727 on 18 December 1971, thus releasing the RC-type coaches for Route 723 at Grays. As the other deliveries were received between January and April 1972, they were introduced on the remaining Routemaster crew-operated routes (with the exception of Route 709), thus expediting the completion of one-man operation on Green Line services. This programme was completed with the conversion of Routes 717 and 715A on 29 April.

February 1973 saw the arrival of the first Leyland National coaches. Although classified by London Country as the LNC (Leyland National Coach) type, they were merely the Leyland National bus dressed up as a coach. Although the exterior was nicely painted up in National green up to the waistband, and then in white up to and including the roof, with the fleet name and National logo in green on the roof sides, and 'GREEN LINE' in large white lettering across the front below the windscreen, the interior of the vehicle was distinctly austere with somewhat hard PVC seating being provided. The first of these new vehicles were sent to Romford for Route 721 on 17 February, the allocation for this route being completed by 3 March. To the passengers boarding them on the first day of operation, the austere interiors must have compared very unfavourably with that of the RP-type coaches they superseded.

An isolated LNC-type coach was rumoured to have been operating out of Tring Garage on Route 706 early in April 1973, and by 1 May, the whole allocation at this garage consisted of the new type of vehicle. The logical sequence would have been for the Chelsham allocation on this route to go over to the new vehicles, but there were space difficulties, so the next delivery was sent to High Wycombe for Route 711, and appeared on this route on 26 May. The whole route was completely converted to LNC-type on 11 June, when Reigate garage received its allocation of the new coaches.

The next batch was received in November 1973, being reclassified as the SNC-type. These were allotted to Two Waters and East Grinstead garages for Route 708, appearing on that service during December. More SNC types were delivered in January 1974, and went to Garston and Swanley for Route 719, their first day of operation being 26 January.

Dorking, St. Albans and Luton garages were the next on the list to change over to the new vehicles, which appeared on Routes 712/713 on 6 March 1974 and on Route 714 three days later.

The next batch of SNC-type coaches incorporated a number of modifications making them more suitable for Green Line operation. Luggage racks were installed, also more comfortable seating with high backs. The first alloca-

One of the new RC-type coaches on the early part of its express run from Hammersmith to Windsor on route 705. (F. Mussett).

RCL-type Routemaster coach on stand at Hertford. (J. G. S. Smith).

RCL-type Routemaster coach in Aldgate Bus and Coach Station. (J. G. S. Smith).

Alexander-bodied A.E.C. Swift SMA 14 nearing the end of its journey in London Road, Dartford. (J. G. S. Smith).

Alexander-bodied AEC Swift SMA3 in London Road, Dartford, en route to Gravesend. (J. G. S. Smith).

Alexander-bodied A.E.C. Swift SMA2 in the forecourt of Northfleet Garage before starting the long trip to Windsor on route 726.

tion went to Grays garage for Route 723 on 3 August, the RC-type coaches they replaced being transferred to Hertford.

There were two deliveries in September 1974. The first went to Tring for Route 706 on 9 September. The Tring allocation of LNC-types were reclassified as LNB and sent elsewhere for bus work. The second batch appeared on 21 September, and were allotted to Staines and Northfleet Garages for Route 701.

A small delivery was received in October 1974 and appeared at High Wycombe on Route 711 on 4 November, the LNC-types they replaced being reclassified as LNB and turned over to bus work.

There were no further SNC deliveries until September 1975. By this time the space difficulties at Chelsham Garage had been resolved, and the opportunity was taken to convert their RF-allocation on 706 to the new vehicles, which appeared on this route on 4 October. The rest of the delivery went to Route 724, on which the Staines allocation went over to the new type also on 4 October. A start was also made on the Romford allocation of this route with the remainder of the September delivery, but was not completed until the next batch was received from Leyland National in January 1976, the whole route being operated by the new vehicles from 7 February. Sufficient vehicles were also received in the January delivery to allow for the conversion of the Reigate allocation of Route 711, which was also carried out on 7 February.

The last batch of SNC-types was received in May 1976, and was sufficient to allow for conversion of the last crew-operated Green Line service 709 to one-man operation, which commenced on 15 May.

In the meantime, the Traffic Section had been having some thoughts about revitalising the Green Line fleet and route network, and agreement on the idea having been reached, a new fleet of A.E.C. Reliance coaches was ordered lease-purchase, from Kirkby Central Organisation of Aston, near Sheffield. These coaches were to be delivered at the rate of 30 each year for five years, and half of each delivery were to be bodied by Plaxton and half by Duple. The Plaxton body to be used as the 49-seat Supreme, to be known as the RS-type, while the Duple body was to be the 53-seat Dominant 2 version, and would be labelled the RB-type. These coaches would replace all the existing RP, SMA and SNC coaches, which would be either diverted to bus work or withdrawn and sold. The new coaches, the first of which was received in December 1976, were the Plaxtons, and were the most luxurious coaches ever to enter service on the Green Line network, being designed not only for Green Line operation, but also for private hire, tours and excursions.

The first five RS-type went to St. Albans Garage enabling the new Luton – Victoria routes 707/717 to commence operation on 29 January. The rest of 1977 deliveries went to Windsor for new express Route 700; Guildford for the peak-hour semi-express Route 710; Windsor and Northfleet for orbital route 726 and to Reigate to increase the service on Route 727 between Crawley and Heathrow Airport for the summer. After the summer season was finished, the Windsor allocation on Route 700 was transferred to Amersham to provide the service on the new Route 790, which operates jointly with City of Oxford Route 290.

This completes the story of the vehicle types which have served as Green Line coaches, and it will be interesting to see what the future has to offer.

Country Bus Atlantean AN 37 (on loan from Guildford Garage) drops its passengers at the entrance to Brands Hatch Stadium. (J. G. S. Smith).

RP31 takes up a passenger in Bishops Rise, South Hatfield. (J. G. S. Smith).

RP1 newly painted in the later livery used for Green Line, sets down passengers at Ware College. (J. G. S. Smith).

← *RP-type coach crossing Elizabeth Bridge (Victoria) en route to Tunbridge Wells (J. G. S. Smith).*

A.E.C. Reliance RP1 about to leave Stevenage Bus Station for London on a quiet Sunday morning.

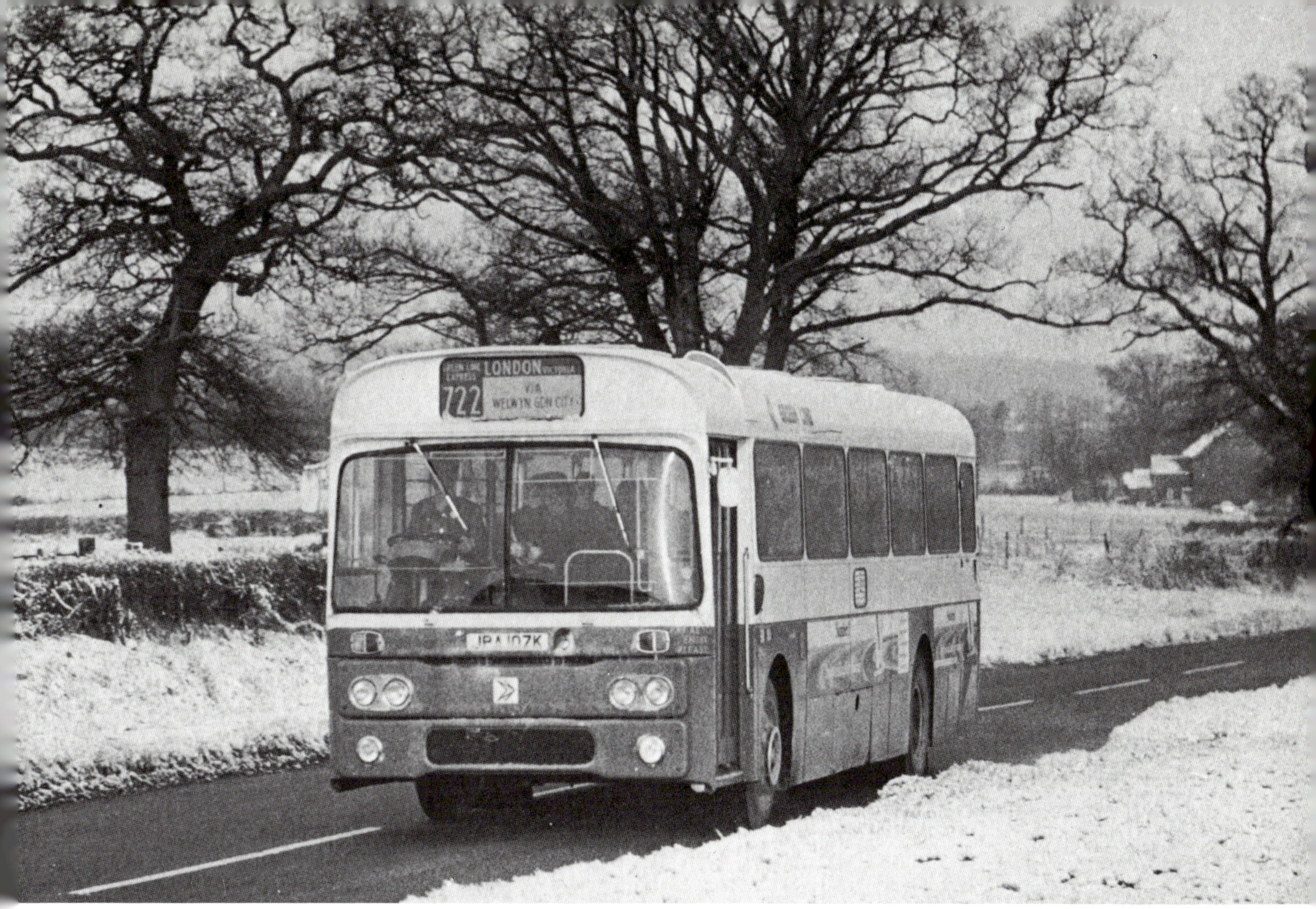
GREEN LINE EXPRESS LONDON VICTORIA
722
VIA WELWYN GDN CITY
JPA 107K

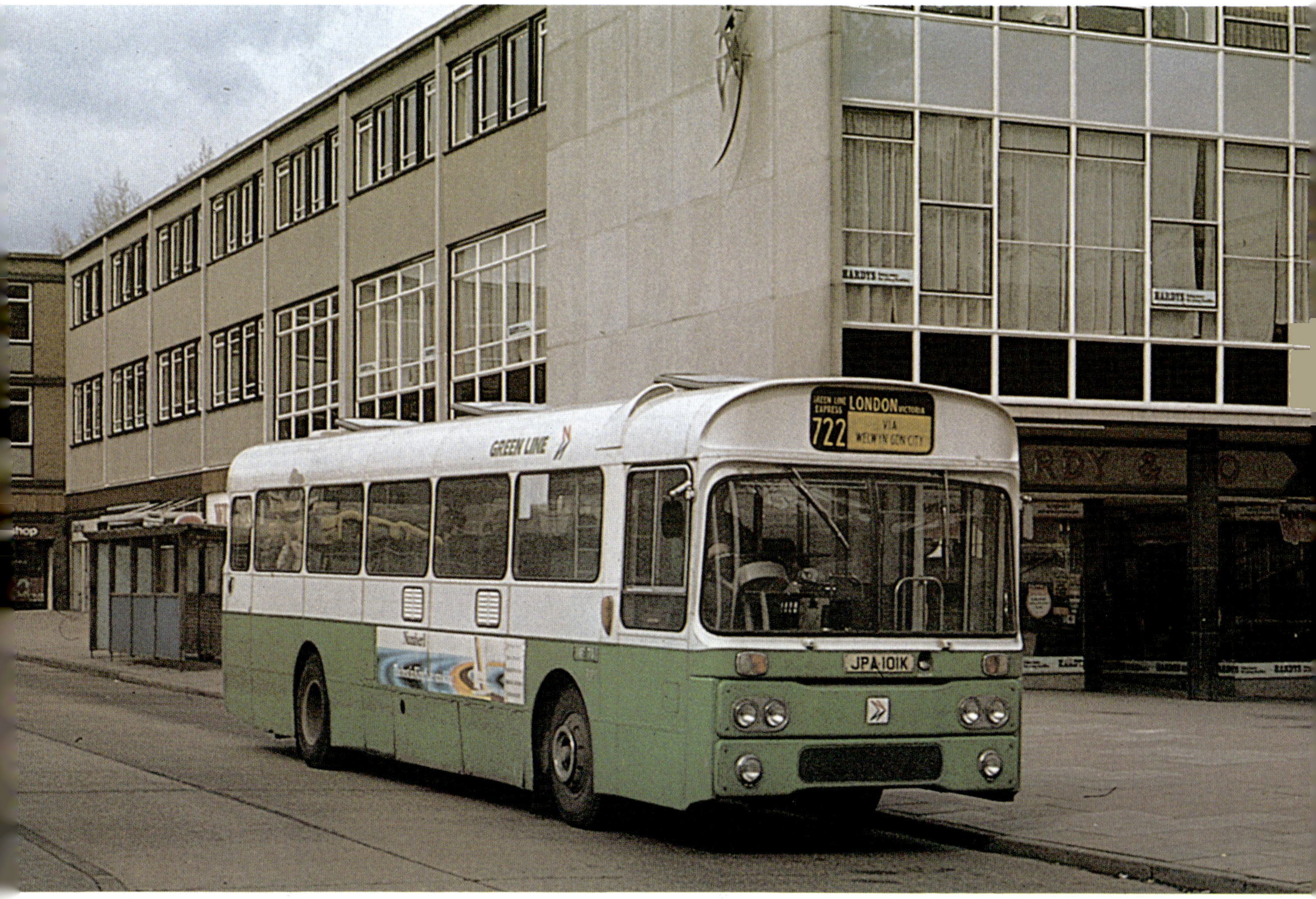
GREEN LINE EXPRESS LONDON VICTORIA
722
VIA WELWYN GDN CITY
GREEN LINE
JPA 101K
HARDYS

RP65 leaving the stop at 'The Cherry Tree', Welwyn Garden City on its way to Victoria via Brent Cross.

Leyland National single-deck bus covering a Green Line duty at the finish of its journey in St. Albans. (J. G. S. Smith).

Leyland National Country Bus SNB315 on Green Line Duties in Howlands, Welwyn Garden City. (J. G. S. Smith).

Leyland National bus SNB316 working a Green Line duty at Potters Bar. (J. G. S. Smith).

Leyland National Country Bus SNB 251 at Victoria on Green Line relief duty on Motor Racing Special Route 739 to Brands Hatch. (J. G. S. Smith).

Leyland National Country Bus SNB 342 at Victoria working a trip on Green Line 790 to High Wycombe. (J. G. S. Smith).

A.E.C. Reliance RP49 leaves Heathrow Airport for Windsor on route 704.

Leyland National coach SNC 76 passes through some pleasant countryside near Shenley on its way to Dorking. (J. G. S. Smith).

Leyland National coach SNC135 on route 724 from Harlow to Windsor.

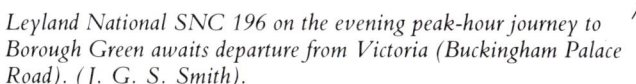

Leyland National coach en route to Bishops Stortford picks up a passenger in Old Harlow. (J. G. S. Smith).

Leyland National SNC 196 on the evening peak-hour journey to Borough Green awaits departure from Victoria (Buckingham Palace Road). (J. G. S. Smith).

Leyland National coach SNC 245 passes through Potter Street on its way to Windsor. (J. G. S. Smith).

Plaxton-bodied A.E.C. Reliance coach (ex-Barton Transport) picking up passengers on Eccleston Bridge (Victoria) before departing to Dorking. (J. G. S. Smith).

Duple-bodied A.E.C. Reliance coach on London – Windsor Express Route at Windsor Castle. Illustrating special 'Jubilee' insignia. (J. G. S. Smith).

Plaxton-bodied A.E.C. Reliance Coach turning on to Elizabeth Bridge (Victoria) on Windsor semi-fast route. (J. G. S. Smith).

Duple-bodied RB 46 picking up passengers at Victoria before starting its journey to Windsor. (J. G. S. Smith).

Duple-bodied RB 54 at Welwyn Garden City (Parkway) on its way to Windsor. (J. G. S. Smith).

Duple-bodied RB27 proceeding along London Road, Horns Cross on its way to Northfleet Garage. (J. G. S. Smith).

Plaxton-bodied A.E.C. Reliance coach about to depart for Tunbridge Wells. (J. G. S. Smith).

← *Plaxton-bodied RS 34 passes through Shepherds Bush on its way to Guildford on semi-fast service 710. (J. G. S. Smith).*

1979

← *Plaxton-bodied A.E.C. Reliance coach at Heathrow Airport on coach – rail – air link route 727.*

↓ *Plaxton bodied RS 39 stops to pick up a passenger at Cheshunt on its way to Hertford. (J. G. S. Smith).*

Plaxton-bodied RS37 stops at Welham Green on its way to London. (J. G. S. Smith).

Former Green Line Q-type coach now demoted to Central Bus duty on route 210 at Golders Green in 1952. (F. Mussett).

Former Leyland TF-type Green Line coach now on bus duties takes its layover in Hertford Car Park in 1954. (F. Mussett).

Former Green Line 9T9 coach now demoted to bus duties leaving Gravesend for Ash on a summer Sunday in 1950. (F. Mussett).

A study in contrasts. Former 10T10 Green Line coach now demoted to bus duty on route 394 (when it still had a Sunday service) stands beside post-war 15T15 bus, which awaits its turn as a relief to the 3.15 departure on route 703 on a Sunday in 1953, at Amersham Garage. (F. Mussett).

Former Leyland TF-type coach, still in Green Line livery, but demoted to bus duty at St. Albans in 1954. (F. Mussett).

TICKET SYSTEMS
CHAPTER ELEVEN

Before discussing the various types of tickets used by Green Line Coaches Limited and London Transport, a few words are necessary on the systems used by the operators mentioned in Chapter Two, many of whom were on the road before the birth of the Green Line organisation.

There are no fewer than thirty-six companies mentioned in that chapter, half of which used the Bell Punch system of pre-printed tickets in differing colours to indicate the fare value. These were cancelled in the presence of the passenger by passing them through the Bell Punch. A fair number of the remaining operators used a combination of Bell Punch and paper tickets, whilst five companies are known to have used the Bell Punch system at the commencement of operations, switching over to ticket issuing machines when these became available. There were also a few operators who issued paper tickets only.

The early operators of short-distance express coach services, namely those which started in 1927/8, usually ran only about five to eight trips per day, far less than their later counterparts. The coaches were usually one-man operated, and, in order not to place the responsibility for collecting fares on the driver, all tickets were pre-booked, the company usually maintaining offices in the two terminal towns, and agencies along the line of route. The fare scale was simple, and consisted of fares from London or the outer terminal to towns and villages along the route, and there were no intermediate fares between the places on line of route, this traffic being left to the local bus services for quite a number of years.

The paper tickets were simple in lay-out, and were printed in triplicate, and made up in books of 50 or 100 tickets. There were spaces for the booking clerk or agent to write in the particulars of the journey to be taken, the fare charged, and whether it was a single or return ticket. There was also a space on the ticket for the agent or booking office to enter details as to who issued the ticket, this being necessary in order that the operator could balance the monthly accounts submitted by the agency, and to ensure correct payment of the commission due to the agent. Two copies of the ticket were handed to the passenger, one copy remaining in the book for reference and audit purposes.

Before setting out on his journey, the driver was usually supplied with envelopes, on the front of which would be written the details of the trips he was working, together with a list of the places at which he could expect to pick up passengers, and in some cases, the number of people to be picked up at each point. On entering the coach, the passengers would hand their tickets to the driver, who would check them and retain the two copies if the ticket tendered was for a single journey. If he had been given a return ticket by the passenger, he would enquire at what time and date the passenger was proposing to make the return journey. If he got this information from the passenger, he would then enter it on both copies of the ticket in the space provided, and then return one copy to the passenger. If the answer was in the negative, one copy of the ticket would be returned to the passenger, and they would be requested to contact the Company's office or booking agent in the town of his destination at least 24 hours before making the return journey.

This ticket system had the advantage of being reasonably cheap to supply and operate. It ensured that all monies due to the Company were paid to them. With the retention of all tickets by the drivers and their subsequent return to the office in their respective envelopes, the Company had useful statistics covering the traffic they were carrying.

Some of the operators who came on the scene at a later date, with more frequent services and conductors issuing Bell Punch tickets on the coaches, also used agencies and booking offices along the line of route. The combination of two systems was greatly favoured by those organisations that did not wish to go to the expense of licensing their coaches as Metropolitan Stage Carriages in the London area. A typical example of this was the original operator on the Ongar – London route. Passengers were picked up anywhere on the section between Ongar and 'The Wake Arms' (Epping Forest), where the coach entered the Metropolitan Police District. From this point to Liverpool Street in both directions, passengers had to be in possession of a ticket before boarding the coach, and, as a pre-booked service over this section, it was considered the coaches were not plying for hire.

In an earlier paragraph, it has been said that at least five operators later used ticket issuing machines when they became available. These operators were: The City Coach Co. Ltd., Premier Line; Hillmans Saloon Coaches; Thackray's Way and Birch Brothers Limited. The first four used the original Setright machine, known as the 'insert' type, so called because the actual tickets were pre-printed and issued in packs of 100 like their Bell Punch contemporaries. There was one difference, however. The overall colouring of the ticket indicated the class (Single; Return; Child; Workman) rather than the fare value. As a general state of affairs, fare values were not pre-printed on the tickets, which, in the case of Singles carried a blank space at the bottom, and in the case of Returns, a blank space at top and bottom. The ticket was placed in the machine, and after various dials at the side had been altered to indicate the fare value required and the number of the farestage at which the passenger boarded, these details were printed on the ticket when the main handle was turned. Dials on the reverse side of the machine kept a running total in both shillings and pence of the amount of cash taken by the conductor. By turning the fare-value dial to 'X' and the farestage dials to the number of the stage boarded, and then printing these details on the remaining blank space on the ticket, returns tendered on the return journey could be cancelled. There was a dial on the reverse side of the machine which recorded the number of passengers the conductor had dealt with, and the cancellation of a return ticket would be recorded as one passenger on that dial, but by use of the symbol 'X', the cash-recording dials would not be affected.

Messrs. Birch Brothers Limited, the fifth operator, did not take up the Setright insert machine, but decided on the Bell Punch 'Bellgraphic'. This machine was manufactured by the Bell Punch Company, and, in the opinion of the writer, was the best of the early ticket machines. The tickets were pre-printed, and on the front side bore the name of the issuing operator, with blank spaces for recording the fare value, class of ticket, plus the numbers of the farestage boarded and the alighting point. The reverse side of the ticket could be used for advertising purposes, although it usually carried a resumé of the conditions of issue, plus a grill of numbers from 1 to 12 under the heading 'Hour of Return'. This side of the ticket usually varied according to the requirements of the issuing authority, sometimes carrying sections for use if a transfer facility was granted. The tickets were printed on thin paper, with a duplicate copy underneath, and were perforated at the side in order that the conductor could tear them off. The whole packet of tickets was placed in the machine, care being taken to feed the bottom copy underneath the reel of carbon paper. This was a useful point, as, once the machine was locked, the rolls of tickets could not be interfered with. The first ticket to be issued could be seen in an aperture in the top of the machine, and the conductor could enter all the details required with an indelible pencil or ball-point pen. Upon manipulation of the handle at the side of the machine, the top copy of the ticket would be ejected at the side of the machine, and then torn off by the conductor and handed to the passenger. The carbon copy of that ticket would remain in the machine, to be withdrawn by the Depot Inspector when the conductor paid in. The carbon reel in the machine was usually double-sided, so that an impression of what was written on the front of the ticket also appeared on top of the lettering on the reverse side, thus offering a further deterrent to any dishonest conductor. The only disadvantage with this machine was the fact that the conductor had to pay in his cash without any cash figures to guide him, as there was with a normal BELL Punch and ticket waybill. The usual thing was for the Depot Inspector to empty the Bellgraphic machine of the tickets issued in front of the conductor, seal them in an envelope, together with the simple waybill used with this type of machine, and on which was recorded the amount paid in by the conductor, any overpayment of cash or shortage of payment by the conductor being assessed by the Traffic Audit Department, and dealt with later. Having a carbon copy of every ticket issued also ensured that the Traffic section had intimate knowledge of the traffic movement over all sections of its routes, and could plan ahead accordingly.

We now come to the tickets issued by Green Line Coaches Limited and London Transport. It will be remembered that Green Line was a direct descendant of the coach services started by the London General Omnibus Company and its associates (East Surrey; Autocar and National), but as the L.G.O.C. were operating the largest number of routes, when the Green Line company took over, it was their ticket system which was inherited and used on the new services started by Green Line in 1930, as well as continuing in use on the original routes.

Although these tickets were of the Bell Punch type, certain values of Single and Return tickets on some routes could be used to travel on the Underground railway between certain outer stations and Central London. In consequence of this the early type of ticket had the legend set out in standard railway style. For instance, on the Windsor via Slough route when it first started, there were three sixpenny fares as follows: Windsor Castle to Colnbrook; Slough to 'The Peggy Bedford' (Harmondsworth) and Colnbrook to Cranford, and there was a separate ticket for each one of these fares. This lead to an unnecessarily large number of tickets being carried by the conductor, many of which were not used from one day to another, so, after a while, the system was altered, so that all fares of like value were shown on the one ticket, which was punched at the stage of boarding, the stage to which it was available being printed opposite. Thus there was now only one sixpenny ticket instead of three, with the consequent saving on printing costs. However, where there was a fare with a railway availability, separate tickets were still retained. Once again quoting the Windsor faretable, there were four 1/3 fares on the chart, as follows: Windsor Castle – Osterley (Thornbury Road); Slough to Gunnersbury Station; Colnbrook – Hammersmith and 'The Peggy Bedford' to London (Charing Cross). The first three of these fares were incorporated on one ticket, a separate ticket being provided for the 'Peggy Bedford' – London stage, which was printed in the railway style (see Example 1 in the photographs). The list of stations to which the ticket was available was printed on the reverse side of the ticket.

Return tickets were printed in the same style as the single tickets, and one issued between Staines and London is illustrated.

Incidentally, as it stated on the tickets that they could be used for one journey in either direction between the points printed in large letters, it was usual for return tickets to be punched on the left-hand side on journeys to London, and on the right-hand side on journeys from London, the reason for this being to ensure that passengers holding return tickets did not make two journeys in the same direction. The method of dealing with return tickets on the return journey was extremely simple. The tickets were perforated across the middle by the printers. and on the ticket being handed to the conductor on the return trip, he tore it into two halves, withdrew the half which had already been punched, then punched the other half and returned it to the passenger. The withdrawn halves were then handed in at the end of the duty to account for the extra punchings shown on the ticket punch register.

Green Line were also using booking agencies along the line of the various routes, as well as selling coach tickets at certain Underground stations in London. These agencies, plus the tube stations, simply issued a Bell Punch ticket of exactly the same type as used on the coaches. On boarding the coach, the ticket was handed to the conductor, punched in the ticket punch and returned to the passenger.

As the number of routes began to grow, it was realised that the system as described above was very loose, and would allow both dishonest conductors and passengers very much room to indulge in malpractices, so a new system was introduced, which tightened up the ticket procedure considerably. A new style of ticket was adopted for both single and return tickets, and the old style of ticket was withdrawn at the end of 1930. Agencies and railway stations were issued with different styles of ticket. Agencies were given books of paper tickets on which they only had to stamp the date of issue, write in the fare, and indicate to the conductor whether a single or return had to be issued. The route letter and availability of the ticket were not stated on these vouchers, and the conductor simply issued a ticket of the value and class stated, and punched at the stage where the passenger boarded.

In the case of the railway ticket offices, a different system was adopted. In the case of the Windsor via Slough route, special Edmonson card railway-type tickets were introduced for both single and return trips. The single ticket, at first glance, looked like a standard railway return ticket, being printed in two halves, and perforated down the middle. They were printed on white paper pasted on cardboard and were overprinted with two horizontal green lines. The left-hand half of the ticket was available from Hammersmith to Windsor on the coach, and was cancelled by the coach conductor with special nippers of the railway-type, and then handed back to the passenger. The right-hand half was available from the station of issue to Hammersmith, and was tendered to the ticket collector when passing through the barrier at that station. These tickets were issued at the following Underground stations:

DISTRICT LINE. *Stations between Charing Cross and Barons Court.*
PICCADILLY LINE. *Stations between Leicester Square and Barons Court.*
BAKERLOO LINE. *Stations between Oxford Circus and Charing Cross.*
HAMPSTEAD LINE. *Stations between Tottenham Court Road and Charing Cross.*

The Edmonson-type return tickets were issued from the same group of Underground stations, and were also printed on white paper on cardboard, and overprinted with two green horizontal lines, but were printed in three sections. The left-hand section was available for the return journey from Windsor to London, and was *not* cancelled by the coach conductor but by the ticket collector when the passenger passed through the barrier at Hammersmith Station. The middle portion was for the outward coach journey from Hammersmith to Windsor, being cancelled in the same manner as described for single tickets, whilst the extreme right-hand side of the ticket was available for the outward railway journey to Hammersmith, and was collected by the ticket collector at that station.

There were also through bookings between the Underground and Green Line routes via Shepherds Bush (Central Line) station, and via Camden Town and Golders Green stations on the Hampstead line (now known as the Northern Line), and no attempt was made at this time to introduce tickets of the railway type, instead a stock of the new type tickets used on the routes concerned were carried in the railway booking offices where these tickets could be issued.

Ticket Nos. 2–6 and 11–13 are examples of the new type of ticket issued on the coaches, and, in the cases of those with railway availability, cover journeys via Shepherds Bush, Camden Town and Golders Green. Example No. 2 is a 6d Child Single Ticket issued on a route on which there was no Underground availability, but why it is punched in the emergency section 'G' is somewhat of a mystery. Sometimes, if an additional fare was added to the farescale, it was usual to use these emergency sections to indicate that the ticket was available for the new fare until a fresh printing of the ticket was required. Example No. 3 is a 6d Child Single ticket issued on the Watford – Golders Green route, and carries a fare from Brockley Hill to London, using the coach to Golders Green and then the tube to Central London, the stations to which it is available being printed on the reverse side of the ticket. If this ticket had been punched in that section, it would be tendered to the ticket collector at the station of alighting, and would be accepted in the same way as a railway ticket.

Ticket No. 4 is a 1/6 Single ticket used on the Watford – Charing Cross and Bushey – London – Crawley services, neither of which had fares which had any Underground facility, and is punched for an adult single journey from Watford to Charing Cross. On the Bushey – Crawley service there were two 3/- Adult Single fares, one from Stanmore (Abercorn Arms) to Redhill and one from Cricklewood (The Crown) to Crawley, for which the child fare is 1/6. A child boarding the coach at Stanmore and asking for a single ticket to Redhill would be issued with this 1/6 ticket, punched in emergency section 'A' ('D' in the reverse direction), while Cricklewood to Crawley would be punched in 'B' and 'E' in the reverse direction.

The 1/9 Single (Ticket No. 5) is from the Hitchin – Reigate route, on which a passenger from Hatfield (the point at which the ticket is punched) could travel right through to London by coach, or change at Golders Green to the Underground. It will be observed that the Hatfield farestage is out of geographical order to the rest of the stages on the left-hand side of the ticket, but it was a rule on these new tickets that all fares with Underground availability should be placed at the top of the ticket in order that they could be recognised as such by the Underground staff. In the case of Ticket No. 5, the passenger has continued on the coach to London. It was laid down in instructions to coach conductors that, after leaving the Underground interchange stations on journeys to London, that they should go round the coach and cancel the Underground availability section of the ticket with the special clippers provided.

Example No. 6 is the reverse side of the 1/6 Single ticket of the London – Guildford route, and is included to show the reader how the stations and lines of availability on the Underground were explained to the passenger.

We come now to the Return Tickets of which there are four illustrations, these being examples 10–13. Ticket No. 10 is the 1/6 Adult Return ticket from the Hertford – London route. Here again you will see that the farestage with Underground availability is at the top of both Forward and Return journey sections. To explain how this ticket would be dealt with for such a journey, the appropriate paragraphs from the instructions to railway staff are quoted:

A passenger boarding the coach at an out-town point will be handed a ticket punched in the top section of the ticket. The ticket will be available to London by coach throughout, or by coach and rail via the exchange station shown on the back of the ticket. Should the passenger proceed by coach throughout, the coach conductor, after passing the station of interchange, would cancel the rail availability section with the clippers provided for the purpose. In the case of a passenger changing from the coach to the Underground at the interchange station, the Ticket Collector must clip the section marked "LONDON" at the top of the ticket and allow the passenger to proceed to any station indicated on the back of the ticket. On arrival at the destination station, the Ticket Collector will collect the top portion of the ticket, leaving the passenger with the remaining two-thirds of the ticket for the return journey.

On the return journey, the passenger will have the option of either boarding the coach in London, or proceeding by Underground from the stations printed on the back of the ticket to the point of interchange. Should the passenger proceed by Underground, the Ticket Collector will clip the ticket in the space marked "LONDON" on the lower half of the ticket, and at the interchange station the passenger will be allowed to pass through. When the passenger boards the coach, the conductor will also punch the lower half of the ticket in the section marked "LONDON" and issue an Exchange ticket punched to the stage the passenger is entitled to travel and collect the remainder of the forward journey ticket (middle section) to account for the Exchange Ticket issued.

The exchange tickets in question are illustrated (7–9). In the case of passengers not using the railway facility, but boarding the coach in Central London, the Conductor would punch the section marked 'LONDON' in the return journey portion of the ticket, and then issue an Exchange Ticket as described in the last paragraph, at the same time collecting the top two-thirds of the ticket to account for the Exchange Ticket issued. This procedure also applied on the routes where there was no availability of tickets on the Underground.

Example No. 11 is a good example of a high-value return ticket of this period, which was issued on Route N (Windsor – London via Staines). On the return journey, the Conductor has correctly punched the bottom half of the ticket, but has not cancelled the railway section on the left-hand side, which he should have done after the coach passed the inter-change station at Shepherds Bush. The ticket was probably withdrawn by an Inspector and the Conductor reported for his misdemeanour.

At a later date, probably during the early part of 1932, the railway availability section was withdrawn from the body of the ticket (see Example No. 13 in the photographs), a section being added at the top and bottom of the ticket, which, being perforated, could easily be detached by the Railway Ticket Collector or cancelled by the Coach Conductor, as has been carried out on the ticket illustrated.

The reader will see that Examples 11 to 13 have been overprinted in red across the middle with the legend in red 'THESE TWO SECTIONS MUST BE RETAINED INTACT FOR THE RETURN JOURNEY'. This legend also appeared in 1932, and was rendered necessary by the fact that too many mutilated return tickets were being submitted to the Conductors for acceptance and being refused by them in accordance with their instructions from the Company.

Examples 2–13 remained in issue throughout the life of Green Line Coaches Limited, and also from July to October 1933 by London Transport. As various companies were acquired by Green Line in 1932, their ticket systems were turned over to the same style of ticket but bearing the names of the companies concerned.

It will be remembered that London Transport had a complete route reorganisation on Green Line, which was introduced on 4 October 1933. At the same time some revised fares were introduced, and the only routes to retain fares with Underground availability were the Watford – Golders Green and Whipsnade Zoo – London routes. Many extra farestages were introduced, and a new style of ticket was introduced, examples of which are depicted in examples 14–22 and Exchange Ticket No. 25 in the photographs.

From these examples, it will be seen that the front and back of the tickets were used for fares, and that, in some cases, two and even more routes were appearing on the same ticket.

Examples 14 and 15 are the front and reverse of the same ticket, which is the 1/6 Adult Single ticket for Routes B (Rickmansworth – Wrotham), I (Watford – Crawley) and J (Watford – Reigate). It will be observed that the farestages have been given much clearer definitions than has been used in the past, and when compared with example No. 4, several intermediate fares have been added between Watford and Oxford Circus, and that the distance allowed for some 1/6 fares on the southern half of the route has been extended. To allow for this ticket to be issued to a child for half of the 3/- adult fare, the sections 'A' and 'B' have been added at the bottom of the reverse side (No. 15 on the photographs). If the ticket was issued as a child ticket on journeys into London, then it would be punched in section 'A', and in 'B' on a journey from London.

Example No. 16 was introduced on the Strawhatter route from Luton to Kings Cross when it was acquired by the Board on 1 February 1934. It will be noticed that underneath the fare stages is printed the legend 'AVAILABLE ONLY ON STRAWHATTER SERVICE'. The reason for this is the fact that the fares on the ex-Strawhatter route were very much cheaper than those charged on Green Line route H, which followed the same route from Luton as far as St. Albans. Although there was a fare revision on the ex-Strawhatter route by October 1934, the fares on this route still remained cheaper than those charged on Green Line Route H, and included a 2/6 Cheap Day Return from Luton to London. Despite the discrepancy between the fare scales on the two routes, when the Strawhatter fares were revised, Return tickets issued on either Green Line Routes H and AH and ex-Strawhatter route BH became interavailable for the return journey and the Cheap Day Return fare from Luton to London and in the reverse direction was also issued on Route H, being available on that route between Luton and Baker Street Station.

Example No. 17 is the 1/6 Adult Single ticket issued on the Watford – Golders Green coach service, and carries the detachable coupon at the bottom which allowed the passenger to proceed by Underground from Golders Green to Central London.

Example No. 18 is a 6d Excess Fare ticket. These tickets were introduced with the route reorganisation of 4 October

1

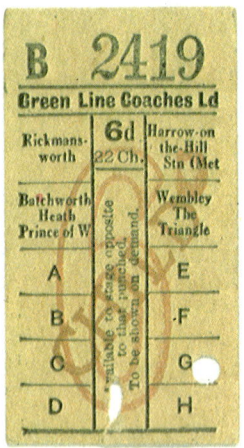

2

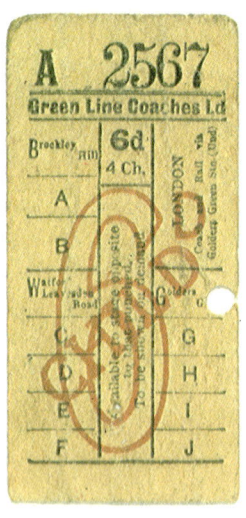

3

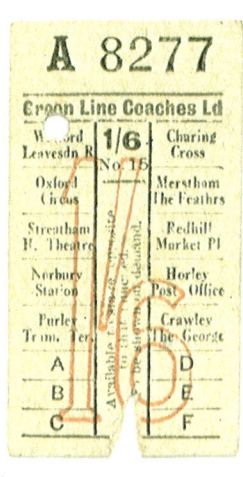

4

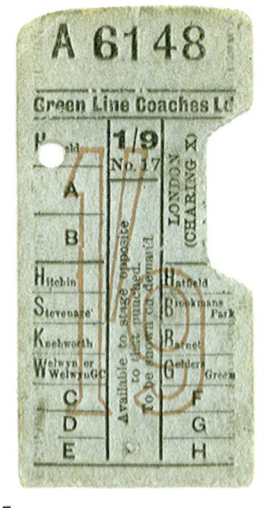

5

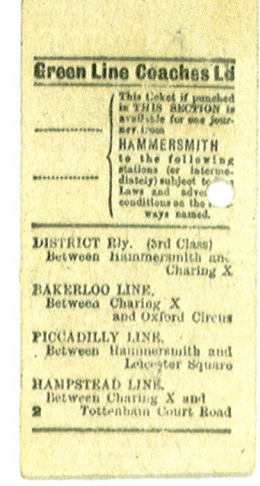

6

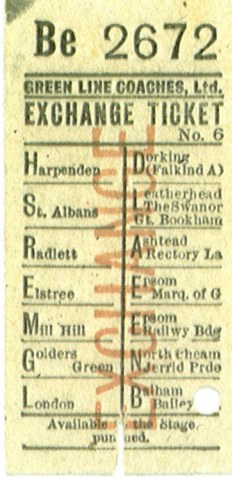

7

8

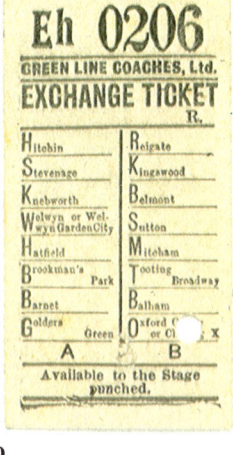

9

10

11

14
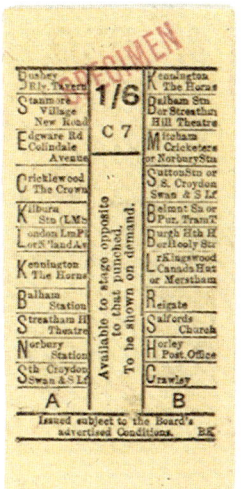
15

16

17

18

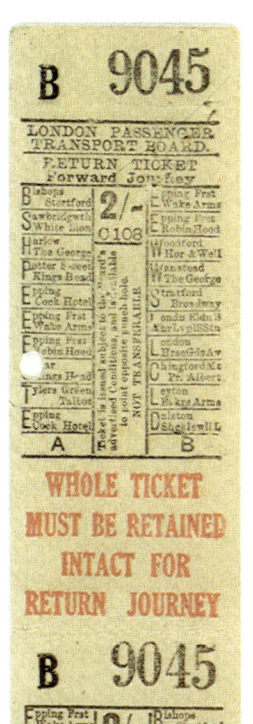
19

20

21
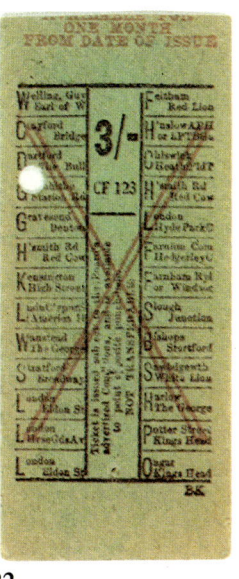
22
23

24
25
26

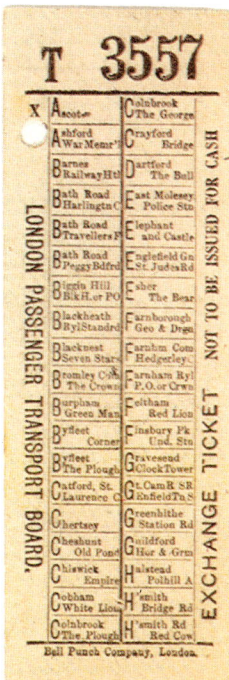

1933. Before that date, it was usual for an ordinary single ticket of the value required to be issued and cancelled by punching it in the serial number at the top of the ticket. This system was evidently felt to be a little haphazard, so 3d, 6d, and 9d Excess Tickets were brought into use on the date stated above. Once again, the ticket covered a group of routes, example 18 being the 6d Excess Ticket for use from Epping Garage on Routes N (Epping – Windsor), V (Bishops Stortford – London) and W (Ongar – London). On issue, it was punched at the stage to which the passenger, having paid the excess fare, was now entitled to travel. It would not be out of place to mention here the method used to assess excess fares where necessary. Excess fares on all buses on the London Transport system at that time were calculated on the difference between the two single fares concerned, with a minimum excess fare of 1d. This system could not be operated on Green Line coaches, as at this time except in certain cases, there was a minimum single fare of 1/-. The principle was the same however, the difference between the two single fares being charged, with a minimum of 3d. The acquisition of the Strawhatter service from Luton, with a Cheap Day Return fare of 2/6, which, as had been stated before was a much lower fare than normally charged on a Green Line service, led to a further ruling on the subject. The official Traffic Notice to the staff dated 30 April 1934, gives the following ruling: 'Conductors are reminded of the instruction covering the issue of excess tickets, which reads: Conductors will charge the difference between the two single fares and *not* the minimum fare for the excess journey. Exception will be made on Route BH, Luton and London, where a cheap day return ticket is in operation. If overriding occurs on a cheap daily return the full charge between must be collected, minimum 1/-'. Incidentally, passengers tendering a return ticket and wishing to ride beyond its availability were also charged the difference between the two single fares, and not the difference between the two return fares.

Example No. 19 is an example of the new-style return tickets issued from 4 October 1933 onwards. Here again, both the front and reverse sides of the ticket were used to accommodate all the farestages and fares for the routes in question. The front of this ticket is for use on Routes V and W from Epping Garage, with the reverse side for use on Routes H and AH from St. Albans and East Grinstead Garages. On issue on the forward journey, the ticket was punched in the top half. Example 19, which has not been used for the return journey, will be seen to have been issued from Ongar (Kings Head), a fact which is indicated by the punch-hole, and is available to Chingford Mount (the stage printed immediately opposite). On the return journey, after ensuring that the whole ticket was intact, the conductor would retain the top or forward half, punch the return half at Chingford Mount, at the same time issuing an Exchange Ticket punched at Ongar (Kings Head) and hand both to the passenger. The top half of the ticket was returned to the office at completion of duty in order to account for the extra punchings registered inside the ticket punch. A simpler system would have been to withdraw the return ticket complete, and simply issue the passenger with an exchange ticket, as there seems to be no point in returning him the bottom half of the return ticket.

Example No. 20 is simply a bottom half of the same ticket as in No. 19, and is merely shown in order that the reader may have some idea of what the reverse side looked like.

The next two examples (Nos. 21 and 22) are a later development of the return tickets, from which it will be seen that a warning has been added that tickets are available for one month from the date of issue, although no arrangement has been made anywhere on the ticket to indicate this date. Both these tickets are the bottom halves, and they were of the same length as Example No. 19. The overprinted 'R' indicating that the bottom half was for use on the return journey has been withdrawn and replaced by a large skeleton overprinted 'X' presumably to remind conductors to issue an Exchange Ticket after punching the bottom half. It will also be noticed that the 'A' and 'B' sections for use when issuing the ticket for a child's fare have now been separated from the normal farestage sections and placed below the operator's title.

Examples 23 and 24 are the front and reverse sides of a new style return ticket which was first introduced in June 1935. It was a much simpler and smaller ticket which saved the repetition of the farestages that had existed on the return tickets depicted in examples 19 to 22. It had a small detachable stub at the bottom, which, on the front side simply carried the words 'LONDON PASSENGER TRANSPORT BOARD', the code number of the ticket (in the case of the examples shown, A 38), the fare value in somewhat larger type, and the serial number of the ticket (in the case of Example 23 it would be U 8610. On the reverse side of the stub was printed the legend: 'THIS PORTION WILL BE RETAINED BY CONDUCTOR ON RETURN JOURNEY' and also carried the ticket code number (A 38) and the fare value 1/6 BK (for back) in small type. The instructions to Conductors for issuing this new type of ticket read as follows: 'The new type ticket has a lower section, with serial number in place of the present return half section. On issue the ticket must be punched in the stage boarded by the passenger, and will be available to the stage opposite that punched. The whole ticket must be handed to the passenger. On the return journey, the ticket must be punched in the stage boarded (opposite original punch-hole) and the lower portion detached and retained. An exchange ticket must be issued, punched to the stage to which the passenger is entitled to travel, to agree with the stage boarded on the forward journey (in the case of Example 23 this would be South Croydon, Swan and Sugar Loaf). The counterfoil section (or stub) must be treated in the same way as the present day forward halves and handed in to the depot office on completion of duty, to agree with the exchange tickets issued.'

The exchange tickets were also altered at this time to the type as depicted in Example No. 26, and it will be observed that the farestages are printed in alphabetical order, instead of the geographical order as shown on Example No. 25.

A revision of Green Line fares took place on 2 May 1937, and the opportunity was taken to introduce new style single and return tickets, and these are depicted in examples 27–35 illustrated. The single tickets were now printed in the style familiar to most users of the contemporary London bus routes before the Second World War, with the stages set up in two adjoining columns, the tickets being punched at the stage of boarding, the availability being to the stage opposite the punch-hole. The special 3d and 6d excess fare tickets were withdrawn, a special section being printed on the reverse side of the ordinary single tickets of those values and also on the 9d single ticket. These tickets, when issued for an excess fare, were punched in Section 'A' on journeys to London, and 'B' on journeys from London. On the very rare occasions when an Excess Fare higher than 9d was required this had to be made up by the issue of two or more low value tickets. Special children's sections were provided on all single tickets on the reverse side, and the punching instructions were the same as for excess fares.

In order to reduce the number of tickets carried by the conductor, single tickets were only produced up to the 2/- value, except on Route U to Whipsnade and Routes K1 and K2, where there was a frequent sale of higher value tickets. When a higher value single fare was asked for on a route with no tickets higher than 2/-, these had to be covered by the issue of two or more tickets in accordance with a special chart carried by the conductor. In the event of a child requiring a single ticket above 2/-, two tickets had to be issued, the higher ticket being punched in the section reading 'TO LONDON' or 'FROM LONDON' as applicable, and the second ticket in the section reading 'A' or 'B'.

It will be observed from an examination of examples 33–35, that the new return tickets were vastly different from those which had been used in the past, and perhaps it might be better to quote the notice of instructions issued on the new style tickets:

RETURN TICKETS:
The new return tickets are of different design and provide:
(1) The farestage names, printed in similar order to those on the existing tickets.
(2) Sections, showing the 12 months of the year (back and front) and the days of the month 1—31 (staggered back and front).
(3) A separate set of sections in which the date of return is to be indicated.
(4) Sections 1—12 on the back in which the hour of return is to be indicated.
Upon issue, these tickets are to be (a) clipped (with clippers) in the stage boarded, and (b) bell punched in the month of issue and again in the day of issue. The punching in the month and day section must be made on the same side (front or back of the ticket) as the clipping in the stage of boarding. Upon the return journey, the following procedure is to be observed:
(a) Agree the validity of the ticket (availability is for one month, i.e., from the 10th of one month to the 9th of the next month, inclusive),
(b) Clip out all the figures in one line, in the cancellation section, to leave the square indicating the date of return.
(c) Clip the section corresponding with the hour of return and return the whole ticket to the passenger.
The new return tickets are printed for fares up to and including the return fare applying between London and the out-town terminal. For fares in excess of this, two tickets are to be issued in accordance with the auxiliary fare charts provided for the route concerned. Children's return fares, with the exception of 9d or 1/-, for which tickets are printed, are to be covered by the issue of adult tickets punched in the emergency sections, as follows:
On journeys to London – clip in section 'A'.
On journeys from London – clip in section 'B'.

Using the above instructions to conductors, let us examine Examples 33 and 34 in the photographs. Example 33 has been issued on 1 June, as indicated by the two punch-holes, for a journey from Bushey (Aldenham Road) to Kilburn Station (L.M.S.). The passenger concerned travelled back on the same date, as the number '1' has been left unclipped in the 'Date of Return' section. There is one thing wrong with this ticket. The arrow-point clipping in the Bushey farestage should have the head of the arrow pointing towards Kilburn (the stage of alighting). Looking at Example 34, which is the reverse side of a Return Ticket, we find that the hour of return was 5 pm, this fact being indicated by the arrow-head of the clipping which faces right. In the unlikely circumstance that the passenger had returned at 5 am, the arrow-head would have been pointing to the left. All of this is better illustrated in Example 35, as all the necessary details are on the front of the ticket. This example was issued from Grays (War Memorial) to East Ham Town Hall on 20 March, the passenger returning on the same day at 9 pm in the evening from East Ham.

Example 36 is a very interesting ticket, being the through ticket from London to Whipsnade Zoo on Route U. This ticket was introduced on 15 May 1937, when additional travelling facilities were introduced on that route. The following instructions were issued to coach conductors:

On and from 15 May 1937, additional facilities will be provided on Route U, London to Whipsnade.
From Underground Stations there will be three routes. Underground to Marylebone Station and thence by coach route U. Underground to Golders Green Station, thence coach route U. Or Underground to Kings Cross, St Pancras Station, thence by L.M.S. Railway to St. Albans and thence to Whipsnade by bus route 368.
From Whipsnade the return journey may be made by any of these three routes.
Passengers booking at Underground Stations and joining the coach at Marylebone or Golders Green Station will be issued with vouchers, similar to those now in use. These will be accepted by coach conductors and coach tickets issued in exchange.
New type coach return tickets will be issued and these are to be cancelled in accordance with the following instructions:
ON FORWARD JOURNEY:
(a) Clip (with clippers) in the stage boarded and (b) Bell Punch in the month of issue and again in the day of issue. Tickets issued on journeys to Whipsnade are also to have the Underground Railways section at the top of the ticket cancelled with the special arrow-head clippers.
ON RETURN JOURNEY:
(c) Agree validity of the ticket (availability is for one month – i.e. from the 10th of one month to the 9th of the next month, inclusive).
NOTE: (In the opinion of the writer, availability of tickets on the Whipsnade route for one month was unnecessary, as the tickets were not available for the return journey on other coach routes, and the passenger would only be visiting Whipsnade for one day).
(d) Clip out all the figures in one line in the cancellation section, to leave the square indicating the date of return.
(e) Clip the section corresponding with the hour of return, and return the whole ticket to the passenger.
Coach tickets presented for return travel on bus route 368, must be cancelled by clipping the hour section only, and the ticket returned to the passenger for presentation to the booking clerk at St. Albans Station for exchange for a railway ticket to London.
RAIL CARD TICKETS:
Rail Card Tickets, which will be issued outwards to passengers travelling by railway to St. Albans and bus 368 to Whipsnade, are to be cancelled as follows:
On bus journeys to Whipsnade – clip in the wording L.P.T.B.
On bus journeys from Whipsnade – clip in the hour of travel.
On coach journeys to London – clip in the hour of travel.

From the use of these instructions, and looking at Example No. 36 in the photographs, we find that the passenger travelled by coach direct from Marylebone, as the top Underground portion has been cancelled by the coach conductor. He travelled on 20 May (the date 20 is on the reverse side of the ticket), and travelled back at 7 pm on the same day, using the coach as far as Golders Green, where he transferred to the Underground. This is indicated by the fact that the Underground section for the return journey at the bottom of the ticket has been torn off by the railway Ticket Collector.

All these styles of ticket remained in issue from 1937 until an increase of fares was introduced on 27 August 1939, when a similar type of ticket was produced which showed the Board's title as 'LONDON TRANSPORT

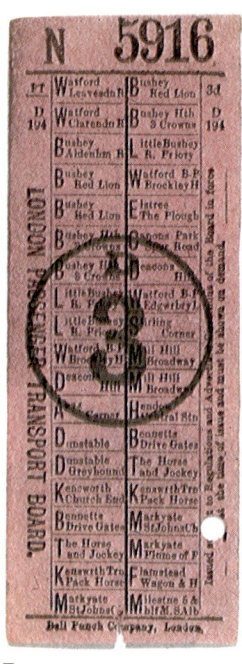

27

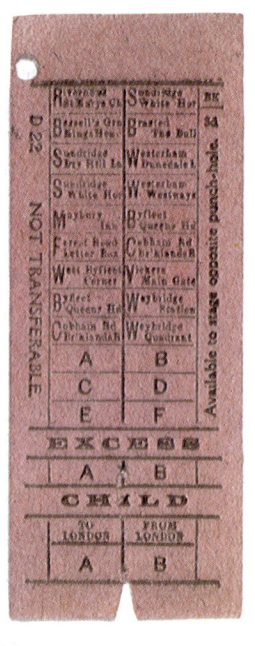

28

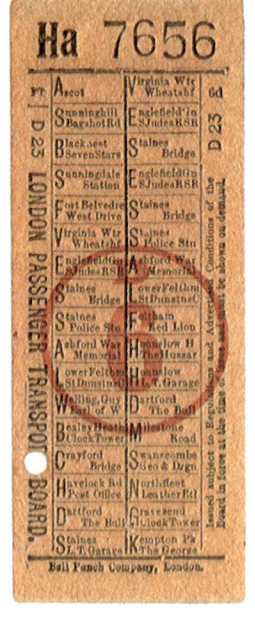

29

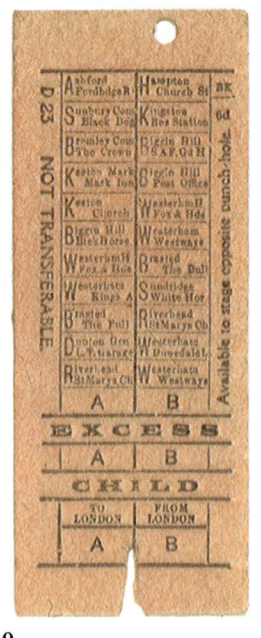

30

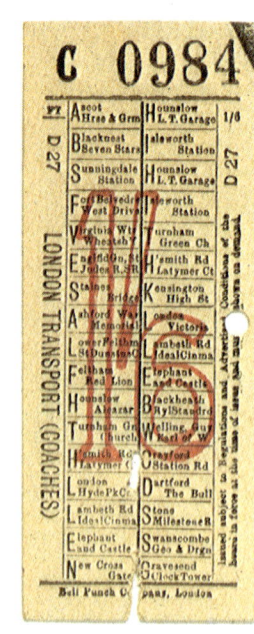

31

32

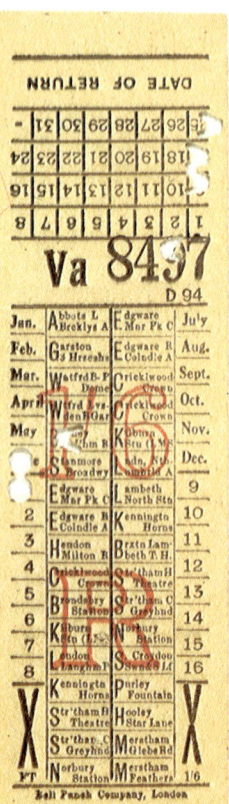

33

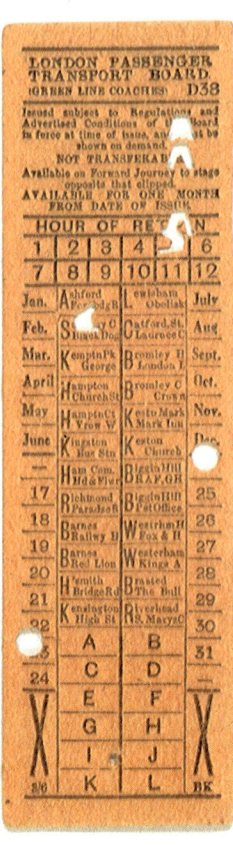

34

35

36

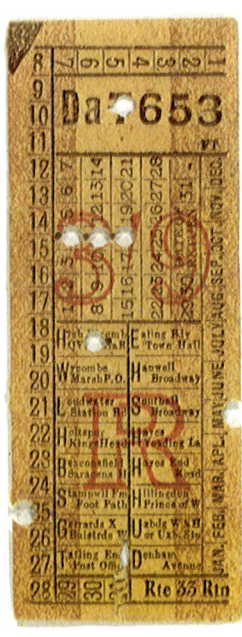

37

38

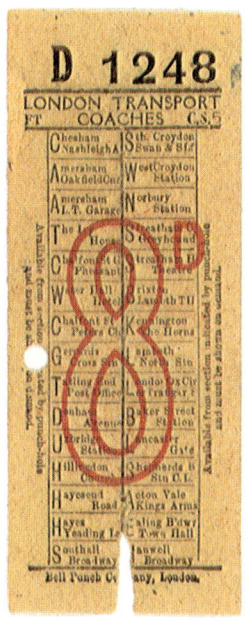
39

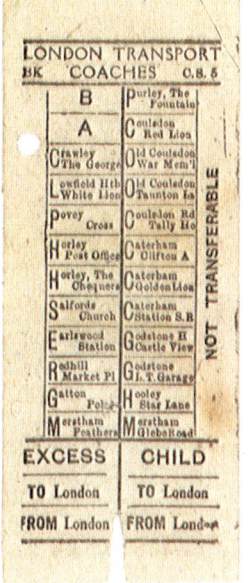
40

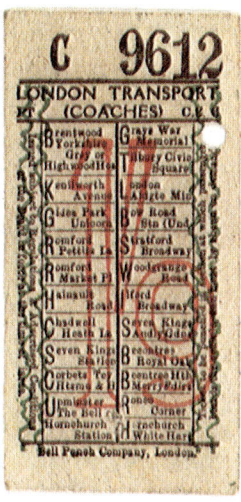
41

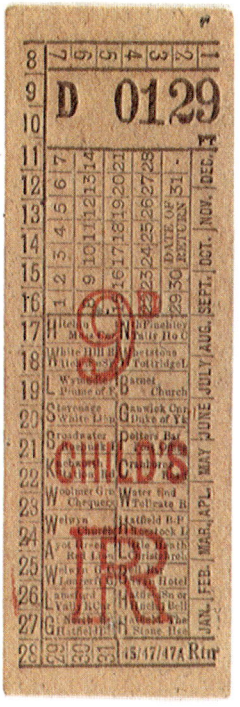
42

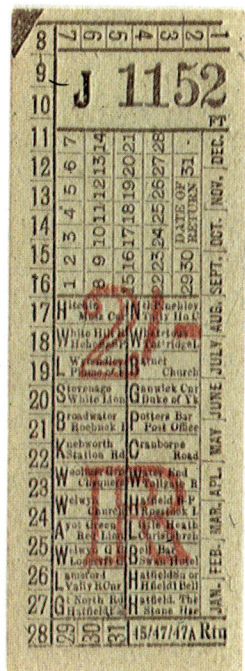
43

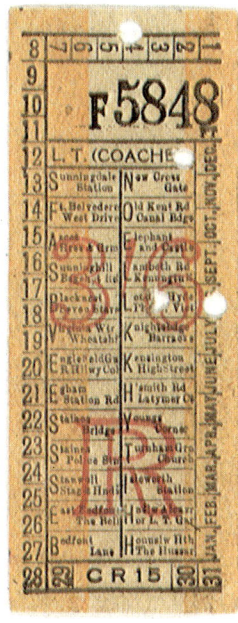
44

45

46

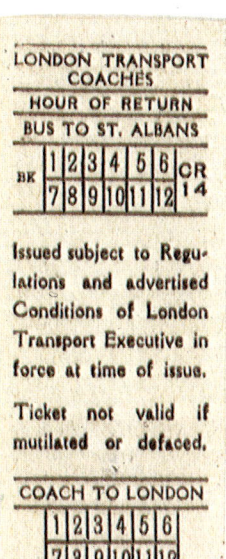
47

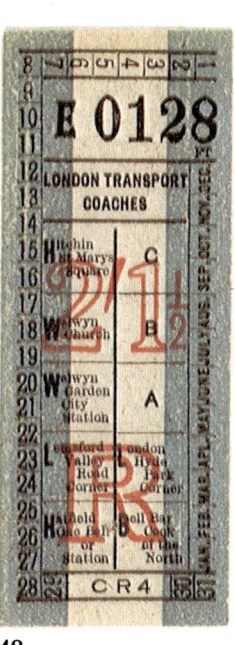
48

49

50

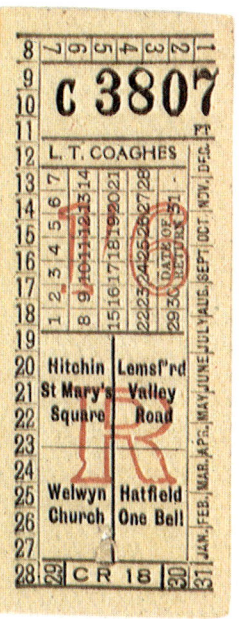
51

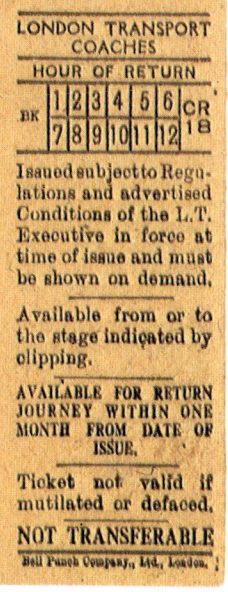
52

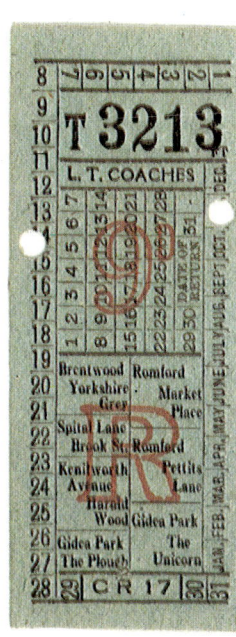
52A

(COACHES)' instead of 'LONDON PASSENGER TRANSPORT BOARD' (see Examples 31 and 35 in the photographs). On the new return tickets, the day and month sections were only printed on the front side of the ticket, and not on both sides as had been the practice previously. These tickets had only been in issue for a few days when war was declared on Germany, and the coach services were withdrawn.

Services were gradually replaced on some routes in November 1939, and also in the early part of 1940, and as the August 1939 faretables still applied, these tickets were used on those routes.

A further increase in coach fares was introduced on 3 July 1940, but the Board did not immediately supply new tickets to cover these increased fares, preferring to use up the old tickets, and the following instructions were issued to coach conductors:

SINGLE TICKETS: *Excess single tickets to cover the appropriate increase punched in the serial number will be issued, and the normal coach ticket at the old fare will be punched at the stage of boarding as per the normal procedure.*

RETURN TICKETS: *Excess single tickets to cover the appropriate increase punched in the serial number will be issued on the forward journey. The return ticket will be punched and clipped in accordance with the existing procedure thus:*

A passenger travelling a journey for which the return fare has been increased from 1/6 to 1/9 will be issued with a 1/6 return ticket punched and clipped as at present and a 3d excess single ticket punched in the serial number. On the return journey, the 1/6 return ticket should be honoured in accordance with the punching and clipping, the tickets being clipped in the hour and date in accordance with the standard procedure.

Soon after this, the blitz on London started, and Routes A1/A2, C and H, all of which had resumed their cross-London runn ng, were curtailed at Victoria from 23 October 1940. The traffic office realised that through return tickets issued up to 22 October would be available for one month from the date of issue, and issued an instruction to coach conductors, that, if they were presented with through return tickets dated prior to 23 October, they were to be cancelled in the usual way and entered on an auxiliary waybill, which was to be handed to the Inspector on duty at Victoria, and who would transfer the passengers to another coach.

As the main-line railways had suffered much disruption through the bombing, the Government decided upon a more or less complete resumption of Green Line services, with the exception that all the routes would terminate in London, and resumption was made during December, and, at the same time, a further increase in fares was applied. Once again, the procedure which applied to the increase in July, and dealt with in a previous paragraph was applied, in which the August 1939 standard coach tickets were still used, plus excess tickets to cover the increase.

Evidently, the 1939 series of tickets became exhausted in the early part of 1941, as the Traffic Notice to staff dated 4 April 1941 had an item concerning the new type of Green Line Coach Tickets. These instructions are quoted herewith:

'*All existing coach tickets are being withdrawn and new tickets, in accordance with revised fares which came into operation on 3 July 1940 and 1 December 1940, will be issued to conductor's ticket boxes for use on and from Monday, 7 April 1941.*

SINGLE TICKETS:
Standard type bus tickets will be issued for all single fares. Farestages will be numbered on the faretables, and single tickets will be punched on issue in the point number corresponding with the stage at which the passenger boards. The following denominations will be supplied to boxes as necessary in accordance with the fares of the routes operated: 1d. to 1/- inclusive, 1½d and 2/-. For fares in excess of 1/- or 2/-, a 1/- or a 2/- ticket will be issued, together with a "balance" ticket to make up the full fare. Both tickets, which will be issued at the time of boarding, will be punched in the stage boarded and clipped in the stage to which passenger is entitled to travel.

RETURN TICKETS:
A new type of return ticket having an overprinted price, will be issued to boxes in denominations to correspond with all return tickets applicable to the routes operated.

These tickets are printed with all the stage names of the route/s which are operated from the garage. On the forward journey, conductors will (a) clip the stage boarded, and (b) punch in the month of issue and again in the date of issue. Tickets will be valid for one month from the date of issue (e.g. a ticket issued on 15 February 1941 will be valid up to and including 14 March 1941), and available to the point corresponding with that shown on the fare-table in accordance with the point boarded and the fare paid.

On the return journey, the conductors will (a) clip out all the figures in one line, in the cancellation section, to leave the square indicating the date of return, and (b) clip the section corresponding with the hour of return. The ticket will then be handed back to the passenger.

CHILDREN'S FARES:
Children's tickets will only be printed and supplied where adult tickets of the appropriate value are not issued. In all other cases, adult tickets (single and return) will be issued in accordance with the charges for children as stated on the faretable.

EXCESS FARES:
Single tickets of the appropriate fare value will be issued by conductors for excess fares and will be punched in the serial number. Instructions upon the charging of excess fares are repeated:

Description of Ticket held:	Passenger to be charged:
Single	Difference between the two single fares.
Return	Either direction 'one half of the difference between the two return fares subject to a minimum charge equivalent to the difference between the two single fares'.
Seasons and Workmen's Weekly Tickets (Routes 59 and 59A)	Either direction 'one half of the difference between the return fare for the journey for which the season ticket or weekly workman ticket is available and the return fare for the journey to be made. If there should be no difference between the return fares, an excess charge of 3d is to be made.'

NOTE: Fractions of a penny are to be charged as one penny. Excess fares are not applicable where the passenger has journeyed less than 3 miles within the availability of the season ticket held'.

A further instruction to coach conductors concerning the cancellation of the 'hour of return' on return tickets was issued in June 1941 as follows:

'*To define the hour of return, tickets must be cancelled in the hour section as follows:*
A.M. Clipped with the arrow head pointing to the left.
P.M. Clipped with the arrow head pointing to the right.
In addition, the following rule must be observed: The hour between 12 noon and 1 pm must be considered as pm, and the hour between 12 midnight and 1 am as am.'

The return tickets mentioned in the past few paragraphs were of the type depicted in Examples 37 and 38 in the photographs, and by following the instructions quoted, the reader will be able to decide for himself how and when the passengers to which they were issued had travelled. Examples of the bus single tickets have not been included, as they only displayed farestages numbers and not names, and do not provide any guide to the journey travelled without an accompanying fares table which was unobtainable at the time this book was written.

The method of issuing excess fare tickets on the coaches was revised from 17 October 1941, and henceforth tickets were to be punched on issue in the farestage number corresponding to the point of availability, instead of in the serial number. Any pre-excess tickets which required to be issued were to be punched in the stage number corresponding to the point boarded by the passenger, while excess tickets issued to holders of season and monthly return tickets were to be punched in the stage number corresponding with the expiration point of the season or return ticket.

On 16 February 1942, all return fares on Routes 26 and 26A (London – Windsor/Farnham Common) were increased in price. Fresh return tickets at the new prices were not provided immediately, and the procedure for excessing existing return tickets up to the value of the new fare, as practised in 1939 and 1940 was re-introduced on these two routes.

Apart from these two items, there was no change to tickets or ticket procedure for the remainder of the time that Green Line was in operation during the war period, although, as stated elsewhere, they were finally withdrawn for the second time in September 1942.

When they returned to the scene in 1946, except for two isolated cases, at first Single fares only were charged, and tickets of the style depicted in Examples 39–41 were used, and this style remained in use up to the fare increase introduced in March 1952. Although at first glance these tickets look somewhat similar to those issued pre-war, there is in fact, a great deal of difference. The farestages are set out on the ticket in geographical order, starting from the left-hand side, then working round to the top of the right-hand side, and upon turning over to the reverse side of the ticket, then starting at the top of the right-hand side and working round to the left-hand side. Examples 39 and 40 are front and reverse sides of the same ticket, and were used by conductors working Routes 709 and 710 from Crawley and Godstone Garages. It will be seen that provision was made on the reverse side of the ticket (Example No. 40) for its use as an excess or child ticket, thus rendering special issues for those fares unnecessary. The instructions to conductors on the issue of these new style tickets were as follows:

Single tickets only will be provided, and on issue, the ticket will be punched in the stage boarded by the passenger. When two tickets are issued in combination to make up a fare for which no ticket has been supplied, both tickets will be punched in the section at which the passenger boards the vehicle.

CHILD'S FARES:
Tickets to cover children's fares will be issued, based on half the adult single fare, fractions of 3d being charged as 3d, except in the case of single fares of 2/6 and under, where fractions of 1d, will be charged as one penny. On issue, tickets will be punched in the special child's section, corresponding with the direction of travel. When children's fares are not covered by existing ticket denominations, two tickets are to be issued in combination, both of which will be punched in the "Child" section corresponding with the direction of travel.

EXCESS FARES:
Passengers will be charged the difference between the two single fares when travelling to points beyond which their tickets are available as follows:
(a) ADULT: Tickets will be punched on issue in the "Excess" section corresponding with the direction of travel. When excess fares are not covered by ticket denominations, two tickets in combination are to be issued, both punched in the "Excess" section corresponding to the direction of travel.
(b) CHILD: The same procedure as that for an Adult will be carried out in the case of a child travelling beyond the point to which the ticket held by the child is available.'

The two isolated cases which had return fares in the farescale were Routes 716 and 721. This was due to the fact that another operator shared parts of their route, and still issued return tickets. In the case of Route 716, the route was shared between Potters Bar and Hitchin with Messrs. Birch Brothers Limited London – Rushden route, while 721 ran between Romford and Brentwood over the same roads as the City Coach Company London – Southend route, which also operated a local return fare between Romford and Brentwood. To cover these return fares, stocks of Return Tickets formerly used on wartime services 45/47/A were used on 716 (Examples 42 and 43), and those used on Routes 54/55/58 were used on 721. As the 54/55/58 tickets were similar in design to those used on 45/47/A, a copy has not been included. These were available for one month, and were punched, clipped and cancelled in the same way as when they were issued during the war. Route 721 had only one fare (9d return from Romford Market Place to Brentwood (Yorkshire Grey)), while 716 issued three adult returns between Hitchin and Welwyn Church (1/6), Lemsford (Valley Road) (2/-) and Hatfield (2/3), although there were Child's fares at 9d, 1/- and 1/3. In the case of the 9d and 1/- fares, the old Child's Return tickets were issued, but for the 1/3 fare, the former 1/3 adult ticket was issued. The procedure for issuing these tickets was that issued to the staff in 1941 when these tickets came into use on the wartime services. When supplies of the war-time tickets were exhausted on both routes, they were replaced by Examples 50 and 51 in the Photographs. Example 52 shows the reverse side of a ticket from Route 716, and the same principle was applied on the reverse side of the 721 ticket (Example 50). The fare on 721 was increased from 9d to 10d from 25 February 1951, but, apart from a change in colour from buff to grass green, and, of course, the value overprint altering from 9d to 10d, the layout was exactly as in Example No. 50.

Cheap Day Return Tickets on a limited scale were introduced from 1 October 1946. They were issued on Tuesdays, Wednesdays and Thursdays only, and Return tickets to London were only available on the forward journey on coaches scheduled to arrive in Central London after 10.30 am. They were available for return on the day of issue only, and on coaches scheduled to leave London before 4.30 pm and after 6.30 pm. Tickets from London were available on the forward journey on coaches scheduled to leave London before 4.30 pm and after 6.30 pm, and were available for the return journey by any coach on the day of issue only. These Cheap Day Returns are depicted in Examples 44 (front of ticket) and (45 (reverse side of ticket) in the photographs. For issue to an adult, they were clipped in the stage of boarding, and punched in the Bell Punch twice, once to indicate the month and again to indicate the day of the month. Upon the return journey, they were simply cancelled by the conductor in the hour of return. No special child tickets were issued, an adult ticket being used, which was Bell Punched in the day and month, and clipped in Section 'A' on journeys to London, and in Section 'B' on

168

53 54 55
56 57 58
59 60 61

62

63

64

65

169

journeys from London. These tickets remained in issue until the fare increase introduced on 1 October 1950, when they were all withdrawn, except on Routes 716 and 717 between London and Hitchin, and the 2/9 Cheap Day Return fare from Aldgate to Brentwood on Route 721.

The punching of single tickets issued in combination was altered in March 1948 as follows:
'The highest and lowest denominations of ticket must be selected to make up the fare required. Both tickets must be punched in the section at which the passenger boards the vehicle, and clipped in the section to which the passenger is entitled to travel.'

The issue of cheap day return tickets was extended from Tuesday 1 June 1948, and they could now be issued from Mondays to Fridays, but the restrictions on times of issue and return were not altered at this time, and lasted until a further alteration was made to the issue of this type of ticket, which took place about a year later.

From Saturday, 11 June 1949, the availability of Cheap Day Return Tickets was extended to Saturdays, Sundays and Bank Holidays, and the restriction upon travel out of London between 4.30 and 6.30 pm was withdrawn at the same time. The restriction on travel to London on coaches scheduled to arrive in London up to 10.30 was still retained on Mondays to Fridays, but no such restriction applied on weekends or Bank Holidays. In addition, on Saturdays, Sundays and Bank Holidays, passengers holding Green Line Return tickets issued from London could return by rail after 4 pm if there was a railway route covering the points between which their ticket was available. The ticket had to be taken to the Railway booking office, where it was changed for a special third-class ticket for the rail journey.

When Route 726 (London – Whipsnade) returned for the summer season of 1951, a new faretable was introduced, in which the only cheap day return fare remained in issue. This was from London to Whipsnade Zoo at a fare of 7/- Adult and 3/6 Child. On the return from Whipsnade, three alternative methods of travel were open to holders of these return tickets, as follows:
1. *Direct return to London by Green Line coach route 726.*
2. *By Bus Route 368 from Whipsnade to St. Albans, thence by Coach Routes 712, 713 and 727.*
3. *After 4 pm only. By rail from Luton (L.M.R.) Station to London (St. Pancras).*

The coach tickets used for this purpose were Examples 46 (front of ticket) and 47 (reverse side) in the photographs. The method of cancellation on the return journey was as follows:
1. Direct return to London by Route 726: *The coach conductor will cancel the ticket in the hour of return in the section headed 'COACH TO LONDON'.*
2. Return by bus 368 and Green Line 712/3 or 727: *The bus conductor will clip out the hour of return in the section headed 'BUS TO ST. ALBANS'. On boarding the coach, the conductor will clip out the hour of return from St. Albans in the section headed 'COACH TO LONDON'. This entitled the passenger to travel to Baker Street Station on Routes 712 and 713 or to Kings Cross on Route 727.*
3. By Rail from Luton: *Passengers had to be informed that, if they proposed to use this route to return to London, they would have to travel to Luton by local bus (not operated by London Transport) at their own expense. Upon arrival at Luton Station, the Green Line ticket was handed to the Booking Clerk, who issued free of charge a Third Class Ticket to London (St. Pancras).*

The above return fare was increased from 7/- to 8/4 (4/2 Child) in 1952, and to 8/6 (4/3 Child) in 1953, but the method of return as described in the last paragraph was retained, the only alteration being that bus 368 had been superseded by bus 313, and coach route 727 was extended to Dorking with the number 714, and tickets on this route could now be used to Baker Street also. These return tickets and the alternatives for the return journey remained in issue until the end of the summer season for 1953.

Messrs. Birch Brothers Limited were granted a fare increase to come into operation on 11 May 1952, and accordingly, London Transport also increased fares on the London – Hitchin/Welwyn Garden City section of Routes 716 and 717. The monthly returns between Hitchin and Hatfield (Example 51) were now withdrawn, and the Cheap Day Return tickets were revised, with the child fares being exactly half of the Adult Fares, which resulted in tickets being printed with odd halfpenny values (Example No. 48; 2/1½ Child Return).

The Eastern National Omnibus Company, Limited, which by this time had acquired the services formerly operated by the City Coach Company, had received permission from the Traffic Commissioners to increase their fares from 31 August 1952, and this affected Route 721 which followed the same route between Romford and Brentwood. The 10d return fare from Romford to Brentwood was increased to 1/-, and some intermediate 9d return fares were introduced, thus leading to a new type of return ticket (Example No. 52A). The same printing block was used for both 9d and 1/- ticket, and the method of issue was the same as had always been used for the issue of returns with an availability of one month.

We now come to Examples 53 to 58. When the fare increase of March 1952 was introduced, named stage (6-return journey) weekly tickets, of which we shall hear more later, were altered in style. Hitherto, they had been printed with the farestage mentioned by name, but this had resulted in a large variety of tickets to be carried in stock, and also to be reprinted whenever fares were increased, and these increases now seemed to appear annually, so it was decided to print one series of all values, with numbers to represent the fare stages. A common number was used for all the central points in London, this being No. 35, which represented all the points, such as Aldgate, Oxford Circus, Trafalgar Square, Victoria, Hyde Park Corner or Marble Arch. The new weekly tickets carried stage numbers from 7 to 64, which adequately covered the longest route. In order to assist the conductors to become acquainted with the fare stage numbers on their routes, the new single tickets carried both the number and name of the point, both the new single and weekly tickets coming into operation with the March 1952 fare increase. It will be observed that the special section for punching the ticket when issued to a child has disappeared, child tickets now being punched at the stage of boarding the the same way as for an adult.

These tickets lasted for about one year, as a Staff Traffic Notice dated 6 March 1953 carries a paragraph which states that revised single tickets bearing farestage numbers only would be issued on all Green Line coach routes as and when stocks of the existing type of tickets became exhausted, and when these appeared they were of the type depicted in Examples 59–61. In addition to saving printing costs, these tickets also helped to get the conductors used to the use of numbers to represent the farestages, in readiness for the introduction of ticket machines.

These, in the form of the Setright Speed model, began to appear on the coaches in the latter half of 1954, and by the end of 1955, Bell Punch tickets had disappeared altogether from Green Line Coaches, much to the annoyance of small boys and many transport enthusiasts, who collected them in pursuance of their hobby.

Whilst we are on the subject of ticket machines, it will be remembered that, in the earlier part of this chapter, I mentioned that Premier Line and Hillman's Saloon Coaches had used the Setright insert ticket machine during the latter part of their existence. When these companies were acquired by the Board, that organisation inherited these ticket machines, and decided to concentrate them in one area. As the Brentwood, Upminster and Grays routes were then the busiest on the Green Line network, with at that time, a large proportion of low-value fares, this was the area chosen, and they used these machines up to the time that the coaches were withdrawn just before the commencement of hostilities in 1939.

We now come to the subject of season tickets. It is obvious that once a coach service is established to a regular timetable, it is necessary to attract commuter traffic. This is done by the issue of season tickets for weekly, monthly or quarterly periods. The longer the period for which the ticket is issued, usually shows a greater discount to the passenger over the purchase of daily return tickets, but, at the same time, ensures a regular source of income to the operator.

The London General Omnibus Company was well aware of this fact, as for many years it had regularly issued joint bus and Underground season tickets on certain routes. It is not surprising therefore that, five months after commencing its first two express coach services from Watford, some form of ticket was introduced to attract regular commuter traffic. In April 1930, booklets containing six return tickets from Watford to London at 10/- and from Bushey at 8/6 on either route were sold by coach conductors on Monday mornings.

These tickets, which were printed in black on primrose paper, were of the same style as the standard coach return (see Example No. 1), but instead of the fare being printed thereon, the day of the week on which it was to be used was shown. The ticket to London issued on the Golders Green route was a better proposition to the commuter than that on the direct Charing Cross route, as they were available on the Underground to any of the stations in an area which stretched from Marble Arch, Paddington and Hyde Park Corner in the west to Aldwych, Bank and Mansion House in the east, giving the commuter the choice of travelling to his nearest station to his place of employment.

The issue of these packets of tickets was so successful that the Company decided to try the issue of quarterly season tickets from July 1930. These were issued from Watford or Bushey to Charing Cross on the direct route, but from Bushey to Golders Green only on the coach-rail service, the tickets being of the peculiar oval type represented in Example 62.

Premier Line, who started its Windsor – Aldwych route on a forty-minute frequency on 27 January 1930, began issuing weekly, monthly and quarterly seasons from 6 February, the date on which it stepped up its service to every half-hour, but the L.G.O.C. did not follow suit when it started its Windsor – Charing Cross service over the same route in April.

Seasons were first issued by them from 1 July when the service was stepped up to a ten-minute frequency, and then on a limited scale only. Tickets for the same periods as those of Premier Line were issued from Windsor or Slough to Hammersmith or Charing Cross, and also from Colnbrook to Charing Cross. Unlike the ordinary return tickets, the holders of which could transfer to the Underground at Hammersmith to complete their journey into London, season ticket holders had to carry on into London by coach. Weekly tickets were sold on the coach by Conductors, and unlike those on the Watford routes, could be used for unlimited journeys during the period of availability, and could also be used on Sundays. The monthly tickets, although conductors would supply an application form, had to be obtained either from the local garage at Slough or from the Express Coach Office at 55 Broadway, S.W.1.

When the Company commenced its Windsor – London via Staines route in July 1930, weekly tickets and seasons from Windsor only were issued, at the same fares as those on the route via Slough, but passengers were required, when applying for seasons to and from Windsor, to state which route they proposed to use, as the tickets were not interavailable.

Once again, these tickets were produced in the oval style used on the Watford routes, and which was also to be used for the season tickets issued on the first two routes introduced by Green Line Coaches Limited.

Evidently there were fairly good sales of the weekly and monthly tickets on the Windsor and Watford routes, but the quarterly tickets were slow movers, as when Green Line introduced the Brentwood and Guildford routes, only weekly and monthly tickets were issued. On the Brentwood service they were issued from Brentwood or Romford (Market Place) to Stratford Broadway, Aldgate East Station or Charing Cross, and on the Guildford service from Guildford, Ripley and Esher to Charing Cross only. For some reason or another, the Esher ticket sales were very low, and the issue of seasons from this point was discontinued after 17 October 1930.

The oval style of season ticket was apparently not very popular with passengers, as no suitable type of holder could be purchased to carry them in, and the conductors also were not too happy with them, as they were awkward to carry in their hands when issuing the weekly type on Monday mornings. In consequence of this, the style of ticket depicted in Example No. 63 appeared in issue during 1931.

No weekly or other type of season ticket was issued on the other Green Line routes as they entered service, but when Skylark Coaches; Bucks Express and Associated Coaches (Ongar) were acquired, the various weekly, monthly and quarterly tickets issued by those organisations continued in operation by Green Line.

There were additions to this list in 1933, when Premier Line, Price's Super Coaches and Batten's were acquired by London Transport, and again in the early part of 1934 when Hillman's Super Coaches, Upminster Services, Sunset Coaches and Fleet Coaches were acquired. Strawhatter Coaches, who were acquired in February 1934, had two 6-day return tickets in operation to Kings Cross, one from Luton at 10/-, the other from London Colney at 8/-, and London Transport continued the issue of these, and an example of the ticket (No. 63) is shown in the photographs. This ticket was issued on the coaches on Monday mornings, and the respective journeys were clipped out every day in the squares on the top and bottom of the ticket.

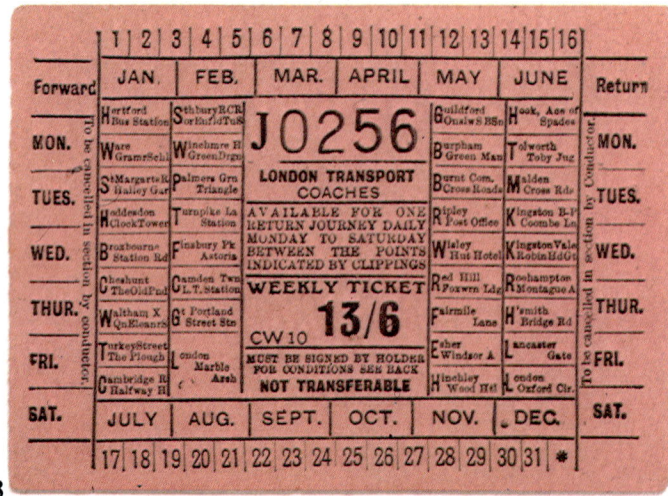

70

71

72

When Batten's Coaches were acquired in December 1933, that company was issuing daily workmen's return tickets, and London Transport extended this facility by the issue of weekly workmen's tickets from Monday, 27 August 1934. They were issued on Monday mornings on all coaches operating journeys before 8 am, and were available for six return journeys on Mondays to Saturdays. The forward journey had to be made before 8 am each day, but the return journey could be made at any time on that day. Like the Strawhatter 6-journey tickets, each respective journey was clipped out by the conductor with special clippers. Unfortunately, it has not been possible to obtain a copy of the ticket, so it does not appear in the photographs.

Since the diversion of a large number of its routes to operate via Eccleston Bridge (Victoria) in October 1933, Green Line had been experiencing a fall in passenger traffic, and in an endeavour to stimulate an increase in the figures, the Traffic Department decided to scrap the present somewhat haphazard idea where some routes issued season and weekly tickets and other routes did not, and to introduce a new season ticket system on all routes with the exception of Route T (Watford – Golders Green) and BH (Luton – Kings Cross). On Route T, the weekly (6-day) tickets from Watford only to Underground Stations were to remain in issue, and were to be the only period tickets on that route. On Route BH, the two weekly tickets mentioned in an earlier paragraph were to be retained in issue, but there would be no tickets for longer periods on this service. The weekly workman tickets were to remain in issue on Route Z, but the season ticket system would be altered to the new one to be introduced. Certain quarterly and special period tickets from the old issues were to continue and be issued as renewals to existing holders only. These tickets would be issued from the Commercial Manager's Department at 55 Broadway.

The new scheme of things was introduced from Sunday, 18 November 1934 and under the new arrangements only two classes of ticket were to be issued as follows:
(a) *Weekly Tickets – Expiring with the last journey on Saturday night.*
(b) *4-weekly Tickets – Expiring with the last journey on the fourth Saturday night.*

Now to describe the tickets. The weekly issues: A new type of weekly ticket was issued which was designed to carry all the necessary farestages of availability on all the routes operating from one garage. On issue on Mondays to passengers, Conductors had to indicate on the ticket, by clipping with special clippers, and not the Bell Punch, the following particulars:
(a) *The two stages between which the ticket was available.*
(b) *The date of expiry.*
(c) *The issue to a female passenger by one clipping in the small square at the top of the ticket. This square to be left blank when issued to a male passenger.*

Passengers were requested, in their own interests, to sign their names and addressses on the back of the ticket.

Conductors were informed that the tickets would be serially numbered and supplied to them together with the special weekly ticket waybill. This had to be completed daily from Saturday–Monday (the period during which the tickets were placed in the Conductor's ticket boxes). Waybills were to be withdrawn every Monday upon completion of duty, and new waybills placed in the ticket box ready for the next Saturday. In cases where Conductors worked on another route than that stated at the head of the waybill (Epping Garage was a case in point), they had to record on the back of the waybill particulars of tickets sold on the other service. The dates on each ticket covered 13 Saturdays, and at the expiry of the period for which the tickets had been printed, fresh tickets were placed in the boxes.

The new weekly tickets could be issued on Saturdays (renewals only) after twelve noon and all day on Sundays and Mondays, and for every fresh ticket issued on Saturdays, Conductors were required to hand in a ticket which had expired. The tickets were available for an unlimited number of journeys during the week for which they had been issued. Once again, it has not been possible to obtain a copy of the ticket for reproduction.

We come now to the four-weekly tickets. Fortunately, an unused specimen has survived and is reproduced in the photographs as Example 65. These tickets were issued on demand after 12 noon on Saturdays (renewals only) and all day on Sundays and Mondays at the coach garages, the enquiry offices at Hertford and Watford, and, in London, The District Messengers Company office at 279 Regent Street (near Oxford Circus). This office could issue 4-weekly seasons for all Green Line routes.

Passengers requiring 4-weekly tickets had to fill in an application form, which could be supplied by conductors or at garages.

On issue, the following particulars were indicated on the ticket by the issuing clerk:
(a) *The two stages between which the ticket was available.*
(b) *The Route letter (in ink).*
(c) *An overstamped 'W' when the ticket is issued to a female passenger.*
(d) *The stamped date of expiry.*
(e) *Name of the person to whom ticket is issued.*

As with weekly tickets, the passengers were requested in their own interests, to sign their names and addresses on the back of the ticket.

On 2 May 1937, revised fares were introduced on all coach routes with the exception of Routes T, U, X, Y1/2 and Z1/2, and new styles of single and return tickets were introduced. The 4-weekly tickets were not altered in style, but a change was made to the weekly tickets. These now showed the Saturday dates of expiry for the whole twelve months, and these were set around the sides of the ticket, the date of the year (1937) also being included on the two side edges. The small square to be clipped out on issue to a female passenger had now been re-sited to the base of the ticket. Issuing procedures remained unchanged. Once again, it has not been possible to obtain a specimen of this ticket for reproduction.

The weekly workmen's tickets issued on Routes Z1/2 were also altered to this style of ticket when the new issue for 1939 was printed.

Wartime rationing of paper and card led to the issue of a new style of Weekly and Workmen's Weekly Tickets, the issue of which commenced with the week which started on Sunday, 29 December 1940. Fortunately, specimens of each type have survived the years, and are reproduced as Examples 66 and 67. 66 is an example of the Weekly Workman's ticket used on Route 59 and 59A from Grays. The ordinary weekly tickets used at both Romford and Grays Garages were to the same design, but printed on pink card. As there were heavy sales of this type of ticket at both garages, the ordinary weekly tickets used by them still carried printed fare stage names, and the only difference to the issuing procedure, was that when the ticket was issued to a female passenger, the star next to the date '31' was clipped out.

On all other Green Line routes, Example 67 was used, and conductors were instructed to enter the farestages between which the ticket was available in indelible pencil (ball-point pens had not then been invented). The date to which the ticket was available was shown by clipping out the month and date of the Saturday of expiry, and again, the star was clipped out if the ticket was issued to a female. This style of ticket remained in issue until the coaches were withdrawn for the second time in September 1942.

When the coaches resumed operation in 1946, no form of season or weekly ticket was introduced until Monday, 30 September in that year, and then they were different to the weekly tickets issued before the war, and the unlimited journey principle which had applied before the war, was not re-introduced, and perhaps it is better to quote the instructions issued to conductors on this occasion:

'Weekly (six return journey) tickets (coloured yellow) will be sold to the public by conductors on Saturdays and Sundays (renewals only), and on Mondays and Tuesdays and will be available from Monday to Saturday for one return journey daily between the points indicated by clippings. These tickets are NOT available for travel on Sundays. Owing to the number of stages on some routes, conductors on these routes will be issued with two tickets of the same price with differing stage points. The colour of both tickets will be yellow and conductors must, therefore, exercise particular care to issue the correct ticket.

Conductors will clip out the month of issue, the date of the Saturday up to which the ticket is available, the stages between which the ticket is available and also the section corresponding with the forward journey on day of issue.

On subsequent journeys, conductors will clip out the section corresponding with the direction and day of travel.

Children's fares: Reduced rates for children do not apply in the case of weekly tickets.'

The tickets were printed in the same style as Example 68. This ticket was introduced with the fare increase in October 1947, when the colour of the tickets was altered from yellow to pink.

The sales of weekly tickets on Routes 721 and 722 at Romford Garage were extremely heavy compared to those from other garages, and the Union complained to the authorities that it was very time consuming to keep locating the position of the various farestages on the old type of ticket, so tickets on the style of Example No. 69 were introduced at Romford, which eliminated the necessity for clipping out fare stages. These tickets were introduced from 12 June 1948.

Tickets of the type depicted in Example 70 were introduced on 1 October 1950, and perhaps it would be better to quote the instructions issued to conductors on this occasion:

'As a result of difficulties with regard to the printing of Coach (6 return journey) tickets, it has been necessary, temporarily, to resort to an emergency type of weekly ticket, as from 1 October 1950, on all routes, excepting 721, 722, where the type of ticket with printed stages will continue to be used. In place of the normal stage points printed on the tickets, there will appear numbers from 1–48, each number representing a fare stage point.

As fare stages are not numbered on coach fare tables, it has been necessary to arrange as a temporary measure for conductors to be supplied with a schedule showing the numbers allocated to the fare stages on the route being operated. In cases where fare stages are common on two or more routes, the stage numbers applicable to each route will be shown on the schedule.'

The procedure for issuing these tickets was the same as before, except that numbers had to be clipped out instead of names, but there was a further instruction to conductors, as follows:

'In the event of a ticket being presented which is clipped in numbers which do not represent the appropriate fare stages covering the section of route on which the ticket is being used, the passenger must be allowed to travel providing the fare denomination of the weekly ticket presented is not less than the weekly ticket rate for the journey the passenger intends to make.'

With the fare increase introduced on Sunday, 2 March 1952, passengers holding weekly tickets issued from one of the Central London Zone points were allowed to return to London on any other route from a point where the weekly ticket rate was the same or less. With the introduction of this concession, farestage numbers appeared on the faretables, and the Central London points at Aldgate (Minories Layby), Victoria (Eccleston Bridge), Hyde Park Corner, Marble Arch, Oxford Circus and Trafalgar Square were given the farestage number 35 in order that the above concession could be implemented. Once again, excepting Routes 721 and 722, tickets in the same style as depicted in Example 71 were used, the procedure for the issue of these tickets remaining unchanged. Incidentally, the rate charged for 6-day weekly return tickets was 9 times the single fare.

After 30 October 1965, the service on Route 722 was reduced to a Monday–Friday peak hour operation, and 6-day (12 journey) tickets were no longer issued. Instead, a new 5-day (10 journey) ticket was introduced at a rate of 7½ times the single fare rounded up to the nearest 3d above. These tickets were printed in the same style as the 6-day tickets and the procedure for their issue was the same, except that the date of the finishing Friday was clipped out instead of the Saturday. They were printed on yellow card to distinguish them from the 6-day ticket, and the type and colour is depicted in Example 72. It is a mystery to the writer as to why they were not adopted on all routes at this time, as the almost universal practice of working a 5-day week had come into use by this time, and the sale of 6-day tickets had dropped considerably. They were also introduced on Route 709 from 31 December 1966 when the operation of that route was confined to Monday-Friday peak hours, plus a couple of Sunday hospital journeys. They were however, confined for issue to and from fare stages 48 (Old Coulsdon, Tudor Rose) to 52 (Caterham, Golden Lion), 6-day tickets being issued where there was an alternative facility on Saturdays, these sections being:

Routes 706/707. South Croydon (Swan and Sugar Loaf) and Brixton.

Route 708 (later 719). Between Godstone L.T. Garage and Caterham Station and also Purley Fountain and Brixton.

Route 710. Coulsdon (Red Lion) and Oxford Circus.

When Route 710 was withdrawn between Crawley and Baker Street on 23 November 1968, the issue of 5-day (10 journey tickets) was extended on Route 709 to cover the section between Old Coulsdon (Tudor Rose) and Purley (Old Lodge Lane).

Further issues of 5-day tickets took place when Route 715A was reduced to operation between Monday and Friday in peak hours only from 8 June 1968. Once again the issue was confined to the sections where 715A was the only service, these being:

Stage 14. Hertford Heath (Townsend Arms) to 16 Wollensbrook (Woodman).

Stage 24. Enfield Highway, Ordnance Road to 30 Seven Sisters Corner.

On 15 February 1969, the Westerham – Chelsham section of 706 was confined to Monday–Friday peak hours only, and

5-day tickets were issued between Westerham (The Crown) (Stage 53) up to Worms Heath (Stage 49), and these tickets were available for stages up to Kilburn High Road, Belsize Road, (Stage 33).

There were no further changes to these types of tickets even when London Country Bus Services assumed the responsibility for Green Line routes, until a fare revision came into operation in June 1973, when the whole structure for the issue of long-issue tickets was revised. Weekly and Monthly tickets were introduced at 9 and 35 times the single fare. The weekly tickets were once again available for use from Sunday to Saturday, and both types of ticket gave unlimited journeys between the two farestages between which they had been issued. This represents a considerable saving to the users of these tickets, as they can be used for local shopping journeys, visits to the cinema and other leisure pursuits.

Thus, over the fifty years of operation of short-stage express services, we have seen ticket issuing methods develop from paper hand-written tickets through tickets of stiffer paper, carrying lists of towns, public houses and roads from which many a transport enthusiast has learned the geography of the routes followed, to the speedy machine-issued ticket that only the ticket inspector or other officials of the company can understand, but which has lightened the conductor's job by reducing the number of waybill entries to be completed before, during, and after completion of his duty, and, at the same time, has eliminated heavy printing costs by reducing the number of tickets to be carried to either a piece of plain paper, or else one on which the only printing requirement is confined to the name of the operator on the front plus a few regulations on the reverse side. Sometimes, these regulations are omitted on the reverse, an abridged version being placed on the front at the bottom of the ticket, whilst the reverse side is rented out for advertisements, thus bringing additional revenue to the operator concerned.

Lapel badge, 1930–1933 *Off duty Inspector* *Cap badge Country buses and coaches, 1933–1970*

Cap badge 1933

District Inspector, 1930–1933 *London Country cap badge, 1970*

INSIGNIA & PUBLICITY
CHAPTER TWELVE

In this chapter I will endeavour to deal with all those ancilliary matters that are, nonetheless an integral part of the Green Line story.

For instance, there is the subject of staff uniforms. After all, one does not expect to see a conductor issuing tickets dressed in civilian clothing, or to have one's ticket demanded by someone, who no matter how smartly he may be dressed, is still in plain clothes but with no visible means of identification as an Official of the Company operating the service.

PART ONE – UNIFORMS:

It is understandable, perhaps, that a company with only three or four vehicles on the road, as was the case with some of the operators mentioned in Chapter Two and Appendix 'A', would initially be working on a shoestring, not affording the luxury of uniforms for their staffs, simply providing them with a peaked cap, plus a metal badge bearing the name of the operator. Whilst this was alright as far as the driver was concerned, as usually, he had little contact with the public, it was not sufficient for the conductor. The writer can speak from personal experience here. He was fortunate enough to be employed by a large organisation which supplied their staffs with a summer weight and winter weight uniform, one suit of which was changed in alternate years. These were manufactured of good quality and hard-wearing cloth, but after two years, with the friction of the cash-bag straps on the shoulders, and the movement of the ticket punch holder on the lower portion of the jackets, they were not much good for further use when exchanged at the annual uniform issue, although the best of them were usually passed on to the garage staff, particularly those employed in bus cleaning.

A glance through my collection of photographs taken in the early days of London coach services, shows that even with the smaller firms, the conductors are wearing a uniform jacket of some sort, and then I remembered that, as a youngster, I had seen redundant bus and tram staff uniforms on sale quite cheaply in shops of the type that nowadays usually go in for the sale of Army surplus clothing, so, presumably, the operating staffs of the smaller companies got their uniforms by purchasing these redundant uniforms quite cheaply.

In the case of the main predecessors to Green Line Coaches Limited (such as Autocar Services, East Surrey and National), the crews working on the coaches wore the same uniform as the bus crews, and were simply senior crews from the bus section of the respective undertaking.

The East Surrey and Autocar men wore a uniform which was made up from a dark navy blue material, with leather cuffs on both jackets and overcoats. From the few photographs I possess showing crews standing alongside their vehicles, the suits do not seem to have been embellished with any coloured piping. Drivers were issued with a uniform suit; greatcoat (for winter use); White dustcoats (for summer use) and a cap. Conductors had a uniform suit and a cap, and, in view of the fact that the buses of those days had rear platforms open to the elements, were also issued with a greatcoat for winter use. The same type of cap was issued both to conductors and drivers, and were of the soft-top type without stiffening wires. A brass cap badge was issued, which was held in position by a metal pin passed through lugs fitted on the back of the badge. It was cut in a similar shape to the bullseye badges used by the London General Omnibus Company, the name of the respective company (East Surrey or Autocar) was picked out in the cross-bar of the badge in the same styling of lettering as used for the fleet-name on the side of the vehicles.

The National Omnibus and Transport Company men also wore a similar type of uniform, but it was embellished with green piping, and, to the best of my recollection, the word 'National' was picked out in green on the lapels of the jackets and greatcoats. Their cap badges were in white metal, and consisted of the word 'National' in script writing.

Although the London General Omnibus Company had been in the bus industry since 1856, and had been operating motor coaches for private hire since 1913, the services from Watford to Charing Cross and Golders Green which they started in 1929, were their first venture with coaches plying for hire. The coaches came from the Private Hire fleet at first, and presumably the drivers (there were no conductors at this time) wore the same uniform as those employed in the Private Hire fleet. This was a navy blue suit made of the same material used for inspectors uniforms, with black bakelite buttons inscribed with the word 'GENERAL' in script writing. The caps were of the soft-top type without stiffening wires, and carried a small circular badge about

1.2" in diameter. It was made of white metal, with a dark blue circle round the edges, and a large 'G' in Gill Sans lettering in the centre.

When the Windsor route started in April 1930, the crews recruited to operate it were not fitted out with either the L.G.O.C. bus uniform or the Private Hire uniform, being issued instead with the standard white dustcoat with brown-coloured shoulder lapels worn by their colleagues on the London buses in the summer. They were also issued with the soft-top caps worn by the London drivers, but without cap badges.

These conditions continued when Green Line Coaches Limited was formed in July 1930 to take over the services formerly operated by the smaller companies, and to develop services on its own account. Those services which had been started by the original companies were still worked by staff wearing the uniform of that company, and where a new route was started by Green Line itself, the new crews were kitted out with dustcoats and caps, but no cap badges. Inspectors and timekeepers wore ordinary civilian suits with an armband bearing the legend 'GREEN LINE – OFFICIAL', plus a lapel badge circular in shape, also bearing this legend, plus a number, in case passengers wished to lay a complaint against the official in question.

This somewhat haphazard situation ended in the early part of November 1930, when drivers, conductors and inspectors were issued with a smart new uniform in green worsted cloth. The one issued to the crews was made of the same cloth as that used for inspectors, the only difference being, that from the top of the 'V' of the lapel, round the shoulders to the top of the 'V' of the opposite lapel, consisted of black cloth. On this section of the uniform, a small metal badge was fixed on both lapels, which was a replica, on a smaller scale, of the triangular device fixed at the top of the radiator of the coaches. One thing that was missing from the jackets and overcoats was the wide leather band usually fitted to the cuffs, presumably because Green Line was regarded at that time as a luxury type of service. The cuffs were stitched down, and two small white metal buttons were sewn on the inside at the bottom of the sleeve. The caps were also made of green cloth, with a plain black band round the lower half. They were of the bandsman type, being stiffened with circular wire stiffeners. A bullseye type cap badge was supplied, which was enamelled green on white metal, with the legend 'GREEN LINE' (underlined) across the bar.

Conductors were also issued with a leather cash bag; a metal holder for the Bell Punch, complete with leather shoulder strap, a pair of special ticket clippers for the cancellation of certain types of ticket; a wooden ticket rack, capable of holding ten packets of tickets on either side, and a metal key, known as a 'budget' key, which opened and locked the cupboard fitted on the coach to carry his ticket box and any personal belongings. At a later date, when new-type coaches arrived with destination indicator boxes at the rear of the coach, this key also unlocked the flap covering the handle which turned the rear destination blind.

When London Transport took over, changes were made to the uniforms issued to the crews. A standard style in green cloth of a more robust weave was adopted both for Country Bus and Green Line coach crews. Piping in a lighter green than that of the cloth was added around the black neckband of the tunics, and down the hems of the outside of the trouser legs, and also round the new white signalling bands on the sleeves. Leather cuffs also re-appeared to save excess wear caused by the constant dipping into the cash bag for change. The metal triangular badges worn on the lapels on Green Line coach uniforms were withdrawn, and the Green Line cap badge was replaced with a standard London Transport bullseye badge, faced with green enamel.

Later on, when buses had enclosed platforms, overcoats were withdrawn from issue to conductors, and they were issued with light short dust jackets for summer wear, together with a mackintosh for inclement weather.

The inspectors' uniforms, apart from being made from a superior type of cloth, had black cloth braid fixed over the outside seams of the trousers, and also in an ornamental scroll (as can be seen on bandsmen's tunics) on the lower portion of each sleeve. Their caps, like those of the crews', were of the bandsman type, but had a hat-band of the same type of cloth braid as used on the sleeves. Incidentally, the neck-band of the tunics on the inspectors' uniforms were of green cloth, and not black. The same type of uniform was worn by both inspectors and District Inspectors, and the difference in rank was emphasised in the type of cap worn, and the colour of the metal used for the cap badge.

District Inspectors had a thin strip of padded black braid round the edge of the peak of their caps. Their cap badge was of the same design as that issued to the inspectors, but was manufactured from silver-gilt.

The ordinary inspector's badge, which did not carry a number, was made of white metal silvered over. The badge itself, was simple but effective, being a replica of the triangular badge bearing the Company's name, which was fitted at the top of the radiator of all the A.E.C. coaches operated by the company. The triangular section was fitted in the centre of a crown of imitation laurel leaves, this being the section which was silvered over. At the bottom of the badge a small metal scroll was fitted, which carried the word 'INSPECTOR' in white on a green background, the same legend being used on both Inspector and District Inspector badges.

Unlike the uniform supplied to the crews when London Transport took over, the Inspector's uniform did not suffer much change. The suits were tailor-made to suit each individual's requirements of a superior type of green worsted cloth, with black bakelite buttons on which was inscribed an image of a griffin bird, the mythical bird which is the emblem of the City of London, and which was adopted by London Transport.

The ornamental black braid was dispensed with, except for the hat band, and the biggest changes were to the cap badges. The inspectors' badges were made of sterling silver and hallmarked, whilst the District Inspectors' (now retitled Chief Inspector) badges were of silver-gilt. The London Transport bullseye was used as a base for the badge, with the roundels outlined in green enamel. It was supported at the base by a pair of griffin birds, facing outwards. The cross-bar of the bullseye carries the words 'LONDON TRANSPORT' picked out in black enamel lettering on the silver background.

PART TWO – PUBLICITY:

As mentioned in the first chapter, publicity is vital if a new coach service is to succeed, and fortunately most operators concerned in the provision of short-stage coach routes in the London area realised this fact.

The writer, who was a youth in his teens when the new type of business began to grow in the late twenties, well remembers seeing the coach booking agents shops in his local area with racks of handbills suspended on strings, and he has seen as many as twenty or thirty different handbills displayed on these racks. Some agents also, if their shop boasted more than one window, would devote a whole window to displays of posters and handbills of the companies for which they held agencies.

Others, with not so much space, would have a display of wooden poster boards standing below their windows. Unfortunately, the local dogs usually found these boards to be an excellent variant as a comfort station, especially in the winter, as they were not so cold to the rear legs, as were the metal lamp-posts of those far-off days.

The smaller operators usually contented themselves with the issue of handbills, which contained the vital information as to times, fares, picking-up points, together with a list of booking offices and agents, plus a double-crown poster which could be pasted on a board, pinned on a wall or displayed in a window, and left it at that.

The more responsible operators, like the City Coach Company, Birch Brothers Limited, Skylark Motor Coach Company and Thackray's Way, all started off with well-produced leaflets, and, as their businesses developed, necessitating them operating more than one route, they provided well-produced timetable booklets.

The booklet issued by Skylark in particular was a most useful publication, as it carried advertisements for tea-shops, restaurants and hotels along the various routes. These not only contributed to the cost of producing the timetable, but gave useful local information to the day tripper.

The Premier Line was one of the larger operators who did not publish a timetable booklet, being content with leaflets for each of its five services. This is somewhat surprising, as in other respects, the company was one of most efficient in operational matters.

Some of the smaller operators, once they got their routes and times well-established, gave up issuing hand bills, and went in for folding card timetables, which were more durable for the regular traveller to carry.

Green Line Coaches Limited, being an offspring of the Underground group, and having as one of its directors the famous Frank Pick, who, in addition to being a great administrator, was particularly interested in the visual arts. It was he who persuaded Edward Johnston in 1916 to design the sans-serif type face which has been a feature of all London Transport notices and signs for many years, and which was an important example of a 'house style' in promotion. He was also responsible for the high standard of poster art which has done so much to stimulate off-peak passenger traffic over the years.

In these circumstances, it is not surprising that Green Line had a distinct advantage in publicity matters over other coach operators of the period. Right from the start, there have been leaflets for each route, giving full information about the route, including a timetable and fares list (at least until constant fare increases made the job impossible). These leaflets have varied in size and style over the years, and during the last war were simply copies of the timetables posted at the stops folded to pocket size. Fortunately, London Country Bus Services, who now operate the services, have kept up and even improved the standard of these route leaflets, printing them on a good quality glazed paper, with an attractive line-drawing on the cover depicting a place of local interest on the particular route.

For the casual passenger, there have always been timetable panels posted at or near the stopping places. Until the fixed stopping place, so familiar a sight in London and the Home Counties today, came into operation on Green Line in the 1933/4 period, the glazed timetable frames were usually fixed to the wall at the side of booking agents for the Green Line services or on the wall of public houses near the stops. These boards were of two types, and would accommodate a timetable 10" by 25" long or two timetables 10" by 12" in size. At places like Poland Street Coach Station; Great Scotland Yard and later Horse Guards Avenue and Victoria (Eccleston Bridge), large display frames were fixed, which carried several frames to accommodate the timetables in both directions for the large number of services which passed these points.

The Underground group (later London Transport) has a large Building Department at Parsons Green, with a well-equipped joiners shop, which manufactures the timetable boards, together with another shop which fabricates all the many bus and Green Line stop posts which one sees in the streets served by London Transport road services. Another section, also at Parsons Green, is responsible for the erection of stop posts, and also makes and fixes the special metal fixing straps, as well as fixing bus stop flags and timetable boards, to the many types of lamp standards carrying bus stop flags. The flags themselves, however, are manufactured by an outside firm.

Turning for a moment to timetable leaflets, the East Surrey and Autocar companies issued a combined folder for the services they operated as early as July 1930, and this was followed a few months later by a combined folder covering the services operated by the L.G.O.C. and Green Line Coaches Limited.

By October, the number of services had increased, and a more ambitious folder was produced which was headed 'GREEN LINE' and contained details of all services then in operation, whether by General, East Surrey, Green Line, Autocar or National.

In the early part of 1931, a predecessor to the later Green Line Coach guide was produced and printed by Waterlow and Sons, which not only included full time and faretables for all routes, but also two very well drawn route maps, one of the country areas served, the other of the inner area of London. Unfortunately, there were several route and frequency changes introduced at the time it was about to be distributed, which immediately made it out of date, and it was never issued to the public.

However, there was still the never-ending spate of leaflets, and to these was added a card folder entitled 'Green Line Coach Service Guide' of which 15,000 were printed and issued to the public. This contained a list of routes with the service intervals and the through single and return fares from London, but no times. The first issue did not carry the route letters, as these had not yet been allocated, although they appeared in the revised issue which appeared later in the year.

I mentioned in an earlier paragraph the high standard of poster art which emanated from the Underground group (later London Transport) Publicity Office. From 1931 onwards, it had four separate organisations for which it had to supply suitable publicity which would help to stimulate leisure and week-end traffic, these being the Tube and District Railways (the Metropolitan Line was not part of the Underground combine in those days); the London General Omnibus Company; Green Line Coaches Limited and three tramway companies (London United; Metropolitan Electric Tramways and South Metropolitan Electric Tramways).

Whilst it is obvious that each of the above organisations had various attractions and events which could only be conveniently reached by using that particular system, there were many places of interest or beauty spots which could be reached by train, bus, coach or tram, or even by combinations of two or more of them. In these cases, an attractive poster would be produced of a popular spot, such as Virginia Water, for instance. There would be a blank space at the foot of the poster on which paper slips could be posted as follows:

(a) By Underground to Hounslow East, then Bus 117.
(b) By Bus 117 from Hounslow Garage.
(c) By London United Tram 57 to Hounslow, then Bus 117.
(d) By Green Line Coach Route A from Charing Cross (Great Scotland Yard).

The poster with slip (a) could then be posted at all Underground stations; with slip (b) at all bus garages; with slip (c) at tram depots and on sites at garages and strategic points on the Green Line system, with slip (d).

As the coach routes had no identifying route letters or numbers before February 1931, no route maps appeared before they were introduced, and the first item to include a route map was a paper folder, folded to size 5½″ by 8″, which was titled on the front as 'The Green Line Coach Guide for Ramblers'. This appeared in March 1932 and contained a list of routes, showing the route letters and Central London terminal points; the route followed; the service frequency, and the single and return fares from the London terminal to the country terminal. The route map, which was well-designed, also showed the location of various villages and beauty spots which were just off the line of routes. This was placed on the reverse side of the folder. Three editions appeared of this guide, and was followed in July 1932, by a new edition, also printed in green on white paper, folded to size 3″ by 8″, but headed 'Green Line – Map of Daily Coach Services – 1932'. Despite the change in title, it contained the same information as the former Ramblers Guide, and this map and list of routes, with various corrections, continued in issue until October 1933, although the print colour was changed from light green to blue for the 1933 issues.

An interesting edition of the map was made in 1932 for staff use only. It was printed on linen-backed card, the front side being a deep green. The reverse side carried the route map printed in grey, and over-printed in red with the location and telephone number of each bus and coach garage which could render assistance in the event of an accident or breakdown.

For display purposes, a quad-royal version of the map and list of routes was produced for posting on Underground stations, bus and coach garages, and later in various passenger shelters erected by London Transport at principal bus and coach stops in suburban and country districts. These maps remained as quad royal size until about 1960, when they were reduced to the normal poster size known as double-royal.

The handbill style of route and timetable information gave way to a folder leaflet (folded size 3″ by 6″) in 1931, thus making it easily portable in a wallet or handbag, and this style lasted for many years, but it was surprising that, having got a network of services on 27 different routes by February 1931, and having acquired a further six routes by March 1932, a timetable booklet was not brought into use at this time, but presumably the Company were awaiting the results of the Committee of Enquiry into London Coach Services, before launching into the expense of printing a timetable book.

The first Green Line coach guide, although not titled as such, was published in October 1933. It had a dark green cover, size roughly 4½″ by 5½″, and was sold to the public for the princely sum of one penny per copy, and gave the times and fares for all routes, but was out-of-date within two months, as by the end of December 1933, four more routes had been acquired, these being the Premier Line services to Windsor and Farnham Common; the Batten Grays and Tilbury route and Price's Super Coaches between East Ham and Aveley.

After the publication of this booklet, there was no further Green Line timetable booklet as such, but the six area timetables produced by London Transport in July 1934, carried a section printed on green paper, which gave complete timetables for all Green Line routes, whether they worked in that area or not.

However, the first Green Line Coach Guide titled as such, was published in February 1936, and was numbered Issue No. 1, 1936. It contained times, fares, weekly and 4-weekly season ticket rates, boarding points, together with diagrams of selected points of boarding. A small pull-out map of routes was provided, with an enlarged plan of the Central Area of London on the reverse, and also a list of Country Bus routes was included. The next two issues, also published in 1936, were of the same style, except that the standard Green Line folder map in a small pocket at the back of the book replaced the former pull-out map. The price per issue of the new Guide was twopence.

The first issue of 1937, published on 2 May, had the first Green cover, and was entirely set in Times New Roman type. It contained an index to places both on or near Green Line routes, as well as route diagrams for each route showing stops and restrictions and including the route numbers of buses serving destinations off line of route at various stopping places. Coach journeys which operated on bus fare scales were specially advertised; there were more boarding point diagrams, and not only were Green Line regulations illustrated with comic drawings and written in a style of English easy to understand, but also Bus, Tram and Trolleybus and Underground Regulations were included. There was a comprehensive list of London Churches worthy of a visit; Museums; theatres and department stores and many other places of interest, complete with instructions of how to get to them. A large folder map of Green Line routes and country bus connections was pasted in the back cover, all for twopence. At this time, the separate route leaflets were printed from the type as used in the Guide.

The second issue for 1937 included an eight-page photogravure section describing a tour of the newly-opened

St. Albans bus garage, which had opened on 26 August 1936, and was one of the most modern garages in the Country Bus and Coach fleet.

The next edition of the Guide, which covered the winter period of 1937/8, was the peak twopennyworth. There was 32 pages of advertisements; and an 8-page Green Line Gazette, all about coach stops, coaches and how to hail them, after which followed a coloured drawing of a 9T9 Regal coach, which bore the announcement that fifty of these new coaches with Weymann bodies were now in service. All these were in the front section, before getting down to producing the actual time and faretables.

Commencing with the first issue of 1938, which appeared in February, much of the extraneous matter was removed, and this trend continued, so that by the time that the second edition of 1939 appeared in April of that year, it carried no route map, no adverts and much less general information. There were two more editions of the Guide in 1939, the last being No. 4, current from 26 July to 3 October. These were both in the same pattern as the second edition, but the withdrawal of all coach routes after the last journeys on 31 August rendered No. 4 redundant after that date.

Although the coaches returned for a period of about two years in the early part of the war, the Green Line Guide did not reappear, although the timetables for Green Line routes appropriate to each area were, of course, published in the local timetable books produced by London Transport in those days.

The coach services had been operating for two years after their post-war resumption before the first post-war Green Line Coach Guide appeared in May 1948. The booklet itself was much smaller in size than its pre-war ancestors, and the contents were entirely confined to a list of places served; time and faretables for each route; plans of the boarding points where split stops applied, and there were no unnecessary frills. The cost to the public was now threepence, and remained the same until the first edition for 1951, when the price was raised to 6d.

Although the Guide remained in the same size, due to increased printing and production costs, the selling price was raised to 9d with the summer 1958 issue, and again to 1/- with the summer 1960 booklet.

The introduction of the 24-hour clock in 1962 necessitated the complete re-setting of all the timetables and caused an increase in the size of the book, all of this being introduced with summer edition for 1963. Fortunately, this upheaval did not cause any increase in the selling price of the Guide, which remained at 1/-.

After this the Guide continued with two issues per year, with amendment leaflets as either times or fares altered within the currency of the Guide, until the final issue was made by London Transport in October 1969.

Turning back to the subject of pocket maps, we left those in July 1933 with an issue still in the large 3″ by 8″ size. This came to an end with the route re-organisation introduced on 4 October 1933. The map produced for this alteration was the same style as those of 1932/3, but the route information was produced in a more compact style, which allowed for a reduction in size, and when folded it was 3″ by 6″. These maps were to scale, and this design remained in issue, with corrections, up to the issue dated April 1935.

The first of what might be described as the standard style of Green Line Map was introduced in the summer of 1935. The routes were shown in a somewhat distorted style, but showed the location of all fixed stops in Central London and suburbs, as well as most of the connecting Country bus routes to places which were off the Green Line network. It was printed on a good quality paper, and was folded to fit the pocket, the size when folded being 3″ by 5½″. I remember, on getting and examining my copy of this map, thinking that Green Line had grown up at last. The layout of the map was slightly altered in 1936, but there were usually two issues per year until the end of 1938.

For 1939, a new style of map was produced, which was drawn to scale, but embodied all the features which had appeared in the maps for the past four years. Four issues were made in that year, the last one appearing just before the war came along and the coaches were withdrawn for a while.

No maps were issued during the period between late 1939 and September 1942, when Green Line reappeared to act as a relief service to the railways during bombings. The Central Bus section of London Transport had also not produced a map since 1940, probably due to a Government restriction on the production of maps in case of an invasion by enemy forces.

When the coaches returned in 1946, a return was made to the style of map published in 1933 and 1934. The first one appeared in May 1946, before the network had been completely restored. It was printed by the Bournehall Press of Bushey, and when folded, the size was 3″ by 6″. Six editions of this map appeared in 1946, but for 1947 and 1948, a return was made to the very excellent style of map produced in 1939.

Presumably these two maps in the 1939 style had been somewhat expensive, as when the 1949 issue appeared in May, an abbreviated style, similar to that of the 1933–1935 period appeared, and remained as the standard Green Line map until the end of 1957. For the years from 1958 to 1960, a combined Country Bus and Green Line Coach Map was introduced as an experiment, being based on the Ordnance Survey Half-Inch District Map of Greater London published at that time. In the opinion of the writer, this was the best route map ever produced and designed by London Transport, and he remembers being extremely disappointed when the experiment was concluded.

Despite the issue of a combined bus and coach map in 1960, for those travellers only interested in a plan of the Green Line routes, a map in the same style as used between 1949 and 1957 was also issued. The style continued to be used until London Transport handed over Country Buses and Coaches to the National Bus Company on 1 January 1970.

From 1963 to 1967 however, experimental issues were made of a Green Line map festooned with colour drawings of various towns and places of interest. The routes were also shown in different colours. Whilst the pictures drew quite a lot of attention to some of the attractions served by Green Line, the production costs were rather high, and the experiment was phased out at the end of 1967.

London Country Bus Services have maintained and even improved on the high standard of publicity which has made the name 'GREEN LINE' famous, not only in the London area, but throughout England. Since they have taken over, improved styles of route maps have appeared, and the standard of folder timetables considerably improved. The Green Line coach map is once again drawn to scale, and has much more information on both sides, designed to stimulate more leisure travel on the coaches. Once again, there is a combined Country Bus and Green Line Coach Map in issue, not only drawn to scale, but also showing the routes of other N.B.C. companies which connect with both Green Line and Country Bus services.

In addition to, this, the company has produced many attractive leaflets in connection with revision of services, for Bank Holiday operations, and also to describe what is to be seen at places such as Windsor and St. Albans. Posters advertising various Green Line routes have appeared once again in bus shelters and on garages, not forgetting the ones which advertise such fare savers as Golders Rovers and Outback tickets.

Thus ends the story of fifty years of well-produced and designed publicity so much a feature of all London Transport artwork.

LIST OF OPERATORS AND SERVICES NOT MENTIONED IN THE TEXT.

Date of Commencement:	Name of Operator:	Route:	Remarks:
August 1927	Glenton Coaches	Victoria – Sevenoaks	Six daily journeys. Pre-booking service. Withdrawn by December 1927
November 1928	Roadways	Aldwych – Welwyn Garden City	Five daily services via Portman Square, Golders Green, Barnet. Date of withdrawal unknown.
January 1929	Grimwoods Parlour Coaches	Trafalgar Square – Egham	Five daily journeys. Increased to nine journeys by January 1930 via Hounslow, Feltham, Ashford. Date of withdrawal unknown.
March 1929	Spencer Park Coaches	Victoria (Vauxhall Bridge Road) – Windsor	Three daily journeys. Route followed and date of withdrawal unknown.
May 1929	St. Albans Coaches (L. Ashby)	Oxford Circus – St. Albans	Eight daily journeys via Edgware, Elstree and Radlett. (Three journeys extended to Wheathampstead on 1 January 1930).
June 1929	Wendrome	Charing Cross – Thame	Via Tring and Aylesbury. Seven daily journeys. Withdrawn July 1930.
June 1929	Renown Motor Coaches	Kings Cross – Dunstable	Via Barnet and St. Albans. Five daily journeys. Withdrawn by October 1930.
October 1929	Gordon Omnibus Co.	East Ham – Tilbury	Via Aveley and Grays. Every 40 minutes. Licence refused by Traffic Commissioners. Withdrawn in late 1932.
November 1929	Direct Roadways	Oxford Circus – Egham	Four daily journeys. Withdrawn by April 1930.
November 1929	Superways	Liverpool Street – Ongar	Twelve daily journeys via Loughton and Epping. Withdrawn by June 1930.
November 1929	Lion and Chimes	Clapham Road Coach Station – Welwyn Garden City	Via Oxford Circus and Barnet. Five journeys Weekdays: three journeys Sundays. Date of withdrawal unknown.
November 1929	Victoria Pullman Coaches	Charing Cross – Dartford	Six daily journeys. Pre-booking service. Date of withdrawal unknown.
November 1929	London and Counties Carriage Co.	Charing Cross – Hertford	Ran approximately hourly daily. Via Bank, Shoreditch, Dalston, Tottenham, Edmonton. Date of withdrawal unknown.
November 1929	Highways Limited	Oxford Circus – Windsor	Hourly service via Slough. Withdrawn July – November 1930 when it was resumed. Licence refused by Traffic Commissioners in 1931.
January 1930	Moseley Grey Coaches Limited	East Ham – Grays	Irregular service. Date of withdrawal unknown.
January 1930	Blue Star Motorways Limited	Oxford Circus – Chesham	Via Uxbridge, Harefield, Rickmansworth, Chalfont Station, Chesham Bois. Three journeys, later increased to seven. Later acquired by Western Star.

Date of Commencement:	Name of Operator:	Route:	Remarks:
January 1930	District Omnibus Services Limited	Oxford Circus – St. Albans	Seven daily journeys via Golders Green, Barnet and South Mimms. Company sold to St. Albans and District Motor Services Limited who increased it to 13 daily journeys. Date of withdrawal not known.
March 1930	Anne Coaches	Victoria Station. (Vauxhall Bridge Road) – Sevenoaks	Four daily journeys via Eltham, Sidcup, Swanley, Farningham and Shoreham. Date of withdrawal not known, but believed to have run for a few months only.
March 1930	Western Star Motorways Limited	Oxford Circus – Seer Green	Via Uxbridge, Gerrards Cross, The Chalfonts and Three Households. Six journeys, later increased to two-hourly, later hourly. Date of withdrawal unknown.
April 1930	Modern Super Coaches Limited	Liverpool Street – Hoddesdon	Half-hourly via Dalston, Tottenham, Edmonton, Waltham X, Wormley. Date of withdrawal unknown.
April 1930	Hemelondon Transport Services	Oxford Circus to Hemel Hempstead	Ten daily journeys via Edgware, Watford-by-pass, Garston, Abbots Langley, Bedmond and Leverstock Green. Withdrawn by June 1930.
May 1930	Pring's Motor Coach Service	Charing Cross – Maidenhead	Five daily journeys via Brentford, Chiswick, Hounslow, Slough. Date of withdrawal unknown.
June 1930	Spartan Coaches	Oxford Circus – Walton-on-Thames	Every 90 minutes. Extended via Oatlands Park to Weybridge by August 1930. Via Kingston, Esher and Hersham. Date of withdrawal unknown.
July 1930	Valliant Direct Coaches	Oxford Circus – Reigate	Hourly via Croydon, Merstham and Redhill. Date of withdrawal unknown.
August 1930	Gleaner Omnibus Services	Marble Arch (Edgware Road) – Chesham	Four journeys. Tickets to be booked in advance. Via Edgware, Watford-by-Pass, Kings Langley, Chipperfield, Bovingdon, Ley Hill. Date of withdrawal unknown.
September 1930	Leighton Coach Company	Aldgate – Tilbury	Twelve journeys via Purfleet. Mainly ran between East Ham and Rainham. Licence to continue service refused by Traffic Commissioners. Withdrawn early 1932.
September 1930	King's Service Coaches	London – Horley (Thorns Hotel) Hourly	Via Tooting, Mitcham, Wallington, and Coulsdon. Some peak hour journeys ran to London Bridge, but were withdrawn in December when alternate journeys from Oxford Circus then ran via Wallington or Croydon until 27 January 1931, after which whole route ran via Wallington, Route withdrawn by order of Traffic Commissioner in October 1931.

Date of Commencement:	Name of Operator:	Route:	Remarks:
October 1930	Bouts Bros. (Tiger Coaches)	Bishopsgate – Ongar	Hourly service via Stratford, Wanstead, Loughton, Epping. Route withdrawn 5 August 1931 by order of Ministry of Transport.
October 1930	Prince Omnibus Company Limited	Liverpool Street – Ongar	Irregular service via Stratford, Wanstead, Woodford Bridge, Chigwell, Abridge and Stanford Rivers. Date of withdrawal unknown.
October 1930	P and S Motor Services Limited	Liverpool Street – Hertford	Hourly service (Two-hourly at certain times of the day). Via Tottenham, Waltham X, Hoddesdon, St. Margarets Ware. Licence to continue refused by Traffic Commissioners.

Note: In the case of those operators for whom dates of their withdrawals are not known, it is possible that some of them withdrew before the new licensing system came into operation on 9 February 1931, and also that licences to continue operation were refused by the Traffic Commissioners in other cases.

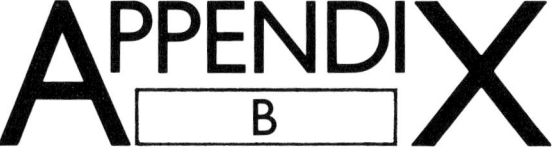

LIST OF LOCAL LICENCES TO APPLY FOR HIRE ASKED FOR BY THE L.G.O.C. OR GREEN LINE COACHES, OR BOTH, PRIOR TO INTRODUCTION OF ROAD TRAFFIC ACT (1930) LICENSING SYSTEM.

The month of application is shown in brackets where known. The single numbers shown in brackets after certain towns refer to notes shown after the respective lists:

LIST A.   APPLICATIONS GRANTED:

AYLESBURY
BALDOCK
BEACONSFIELD (September 1930)
BEDFORD (September 1930)
BERKHAMSTEAD
BISHOPS STORTFORD (1)
CHERTSEY
CHESHAM (2)
DARTFORD
DORKING
DUNSTABLE
HITCHIN
HODDESDON
LEATHERHEAD
MAIDENHEAD (4)
MARLOW (5)
NORTHFLEET
ROYSTON (September 1930)
SAFFRON WALDEN (September 1930)
ST. ALBANS
SAWBRIDGEWORTH (6)
SEVENOAKS

EGHAM	STEVENAGE
EPPING	SWANSCOMBE
ETON	TRING
GRAVESEND	UPMINSTER (7)
GUILDFORD (3)	WALTON-ON-THAMES
HARPENDEN	WARE (8)
HEMEL HEMPSTEAD	WELWYN (9)
HENLEY (September 1930)	WEYBRIDGE
HERTFORD	WINDSOR

Notes:
1. Green Line applied to Bishops Stortford Council in August 1930 and were informed that licences were not required to ply for hire.
2. Green Line applied to Chesham Council in September 1930, October 1930 and December 1930 and were refused on all three occasions. Licences were finally granted on 27 February 1931, subject to timetable modifications. Route was actually operated by Amersham and District.
3. Application was made by the L.G.O.C. in February 1930. Guildford Council refused licences on 24 March 1930, but agreed in June to transfer bus licences to coaches. What exactly is meant by this is not known, as L.G.O.C. operated two bus services to Guildford at that time, 115 on Mondays–Fridays, and 620 on Saturdays and Sundays. Neither route was withdrawn when Green Line service started.
4. Maidenhead Council granted licences to L.G.O.C. subject to the surrender of bus licences. As L.G.O.C. had only ever operated buses to this town on summer Sundays, this presented no problem.
5. Marlow Council was applied to in August 1930, and granted licences subject to certain special conditions. Presumably these conditions were not acceptable to Green Line as operation to Marlow was never taken up.
6. Green Line applied to Sawbridgeworth Council in August 1930 and were informed that licences were not required to ply for hire.
7. At that time, Upminster was in the Romford Rural District Council area. Application was made for licences to them in October 1930.
8. Application was made to Ware Council in July 1930. Licences were refused to Green Line, but upon re-application by the National Omnibus and Transport Company, they were granted to them.
9. Applications were made by the L.G.O.C. to the Welwyn Council in July 1929, and were granted for a service to London via Barnet and Highgate, but these were never taken up; later licences for operation via Barnet and Golders Green were granted easily.

LIST B. APPLICATIONS REFUSED:

ALDERSHOT	(September 1930)	LUTON	(January 1930 & September 1930)
CAMBRIDGE	(September 1930)	OXFORD	(August 1930)
CHELMSFORD	(September 1930)	READING (2)	(August 1930)
CHORLEYWOOD	(September 1930)	RICKMANSWORTH (3)	(September 1930)
FARNBOROUGH (Hants)	(August 1930)	SUNNINGDALE	(August 1930)
FARNHAM (1)	(August 1930)	WINDLESHAM	(July 1930)
FRIMLEY	(August 1930)	WOKING	(July 1930 & September 1930)
GODALMING	(September 1930)	WOKINGHAM (4)	(August 1930)
HIGH WYCOMBE	(September 1930)		

Notes:
1. The application to Farnham U.D.C. was for a service from London via Guildford.
2. The application to Reading Council was for a service from London via Maidenhead.
3. Although Rickmansworth U.D.C. refused licences to ply for hire in the town, the Rickmansworth service ultimately started with pre-booking from a booking agent.
4. In its refusal, Wokingham Council suggested that Green Line should try again when the Road Traffic Act Licensing system came into operation.

APPENDIX C

ORIGINAL PROPOSALS FOR THROUGH LONDON WORKINGS – NOVEMBER 1930

Note: Some of the services shown below were alternatives and some of the frequencies (shown in minutes) are approximate only. Letters in brackets refer to special notes on the service, which will be found at the end of the list.

Windsor – 30 – Staines – 30 – London – 30 – Dartford – 60 – Gravesend.
Windsor – 15 – Slough – 15 – London – Lewisham – (30 – Orpington (a)
                                                               (60 – Sidcup (b)
                                                                (60 – Farningham (c)
Maidenhead – 30 – London – 30 – Westerham Hill – 60 – Sevenoaks.
West Wycombe – 60 – } Gerrards Cross – 30 – London – 30 – Sevenoaks.
Amersham – 60 –
Uxbridge – 30 – London – 30 – Tunbridge Wells.
Beaconsfield – 60 – } Gerrards Cross – 30 – London – 30 – Chelsham – 60 – Edenbridge.
Amersham – 60 –
Uxbridge – 60 – London – 60 – Caterham-on-the-Hill.
Chesham – 60 – Northwood – 30 – London – 30 – Redhill.
Harrow Weald – 60 – London – 60 – Caterham-on-the-Hill.
Wendover – 120 – Tring – 60 – } Two Waters – 30 – London – 30 – Godstone – 60 – East Grinstead.
Hemel Hempstead – 60 –
Watford – 30 – London – 30 – Belmont.
Watford – 30 – London – 30 – Chelsham – 60 – Oxted.
Dunstable – 60 – } St. Albans – 30 – London – 30 – Dorking.
Wheathampstead – 60' –
Baldock – 30 – London – 30 – Reigate.
Royston – 60 – } Ware – 30 – London – 30 – Guildford (d).
Hertford – 60 –
Bishops Stortford – 30 – London – 30 – Chertsey (e).
Ongar – 30 – London – 30 – West Byfleet.

Notes:
(a) The choice of Orpington as a final destination is most interesting. Presumably it would have been reached via Eltham, Chislehurst and Petts Wood, as the alternative route via Farnborough would be serviced with a 15-minute service which would be sufficient for the traffic needs of that route.
(b) Presumably the operation to Sidcup would follow Footscray Road, Main Road, Sidcup High Street and Sidcup Hill to Sidcup Garage.
(c) Presumably the Farningham route would leave the other two services at the London end of the Sidcup-by-pass, although this is by no means certain.
(d) This operation was amended to Bishops Stortford – 30 – London – 30 – Guildford to avoid competing with the Skylark Hertford – Guildford operation.
(e) Subsequently amended to Royston – 60 – } London – 30 – Chertsey.
                                 Hertford – 60 –

APPENDIX D

ORIGINAL ALLOCATION OF GREEN LINE ROUTE LETTERS, FEBRUARY 1931

Route Letter	Route and Frequency (in minutes)
A	Dartford – 30 – London – 30 – Virginia Water – 60 – Ascot – 60 – Sunningdale.
B	Charing Cross (Embankment) – 12/15 – Brentwood.
C	Poland Street Coach Station – 30 – Chertsey.
D	Poland Street Coach Station – 30 – Dorking.
E	Bushey – 30 – London – 30 – Redhill – 60 – Crawley.
F	Poland Street – 30 – Hertford (every 20 minutes weekday peak hours).
G	Poland Street Coach Station – 30 – Guildford.
H	Harpenden – 30 – London – 30 – Great Bookham.
I	Poland Street Coach Station – 60 – Farningham.
J	Poland Street – 30 – Chelsham – 120 – Edenbridge.
K	Hemel Hempstead – 60 – London – 60 – Caterham Station.
L	Poland Street Coach Station – 60 – Tunbridge Wells.
M	Poland Street Coach Station – 30 – Maidenhead.
N	Poland Street Coach Station – 30 – Windsor (via Staines).
O	Charing Cross (Embankment) – 30 – Bishops Stortford.
P	Poland Street Coach Station – 30 Rickmansworth.
Q	Poland Street Coach Station – 30 – Uxbridge.
R	Hitchin – 30 – London – 30 – Reigate.
S	Poland Street Coach Station – 30 – Sunbury Common.
T	Aylesbury – 60 – London – 60 – Godstone Green (later curtailed at Tring).
U	Poland Street Coach Station – 60 – East Grinstead.
V	Golders Green Station – 30 – Watford.
W	Charing Cross (Embankment) – 30 – Watford.
X	Poland Street Coach Station – 60 – Sevenoaks via Westerham.
Y	Poland Street Coach Station – 30 – West Byfleet.
Z	Charing Cross (Embankment) – Windsor (via Slough)*

*This service consisted of a 30-minute service on Mondays–Fridays, evenly spaced to give a 15-minute joint service with Route M from Slough to Chiswick (Young's Corner). On Saturdays and Sundays, four coaches per hour at uneven timings on Route Z from Windsor gave a ten-minute joint service from Slough to London with Route M.

LATER ALLOCATIONS OF ROUTE LETTERS.

AF	Oxford Circus – 60 – Hertford Heath (Ex-Skylark route)	(27 April 1932)
AK	Oxford Circus – 90 – Hemel Hempstead (Ex-W. Herts route)	(1 July 1933)
AO	Bishopsgate – 30 – Ongar (Ex-Associated Coaches route)	(27 April 1932)
AQ	Oxford Circus – 60 – High Wycombe (Ex-Skylark route)	(27 April 1932)
AR	King's Cross – 60 – Baldock (Ex-Queen Line route)	(26 April 1933)
AT	Marble Arch – 8 journeys – Aylesbury (Ex-Red Rover route)	(29 November 1932)
AU	Paddington – 60 – East Grinstead (ex-Blue Belle)	(20 July 1932)
AW	Oxford Circus – 15/30 – Watford (Ex Bucks Express route)	(27 April 1932)
BG	Oxford Circus – 60 – Guildford (Ex Skylark route)	(27 April 1932)
BH	Marylebone Station – journeys – Whipsnade (Limited Stop)	(24 March 1932)
BR	Portman Square – journeys – Brookmans Park (Ex-Lewis)	(1 August 1933)
CF	Oxford Circus – 60 – Hertford (Ex-Regent route)	(27 April 1932)

THE SECOND ALLOCATION OF ROUTE LETTERS 4 OCTOBER 1933

Route Letter	Route and Frequency (in minutes)
A	Gravesend – 60 – Victoria – Ascot.
AA	Gravesend – 60 – Victoria – Sunningdale.
B	Wrotham – 60 – Victoria – Rickmansworth.
C	Tunbridge Wells – 60 – Victoria – Chertsey.
AC	Tunbridge Wells – 60 (Sats/Suns only) – Sevenoaks – 60 – Victoria – 60 – Woking via Weybridge and West Byfleet.
D	Sevenoaks – 60 – Westerham Hill – 30 – Victoria – 30 – Sunbury Common.
E	Edenbridge – 120 – Chelsham – 60 – Victoria – 60 – Tring.
F	Tatsfield – 120 – Chelsham – 60 – Victoria – 60 – Hemel Hempstead, via Stanmore.
AF	London (Portman Square) – 90 – Hemel Hempstead via Watford-by-Pass.
G	Caterham – 60 – London (Horse Guards Avenue).
H	East Grinstead – 60 – Victoria – 60 – Harpenden.
AH	East Grinstead – 60 – Victoria – 60 – Dunstable.
I	Crawley – 60 – Redhill – 30 – Oxford Circus – 30 – Watford.
J	Reigate – 30 – Oxford Circus – 30 – Watford – 30.
K	Dorking – 30 – Victoria – 30 – Welwyn Garden City – 60 – Hitchin.
AK	London (Kings Cross) – 60 – Baldock via Hitchin and Letchworth.
L	Great Bookham – 30 – Victoria – 30 – Uxbridge.
M	Guildford – 30 – Oxford Circus – 30 – Enfield – 30 – Hertford.
AM	Guildford – 60 (Sats/Suns) – Esher – 60 – Oxford Circus – 60 – Great Cambridge Road – 60 – Hertford.
BM	West Byfleet Corner – 60 – Oxford Circus – 60 – Great Cambridge Road – 60 – Hertford.
N	Windsor – 30 – Staines – 30 – Portman Square – 30 – Epping.
Q	High Wycombe – 60 – Oxford Circus.
R	Amersham Garage – 60 – Oxford Circus.
AS	Aylesbury – approx. 60 – Tring – approx. 60 – Marble Arch via Watford-by-Pass.
T	Watford (Leavesden Road Garage) – 30 – Golders Green Station.
U	Whipsnade Zoo – Marylebone Station (Limited Stop. Irregular service).
V	Bishops Stortford – 30 – Liverpool Street (Eldon Street). Extended to Horse Guards Avenue Saturdays pm and Sundays.
W	Ongar – 30 – Liverpool Street (Eldon Street).
Y	Brentwood – 10/20 – Romford – 5/10 – Aldgate. Extended to Horse Guards Avenue every ten minutes on Saturdays pm and Sundays.

LATER ADDITIONS TO ABOVE LIST

BH	Luton – 30/60 – London (Kings Cross) (Taken over 1 February 1934).
O	Windsor Hospital – 15 – London (Cockspur St.) (Taken over 20 December 1933).
P	Farnham Common – 30 – London (Cockspur St.) (Taken over 20 December 1933).
S	Aylesbury approx. 60 – Victoria (Coach Station) (Taken over 17 January 1934).
X	Gidea Park – 60 – Romford – 30 – Aldgate (New route 25 October 1933). Extended to Horse Guards Avenue on Saturdays pm and Sundays.
AY	Upminster – 5/7 – Aldgate. (Taken over 10 January 1934).
Z	Tilbury – 60 (Weekdays only) – Grays – 20 – Aldgate (Taken over 23 December 1933).
AZ	Aveley – 45 – East Ham. (Taken over 1 December 1933).

APPENDIX F

THE THIRD ALLOCATION OF ROUTE LETTERS INTRODUCED 1935–1937

Route Letter	Route and Frequency (in minutes)
A1	Gravesend – 60 – Victoria – 60 – Ascot.
A2	Gravesend – 60 – Victoria – 60 – Sunningdale.
B	Wrotham – 60 – Victoria – 60 – Wendover – 120 – Aylesbury.
C1	Tunbridge Wells – 60 – Victoria – 60 – Chertsey.
C2	Tunbridge Wells – 60 – Victoria – 60 – Woking.
D	Sevenoaks – 60 – Westerham Hill – 30 – Victoria – 30 – Staines.
E	Chelsham – 60 – Victoria – 60 – Tring – 120 – Aylesbury.
F	Edenbridge – 120 – } Chelsham – 60 – Victoria – 60 – Hemel Hempstead. Tatsfield – 120 – }
G	Caterham – 60 – Horse Guards Avenue.
H1	East Grinstead (via Felbridge) – 60 – Victoria – 60 – Luton.
H2	East Grinstead (via Baldwins Hill) – 60 – Victoria – 60 – Dunstable.
BH	Kings Cross – 30 – Luton (re-lettered H3 29 July 1936).
I	Crawley – 60 – Redhill – 30 – Oxford Circus – 30 – Watford – 60 – Abbots Langley.
J	Reigate – 30 – Oxford Circus – 30 – Watford.
K1	Dorking – 60 – Leatherhead – 30 – Victoria – 30 – Valley Road Corner – 60 – Welwyn Garden City or 60 – Baldock.
K2	Horsham – 120 (60 Sat/Sun) – Dorking – 60 – Victoria – 60 – Welwyn Garden City – 60 (Sat/Sun) – Hitchin.
L	Great Bookham – 30 – Victoria – 30 – Uxbridge.
M1	Guildford – 30 – Oxford Circus – 30 – Hertford via Enfield.
M2	Byfleet – 60 – Oxford Circus – 60 – Hertford via Great Cambridge Road and Hertford Heath.
M3	Guildford – 60 (Sat/Sun) – Esher – 60 – Oxford Circus – 60 – Hertford via Gt. Cambridge Road and Ware.
N	Windsor (via Staines) – 30 – Portman Square – 30 – Epping – 60 (Sat/Suns) – Bishops Stortford.
O	Windsor (via Slough) – 15/20 – Trafalgar Square.
P	Farnham Common – 60 (30 Sat/Sun) – Trafalgar Square.
Q	High Wycombe – 60 – Oxford Circus.
R	Chesham – 60 – Oxford Circus.
T1	Watford – 60 – Golders Green via Watford-by-Pass.
T2	Watford – 60 – Golders Green via Elstree Village.
U	Whipsnade Zoo – Marylebone – Limited stop – Irregular service.
V	Bishops Stortford – 30 – Liverpool Street – 30 (Sat/Sun) – Horse Guards Avenue.
W	Ongar – 30 – Liverpool Street.
X	Gidea Park – 15 – Aldgate – 15 (Sat/Sun) – Horse Guards Avenue.
Y1	Brentwood – 7½/15 – Romford – 5/15 – Aldgate – 15 (Sat/Sun) – Horse Guards Avenue.
Y2	Corbets Tey or Hornchurch Station – 12/15 – Aldgate.
Z1	Tilbury – 60 – Grays – 20 – Aldgate via Purfleet.
Z2	Grays – 60 – Aldgate via Aveley.

APPENDIX G

WARTIME ALLOCATION OF ROUTE NUMBERS DECEMBER 1940

Route number	Former Letter	Date of Operation	Route and Frequency (in minutes)	Notes (see below)
2	A	4.12.40	Gravesend – 30 – Victoria	
3	B	4.12.40	Wrotham – 60 – Victoria	
5	C	4.12.40	Tunbridge Wells – 30 – Victoria	
8	H	4.12.40	East Grinstead – 30 – Victoria	(a)
9	I	4.12.40	Crawley – 60 – Redhill – 30 – Oxford Circus	
10	J	4.12.40	Reigate – 30 – Oxford Circus	
14	K1	18.12.40	Dorking – 30 – Epsom – 30 – Victoria	(b)
15	K3	18.12.40	Dorking – 30 – Kingston – 30 – Victoria	
18	M1	4.12.40	Guildford – 30 – Oxford Circus	(c)
20	C	4.12.40	Chertsey – 30 – Victoria	(d)
21	D	18.12.40	Staines – 30 – Kingston – 30 – Victoria	
23	A1	4.12.40	Ascot – 60 – Victoria	
23A	A2	4.12.40	Sunningdale – Victoria (hourly)	
26	G	18.12.40	Windsor – 20 – Victoria	(e)
26A	P	18.12.40	Farnham Common – 60 – Victoria	(e)
33	Q	4.12.40	High Wycombe – 30 – Oxford Circus	(c)
34	R	4.12.40	Chesham – 60 – Amersham – 30 – Oxford Circus	(c)
35	B	4.12.40	Aylesbury – 60 – Amersham – 60 – Victoria	
40	E	4.12.40	Aylesbury – 30 – Tring – 30 – Victoria	
40A	F	4.12.40	Hemel Hempstead – 30 – Victoria	
45	H1	4.12.40	Luton – 30 – Radlett – 30 – Victoria	
46	H3	4.12.40	Luton – 30 – Barnet – 30 – Victoria	(f)
47	K1	18.12.40	Hitchin – 60 – Victoria	
47A	K2	18.12.40	Welwyn Garden City – 60 – Victoria	
49	M1	4.12.40	Hertford – 20 – Oxford Circus	
52	N	4.12.40	Epping – 30 – Oxford Circus	(g)
53	V	4.12.40	Bishops Stortford – 30 – Aldgate	(h)
54	X	18.12.40	Romford – 20/30 – Eastern Avenue – 20/30 – Aldgate	
55	Y1	4.12.40	Brentwood – 30 (Sats pm 20: Sundays 15) – Romford – 6/10 – Aldgate	
58	Y2	18.12.40	Corbets Tey – 30 – Hornchurch – 10/15 – Aldgate	
59	Z1	4.12.40	Grays – 20/30 – Purfleet – 20/30 – Aldgate	
59A	Z2	4.12.40	Grays – 20/30 – Aveley – 20/30 – Aldgate	

Notes:

(a) Re-routed between Kennington Oval and Victoria via Harleyford Road and Vauxhall Bridge instead of Kennington Road, Lambeth Bridge and Millbank.

(b) Re-routed at Stockwell via South Lambeth Road and Vauxhall Bridge instead of Clapham Road, Kennington Road, Lambeth Bridge and Millbank.

(c) Inward route via Bayswater Road and Oxford Street. Outward via Portland Place, Marylebone Road and Sussex Gardens.

(d) Re-routed via Kingston Bridge, Hampton Court Road, Hampton Court Bridge and Bridge Road instead of the pre-war route via Portsmouth Road, Thames Ditton, Embercourt Road, Imber Lane and Esher Road.

(e) Ran via Slough and diverted at Hyde Park Corner to Victoria instead of running via Piccadilly and Trafalgar Square to the pre-war terminal at Horse Guards Avenue.

(f) Diverted at North Finchley (Tally Ho Corner) to run via Golders Green, Finchley Road, Baker Street and Park Lane to Victoria instead of running via East Finchley and Highgate to its pre-war terminus at Kings Cross Coach Station.

(g) Diverted at Great Portland Street Station to Oxford Circus instead of running to Portman Square as was the practice with former Route N.

(h) Diverted at Mile End Gate to run to Aldgate (Minories Bus Station) instead of using the pre-war terminal at Liverpool Street.

POST WAR ALLOCATION OF ROUTE NUMBERS

Route 700:
21 May 1977 — New Daily Express Route between London (Victoria) and Windsor (Bus Station). Via M4 Motorway, stopping only at Windsor Castle. Runs during Summer Season only.

Route 701:
22 June 1946 — Gravesend – Dartford – Welling – Victoria – Chiswick – Hounslow – Staines – Virginia Water – Ascot (Hourly).

31 October 1965 — On Mondays–Fridays, service divided in London as follows: Ascot – Victoria (Hourly); Hammersmith – Gravesend (30 minutes).

18 May 1968 — Through service on Mondays–Fridays resumed hourly from Gravesend to Ascot. Service increased to half-hourly during Monday–Friday peak hours between Gravesend and Hammersmith.

23 November 1968 — Route converted from crew to one-man operation.

3 October 1975 — Last day of operation. No replacing service.

20 May 1978 — *New Daily Route:* London (Victoria) – Windsor (via Slough). Runs non-stop between Hammersmith and Heathrow Airport Central via the M4 motorway. Hourly service. Extended to Windsor Safari Park daily during summer season.

Route 702:
19 June 1946 — Gravesend – Dartford – Welling – Victoria – Chiswick – Hounslow – Staines – Virginia Water – Sunningdale (Hourly).

31 October 1965 — On Mondays–Fridays an hourly service works between London (Victoria) and Sunningdale only. On Saturdays and Sundays runs hourly Sunningdale – Gravesend.

18 May 1968 — Monday–Friday service consists of two peak hour journeys from Victoria – Sunningdale. Runs on Saturdays and Sundays from Sunningdale – Gravesend, but no early morning or late evening journeys operated.

20 February 1971 — Saturday and Sunday service withdrawn.

17 June 1972 — Monday–Friday service reduced to one coach in each direction in peak hours.

6 July 1973 — Last day of operation. No replacing service.

2 April 1978 — *New Daily Route:* Bishops Stortford – Walthamstow Central Station via Harlow Bus Station and Epping. Hourly.

Route 703:
3 April 1946 — Wrotham – Sidcup – Lewisham – Victoria – Harlesden – Harrow – Rickmansworth – Chorleywood – Amersham (Hourly).

3 November 1964 — Last day of operation. Replaced between Wrotham and Victoria by extension of Route 717.

31 May 1975 — *New Daily Route:* Dorking – Leatherhead – Epsom – Tooting – Clapham – Victoria – Marble Arch – Baker Street (Hourly).

1 October 1976 — Last day of operation. No replacing service.

2 April 1977 — *New Monday–Saturday Route:* Bishops Stortford – Waltham Cross via Harlow and Waltham Abbey. Hourly. No evening service.

20 August 1977 — Service introduced on weekday evenings and Sundays from midday due to withdrawal of LT bus route 217A.

20 May 1978 — Route withdrawn. Replaced by new Green Line Route 712 and Country Bus Route 329.

Route 704:
6 March 1946 — Tunbridge Wells – Sevenoaks – Bromley – Victoria – Chiswick – Great West Road – Heathrow Airport North – Slough – Windsor. Daily. Every half-hour.

16 April 1965 — Duplicate vehicles between London and Windsor to run non-stop between Hammersmith and Langley via M4 motorway.

12 June 1966 — RCL-type double-deck Routemasters introduced on this route.

2 December 1967	Tunbridge Wells Garage closed and operations transferred to Dunton Green Garage. Alternate coaches to run between Windsor and Sevenoaks only, except during Monday–Friday peak hours and Saturday shopping hours. Service now: Windsor – 20 minutes (joint with 705) – Bromley – Alternately every 20/40 minutes – Sevenoaks – 60 (20/40 MF peaks and Sats until evenings) – Tunbridge Wells.
19 April 1969	Emergency timetable brought into operation due to staff shortage at Windsor Garage. Windsor – Sevenoaks journeys withdrawn when due to be worked by Windsor-based crews, leaving an irregular service between Windsor and Bromley.
4 October 1969	Revised service. Windsor and Tunbridge Wells hourly daily. Joint half-hourly service between Windsor and Bromley with Route 705.
4 July 1971	Summer Sundays only. Certain journeys extended to Windsor Safari Park. Hourly service until midday; half-hourly service in afternoons jointly with Route 705.
25 March 1972	Route converted to one-man operation with RP-type coaches.
21 May 1977	Re-routed to make a double-run to and from Heathrow Airport Central Bus Station. Certain Sunday journeys diverted at Knockholt Station via Halstead and Knockholt Pound. Runs on summer Sundays to Windsor Safari Park.
30 September 1977	Last day of operation of Safari Park journeys.
20 May 1978	New timetable. Hourly service operates on Mondays–Saturdays. Two-hourly service on Sundays. Hourly between Windsor and Bromley with Route 705. Two journeys in each direction diverted via Halstead and Knockholt Pound on Sundays.

Route 705:

29 May 1946	Sevenoaks – Westerham – Bromley – Victoria – Chiswick – Great West Road – Heathrow Airport North – Windsor. Daily. Every half-hour.
3 October 1954	Due to staff shortage at Windsor Garage, this route is temporarily withdrawn between Windsor and Victoria. Half hourly service is maintained between Victoria and Sevenoaks.
20 October 1954	Normal operations resumed between Windsor and Victoria.
15 October 1958	Diverted between Bromley South and Keston Mark via Westmoreland Road, Hayes Lane, Baston Road and Croydon Road in order to serve Hayes Village.
28 August 1963	Express service introduced between London (Victoria) and Windsor Bus Station.
2 December 1967	Service reduced from half-hourly to hourly. Express single-deck service withdrawn. Normal stopping service resumed with Routemaster double-deck coaches.
4 July 1971	Summer Sundays only. Certain journeys extended to Windsor Safari Park, jointly with Route 704.
25 March 1972	Route converted to one-man operation with RP-type coaches.
21 May 1977	Re-routed to serve Heathrow Airport Central Bus Station. Some journeys on Wednesdays, Thursday, Saturdays and Sundays to double-run to Chartwell House. Journeys extended to Windsor Safari Park on summer Sundays.
30 September 1977	Last Day of operation to Windsor Safari Park.
20 May 1978	Weekday service withdrawn, except for one late journey from Tunbridge Wells to Westerham. Sundays: Two-hourly service from Windsor – Tunbridge Wells via Biggin Hill and Westerham. Supplemented by two-hourly short workings between Bromley North Station and Sevenoaks.

Route 706:

26 June 1946	Westerham – Chelsham – Croydon – Victoria – Edgware – Watford – Boxmoor – Berkhamsted – Tring – Aylesbury. Daily service hourly.
19 May 1948	Route diverted via Tatsfield in both directions.
10 July 1966	Certain journeys in the Summer Season extended from Westerham via Hosey Common to Chartwell House on Wednesdays, Thursdays, Saturdays and Sundays.
15 June 1968	Sunday service now half-hourly between Aylesbury and Chelsham due to the withdrawal of Route 707 on that day.

15 February 1969	Route 707 now withdrawn. Route 706 converted to one-man operation. Service between Aylesbury and Chelsham now half-hourly, extended hourly in Monday–Friday peak hours to Westerham. Chartwell journeys as in previous Summer Seasons.
1 April 1972	Service now hourly between Aylesbury and Chelsham. Extra journeys operated in Monday–Friday peaks from Tring to Victoria and Victoria to Westerham. Chartwell journey as in previous summers.
7 July 1973	Peak hour journeys to Westerham reduced to one up to London (mornings) and one down (evenings).
31 May 1975	Except for Summer Season journeys to Chartwell, all journeys south of Chelsham withdrawn.
1 April 1977	Last day of operation. See Route 708.

Route 707:

26 June 1946	Oxted – Chelsham – Croydon – Victoria – Edgware – Watford – Boxmoor – Berkhamsted – Tring – Aylesbury. Daily service hourly.
3 October 1965	Sundays service extended from Oxted via Hurst Green to Holland to replace Bus Route 464 withdrawn on that day.
15 June 1968	Route withdrawn on Sundays. Increased service on 706.
14 February 1969	Last day of operation. See Route 706.
29 January 1977	*New Daily Route:* Victoria – Golders Green – North Finchley – Barnet – St. Albans – Harpenden – Luton – Luton Airport. Daily service, joint with 717.

Route 708:

1 May 1946	East Grinstead – Felbridge – Lingfield – Godstone – Caterham – Kenley – Croydon – Victoria – Edgware – Watford – Hemel Hempstead (Daily. Half-hourly).
2 October 1946	Extra service introduced between Victoria and Watford (Pond Cross Roads) Daily.
April 1947	Watford – London extra service withdrawn (Actual date of withdrawal not known).
19 May 1948	Two journeys morning and evening diverted between Blindley Heath and Newchapel via Eastbourne Road (A22).
2 March 1949	Above journeys return to normal route via Lingfield.
30 December 1967	Converted from single-deck crew operation to double deck Routemasters. Service now hourly daily.
15 February 1969	Converted back to single-deck one-man operation. Service still hourly daily.
2 April 1977	Extended from Hemel Hempstead to Aylesbury to replace withdrawn Route 706. Extra journeys worked in Monday–Friday peak hours from Victoria to Hemel Hempstead giving a half-hourly service over this section. One of these peak hour journeys is extended to Tring.
19 November 1977	Certain journeys in both directions on Mondays to Saturdays diverted via Brent Cross Shopping Centre.
1 April 1978	Withdrawn between East Grinstead and Victoria (see Route 719).

Route 709:

6 March 1946	Caterham Station – Old Coulsdon – Coulsdon – Croydon – Streatham – Brixton – Westminster – London (Baker Street). Hourly service daily.
2 October 1946	Garage journeys between Caterham Station and Godstone Garage which were formerly worked 'out of service' now to be worked in service.
12 November 1947	Extended from Baker Street to Chesham (Nashleigh Arms) daily. Hourly service to replace Route 725.
4 November 1964	Diverted between Shepherds Bush and Uxbridge via Western Avenue and to run as an Express Service from Oxford Circus to Chesham. On Sundays to run from Godstone to London (Baker Street) only.
1 November 1965	Withdrawn between Chesham and London (Baker Street). Now runs hourly between Baker Street and Godstone daily.

31 December 1966	Service reduced to two 'up' journeys on Monday–Friday morning peaks plus two 'down' journeys in evening peaks, plus two round trips on Sundays for hospital traffic to St. Lawrence's Hospital, Caterham. Monday–Friday journeys down to Godstone after morning peak, and up to London before evening peak operated 'out of service'.
25 February 1967	Journeys formerly worked 'out of service' commence to operate in service.
23 November 1968	Monday–Friday peak hours. One additional journey in each direction morning and evening added due to withdrawal of Route 710.
15 May 1975	Monday–Friday peak journeys reduced to two journeys in each direction.

Route 710:

6 March 1946	Crawley – Redhill – Coulsdon – Croydon – Streatham – Brixton – Westminster – Baker Street. Daily. Hourly.
12 November 1947	Extended from London (Baker Street) to Amersham Garage daily. Hourly service to replace Route 725.
3 October 1954	Route temporarily withdrawn due to staff shortage at Amersham Garage.
27 October 1954	Normal service resumed between Amersham and Crawley.
2 August 1957	Route diverted at Horley along new A23 road passing Gatwick Airport. Povey Cross and Lowfield Heath areas no longer served either by coach or bus.
4 November 1964	Route extended to Chesham on Sundays, replacing Route 709. Withdrawn in London on that day.
1 November 1965	Route extended to Chesham daily. Additional journeys during Monday–Friday peak hours to cover withdrawal of Route 709.
23 November 1968	Route converted to one-man operation and curtailed to operate Amersham Garage – London (Baker Street) only.
20 February 1971	Withdrawn between Uxbridge Station and Baker Street.
13 October 1972	Last day of operation. No replacing service.
2 April 1977	*New Route:* Guildford – Oxford Circus via Kingston-by-Pass. Monday–Friday peak hours only. Semi-Express service. Runs express Guildford – Cobham and Hammersmith – Oxford Circus.

Route 711:

3 April 1946	Reigate – Kingswood – Sutton – Tooting – Oxford Circus – London (Baker Street). Daily service every half-hour.
12 November 1947	Extended from London (Baker Street) to High Wycombe to replace Route 724. Daily. Half-hourly service.
31 December 1966	Diverted at Belmont via Downs Road, Sutton Lane, Banstead High Street and Garratts Lane to Brighton Road.
23 November 1968	Route converted to one-man operation. Hourly service High Wycombe – Reigate (Saturday shopping hours half-hourly). During Monday–Friday peak hours extra hourly service between Reigate and Baker Street and High Wycombe and Baker Street. Diverted at Gerrards Cross to make a double-run to serve the southern end of the village.
17 June 1972	Extra peak hour journeys between Reigate and Baker Street reduced from three journeys to one in each direction.
7 July 1973	Remaining peak hour journey from Reigate withdrawn. One peak hour journey from High Wycombe withdrawn, leaving two in operation. Saturday service now hourly.
29 November 1975	Peak hour journeys from High Wycombe to Baker Street reduced to one journey in each direction.
8 August 1977	Emergency timetable introduced, due to staff shortage at High Wycombe Garage. Service now: Reigate – hourly – Baker Street – Two-hourly – High Wycombe on weekdays. Sundays. Two-hourly Reigate to High Wycombe.
1 October 1977	Route 711 withdrawn. For High-Wycombe to London section see Route 790. Route 711 replaced between Sutton and Reigate on weekdays by Route 422 bus.

Route 712:

29 May 1946	Dorking – Epsom – Tooting – Victoria – Golders Green – Mill Hill – Radlett – Shenley – St. Albans – Luton. Daily service hourly.
11 July 1956	Intermediate route diversion between Borehamwood and Radlett via Shenley Road, Eldon Avenue, Brook Road, Leeming Road, Aycliffe Road and Theobald Street in order to serve northern section of Borehamwood L.C.C. Estate.
23 November 1960	Intermediate route diversion between Radlett and St. Albans via Colney Street, Park Street, North Orbital Road, Driftwood Avenue, Watford Road (A412), St. Stephen's Hill and Holywell Hill to Chequer St.
22 May 1963	Diverted at Park Street via Park Street Lane and Tippendell Lane to Watford Road in lieu of North Orbital Road and Driftwood Avenue. Certain journeys in Summer Season diverted at St. Albans to Whipsnade Zoo as Route 712A.
4 November 1964	Certain journeys diverted at St. Albans via Redbourn and Markyate to Dunstable as Route 712B.
14 April 1965	All 712A and 712B journeys now renumbered to 712. This route number now indicates that coaches showing it operate via Park Street and St. Stephens whether running to Luton, Dunstable or Whipsnade Zoo.
2 June 1965	Dunstable and Whipsnade journeys now operate from St. Albans via Harpenden Road and Batchwood Drive in lieu of Catherine Street, Folly Lane and Verulam Road.
15 February 1969	Route converted to one-man operation.
20 February 1971	With the exception of the summer extension to Whipsnade Zoo, this route is withdrawn north of St. Albans.
31 May 1975	Withdrawn between Dorking and Victoria (see Route 703). Now operates Victoria and St. Albans on weekdays only.
28 January 1977	Route withdrawn. See new Routes 707/717.
20 May 1978	*New Route:* Bishops Stortford – Harlow Bus Station – Epping – Theydon Bois – Abridge – Chigwell Row – Collier Row – Romford. Hourly service weekdays. Sundays: Harlow – Romford. Two hourly service.

Route 713:

29 May 1946	Dorking – Epsom – Tooting – Victoria – Golders Green – Mill Hill – Radlett – Shenley – St. Albans – Dunstable. Daily. Hourly service.
11 July 1956	Intermediate diversion at Borehamwood to serve the Northern part of the Borehamwood L.C.C. Estate (see 712).
4 November 1964	Certain Monday–Friday peak hour journeys diverted via Harpenden to Luton as Route 713A.
14 April 1965	Luton journeys renumbered 713. This number now indicates that all coaches bearing it operate via Shenley and London Colney irrespective of final destination.
2 June 1965	All Dunstable and Whipsnade Zoo journeys now run from St. Albans via Harpenden Road and Batchwood Drive to Redbourn Road in lieu of Catherine Street, Folly Lane and Verulam Road to Redbourn Road.
15 February 1969	Route converted to one-man operation.
20 February 1971	Luton journeys withdrawn. Operates between St. Albans and Dunstable during Monday–Friday peak hours and on Sundays only.
31 May 1975	Route between St. Albans and Dunstable withdrawn without replacement. Also withdrawn between Victoria and Dorking (See Route 703).
28 January 1977	Route withdrawn. See New Routes 707/717.

Route 714:

1 May 1946	Dorking – Leatherhead – Kingston – Richmond – Barnes – Hammersmith – Kensington – London (Baker Street). Daily. Half-hourly, except during late evening on weekdays, when service is hourly.
30 September 1951	Extended from Baker Street via Euston Road, Kings Cross, Highgate, Barnet and St. Albans to Luton, replacing withdrawn route 727. Half-hourly service daily.

1 November 1965	Due to heavy traffic congestion in Central London, now works in two sections on Mondays to Fridays: Luton – Baker Street; Baker Street – Dorking.
31 December 1966	Through operation recommences on weekdays. Diverted daily at Marble Arch via Oxford Street, Oxford Circus and Portland Place.
23 November 1968	Converted to one-man operation.
29 January 1977	Route withdrawn Luton and Hyde Park Corner (see New Route 707) and diverted to terminate at Victoria.

Route 715:

6 February 1946	Guildford – Esher – Tolworth – Roehampton – Barnes – Shepherds Bush – Oxford Circus – Finsbury Park – Palmers Green – Enfield – Waltham Cross – Cheshunt – Hoddesdon – Ware – Hertford. Daily, half-hourly until May 1946, then every twenty minutes.
29 August 1962	Route converted from single-deck to double-deck operation with RMC-type Routemasters. Frequency now half-hourly.
March 1969	Sunday service reduced to hourly.
15 May 1971	Alternate Saturday journeys diverted via Kingston. (See Route 715A).
29 April 1972	Route converted to single-deck one-man operation. Frequency now hourly daily, with extra hourly service on weekdays from Oxford Circus to Hertford.
2 April 1977	Route diverted to double-run to and from Cobham Village Centre, also diverted via Kingston daily. Revised timetable. Frequency now: Guildford – 30 (weekdays) 60 Sundays – Kingston – 60 (30 Saturdays) – Oxford Circus – 30 (Weekdays), 60 Sundays – Hertford.

Route 715A:

11 July 1956	Hertford – Hertford Heath – Hoddesdon – Waltham Cross – Edmonton – Tottenham – Finsbury Park – Oxford Circus – Marble Arch. Hourly service Daily.
29 August 1962	Route converted to double-deck operation with Routemaster coaches.
12 June 1966	Converted to single-deck operation.
14 February 1969	Last day of operation. No replacement service.
15 May 1971	New Route. Saturdays only. Guildford – Hertford via Kingston. Hourly service (Two Hourly evenings).
2 April 1977	To run daily and renumbered to 715.

Route 716:

27 February 1946	Chertsey – Weybridge – Kingston – Kensington – Marble Arch – Golders Green – Barnet – Hatfield – Welwyn – Stevenage – Hitchin. Daily service, hourly.
25 August 1948	Chertsey terminus altered from Bell Corner to Chertsey Bridge.
23 November 1960	Intermediate diversion at Stanborough (The Bull) via Stanborough Lane, Broadwater Road, Holwell Road, Pear Tree Lane, Bridge Road East, Welwyn Garden City Town Centre, Knightsfield and Digswell to original line of route at Welwyn Village.
2 January 1963	Route converted from single-deck to double-deck Routemaster coaches (RMC-type).
11 March 1972	Route converted to single-deck one-man operation.
14 October 1972	Route diverted in Stevenage to serve the New Lister Hospital.
15 May 1976	Existing route withdrawn. Route 716A extended from Welwyn Garden City to Hitchin and renumbered 716.
14 January 1978	Route withdrawn between Hitchin and Marble Arch and diverted to work Oxford Circus to Woking hourly. Hitchin section now worked by new routes 722/732.

Route 716A:

5 October 1955	Former Route 717 (Woking-Welwyn Garden City) withdrawn between Valley Road Corner and Welwyn Garden City and extended via Ayot Green, Welwyn and Knebworth to Stevenage. Hourly service daily.
2 February 1963	Route converted from single-deck to double-deck Routemaster coaches (RMC type).

2 December 1967	Re-routed at Little Heath Church to operate via Brookmans Park, Welham Green, South Hatfield, Mill Green, Howlands, and Welwyn Garden City Centre to Valley Road Corner to replace withdrawn route 717.
11 March 1972	Converted to single-deck one-man operation.
15 May 1976	Extended to Hitchin and renumbered 716.

Route 717:

1 May 1946	Woking – Woodham – Addlestone – Weybridge – Kingston – Kensington – Marble Arch – Golders Green – Barnet – Hatfield – Welwyn Garden City Station. Daily. Hourly.
3 December 1952	Diverted between Woking and Woodham Lane via Sheerwater L.C.C. Estate.
5 October 1955	Withdrawn between Welwyn Garden City Station and Valley Road Corner and diverted to Stevenage (renumbered 716A). New Route 717 hourly from Victoria to Welwyn Garden City Station via Golders Green, Barnet, Potters Bar, Little Heath, Brookmans Park, Welham Green, Dixons Hill Road (east), Gt. North Road, Hatfield and Stanborough.
18 April 1956	Diverted at Welham Green via Dixons Hill Road (west), Barnet-by-Pass, Bishops Rise and Cavendish Way to serve the new South Hatfield area.
12 June 1957	Extended in Welwyn Garden City to Cole Green Lane.
23 November 1960	Route diverted at Hatfield via Mill Green, Howlands, Hollybush Lane, Cole Green Lane, Ludwick Way and Pear Tree Lane to Welwyn Garden City Station.
22 May 1963	Diverted at junction of Hollybush Lane and Howlands via Howlands, Great Ganett and Heronswood Road to serve the new Queen Elizabeth Hospital at Welwyn Garden City.
4 November 1964	Extended from London (Victoria) to Wrotham to replace withdrawn Route 703. Single-deck coaches replaced by double-deck Routemasters (RMC type).
2 December 1967	Route withdrawn between Welwyn Garden City and London (Baker Street) See Route 716A.
30 December 1967	Converted from double-deck crew operation to single-deck one-man operation.
23 November 1968	Route withdrawn and replaced with extension of Route 719.
29 January 1977	*New Route:* London (Victoria) – Luton Airport via Golders Green – Brent Cross Shopping Centre – Mill Hill – Borehamwood – Shenley – St. Albans – Harpenden. Weekday service: Two hourly. Sundays: One journey each way to serve Shenley Hospital. Omits Brent Cross en route.

Route 718:

3 April 1946	Windsor – Staines – Kingston – Victoria – Marble Arch – Baker Street – Finsbury Park – Tottenham – Walthamstow – South Woodford – Woodford Green – Loughton – Epping. Daily service every half-hour.
10 May 1950	Diverted at Walthamstow via Chingford Mount and Chingford to Woodford Green.
11 July 1956	Extended from Epping to Harlow New Town (Bus Station) via Potter Street, Southern Way and Tillwicks Road. Daily service every half-hour.
24 October 1962	Route converted to double-deck Routemaster coaches.
1 November 1965	Timetable change for winter: Monday–Friday: Harlow – 60 (30 peaks) – Baker Street – 60 – Victoria – 60 (30 peaks) – Windsor. Saturdays, every 30 minutes, except early morning and late evening. Sundays: 60 minutes with two additional journeys Harlow – Baker Street in the evenings.
15 May 1966	Half-hourly service throughout the route daily for the Summer Season.
2 October 1966	Winter Service. Hourly service throughout on Mondays–Fridays and Sundays. Half-hourly on Saturdays. Peak hour service Mondays–Fridays as for 1 November 1965.
31 December 1966	Diverted between Marble Arch and Albany Street via Oxford Street, Oxford Circus and Portland Place. Peak hour 'shorts' from Harlow now terminate at Oxford Circus.
13 May 1967	Summer service: Monday–Friday: Harlow – 60 – Victoria – 30 – Windsor, plus three peak-hour 'short' workings Oxford Circus – Harlow. Saturdays and Sundays, Half-hourly service throughout the route.
7 October 1967	Revised service. Hourly frequency now provided throughout the route permanently.
8 June 1968	Intermediately diverted between Kingston Vale and Putney Heath (Green Man) via Roehampton Lane, Roehampton Village and Putney Heath (North Side).

5 February 1972	Route converted to single-deck one-man operation.
2 April 1977	Withdrawn between London (Victoria) and Harlow.

Route 719:

11 July 1956	Hemel Hempstead – Leverstock Green – Bedmond – Garston – Watford – Stanmore – Queensbury – Kingsbury – Neasden – Willesden – Kilburn – London (Victoria). Daily. Hourly.
29 May 1957	Frequency increased to half-hourly.
21 November 1962	Route converted from single-deck to double-deck Routemasters (RMC-type).
30 December 1967	Converted from double-deck to single-deck crew operation.
23 November 1968	Extended from Victoria to Wrotham to replace withdrawn Route 717. Hourly service introduced with Victoria – Garston section increased to half-hourly during Monday to Friday peak hours and Saturdays until early afternoon.
15 July 1972	Monday–Friday peak and Saturday extra journeys withdrawn.
1 April 1978	Route withdrawn between Victoria and Wrotham (see 729). Now runs to East Grinstead hourly, replacing Route 708.

Route 720:

6 February 1946	Bishops Stortford – Sawbridgeworth – Old Harlow – Potter Street – Epping – Loughton – Woodford – Wanstead – Leytonstone – Stratford – London (Aldgate). Daily. Half-hourly service.
24 October 1962	Route converted to double-deck Routemaster coaches.
22 May 1963	Certain journeys in both directions diverted at Old Harlow to double-run via First Avenue to Harlow New Town (Bus Station).
4 November 1964	Route converted to single-deck crew operation.
31 October 1965	Diverted between Potter Street and Old Harlow via Southern Way, Tillwicks Road, Second Avenue, Howard Way, Harlow Bus Station and First Avenue in place of withdrawn Route 720A.
23 November 1968	Route converted to single-deck one-man operation.
4 May 1974	Extended from Bishops Stortford to Stansted Airport.
2 April 1977	Route withdrawn. Partly replaced by new Routes 702/703.

Route 720A:

30 June 1954	Harlow New Town (The Stow) – Potter Street – Epping then as Route 720 to Aldgate. Daily. Hourly service.
3 October 1954	Route temporarily withdrawn due to staff shortage at Harlow Garage.
20 October 1954	Route resumes normal operation.
11 July 1956	Route diverted at Potter Street via Southern Way, Tillwicks Road, Second Avenue and Howard Way to Harlow Bus Station.
24 October 1962	Route converted to double-deck Routemaster coaches.
4 November 1964	Route converted to single-deck crew operation.
30 October 1965	Last day of operation. Replaced by diversion of 720.

Route 721:

6 March 1946	Brentwood – Romford – Ilford – Bow – London (Aldgate). The service provided at first was every twenty minutes from Brentwood, ten minutes from Romford, but was increased later. It has varied considerably throughout the years of operation and no further frequencies will be quoted.
28 July 1957	Extended on Sunday afternoons from Brentwood (Yorkshire Grey to Highwood Hospital).
15 October 1958	Extended daily to Brentwood (Highwood Hospital).
2 June 1965	Route converted from RT-type double-deck to Routemaster double-deck coaches (RCL-type).
1 January 1972	Converted to one-man operation with single-deck RP type coaches.
2 July 1977	Route withdrawn without replacement. Romford Garage closed.

Route 722:

3 April 1946	Corbets Tey – Upminster – Hornchurch – Rush Green – Becontree – Ilford – Stratford – London (Aldgate). *Frequency:* Corbets Tey – Half-hourly – Hornchurch – every 15 minutes – Aldgate. This frequency was increased later, and like 721, the frequencies have varied over the years.
8 January 1958	Route diverted at Rush Green via Oldchurch Road and South Street (Romford) to serve Oldchurch Hospital.
14 October 1959	Proposal to divert part of the service to North Romford (Chase Cross) as Route 722A. Proposal dropped due to opposition from local Central Bus crews.
4 July 1962	Hornchurch Station journeys now withdrawn.
18 November 1963	Route extended from Corbets Tey to Dartford via North Ockendon, Belhus Estate and Dartford Tunnel. Hourly service daily.
3 November 1964	Last day of operation between Corbets Tey and Dartford.
16 June 1965	RT-type double-deck coaches replaced by Routemasters (RCL-type).
31 October 1965	Route to operate during Monday–Friday peak hours only.
13 June 1966	Routemasters replaced by double-deck RT-types.
2 August 1968	Last day of operation. No replacement service.
14 January 1978	*New Route:* London (Victoria) – Golders Green – North Finchley – Barnet – Hatfield – Welwyn Garden City – Welwyn – Knebworth – Stevenage – Hitchin. Joint hourly service with 732 weekdays. Sundays hourly. Replacing Route 716 withdrawn in London.

Route 723:

6 March 1946	Tilbury – Grays – Purfleet – Aveley – Rainham – Dagenham – Barking – East Ham – London (Aldgate). Daily. Service every 15 minutes to Grays, hourly to Tilbury.
4 July 1951	Two journeys per hour daily diverted between Grays and Aveley via Hogg Lane, North Stifford, Ford Place and Stifford Road and renumbered 723A.
30 June 1954	Converted from single-deck to double-deck RT-type coaches, and diverted between Grays and Tilbury via Woodside Estate and Chadwell St. Mary. Service now: Aldgate – 30 – Grays – hourly – Tilbury.
4 November 1964	Route 723 re-routed between Grays and Aveley via same route as route 723A.
June 1965	Route converted from RT-type double-deck to RCL-type Routemaster double-deck coaches.
20 February 1971	Alternate journeys re-routed in Belhus Estate via Foyle Drive, Erriff Drive and Daiglen Drive and renumbered 723A.
1 January 1972	Converted to one-man single-deck operation with RC-type coaches and re-routed at Belhus via 723A route. Route 723A withdrawn.
5 May 1973	Route withdrawn between Grays and Tilbury. Timetable revised to half-hourly service with extra journeys between East Ham and Grays during Monday–Friday peak hours and Saturday shopping hours.

Route 723A:

4 July 1951	Two journeys per hour ex route 723 diverted between Aveley and Grays via Belhus Estate, North Stifford and Hogg Lane. One journey per hour extended to Tilbury via Dock Road and East Thurrock.
30 June 1954	Converted from single-deck to RT-type double-deck coaches and Tilbury journeys withdrawn.
5 October 1955	Route diverted at Barking via Movers Lane and Barking-by-Pass also at Wennington via Sandy Lane (B1335) and Mill Road to Aveley village.
4 November 1964	Extended to Tilbury Ferry via East Thurrock and Dock Road.
June 1965	Route converted from RT-type double-deck to Routemaster double-deck coaches (RCL-type).
31 December 1966	Route withdrawn.
20 February 1971	Alternate 723 journeys diverted in Belhus Estate and renumbered 723A.
1 January 1972	Route withdrawn and replaced by diversion of Route 723.

Route 723B:

30 June 1954	Tilbury Ferry – Dock Road – Grays – South Stifford – Stonehouse Corner – Aveley – Rainham – Dagenham – Barking – East Ham – Aldgate. Daily. Hourly service. Operated by double-deck RT-type vehicles.
4 November 1964	Withdrawn between Tilbury and Grays. See Route 723A.
June 1965	Route converted from RT-type double-deck to Routemaster coaches (RMC-type).
31 December 1966	Withdrawn between Aldgate and East Ham Town Hall and to operate during Monday–Friday peak hours and on Saturdays only.
4 October 1968	Last day of operation. No replacing service.

Route 724:

3 April 1946	High Wycombe – Beaconsfield – Gerrards X – Uxbridge – Southall – Ealing – Shepherds Bush – Oxford Circus. Daily service. Hourly until May, then every 30 minutes.
12 November 1947	Route withdrawn and replaced by extension of Route 711.
10 July 1967	*New Daily Orbital Route:* High Wycombe – Amersham – Rickmansworth – Watford – St. Albans – Hatfield – Welwyn Garden City – Hertford – Harlow – Romford. Hourly Express Service.
3 June 1972	Withdrawn between High Wycombe and Rickmansworth and diverted via Uxbridge and Heathrow Airport to Staines.
2 April 1977	Withdrawn between Romford Station and Romford Market Place and extended from Staines to Windsor via Runnymede and Datchet. Hourly service.
20 May 1978	Withdrawn between Romford and Harlow Bus Station. Replaced over this section by new route 712.

Route 725:

19 June 1946	Chesham – Amersham – The Chalfonts – Gerrards Cross – Uxbridge – Southall – Ealing – Shepherds Bush – Oxford Circus. Daily. Half-hourly from Oxford Circus to Amersham, hourly to Chesham.
12 November 1947	Withdrawn. Replaced by the extension of Routes 709/710.
1 July 1953	*New Orbital Route:* Windsor – Staines – Kingston – Sutton – Croydon – Beckenham – Bromley – Sidcup – Crayford – Dartford – Gravesend. Daily. Hourly service.
28 April 1954	Half-hourly service introduced between Windsor and Dartford (Market Street).
4 November 1964	Intermediate diversion to serve Ashford Town Centre.
12 February 1969	Route converted to one-man operation.
21 May 1977	New timetable. Hourly service introduced from Windsor to Dartford with some journeys (mainly during Monday–Fridays peak hours) to Gravesend. See also Route 726.
28 October 1978	Intermediately diverted at Croydon to serve East Croydon Station, also at Bexley to serve Bexleyheath Clock Tower and shopping area.

Route 726:

17 July 1946	London (Marylebone, Harewood Avenue) – Whipsnade Zoo. Limited Stop. Irregular Service. Summer only. Daily.
26 March 1948	London terminus now Baker Street Station (Allsop Place).
19 May 1954	Route extended to Romford Market Place.
19 May 1957	Sunday service extended to Harold Hill Estate.
11 September 1960	Last day of operation to Harold Hill on Sundays.
6 May 1964	Route diverted at Golders Green to run via Hendon Central, Mill Hill and M1 motorway to Friars Wash.
18 May 1968	Additional picking up point introduced at Oxford Circus.
6 September 1968	Last day of operation.
21 May 1977	*New Orbital Route:* Gravesend – Windsor via Route 725 to Ashford, thence via Heathrow Airport and M4 motorway. Daily, hourly service.
28 October 1978	Intermediately diverted via East Croydon Station.

Route 727:
29 May 1946	Luton – London (Kings Cross) via St. Albans and Barnet. Daily service. Every half-hour.
30 September 1951	Route withdrawn and replaced by extension of Route 714.
4 November 1964	*New Express Service:* Tring – London (Victoria) via Berkhamsted, Hemel Hempstead, M1 motorway, Golders Green, Oxford Circus, Charing Cross, Westminster. Daily. Hourly service.
30 October 1965	Last day of operation. No replacing service.
13 May 1967	*New Orbital Express Service. Daily. Hourly:* Crawley – Reigate – Epsom – Kingston – Heathrow Airport – Uxbridge – Watford – St. Albans – Luton Station.
20 March 1971	Route extended to Luton Airport.
21 May 1977	Half-hourly service Crawley – Heathrow for summer season.
30 September 1977	Crawley – Heathrow service reduced to hourly for the Winter months.
20 May 1978	Crawley – Heathrow Airport. Half-hourly service introduced permanently.

Route 729:
1 April 1978	Borough Green – Wrotham – Sidcup – Lewisham – Victoria. Monday–Friday peak hours only. One journey am and pm.

Route 732:
14 January 1978	London – Hitchin via Brent Cross Shopping Centre. Two-hourly service on weekdays during shopping hours.

Route 737:
7 May 1977	London (Victoria) – Whipsnade Zoo via M1 motorway. Express service Summer Season only.

Route 739:
1 April 1978	London (Victoria) – Brands Hatch Stadium. Special service operated for Motor Racing meetings. Number of journeys operated varies in accordance with the importance of the Race Meeting.

Route 790:
1 October 1977	London (Victoria) – High Wycombe – Amersham Garage. Daily service. Two hourly service Victoria – High Wycombe, four daily journeys extended to Amersham.

INDEX

A
Abbots Langley 25 26 73 91 95
Abridge 9 10 106
Acme Pullman Services Ltd 18 44 58 63 66 68
Addiscombe 125
Addlestone 44 91 95 119
Addlestone Garage 44 55 111
Adeyfield 95
A.E.C. Ltd. 6
A.E.C. Regal Coaches (T-type) 18 130 133 134
A.E.C. Regal Coaches (RF-type) 137
A.E.C. Reliance Coaches (R-type) 130
A.E.C. Reliance Coaches (RB & RS) 119 143
A.E.C. Reliance Coaches (RP-type) 114 115 141
A.E.C. Ricardo Engine (Q-type) 133
A.E.C. Swift 141
A.E.C. 4U2A Coaches (RC-type) 141
Agencies 156 158 179
Aldershot 30 31 43
Aldershot and District Traction Company Ltd 22 30 133
Alder Valley 113 116
Aldgate 24 29 30 33 36 55 67 70 71 79 86 87 93 95 98 106 109 137 171
Aldwych 18 20 21 31 32 41 66 171
Amalgamated Omnibus Services and Supplies Limited 23
Amersham 14 15 32 37 49 63 73 77 86 88 95 101 103 105 106 115 123 133
Amersham and District Omnibus and Haulage Company 32 37 63 65 73 133
Amersham Garage 16 87 93 103 111 123 143
Amersham-on-the-Hill 63
Annual Passenger Figures 93 95 96 101
Apsley 25
Arkley 10
Ascot 9 13 28 43 49 50 52 55 68 87 88 105 109 115 116 133
Ashford (Middx) 37 50 91 123
Associated Coaches (Ongar) Limited 29 56 171
Autocar Services Limited 6 14 38 42 130 133 157 177
Aveley 10 24 67 70 73 86 88 93 103 113
Aylesbury 14 16 17 32 37 55 56 58 63 65 66 73 87 88 91 109 111 114 119
Aylesbury Bus Company 66 70 73

B
Badges (Cap) 177
Bagshot 30 31
Baker Street 56 80 93 95 101 103 105 106 109 111 113 115 116 119
Baldock 14 49 59 63 66 77 87
Baldock Motor Transport Company 17 58 63 64 66 79

Baldwins Hill 87
Banstead Village 106
Barking 24 36 55
Barnes 22 32 42 44
Barnet 17 20 21 33 34 43 56
Barnet-by-Pass 17 18 79 88 93 95
Barnet Lane 77
Barnet Urban District Council 67
Basingstoke 31
Batchworth Heath 88
Bath Road 125
Batten's Luxurious Coaches 24 36 67 70 171
Bayswater Road 111
Beaconsfield 23 32 49 55 63
Beare Green 23
Beaumont Saloon Coaches 13 63 65
Beaumont Safeway 13 21
Beckenham 35
Becontree Heath 30 55 88 96
Bedfont 41 43 50 91 123
Bedford 13 14 17 20 43
Belhus Estate 93 103 106 113 114
Bell Common 19 29 106
Bellgraphic Tickets 157
Bell Punch Tickets 79 156 157 171
Belmont (Surrey) 9 49
Berkhamsted 16 33 37 43 49
Bexley 125
Bexleyheath 55 125
Biggin Hill 35 44
Biggleswade 17
Birch Brothers Limited 13 14 20 63 66 93 101 103 105 157 170 179
Birmingham Railway Carriage and Wagon Company 133 134
Bishopsgate 29
Bishops Stortford 18 20 29 44 49 58 63 66 68 73 77 86 87 101 105 115 119 125
Bishops Stortford Garage 44
Blackheath 55
Blitz on London 87 88
Blue Belle Motors Limited 34 58
Blue Line Coaches Limited 42
Bordon (Hants) 30
Borehamwood 77 78 95 96 119
Borough Green 123
Botley Hill 49
Bournemouth 70
Bow 22 70
Boxmoor 9 16 25 43
Bracknell 13 28
Brands Hatch 125
Brasted 44 91
Brent Bridge 125
Brent Cross 119 123
Brentford 55 103
Brentwood 9 10 12 21 24 29 30 33 43 49 70 77 79 86 93 96 137 171
Brighton 8 63
British Rail 95 98 101 106 163 170

Brixton 35 38 41 43 49 55 58 93
Brockley Hill 16 43 73 158
Bromley (Kent) 12 14 35 41 91 95 96 109 111 125
Bromley Common 44 125
Brookmans Park 33 34 67 68 95 109
Broxbourne 77 86
Bucks Expresses Limited 26 41 56 67 171
Buckhurst Hill 8 9 29
Buckingham 16
Building Department (LPTB) 179
Buntingford 49
Burnham Beeches 8 9 77 79
Burpham 22
Burton Latimer 20
Bushey 26 40 41 55 63 65 158
Bushey Heath 26 40
Bush House 18 20 21 31 32 41 66
Byfleet 9 55 63 65 91

C
Camberley 30 31
Cambridge 20 43
Camden Town 11 44 158
Canons Park 49
Cap Badges 177
Capel 23
Cardington Camp 21
Caterham 8 9 35 36 55 65 79 93 106
Caterham-on-the-Hill 35 49 50
Central Bus Route 617 (Night) 73
Central Line 93
Central London Road Transport Station 17 18
Chadwell Heath 9 88
Chadwell St. Mary 95 103 106
Chalfont Station 49 63
Chalfonts, The 32 49
Charing Cross 8 10 13 19 24 30 33 38 41 42 43 44 50 55 58 63 64 73 103 109 157 158 171
Chartwell 106 109 111 114 116 123 125
Chase Cross 96
Chatham 36
Cheap Day Return Fares 93 96 101 103 105 106 109 111 113 114 115 119 167 170
Chelmsford 22 29 30 43
Chelsea 91 123
Chelsham 15 37 49 73 109 11 114 115 116 141 143
Chertsey 10 44 49 50 52 63 65 87 95 119
Chesham 15 37 49 63 65 79 87 90 93 95 101 103 105 111 133
Cheshunt 14 27 49 67 73
Chessington 77 80
Chigwell Row 8 9 10 106
Chingford 8 9 29 30 56 93
Chingford Mount 30 93 162
Chislehurst 44
Chiswick 30 31 41 43
Chiswick Works 90 133 134

203

Chorleywood 49 62
Cippenham (Berks) 32
City Coach Company Ltd 11 156 170 179
City of Oxford Motor Services 123 143
City Omnibus Company Limited 11 12
Clandon 23
Clapham 38
Clapham Road Coach Station 17 35 36
Clapton 19 29
Clophill 13 20
Coach (Lord Mayors Show) 56
Coach Operators 156
Cobham 22 42 55 63 65 91 119
Cockspur Street 32
Codicote 14 20
Colchester 22
Collier Row 96 106
Colliers End 49
Colnbrook 28 31 41 103 134 157
Colnbrook-by-Pass 31
Colney Street 91 96
Comfy Cars Limited 43
Commercial Managers Department 174
Committee of Enquiry 28 32 34 55 58 61 62 64 65 66 67
Conductors 60 156 157 158 162 166 174 178
Corbets Tey 77 87 95 103
Corbets Tey Road 73 77
Coronation Year (1952) 95
Coulsdon Common 50
Coulsdon Court 91
Coulsdon Town Centre 91 111
Cranford 157
Crawley 27 49 50 55 63 64 73 93 106 111 114 123 125 137 143 158
Crayford 9 13 55 125
Crayford Garage 55
Cricklewood 16 25 26 41 93 123 158
Crockham Hill 35 50
Croydon 35 38 41 43 49 55 91 95
Croydon Airport 79
Crystal Palace 35
Curtis and Thompson 29

D
Dagenham 24 36 77 93
Daily Workman Return Tickets 174
Daimler Double-deck Coaches 134
Dalston 19 29
Dartford 10 13 44 50 55 64 73 95 103 123
Dartford Garage 95 114
Dartford Tunnel 103
Datchet 33 119
Denham 50
Denham Cross Roads 23
Diesel Operation (Railways) 101
Digswell 96
District Messengers Company Ltd 174
District Railway 8 109
Dixons Hill Road 95
Dorking 6 8 9 10 18 23 41 43 44 49 50 52 77 79 80 91 93 95 96 106 116 119
Dorking Garage 44 77 79 80 114 115 134 141
Double-deck Coaches 56 95 98 101 105 109 113 134 137 141
Drivers 60 177 178
Dunstable 14 25 36 49 62 65 73 86 87 103 114
Dunton Green Garage 44 64 79 109 114
Duple Dominant Bodies 119 143

E
Ealing 23 37

East Croydon 125
East Grinstead 14 35 36 49 50 52 87 91 109 123 141 162
East Ham 24 55 67 70 73 86 93 106
East Kent Road Car Company 60
East Molesey 44 91
East Surrey Traction Company Ltd 6 38 42 53 130 133 177
East Thurrock 95
Eastern Avenue 70 93 96
Eastern National Omnibus Co. 12 18 20 22 58 68 70 77 88 115 170
Eastern Traffic Commissioners 67
Eastward Coaches 29
Edenbridge 35 49 50 52 73 86 87 91
Edgware 16 25 26 41 55
Edgware Road 26 49
Edgware Way 73 77
Edmonson-type Tickets 158
Edmonton 14 27 95 111
Effingham 23 62
Egham 8 9 28 31 43 50
Elephant and Castle 55
Elstree 43 73 77 79
Eltham 44 45
Enfield 14 50 67 79 88
Enfield Wash 93
Englefield Green 41
Enterprise Coaches 26
Epping 8 9 10 18 29 66 73 77 86 93 95 106 125 134 162
Epping Forest 8 44 63 87
Epping New Road 18 29 93 115
Epsom 8 9 23 41 106
Esher 8 9 22 23 42 63 65 88 91 113 119 171
Eton 32 41
Evans Coaches 29
Excess Fare Tickets 159 162 166 167
Exchange Tickets 159 162
Express Routes 101 103 105
Eynsford 50

F
Fares 73 77 103 109 111
Fare Revisions 93 101 103 105 109 111 113 115 116 119 162 166 174 175
Fares–Children 166 167
Fares–Excess 166 167
Farnborough (Hants) 30
Farnborough (Kent) 8 9 14 44
Farnham 30 43 113 116
Farnham Blue Coaches 30
Farnham Common (Bucks) 31 65 66 70 77 91
Farnham Royal (Bucks) 31
Farningham 9 10 13 44 50 55 64 68 73 86 88
Felbridge 87 91
Felcourt 91
Feltham 50 91
Fenchurch Street 103 109
Festival of Britain 93 95
Finchley 21
Finchley Central 119 123
Finchley Road 96 119
Finsbury Circus 29
Finsbury Park 9 11 23 27 44
Five-Day Tickets 105 106 115 175
Flags (Bus Stop) 179
Flamstead (Herts) 101 123
Fleet Transport Services Limited 36 70 71 171
Frimley 30
Fuel Supplies 87 90 93 95 96

G
Ganwick Corner 21
Garston (Herts) 25 26 50 91 95 111 115 141
Gatwick Airport 96 106 123
Gerrards Cross 32 37 49 63 65 111
Gidea Park 33 43 70 79
Gidea Park Garage 43
Gilford Coaches 133
Gilford Motor Company Limited 30
Gillingham (Kent) 13
Glenton Coaches 6
Gloucester Place 111
Godalming 43
Godstone 8 9 35 50 65 105
Godstone Garage 43 55 79 93 115 119
Godstone Green 43 55
Golden Rover Ticket 115 116 119
Golders Green 8 33 40 42 43 49 56 65 79 91 119 123 158
Gordon Omnibus Company Ltd. 24 67
Graveley 63 64 66
Gravesend 13 43 50 68 70 87 90 91 95 105 109 113 123
Grays 10 24 25 36 67 70 73 77 86 87 88 95 103 105 106 114 171
Grays Garage 114 115 134 137 141 143
Great Bookham 43 49 50 62 65 79
Great Cambridge Road 23 27 79 88 93
Greater London Council 109 111 123
Great Missenden 32 77 86
Great North Road 17 63 64 96 106
Great West Road 31 41 55 103 123
Green Line Coaches Limited 6 15 16 18 22 23 27 32 33 34 36 37 41 44 56 58 62 63 64 66 67 68 133 156 157 177 178 179
Green Line Coach Tickets 156 157 158 159 162 166 167 170 174 175 176
Green Street Green (nr. Farnborough) 10 12
Grey Coaches Limited 62
Grey-Green Coaches Limited 24
Guildford 6 9 10 22 23 42 49 50 62 63 65 91 96 114 119 137 143 171
Guildford Garage 42 115
Gunnersbury 55 157

H
Hackney Wick 70
Hadley Woods 9
Hainault Forest 8
Halstead (Kent) 123 125
Ham Urban District Council 32 66
Hammersmith 30 31 32 41 42 43 44 91 103 105 115 119 125 157 158
Hampton Court 8 9 32 37 55 91 113 119
Hampton Urban District Council 32 66
Handcross 8
Harefield 88
Harlesden 14 55
Harlow 18 106 114 123 125 137
Harlow New Town 95 98 105 119
Harmondsworth 31 41 157
Harold Hill Estate 98
Harold Wood 33 98
Harpenden 9 36 49 50 62 65 73
Harpenden Garage 43
Harrow-on-the-Hill 14 49
Harrow Weald 49
Hatfield 8 17 20 21 43 79 88 93 95 96 111 158
Hatfield Garage 77 80
Hayes (Kent) 96
Hayes (Middlesex) 133
Heath End 30

204

Heathrow Airport 31 106 115 123 125 143
Hemel Hempstead 8 25 49 55 65 68 73 87 95 101 103 109 119 123 137
Hendon Central 40 41 43 119
Henley-on-Thames 43
Henlow 13 14 20
Henlow Camp 21
Hersham 63
Hertford 9 14 23 27 49 50 52 63 66 77 86 87 93 95 101 105 106 111 114 115 119 137 174
Hertford Heath 23 77 86 93 95 111
High Beech 8 9
Highgate 17 20 21
Highways Limited 66
Highwood Hospital (Brentwood) 33 70 96
High Wycombe 23 37 49 65 79 87 90 93 101 103 106 111 115 123 137 141 143
Hillman Saloon Coaches Limited 21 30 33 43 70 156 171
Hitchin 13 14 17 20 49 63 66 77 79 93 101 105 116 123 158
Hitchin Garage 77 80
Hockliffe 14
Hoddesdon 14 67 77
Holland (Surrey) 105 109
Hook (Surrey) 77
Horley 50 96
Hornchurch 30 37 55 71 95
Hornchurch Station 77 87 88
Horse Guards Avenue 20 36 70 79 179
Horsham 23 77 79 80 87 91
Horsley 23 62
Horton Kirby 86 88
Hosey Common 35 106
Hounslow 8 41 43
Hounslow Heath 50 91
House of Commons 103
Howlands (Hatfield) 96 109
Hurst Green 105
Hyde Park Corner 22 35 41 58 101 171

I
Ifield 137
Ilford 22 30 33 36 55
Imperial Motor Services 6 13 18
Instructions to Conductors 162 163 166 170 174 175
Interavailability of Tickets 56
Isleworth 55
Ivychimneys 106

K
Keith Coaches Limited 16
Kempton Mark 37 55
Kenley 9 35 43 55
Kennington 49
Kensal Green 55
Kensington 22 30 93
Kent County Council 123
Kentish Town 11
Keston 10
Keston Mark 35 44
Kettering 20
Kew 43
Kew Gardens 9
Kilburn 26 41 55 95
Kingsbury 95 *Kings Cross:*
  Central London Coach Station 17 18
  Coach Station 28 90 93 171
  Kings Cross St. Pancras Station 79
  York Road 13 14 18 27
Kings Langley 16 25 43 55
Kingston 31 32 37 44 55 65 66 77 80 91 95 106 113 114 119

Kingston-by-Pass 22 42 119
Kingston Road 109
Kingston Vale 114
Kingswood (Surrey) 38 41 123
Kirkby Central Organisation 143
Knightsfield 96
Knockholt Pound 123 125
Knockholt Station 123
Knotty Green 32

L
Laindon (Essex) 12
Lambourne End 8 9
Langley (Bucks) 41 103
Lea Bridge Road 19
Leatherhead 8 9 23 41 43 79 85
Leatherhead Garage 43 77 80 91
Leaves Green 44
Ledbury Transport Limited 27 28
Leicester Square 41
Leighton Buzzard 14
Leighton Coaches Limited 36
Letchworth 17 19 64
Leverstock Green 95
Lewisham 14 41 44 55
Lewis's Cream Line Coaches Ltd. 33 67 68
Leyland Vehicles:
  Nationals 115 116 119 141 143
  Olympic 137
  TF-type 134
  Titan and Tigers 133
Leyton 29 70
Leytonstone 70
Licences:
  Conductors 60
  Drivers 60
  Express Service 61
  Short Stage Express 61
  Stage Carriage 61
  Licensing Decisions– Appeals 64 65 66 67
Limited Stop Service 56
Limpsfield 35 50
Lingfield 91
Lion Coaches Limited 29
Little Heath (Herts.) 33 95 109
Little Missenden 77
Liverpool Street 18 19 20 29 37 79 93 98 101 156
London and North Eastern Railway 34 66 67
London Blitz 87
London Coastal Coaches Limited 12 14 15
London Colney 73 91 96 103 171
London Country Bus Services Limited 6 18 111 113 119 125 141 176 179
London County Council Tramways 30
London General Omnibus Company Limited 6 8 19 26 37 38 44 58 68 157 171 177
London Motor Omnibus Company Limited 8
London Passenger Transport Act 68
London Terminal Coach Station 17 35
London Traffic Act (1924) 10
London Transport 6 13 14 16 18 19 22 23 24 25 30 33 34 36 38 68 70 96 101 103 106 109 111 114 119 125 133 141 156 157 171 178 179 181
London Transport Executive 109 111 113 123
London Transport (Building Dept) 179
London United Tramways 8 133

Longcroft Green (Welwyn Garden City) 96
Loughton 9 19 29 44
Lower Feltham 37
Lower Kingswood 8 9 10
Lowfield Heath 50 96
Lupus Street Coach Station 12 14
Luton (Beds) 13 18 20 49 62 65 70 73 87 90 93 95 101 103 105 106 113 114 119 143
Luton Airport 113 119
Luton Garage 18 70 115 119 134 141
Luton Station 106

M
Maidenhead 8 27 31 32 33 43 44 52 63 65 66 70 133
Maidstone 13
Maidstone and District Motor Services Ltd. 12 13 37 50 60 68 77 123 133
Manor House 95 111
Manor Park (Slough) 33
Mansion House 41 171
Marble Arch 32 35 41 58 73 95 101 111 123 171
Margate 70
Marlow 43
Marlpit Lane 91
Marylebone Station 21 56 79
Maximum Single Fare 106
Maybury (nr. Woking) 55 63 91
Meadway 91
Merrow 50 62
Merstham 9 38 41
Merton Garage 137
Metro-Cammell-Weymann 137
Metropolitan Police 60
Metropolitan Police District 10 60 156
Metropolitan Railway 14 32 49 66 68 103
Metropolitan Stage Carriages 35 61 156
Metropolitan Stage Carriage Act 60 61
Metropolitan Traffic Commissioners 62 64 67
Mile End 19 29 30 87
Mill Green (Herts) 96
Mill Hill 40 43 73 77 101 103 119 123 125
Minister of Transport 64 66 67 68
Ministry of Transport 10 50 56 60 62 63 66
Ministry of War Transport 88
Missendens, The 14 32
Mitcham 41
Monthly Seasons 171 174 176
Morden 41
Motor Hirers and Coach Services Association 62
Motorways:
  M1 103 125
  M4 103 123 125
Mutton Lane (Potters Bar) 93

N
National Bus Company (NBC) 10 125 181
National Omnibus and Transport Co. Ltd. 25 29 42 43 44 50 157 177
Neasden 95
New Barnet 88
Newbury 28
Newbury Park 93
Newchapel 91
New Cross 14 55 93
New Empress Saloons Limited 11
New Hatfield 79
New Haw 91

205

Newlands Corner 50
Newmarket 18 20 58 68
New Towns 95 98 101 119 137
Night Bus Route (617) 73
Northchurch 43 49
North Circular Road 125
North Finchley 17 33 119
Northfleet Garage 95 115 133 143
North Romford 96
North Stifford 93
North Watford 25
North Weald 29 56
Northwood 10 14 49 55 88
Norwood 35

O
Off-peak Traffic 96 98
Oldchurch Hospital (Romford) 96
Old Coulsdon 91
Oldings Corner (Hatfield) 79
Old Harlow 18
Old Windsor 41 119
Old Woking 55
One-man Operation 109 113 114
Ongar 12 29 49 56 73 86 87 93 156 162
Ongar Garage 29 56
Orpington 44
Osterley 157
Otford (Kent) 50
Oxford 123
Oxford Circus 14 17 18 20 22 23 27 33 41 43 44 55 79 87 91 93 101 103 105 106 109 119 123 133
Oxford Road 111
Oxford Street 64 109
Oxted (Surrey) 35 49 50 73 91 105 109

P
P and S Motor Services Limited 67
Paddington (Spring Street) 35 58
Paddington Station 41 171
Paines Hill (Cobham) 63
Palmers Green 14 50
Pampisford 19
Paper Tickets 156 158
Park Lane 32
Park Street (St. Albans) 91 96 103
Pear Tree Village 96
Penge 35
Petersham 32
Petts Wood 44
Piccadilly 32 43 44 64
Piccadilly Circus 55
Pinner 9 14 55
Plaxton Supreme Bodies 119 143
Poland Street Coach Station 36 44 50 52 55 68 179
Ponders End 50 79 93 95
Poplar 24 55
Portman Square 26 68 73 87
Posters 179
Potter Street (Essex) 73 95
Potters Bar 10 20 21 33 34 80 93
Povey Cross 96
Premier Line Limited 31 32 38 58 66 156 171
Premier Omnibus Company (London) 31
Premier Omnibus Company (Watford) 25 26 68
Price's Super Coaches 24 70 171
Priest, Arthur 14
Priest, Ralph 13 18
Private Hire Fleet (LGOC) 130 177
Private Hire Fleet (London Transport) 134 137

Proposed Route Alterations 62 63 64
Public Carriage Office 60
Publicity:
   Green Line Guide 180 181
   Handbills 179
   Leaflets 179
   Maps 180 181 182
   Posters 179 180
   Special Displays 179
   Timetables 179 180
   Timetable Boards 179
Publicity Office (London Transport) 179
Public Service Vehicle Licences 80
Puckeridge (Herts) 49
Purfleet 24 36 77 88 103
Purfleet-by-Pass 86
Purley 35 43 50
Purley Way 35 36 58 79 91
Putney 77 80 91
Putney Heath 109

Q
Quarterly Season Tickets 171
Queen Line Coaches Limited 17 18 49 58 66
Queensbury 95

R
Radlett 43 73 88 91 95 96 103
Rainham (Essex) 9 10 24 36 73 77 78 93
Railway (Diesel Operation) 101
Railway Electrification 98
Railway Strike 95
Ranger Tickets 101
RC-type Coaches 114 115 141
Reading 13 17 28 43
Redcar Services Limited 6 12 14 63 64 77 133
Red Line Coaches Limited 42
Red Rover Saloon Coaches 16 32 58 66
Redhill 6 8 10 23 27 38 41 44 49 50 64 123
Regent Motor Services 14 27 56
Reigate 6 8 10 23 27 38 41 44 49 50 65 93 106 109 111 114 115 123 141 143 158
Reinstatement of Services 86 90
Return Tickets (Green Line) 159 162 163 166 167
RF-type Coaches 137
Richmond (Surrey) 8 32 44 66 91
Rickmansworth 14 37 49 50 55 73 103 115
Ripley (Surrey) 22 42 114 171
Rippleside 9
Road Service Licences 50 55 58 62 63 67 68
Road Traffic Act (1930) 6 10 14 15 18 25 50 60 62
Roehampton 91 109
Rolling Stock Department 133 134
Romford 8 11 22 24 33 36 55 70 79 86 88 93 95 96 106 111 119 125 171
Romford (London Road) Garage 70 105 109 114 115 116 123 134 137 141 143
Romford (North Street) Garage 43
Romford (Roneo Corner) 96
Route Alterations 62 63 64 116
Route Letters 55 188 189 190
Route Numbers 87 90 191 192
Routemaster Buses 137
Routemaster Coaches 101 102 105 109 111 113 114 115 137 141
Royston (Herts) 43 49
RT-type Buses 136
RT-type Coaches 95 105 106 134 137
RT-type experimental Coach (RTC) 134

Rubber supplies 87
Runnymede 119
Rushden 20 21
Rush Green (Romford) 30 96

S
St. Albans 8 9 10 14 20 26 43 49 50 73 79 86 91 95 96 103 106 113 114 116 119 143
St. Albans City Station 79
St. Albans Garage 109 114 119 134 141 162
St. Pancras 79 101
St. Stephens 96
Safeway Motor Services 13
Saffron Walden 18 43 58
Salt Hill (Slough) 31 33
Sanderstead 50
Sawbridgeworth 18
Season Tickets 73 115 171
Selsdon 50
Setright Ticket Machines 157 170
Seven Kings 71
Sevenoaks 12 13 14 41 44 50 52 63 64 65 77 79 86 88 91 109 111 123 125
Seven Sisters 101
Sheerwater Estate 95
Shefford 13 14 20
Shenley 91 103 119
Shenfield 98
Shepherds Bush 23 31 41 87 103 158
Shere (Surrey) 50
Shooters Hill 55
Shortlands 35
Sidcup 8 9 44 45
Sidcup-by-Pass 44
Single-deck Coaches 103 106 109 113 114
Single Tickets (Green Line) 157 158 166 167
Skylark Motor Coach Company Limited 22 42 56 65 67 93 171 179
Slough (Bucks) 6 8 10 27 31 32 41 44 66 79 91 125 133 157 158
Slough (Alpha Street) Garage 41 43 44
Slough (Bath Road) Garage 33 133
Southall Garage (AEC Works) 55
Southbury Road (Enfield) 93
South Croydon 50
Southend-on-Sea 11
Southern Railway 32 63
Southern Traffic Commissioners 66
Southern Way 93
South Hatfield 95 109
South Wales Transport Ltd. 141
Staff 95
Staines 8 10 13 28 43 50 70 79 88 91 96 115 119 133 157
Staines Garage 41 44 79 115 116 133 143
Stanborough (Herts) 96
Stanmore 26 41 49 55 95
Stansted Airport 115
Stapleford Abbots 10
Staples Corner 103 123 125
Stevenage 14 17 95 137
Stirling Corner 77
STL-type Buses 87 134
Stoat's Nest 91
Stoke Common 32
Stoke Newington 14
Stonehouse Corner (Hatfield) 79
Stonehouse Corner (Purfleet) 77
Stop Posts 179
Stotfield 14
Stratford 18 19 21 22 29 30 33 36 55 98 171

Strawhatter Coaches Limited 13 18 49 70 162 171 174
Streatham 43 45
Strike (1958) 96
Sudbury (Middx) 49 55
Sunbury 37
Sunbury Common 32 55 66 70
Sunbury Garage 55 70
Sunningdale 30 31 43 49 50 52 55 68 87 105 109 113 133
Sunshine Saloon Coaches 37
Sunset Pullman Coaches Limited 22 23 36 43 70 171
Superways Limited 29
Surbiton 77
Surrey County Council 119
Sussex Gardens 35 111
Sutton (Surrey) 23 38 41 95 123
Swanley 71 141
Swanley Garage 55 115
Swanley Junction 55 86

T
T-type Coaches 130 133
Taplow (Bucks) 32
Tatsfield 86 87 91 93 111
Thackray's Way 14 17 23 156 179
Thames Ditton 44 91
Thames Valley Traction Company Limited 28
Theobald Street 95
Theydon Bois 106
Three Bridges 137
Tibbetts Corner (Putney Heath) 109
Tickets:
   Cheap Day Returns 93 96 103 105 106 109 111 113 114 115 119 162 166 167 170
   Daily Workman Return 174
   Excess Fare 159 162
   Exchange 159 162
   Five-day 105 106 115 175
   Golden Rover 115 116 119
   Instructions to Conductors 162 163
   Instructions to Railway Staff 159
   Interavailability of 56
   Methods of Issue 156 157 158 159 162
   Monthly Season 171 174 176
   Packets 171
   Quarterly Seasons 171
   Railway Card Type 163
   Ranger 101
   Season 73 115 171
   Setright 157
   Single 95 114, 157 158 166 167
   Systems 156 157
   Through Booking 158 159 163
   Underground/Bus 156
   Underground/Coach 157
   Weekly 73 93 106 115 170 174 175 176
   Weekly Workman 174
Tilbury 24 36 67 73 77 87 90 95 103 106 115
Tilbury Dock Station 24 70
Tilbury Ferry (Riverside) Station 95
Titsey Park 49
Tolworth 88
Tonbridge 12 41 88
Tooting 23 38 41
Tottenham 14 95 111
Tottenham Court Road 41
Tottenham Hale 44
Tower Hill 67
Trafalgar Square 32 79
Traffic Areas 60

Traffic Audit 157
Traffic Circulars 87 166 170
Traffic Commissioners 10 14 18 27 28 31 32 33 34 36 37 38 50 55 60 62 64 65 66 67 115 125 170
Transport Act (London) (1969) 111
Transport (London) Bill 111
Transport, Minister of 64 66 67 68 101 103 109 111
Transport, Ministry of 10 50 56 60 62 63 66
Tring (Herts) 16 17 43 49 55 65 73 87 103 105 114 115
Tring Garage 119 141 143
Tulse Hill 35
Tunbridge Wells 6 12 13 41 44 52 63 64 77 86 87 88 91 96 109 125
Tunbridge Wells Garage 109
Turnpike Lane Station 93
Two Waters 49 55 114 141

U
Underground Group, The 6
Underground Railways 68 79 109 157 158 179
United Counties Omnibus Co. 21
United States Army 90 134
Uniforms:
   Conductors 177 178
   Drivers 177 178
   Inspectors 178
Upminster 9 10 55 56 70 73 109 171
Upminster Services Limited 29 30 70 171
Uxbridge 9 10 23 37 44 49 50 55 65 70 103 106 113 115 133

V
Varsity Motors Limited 20 68
Venture Transport Services Ltd. 13 14 17 18 49
Victoria Area: 12 13 14 15 17 30 31 35 41 70 73 77 79 87 91 95 101 103 105 106 109 111 113 114 115 116 119 123 125 143 174 179
Victoria Embankment 34
Victoria Line 101 111 119
Victoria Park 70
Virginia Water 8 9 30 50 116

W
Wadesmill (Herts) 49
Wake Arms 8 19 29 44 63 115 119 123 156
Waltham Abbey 119
Waltham Cross 14 27 79 88 93 111 119 123 125
Walthamstow 29 44 93 98 115 119
Walthamstow Central Station 119
Walton-on-the-Hill 8 9
Walton-on-Thames 44
Wanstead 8 18 19 29 70
Ware (Herts.) 14 23 49
Warlingham 50 86
Warren Wood House 8 9
War Transport, Ministry of 88
Watch Committee 60
Water End (Herts) 93
Watford 8 9 10 16 25 26 40 42 43 49 50 65 71 73 79 91 106 115 130 133 158 171 174
Watford Junction Station 106 115
Watford (Leavesden Road) Garage 16 40 43 55 62 73 87
Watford Way 40 96 103
Waybills 166
Wealdstone 49

Weekly Tickets 73 115 170 174 175 176
Weekly Workman Tickets 174
Welham Green 95 109
Welling (Kent) 55
Wellingborough 20
Welwyn 13 14 20 21 96
Welwyn Garden City 17 18 43 49 50 64 66 77 79 93 96 106 116
Wembley 14 49 55
Wendover 14 32 49 77
Wennington 24 93
West Byfleet 49 55 87 91
West Croydon 125
Western Avenue 103
West Herts. Motor Services Ltd. 25
West Kingsdown 13
West London Coaches 14 37 49 55 65 70 73
Westminster 103
West Molesey 44
Westoning 21
West Wickham (Kent) 9
West Wycombe (Bucks) 9 49
Westcliff Motor Services Ltd 11 12
Westerham 35 44 50 63 79 87 91 114 115 123 125
Westerham Hill 8 9 35 44 63 64 65 79 91
Weybridge 44 63 65 87 91
Weybridge Station 91
Wheathampstead 49
Whipps Cross 19
Whipsnade Zoo 56 77 79 90 95 101 105 109 116 123 125 163 170
Whitchurch (Bucks) 16
Whitechapel 24
Whitehill (Hants) 30
Whyteleafe (Surrey) 35 43 55
Willesden 95
Windsor 6 8 9 10 32 33 37 41 44 50 63 65 66 70 95 96 103 105 106 109 111 114 119 123 125 133 157 158 171
Windsor Garage 79 111 114 125 133 134 137 143
Windsor Safari Park 114 123 125
Woking 10 13 43 50 63 65 87 91 95 116 123
Woking Urban District Council 55
Woodford 18 19 29 44
Woodford Bridge 8 9
Woodford Wells 86 93
Woodgrange Coaches 29
Wood Green 11 23 27 50
World War II 86 90
Wormley (Herts.) 8 9 10 23 27
Wrotham 13 68 73 86 88 91 103 111 123 125
Wrotham Heath 68

Y
Yellow Line Coaches Limited 42
Yorktown (Camberley) 31

ERRATA
Page 5:-Appendix B should read
applied for by L.G.O.C. or Green Line.

NOTE:
The dates quoted below the drawings of coaches in the text are those during which the livery depicted was in use.